China's Future

China's Future

Constructive Partner or Emerging Threat?

Edited by

Ted Galen Carpenter
and James A. Dorn

CATO
INSTITUTE
Washington, D.C.

Library of Congress Cataloging-in-Publication Data

China's Future : constructive partner or emerging threat? / edited by
Ted Galen Carpenter and James A Dorn.
   p. cm.
   "This book is the outgrowth of a September 1999 Cato Institute
conference 'Whither China? The PRC at 50' " —p. ix.
   Includes bibliographical references and index.
   ISBN 1-882577-87-6—ISBN 1-882577-88-4
   1. United States—Relations—China—Congresses. 2. China—
Relations—United States—Congresses. 3. United States—Foreign
relations—1989—Congresses. 4. China—Politics and government—
1949—Congresses. 5. China—Economic policy—Congresses.
I. Carpenter, Ted Galen. II. Dorn, James A. III. Cato Institute.
E183.8.C5 C5375 2000
303.48'273051—dc21   00-031529

Cover design by Elise Rivera.

Printed in the United States of America.

CATO INSTITUTE
1000 Massachusetts Ave., N.W.
Washington, D.C. 20001

Contents

v

Acknowledgments

This book is the outgrowth of a September 1999 Cato Institute conference, "Whither China? The PRC at 50," attended by nearly 200 people. We wish to express special thanks to FDX Corporation for its generous financial support of that event.

Many individuals deserve appreciation as well. Edward H. Crane and William A. Niskanen, respectively president and chairman of the Cato Institute, provided consistent and enthusiastic backing for the conference and the subsequent book. Laura Major, Laura Cooper, Gary Dempsey, and other members of the Institute's staff did an excellent job of handling the conference's many logistical requirements. Doug Bandow, Jo Kwong, and Stuart Anderson generously donated their time to moderate some of the panels.

An additional debt of gratitude is owed to those people who have helped to make the book possible. David Boaz, Cato's executive vice president, presided over the project along with his numerous other duties; and David Lampo, the Institute's director of publications, helped keep us on schedule with punctual reminders of deadlines. Megan Brumleve and Terri Williams labored long and diligently to incorporate the revisions made by the authors. Paul Benjamin tracked down occasionally elusive sources for the various chapters. Elise Rivera did a splendid job of designing an appealing book jacket, and Shirley Kessel indexed the book with great thoroughness and accuracy. Our copyeditor, Laura Goetz, worked hard to improve the style of the manuscript and prepare it for publication. Any errors that may have escaped her rigorous screening are solely the responsibility of the editors.

Most of all, we want to thank the authors for their cooperation and enthusiasm. It has been a pleasure to work with them, and we believe that our collective endeavor has produced a book that offers some important insights about the complex puzzle that is China at the dawn of the 21st century.

Introduction: The Future of U.S.-China Relations

Ted Galen Carpenter and James A. Dorn

Relations between the United States and the People's Republic of China have become increasingly unsettled. A short time ago, both governments spoke of a "strategic partnership" and sought ways to enhance already substantial economic and political ties. The bombing of the Chinese embassy in Belgrade, the release of the Cox report alleging systematic nuclear espionage by the PRC, and angry Chinese reactions to both developments, however, have produced a new round of tensions. So, too, has China's renewed threat to use force against Taiwan to regain the "renegade province." On the positive side, China's probable accession to the World Trade Organization, followed by Taiwan's inclusion, offers hope that future U.S.-Chinese relations will improve.

Is China a rising colossus that intends to bully its neighbors and dominate Asia? Should Washington adopt a more hard-line policy toward the PRC on trade, human rights, and national security issues? Or is China a country that has already moved far along the road to a market economy and a more open society and is committed to being a stabilizing, cooperative power? The distinguished contributors to this book examine those questions by considering both the short- and long-run prospects for the evolution of a peaceful and prosperous New China, despite the background of 50 years of communist rule.

The dark side of the Chinese Communist state is disturbing and must not be ignored. But that unsavory record should not be allowed to hide the progress that the Chinese people have made since economic reforms began in 1978. The expansion of markets relative to state planning has given millions of people new opportunities and has substantially raised living standards. China's leaders have reluctantly accepted economic competition while trying to maintain their monopoly of political power. But as people have acquired greater

1

economic freedom, they have also sought greater personal freedom. The dilemma for the Chinese Communist Party is how to grow the productive nonstate sector and at the same time prevent an erosion of the party's power as market participants demand greater civil liberties.

The United States and other countries are betting that China's accession to the WTO will make China a more open society and eventually lead to democratic rule as well as a more stable and peaceful international policy by Beijing. However, while free trade is necessary for peace, it is not sufficient. The CCP may be willing to sacrifice substantial gains from trade in order to protect its power and privilege. Witness, for example, Beijing's latest White Paper and its threats against Taiwan, one of China's major trading partners.

The challenge is to exploit opportunities for further gains from trade and move closer toward a constructive partnership with the PRC while protecting vital American interests. Unfortunately, the U.S. policy debate has been largely a contest between the inconsistent Clinton approach and the extremely confrontational approach advocated by many conservatives. The latter strategy risks creating a self-fulfilling prophecy of China's becoming an enemy. Indeed, a growing chorus of voices in Congress and the U.S. foreign policy community argues that the PRC is a belligerent dictatorship and a future enemy of the United States.

Painting China as an emerging global economic "superpower" and carrying that military metaphor over to foreign policy are dangerous. Free trade is mutually beneficial—both China and other countries gain from trade liberalization. If the Chinese people become richer, is that a cause for concern in the West? There is no doubt that, as the Chinese economy grows, so will the Chinese military budget.[1] But that is not unusual for a large nation state, and thus far China's military modernization effort has been relatively modest.

It is true that no one can be certain how the PRC will behave on security issues in the future. Unlike Nazi Germany or the USSR, however, the PRC is not a messianic, expansionist power; it is a normal rising (or reawakening) great power. That can be difficult enough for other countries to deal with at times, but such a country does not pose a malignant security threat.

The most prudent course is to treat China as a normal (albeit sometimes repressive and prickly) great power but avoid the

2

extremes of seeing the PRC as either enemy or strategic partner. The United States would also be wise to encourage other major countries in Asia to think more seriously about how *they* intend to deal with a rising China.

Beijing's behavior toward regional neighbors has been a curious amalgam of conciliation and abrasiveness. Examples of conciliation include efforts to dampen the border disputes with such important land neighbors as India, Vietnam, Russia, and Kazakhstan and a campaign to build close political and economic ties with South Korea. (The PRC has also been helpful in trying to discourage the North Koreans from pursuing a nuclear-weapons program.) At the same time, China's relations with Japan, the Philippines, and other countries (primarily its oceanic neighbors) remain tense, and Beijing still aggressively pushes its territorial claims in the South China Sea.

The Taiwan issue remains an especially dangerous flash point. Any move toward independence by Taipei would surely provoke military action by Beijing. Yet China's economic future depends strongly on Taiwan's prosperity, so military action must be seen as a last resort. The election of Chen Shui-bian as president in March and the defeat of the long-dominant Nationalist Party are stern reminders to the CCP that its future is highly uncertain.

The tension created by Beijing's strategy of opening China's economy to the outside world while preventing meaningful political change has to be released sooner or later. The question is how far and how fast will China go toward creating a fully open society based on private property and limited government. Gradualism appears to have worked reasonably well thus far, but the inefficiency of China's nonstate sector is apparent and corruption is rampant.

Part I of this book examines the first 50 years of the PRC and the significant transformation that has occurred in the post-Mao era. Slowly but surely China is moving from political to civil society, with the driving force being the market-oriented reforms initiated by Deng Xiaoping. Chinese intellectuals are now reading Hayek and Friedman rather than Marx and Engels. But whether China will go all the way toward a true free-market system remains highly uncertain.

Part II considers the erratic and contradictory nature of U.S. foreign policy toward the PRC. Instead of painting China as a serious threat one day and as a de facto strategic ally the next, the United States needs to formulate a balanced view consistent with our own principles—one that recognizes our long-run interest in engaging China while at the same time protecting our national security. The PRC's claims to the South China Sea islands and its relations with Japan and Taiwan are discussed from that perspective.

Part III deals with the relationship among trade liberalization, national security, and human rights. That relationship is especially important in light of China's pending accession to the WTO. What are the costs and the benefits of admitting China to the WTO? How should the United States balance free trade and security? What have been the successes and failures of China's trade regime? Those and related questions receive close attention.

Part IV looks toward the future of economic, political, and social reform in China and how that future may be shaped by the liberal influence of Hong Kong and Taiwan. Will freedom from those sources spill over to the mainland or will Chinese Communism slowly corrupt the rule of law and weaken the free market in Hong Kong and seek to absorb and subordinate Taiwan? It seems clear that without privatizing state-owned enterprises, China faces continuing problems of corruption and inefficiency. But wholesale privatization would undermine the last vestiges of party power. So the challenge for China's leadership is stark.

Ultimately, the creation of real markets as opposed to pseudomarkets in China will require the full recognition of private property rights. The recent amendment to the PRC constitution, which places the nonstate sector and private enterprise on a par with state-owned enterprises, is a step in that direction. But without further constitutional and political reform that places rights to life, liberty, and property above the party, and allows for both economic and political freedom, there can be no certainty of ownership.

That is why it is so important for China to face foreign economic competition and to be exposed to new ideas. Every step in the direction of greater economic freedom will provide further opportunities for the Chinese people to enlarge their private space and shrink the relative size of the state. Pressures will then build for greater social and political freedom. As William McGurn of the *Wall Street Journal* points out in his chapter:

> The slow accretion of experiences has persuaded me that the transformations we see in China are real, not because its leaders want such change but because those openings as they

have created constitute cracks in a system that people are quick to exploit. In the grossest terms, the bankruptcy of the socialist system, as much as real market openings, means that much of what was once provided by the state—housing, health care, retirement, livelihood—has become something the Chinese people are doing for themselves. It is inconceivable that even on this level such a shift would be without social and political consequences.

To agree with McGurn's conclusion does not mean that we should ignore the human rights abuses of the Beijing regime. But cutting off—or even obstructing—trade with China in the hope of improving human rights would be self-defeating. Isolating China would strengthen the party and the state while harming the nascent market sector and reducing economic freedom. If free trade is restricted, the probability of conflict between the PRC and the United States will also increase. The United States should do everything in its power to increase contacts with the Middle Kingdom and push for liberal reforms.

The best answer to the question of "whether China will be a constructive partner or an emerging threat" is given by Liu Junning in his chapter. According to Liu, an independent scholar who was recently purged from the Chinese Academy of Social Sciences, the answer will "depend, to a very great extent, on the fate of liberalism in China: a liberal China will be a constructive partner; a nationalistic and authoritarian China will be an emerging threat."

Notes

1. The PRC is modernizing its military, but military expenditures (estimates range from $35 billion to $50 billion) remain typical of those of other major powers and are dwarfed by the U.S. military budget of $280 billion.

PART I

A HALF-CENTURY OF TURBULENT CHANGE

1. Fifty Years of China's Economy with Its Background in Politics and Society

Mao Yushi

From Plan to Market

Soon after the founding of the People's Republic of China in 1949, the government spent three years to rebuild the war-torn economy and strove to overcome many difficulties (e.g., shortages, monetary instability, and trade sanctions). As soon as the economy had recovered, the government decided to take firm and well-contrived steps to bring forth its great plan of nationalizing the economy. Around 1956, China began to turn all private enterprises, firms, and even shops in urban areas into "joint ventures" shared by the government.[1] Very quickly during the next few years they were entirely restructured as state-owned enterprises (SOEs). The original owners received limited, fixed dividends for about 10 years. In rural areas, peasants were organized in cooperatives under collective ownership in 1955.[2] Those cooperatives gradually grew from lower to higher levels, culminating in the creation of the nationwide People's Commune in 1958. Property rights of all farmlands were turned over to the state, but the right to land use, as well as to all means of production, belonged to the cooperatives. So in rural areas collective ownership predominated, unlike in the former Soviet Union, which adhered to the single system of state-run farms with workers instead of peasants. Along with the nationalization of the private sector, SOEs, consisting mainly of formerly state-run and confiscated comprador enterprises, had been greatly strengthened. Moreover, with the help of the USSR, the PRC built many new factories in heavy industry.[3] Thus, by 1956, China had successfully nationalized its industrial, commercial, banking, transportation, and service sectors[4] and collectivized agriculture. The overall ownership scheme was termed "public ownership," which constituted the main feature of China's socialist economy.

9

Under the socialist belief that common ownership is better than private ownership, and that planning can eliminate all waste attributable to blind competition in a market, central planning of the economy goes hand in hand with public ownership, like twin brothers. Under total public ownership, all enterprises, firms, and rural cooperatives have only one boss—the state. No enterprise can behave of its own accord but must turn out products according to mandatory planning.

As a weak nation, China had suffered so much from foreign aggressors that it felt an urgent need to develop its economy and gain national strength. The PRC wanted to expand its heavy industry at a rapid pace and strengthen its military by efficiently mobilizing national resources through central planning. During the first few years of this experiment (1953–56), China achieved remarkable success. Industrial output grew 84 percent, agricultural output increased 32 percent, commodity retail sales expanded 66 percent, and wages increased 28 percent.[5] Economic aid from the Soviet Union played an important role (as manifested by 156 projects mostly in heavy industry), and the price system—left from the days before the founding of the PRC—promoted efficient resource allocation.

China's success, however, was short-lived. During the 20-year period from 1957 to 1976, China's centrally planned economy was a disaster. The price system did not function effectively because there was no competitive market system to give birth to correct price signals. Prices were used not for resource allocation but for accounting purposes only. Although the macroeconomy was in balance, there were serious disequilibria of supply and demand for various commodities and services.

Under public ownership, low efficiency in resource allocation and in enterprise management had been constantly worsening the national economy. Most of the surplus collected was allocated for military production, the iron and steel industry, and satellites, which did achieve some success. However, as in the former Soviet Union, there was a serious shortage of daily necessities, such as food, apparel, and fuel. Urban people had low incomes, and many products were subject to rationing. Life was hard for everyone, but for peasants, it was even more miserable.

Because of price distortions, it was difficult to estimate the PRC's actual gross national product; hence, it was not possible to determine the country's true economic growth. Official figures were based on the physical output of all products, including intermediate products, rather than on the economic value of final goods and services. Thus, those figures were of little economic significance. Everything was produced, exchanged, and consumed as planned, with no official unemployment and no reported domestic or foreign debt. All of those economic results were flaunted as highlights of China's socialist economy.

The planned economy was especially subject to violent shocks caused by political incidents. In 1959 China's top leaders were determined to uphold a policy comprising the Great Leap Forward and the rural People's Commune in a bid to start an ambitious campaign of spurring the national economy to surpass that of England within 10 years. That campaign led to the Great Famine (1959–61), which claimed the lives of some 15 to 30 million people, most of whom lived in the countryside.[6] The Great Famine was no natural disaster; it was a man-made catastrophe brought on by political turbulence and the suppression of the market.[7] Without exception, mass starvations in modern society are always linked to the lack of free markets.

The Cultural Revolution, spanning 1966 to 1976, imposed another calamity on the national economy. In the planned economy, every enterprise was led by officials and a party secretary appointed by the government. All enterprises were just subsidiaries to the government and ruled by governmental administration. When the Cultural Revolution was sweeping the country, with turbulence and violence, all officials and party committees everywhere were disabled, leaving enterprises in a mess. Production drastically declined. The national economy was brought to the brink of collapse. People suffered more than ever, but this time those who suffered most were intellectuals, governmental officials, and party cadres, not peasants. Formerly, people had believed in at least the illusion of communism; now, even that illusion was gone. After President Nixon's visit to China, the Chinese people could peer through a narrow rift at the outside world, and, to their astonishment, they found how miserably China had lagged in economic development.

Beginning in 1978, China turned to the market-oriented reform of its national economy. The principal feature of the reform was what economists call dual-track Pareto improvement—that is, no one would be worse off because of the reform, and a portion of people could benefit at each step of the change. To ensure a smooth, sustaining process of reform, with the fewest shocks and the least resistance or counteraction, dual-track reform proved a desirable strategy. Keeping in mind the goal of building a market economy, China could not abolish the old planned economy all of a sudden, so it resorted to a gradual restructuring. The planned economy was allowed to exist for a period but put under continual reform. All benefits that were part of the old system were thus retained—for instance, guaranteed employment, lodging, medical care, and subsidized prices of some necessities. The market economy, which was the newcomer, needed to be staged, established, and constantly improved. It afforded an additional area of economic activity, an area of vital importance for the reform. The dual-track system should have ended in 1993, merging into a single market system when the government would have formally abandoned the planned economy. But, in fact, the dual-track system is still in operation. It dies hard.[8]

In the market track, non-state-owned enterprises play the leading role. At the beginning, the breeding ground for the market emerged in the countryside. It was fortunate that previously China had not totally nationalized its economy—farmers were treated as household workers, not as workers on state-run farms. At the beginning of reform in 1977, farmers in Anhui Province initiated, at the risk of severe punishment, a household contract responsibility system in which each family received a piece of land distributed by a local production brigade and was entitled by a contract to use that land for growing farm products. After the harvest, each family paid the local government an agricultural tax and sold the remaining produce at market prices.

The household responsibility system released a large amount of surplus labor in rural areas. There soon emerged a multitude of factories and workshops—the so-called township and village enterprises (TVEs)—that were collectively owned and competed with SOEs.[9]

Another remarkable change taking place on the market-economy track was the policy of trading with the outside world. Previously, Chinese foreign trade was strictly controlled by a few national trading companies, but gradually it opened to more and more SOEs, and finally private companies could also participate in trade. The trading volume increased from $20.6 billion in 1978 to $340 billion in

1998, with an annual growth rate of 15 percent. The Special Economic Zones, which were established in coastal areas that had freer and more flexible economic policy, contributed significantly to increased trade.[10] SEZs attracted huge foreign investment and produced mostly for export.

The nonstate sector—TVEs, cooperatives, partnership enterprises, incorporated companies, individual proprietors, foreign-funded enterprises, and joint ventures—has given China a gigantic push on the market track. To a large extent China's rapid economic growth has been the result of this dynamic sector.

The task of reforming SOEs is formidable. The inefficiency of SOEs is a common phenomenon not only in China but also around the world. What is particular in China's case is that the Chinese Communist Party firmly insists on a socialist market economy in which SOEs dominate, since it seems that SOEs form the foundation of the regime. So long as SOEs remain inefficient, the task confronting China's government is to reform them and make them perform as efficient and vigorous competitors in a market environment. Unfortunately, that task has not been successful, and it does not seem likely that it can be successful. A large number of SOEs are still losing money or running into difficulty. Since 1998 the central government has sent senior auditors to inspect large SOEs. But those auditors can at best only determine the status of assets, profit, and debt but can seldom help SOEs become market oriented and profitable.

China's social welfare system has been difficult to change. For instance, commercialization of urban apartments is no easy task. Ownership and transaction problems have hindered the development of China's housing market.

Moreover, China has not yet developed its financial market. Financing activities remain under the strict control of the state. Almost all banks are state owned. Private banks are prohibited. The risk of a financial crisis poses a huge potential disequilibrium for China's economy. In the past 20 years, China's growth came from investment that was supported by some 40 percent of people's savings, mostly bank deposits. A large part of those funds was poured into SOEs, which simply wasted the money. Meanwhile, nonstate enterprises have found it difficult to get loans from state banks. Nearly 25 percent of bank deposits have been eaten up by SOEs' bad debts, a situation that breeds financial instability.

As part of economic liberalization, most commodity prices have been set free. However, state monopoly still exists in many industries and gives rise to distorted prices (e.g., in the petroleum industry, telecommunications and post, electric utilities, and railroads). The government still exerts administrative control over the prices of grain, cotton, and coal and infringes on the property rights of citizens by ordering the shutdowns of well-run coal mines to reduce the oversupply of coal and to raise prices for the sake of rescuing inefficient state-owned coal mines. The government instinctively has a strong preference for SOEs, even at the expense of economic efficiency, just because they serve as the basis for the government's political power.

The conflict between efficiency and political power has a profound implication. Because the use of resources was inefficient, the per unit output of pollution was very high during the prereform period—that is, prior to 1979. Although the market has improved efficiency, and pollution has decreased, rapid economic growth has created serious pollution and high consumption of natural resources. The Chinese government is now paying more attention to environmental protection. Spending on pollution reduction and resource protection is approaching 1 percent of GNP.

The success of China's economic reform has won remarkable attention worldwide. Average annual growth of GDP has been nearly 9 percent for over 20 years, making China the fastest-growing economy in the world.[11] The core of successful reform lies in the dual-track Pareto improvement, a gradual, acceptable process that has already changed China enormously. Meanwhile, however, many difficulties and tough problems have accumulated. Political power competes against the market for resource allocation, leading to distorted income distribution and diminished social justice. Political power also erodes economic efficiency.

The Link between Economic Reform and Political Power

In China, politics is linked with the economy. On the one hand, a centralized planned economy requires a centralized authoritarian political regime (more properly termed totalitarianism) to ensure that implementation of mandatory planning and initiation of economic activities be put into effect across the country. On the other hand, a totalitarian regime can reinforce a planned economic regime, because the former puts everything and every citizen under state control and proscribes any obstruction or dissension. Communism prevents private property and individual ownership, so there can be no true markets in a planned economy under a centralized authoritarian regime. Therefore, it is true both theoretically and empirically that state ownership, central planning, and totalitarianism form an iron triangle of communistic conjugation.

Under a centrally planned economic system, the state (represented by its government) is the sole employer of all citizens. Nobody can escape the control of and the persecution by the government. Control by economic means is the most effective and forcible ever used in human history, since that control penetrates every corner of the society. Everybody must join a *danwei* (work unit), which is subordinate to the government. Everyone is assigned to a post and has no right to move. Every organization must accept and accommodate workers assigned by its superior or relevant authorities and has no right to accept or dismiss anyone at will. Thus, everybody is pinned to a particular organization that is just a ring on a huge chain—the government. This form of personal appendage is a characteristic feature of all planned economies.

Personal subsistence is entirely determined by the organization to which an individual is attached. It affords him salary and lodging, usually no more than is barely necessary for his family's daily living. All surplus labor contributions are collected by the state—implicitly, of course. Then the local government authorities will, at the request of the organization, offer that individual the necessities for urban living: registration card, various quotas, and coupons for such items as grain, edible oil, meat, bean products, cloth, coal, and tea. When an individual is detached from his danwei—the equivalent of being expelled from society—he is incapable of surviving. If a person is reproached by his organization, he suffers, mentally and physically, and is doomed to a miserable life.[12] The government can rigorously control and persecute anybody. No one can escape. This structure gives "power" a unique importance.

Compare that situation with one under a market economy, in which various organizations not affiliated with the government emerge. Nobody needs to fear living in bondage to government authority. People have more freedom to live where they can make a better living. No longer subject to quotas and coupons, they can

15

buy their necessities with money. Money is a powerful means for democracy because money demolishes the system under which government determines the distribution of material benefits. The market, however, has its own problem: without money, the necessities of the poor cannot be transferred to producers; thus, the poor are ignored. This distortion of income distribution incenses people, especially when money is used to acquire power.

In China's planned economy, everybody lived under control of his danwei, and every danwei operated under control of the government—actually under control of the CCP. The all-encompassing reach of the CCP effected totalitarian rule throughout the country. Several small parties (called democratic parties) were all dependent on, and subject to the leadership of, the CCP. With some 61 million members, the CCP erected a nationwide network from the top political bureau and central committee to party committees and branches at every danwei. All governmental administration (including economic activities) had to obey the rule of party organizations. That regime has long proved to be very effective, efficient, and overwhelming. Whenever the top leaders (headed by Mao Zedong) made a policy decision, it was passed down very quickly through the party network to every danwei across the country. The CCP could mobilize the masses to take immediate action and carry out any decision. It is by that mechanism that the party has repeatedly launched vast political campaigns aiming at disciplining and persecuting officials and intellectuals, usually leading to disasters nationwide. That mechanism is still in place today but is not so strongly enforced because of the emerging private sector.

A typical political campaign that led to the Great Famine in the early 1960s was the notorious Anti-right Opportunism campaign, which was instigated at the 1959 Lushan session of the political bureau. At that time the economic situation had worsened, largely because of improper economic policies supporting the Great Leap Forward—for example, establishment of the People's Commune, overestimation of farm produce, imposition of high levies on grain, inefficient collection of crops, and coercion to join the common dining hall that had replaced household cooking. The session had been scheduled to discuss ways for improving the economic situation. Peng Dehuai, then minister of defense and also a member of the political bureau, offered his opinion and some criticism on the matter in a letter to Mao. Peng's criticisms were quite correct and conducive to improving the CCP's policy. However, Mao could not accept the criticism and was terribly upset. He used his full authority and influence to convert the session into one condemning Peng, accusing him of "right opportunism" and of heading an "anti-party gang," a term frequently used for persecution. The nationwide Anti-right Opportunism campaign, which tragically strengthened all wrongdoings in rural areas and crushed all dissent, was soon launched. Under the pressure of that campaign, people were encouraged to lie in order to protect themselves and to destroy the reputations of anyone who may have been suspected of party disloyalty.

Then came the Great Famine (1959–61). The famine was brought on not by a natural disaster or shortages due to foreign conflicts.[13] The cause of the Great Famine was due mainly to political misdoing—the destructive Anti-right Opportunism campaign.

Another feature of the PRC's totalitarian politics was the intrinsic and ongoing discrimination against intellectuals. In the early 1950s Chinese intellectuals paid hearty respect to the party and the newly founded PRC and were enthusiastic to join. Many Chinese scholars studying abroad (largely in the United States and England) hurried home and worked fruitfully in a very friendly relationship with the party. A few years passed, and things began to change. In 1954 the party launched a campaign against the Hu Feng counterrevolutionary clique. The campaign badly hurt many writers, poets, and literary critics. The next incident, in 1955, the campaign of "wiping out counterrevolutionaries," was much broader geographically and brutally hurt many innocent people, including Kuomintang officials and military staff, who had already put down arms and surrendered.

The true catastrophe for Chinese intellectuals was the calamitous Anti-rightist movement, which occurred in 1957. Initially, Mao declared that the CCP should rectify its working style. He ordered that every party committee and party branch should give ear to opinions and criticism coming from all intellectuals, officials (called "cadres" in China), and party members. He coaxed party members "to say all you know and say it without reserve" in their criticism of the party's working style. Soon a bumper crop of frank, earnest, and helpful opinions filled the newspapers for about one month. Then Mao abruptly proclaimed that there were rightists ferociously attacking the party with the aim of overthrowing the ruling party

17

and smashing socialism. He ordered an immediate nationwide crackdown on the rightists. Thus, the campaign to rectify the party's working style turned into a wave of unexpected class struggle that crushed hundreds of thousands of naive intellectuals. Mao called the campaign an open fight, not a conspiracy.

The victims who were labeled rightists were treated as enemies, antagonists of the society. They were openly deprived of their human rights and thus lost all protection against various violations. They were never convicted by law but condemned by the logic of class struggle. It was reported that the rightists, all talented intellectuals accounting for more than 10 percent of the nation's intellectuals, totaled .55 million. China lost its most precious resource—its most productive human capital—because of this campaign. The so-called rightists were expelled from their posts; most were exiled to remote barren areas and compelled to endure strenuous manual labor accompanied by repeated scoldings. Many of their families were ruined. They were not permitted to do the jobs for which they had been trained. Such misery lasted some 22 years, too long for many rightists to survive. However, it should be recognized that, unlike in the Soviet Union, executions of politically persecuted people were limited.

The Anti-rightist movement eliminated all different voices from outside of the party, and the Anti-right Opportunism campaign further eliminated voices from inside. Under such a "one-voice society," harmful policies could bring on extreme situations—such as the Great Famine. Then came the notorious Cultural Revolution, a massive persecution initially within the party. Groups of people fought against each other. Though there is no official figure available, it is estimated that hundreds of thousands of deaths were attributable to persecution, suicide, battle, and executions. Almost all governmental departments, including the police, the courts, and even the railways, were forced to cease operation. Why were people driven mad fighting each other? The answer is the absence of private property and human rights protection; everybody was vulnerable to persecution. The only way to be safe was to grasp more power. When one seizes more power, one is safer; so, seizing power became the top priority for everyone—from Mao and Lin Biao to the "revolters." Dissenters were immediately labeled counterrevolutionary and a miserable situation would be waiting for them. Lin was killed in a plane crash after he lost his fight for power in 1971. Most Chinese people were afraid of being labeled counterrevolutionary as soon as they lost power. History has shown that central planning, whether in China or elsewhere, leads to a political regime in which people fight for power and persecution prevails.

Internal fighting during the Cultural Revolution seriously damaged the industrial structure and the normal functioning of government. National output was declining. After the death of Mao, in 1976, the Cultural Revolution came to an end, but the national economy was on the verge of collapse. Then, a new era of opening and reform began in China.

Since 1978, along with the emerging dual-track economy, China's politics also has been changing into a dual-track system—the in-system track and the out-of-system track, as Chinese scholars call them. The in-system track consists of politics combined with the public sector—that is, SOEs, the party, the government, and the military. On that track things more or less have remained the same. The out-of-system track is politics combined with the private sector. Remarkable changes have been taking place in this newly emerging track. The nonpublic sector is relatively freer: no party rule, no government rule except observation of the laws, no coercive inculcation of ideology, and no political campaigns. A private enterprise is no longer a danwei subordinate to the government. Of course, government authorities do not like the out-of-system track because it reduces their power. However, the authorities tolerate the situation, since it provides the main financial source of the economy.

In politics the double tracks do not merge into one. The two will not merge in the foreseeable future. Their growth rates are different because of the action of economic forces. From the past experience, it can be expected that the out-of-system track will expand, taking the place of the other track. If the government can tolerate such a change, a smooth reform process should continue.

Economic reform has expanded personal freedoms: people are freer to choose an occupation, to move from one danwei to another, to travel abroad, and to speak more openly. The post-Mao government has not launched any political campaigns, the class struggle ideology has been rarely spoken of, and intellectuals are more respected. At the village level, elections are freely held, although they are confronted with huge resistance from vested interest

19

groups. Rule by law (not by the party) has been growing. Up to 1998, the standing committee of National People's Congress had formulated hundreds of laws, largely applicable in economic affairs and copied from the West. China has revised its code of criminal and civil procedure. Lawyers have become popular and some court trials have begun to allow visitors. Changes are apparent, but it is also apparent that political reform lags.

The Economy, Society, and Culture

Under the old regime, Chinese society was highly stratified. The regime's extensive discrimination was based on economic and political factors. For instance, the strict separation of urban and rural residents was enforced by China's household registration system. Urban residents are still given an urban registration card that allows them to acquire various coupons for subsidized goods, while rural peasants have a rural registration card. Peasants are not allowed to move into cities and earn a living there. They are doomed to live under poor and inferior conditions. This discrimination against peasants is the result of the planned economy that requires peasants to be tied to their farms and to fulfil their production plans, while urban factories can employ new workers (mostly family members of currently employed workers) only by mandatory planning. Since 1978 millions of redundant rural laborers have rushed to cities to work because of the booming economy, but they are not permanent residents and have to endure all kinds of hardships.

The old regime called for strong discrimination that was based on class status for older people and on class backgrounds for younger people. Unlike ethnic discrimination, class discrimination is artificial, but both have led to serious social disorder. The party rulers believe that people born to proletarian families are naturally inclined to the proletarian revolution, while people born to bourgeois families must naturally be inconsonant with socialism and communism. (Ironically, many of China's revolutionary leaders did not come from poor families.) This kind of discrimination, especially severe during political campaigns, has now ended.

Discrimination still exists between party members and nonmembers. It is almost always the case, though not regulated by any law, that only party members have the privilege of being promoted to high leading posts. That is why many young people joined the party—not to serve the people but to be in power. The market, on the other hand, is based on free choice and equal status. With the development of a market system, discrimination is gradually receding. By signing the U.N. Human Rights Covenant in 1998, the Chinese government has signaled the dawn of a new human rights movement, but things will not change overnight.

China had a population of .54 billion in 1949 and .97 billion in 1979. During that 30-year period, the population grew annually by 2 percent. After the economic reform began in 1978–79, the population grew more slowly, at about 1.3 percent annually and grew to 1.28 billion in 1999. Today the population is increasing by only 1 percent annually. In China's history that is a record-low number.

During the reform era, about 150 million people have moved from rural to urban areas, setting a record for the greatest population movement in human history, and urban population has increased from 18 percent to 30 percent. Such an increase has completely changed urban areas. The market opening has contributed to that change. Now people have more opportunities to make money and pursue their careers and have begun to realize that having too many children can be a burden. Nowadays many young couples freely choose to marry late and have fewer children. Nevertheless, the government continues to carry out its family-planning project nationwide.

Many people in the West believe that China's family planning is coercive, but it is less so now. Today many women prefer not to have children, and the one-child policy in rural areas is more flexible, with rural couples often having two children.

Improved economic conditions; success in the eradication of poverty; implementation of women and children projects; encouragement of community projects; and, equally important, improvements in sanitation, nutrition, medical care, housing, and education have all combined to bring about a longer life span and a lower infant mortality rate. It is remarkable that the Chinese people have an average life span of 70 years, nearly the same as in developed countries, while in terms of per capita income, China is still a developing country. With prolonged life spans and a one-child policy, China's population is aging quickly and will turn from a country of labor surplus into one of labor shortage. As a result, China's economic growth could be seriously hindered.

China's social security system is not suitable for a market economy and an aging population. Formerly, social security was provided only to urban residents (workers and cadres). Rural people received no pension, medical care, or accident insurance, illustrating the unequal status between urban and rural people. Rural elders fully depended on their families late in their life. Under the old urban security system, expenses were paid from SOEs' current income. But as the structure of the population changes, especially when some factories or danwei go bankrupt, retirees will lose their pensions. The burden is shifting to the government, and social security reform is now under way. However, many financial difficulties lie ahead.

Enormous changes have also occurred in income distribution and civil rights. Under the old regime, society was quite egalitarian in terms of monetary income. The differences in salary between high-ranking officials and ordinary workers were small. But the former could enjoy (not own) a comfortable residence, a car, a villa, servants, a chef, special travelling facilities, and special health care, all provided free by the government, with expenditures usually far exceeding one's salary. The main source of income differences was power, not earnings. Since 1979 economic growth has improved the overall level of income nationwide, with living standards increasing faster in urban areas than in rural areas. The distribution of income has diverged greatly because of market competition.[14] Most urban residents are better off. The poor are mainly retirees, workers laid off from SOEs, and peddlers. The rich are individual proprietors, CEOs of corporations and joint ventures, bankers, and managers of state monopolies. In recent years, some renowned actors, singers, and writers have also joined in the galaxy of the rich. In the early years of the dual-track reform, there emerged not only profiteers who came from a background of political privilege but also tax evaders and smugglers. And worst of all, a new group of rich corrupt officials has emerged.[15]

Corruption of officials is becoming rampant, despite social resentment and government action. Along with the growth of the economy, the crime rate is increasing, with many crimes related to economic affairs. Too much government intervention in the market, including too many government-run businesses, inevitably creates many opportunities for rent seeking, leading to embezzlement and bribes. Moving to a market economy while at the same time sticking to a doctrine that SOEs should dominate the market is a sure way to corruption. A remedy against corruption would be to establish more effective and transparent property rights that limit government involvement in the market economy. That approach, however, is very difficult to implement in the current regime.

Under the planned economy, high-ranking officials are the planners; they make mandatory decisions about huge investments and hundreds of thousands of workers. They also make political decisions or play an important role in political campaigns that determine the fate of millions of citizens. Ordinary citizens have no right to say anything; they must obediently follow orders. The whole society is deeply stratified into planners and workers, the powerful and the powerless, and rulers and subjects. However, even high-ranking officials are not protected by law; they have to keep an eye on what others are doing. A socialist society should be a society with one unified will, coordination, and harmony, but, in fact, because of the lack of legal protection and overwhelming persecution, it has a very unstable structure.

Economic reform has been accompanied by political progress. In addition to greater individual freedom, fighting among party members has weakened. Once a state leader steps down, he is not labeled a counterrevolutionary and can continue to live in peace. Even the term "counterrevolutionary," which has always threatened innocent Chinese people, has been discarded. Nowadays, the main danger of social instability is not class struggle within the party but the inability of the party or the government to maintain social justice. Corruption and abuse of power are the main sources of popular resentment.[16]

The socio-ethical ideas have also undergone changes. In the early 1950s, people were encouraged to serve the public without any thought of themselves. Such ethics of communism, at one time, had succeeded in purifying the social mood and dissolving inconsonance, providing a high moral standard in society: "No one picks up and pockets anything lost on the road; no one needs to shut one's door at night." Unfortunately, this kind of ethics cannot last long. When everyone is selfless, a few cunning people can exploit others. Moreover, the ethics of communism can be easily damaged by people's struggle for power as a means for safety. The death of Lin in a plane crash in 1971 revealed the hypocrisy of communist morality. To

23

establish a new morality—combining traditional ethics with new market ethics—is a difficult task.

China was closed to and excluded from international intercourse for 30 years; then came reform and opening to the outside world for 20 years. The most remarkable change in China's social culture is the influence of foreign (Western) culture. For instance, a constitution is an imported idea, as is protection of the environment. Most Chinese laws are copied from the West. It is now accepted for China to link its laws to an international norm and to import technology. Classical music, once banned during the Cultural Revolution, has become popular again.

In recent years, individual rights (civil rights) have been finding their way into the establishment. The goal of demolishing special privileges has gradually met with general acceptance. Economic planning and totalitarian politics are all founded on privilege. It can be concluded that the whole process of reform is a process of gradually removing privilege rights. It is a hard course because of the resistance coming from the vested interest groups, who take advantage of their privilege rights, and also because of the lack of human rights in Chinese traditional culture. Fortunately, owing to the market system, which has an inherent tendency toward equal status, and to the flexible attitude that the party holds toward social changes, the process of removing privilege rights is making progress. The opening advocated by Deng Xiaoping has encouraged the international exchange not only of goods and services but also of personnel, culture, ideas, and institutions.

People often pay too much attention to the transfer of foreign technology but ignore the importance of institutional transfer. For example, a judicial and legal system, stock exchanges and futures markets, and even universities are all institutions established through many years of trial and error in Western countries. Those fine institutions are the results of a learning process that involves a cost. When China adopts those institutions from the West, a huge learning cost is saved. The catch-up advantage in institution building is no less than the advantage in technology transfer. Therefore, "to keep in line with international norms" is a wise policy for the Chinese government. However, since people are afraid of losing their traditional Chinese culture, the policy faces many obstacles. Thus, the policy has to be modified "in line with an international norm with Chinese characteristics," or simply, a "socialist norm."

China's middle class is growing, yet it has no political representative on behalf of its interests. Nobody in the politburo speaks for the interests of this backbone of society. Recently, some provincial people's congresses and people's political consultative conferences accepted a few business CEOs as members. But the CEOs' voices are not loud enough to protect their interests. They are still a weak component in the stratum of society.[17] China is still a poor country, and it will take decades for its middle class to achieve an influential voice in the political debate.

Prospects for the Next Decade

The experience of the past 50 years is that the market not only provides a better economy but also is conducive to democracy. The call by the May Fourth Movement 80 years ago for democracy and science was entirely correct, but unfortunately China trod down the wrong road. Sixty years after that, in 1978, there was neither democracy nor science, only a collapsing economy. Since then, although democracy and science have been rarely talked of, people have acquired more democracy and science because the market has propelled both. This is not to say that the market will bring about democracy and science automatically, but only that the market encourages people to strive for individual rights and ways to get rich. The market is based on free exchange, and that is possible only if property rights and freedom of choice are protected. Only when people's individual rights are violated will they ask, "Who is governing the state?" The experience of Hong Kong tells us that as long as the Hong Kong people can enjoy individual rights, they are not overly concerned about democracy.

The way to become rich in a market economy is to adopt new technologies and better management, both of which require knowledge of science. Therefore, a market economy encourages people to understand science. Twenty years of reform in China have turned many peasants into adept technicians, managers, and even bankers. Market competition is pushing them to learn more. The market is really a powerful tool for education.

The future of China's economy will depend on how smoothly the market can develop. The major obstacle to developing market institutions in China is the special privilege rights that lie beyond, and conflict with, human rights. The acceptance of human rights

25

in China requires changes in the political system. The party has announced that political reform will proceed. A flexible attitude of the party toward political change is a key factor for the future of China's economy.

It is also important to exchange with the outside world and to learn from different civilizations. Those exchanges will ensure movement toward a more rational system. If there had been no such exchanges in the past, economic reforms would not have been successful.

Over the next 20 years, the current leaders will pass. Who will be the future leaders? According to the experience of Taiwan and other Asian countries, the national authority changes hands from traditional rulers to returned students from the West. That change is happening now in China too, but only at the lower levels. However, it will develop and extend to higher levels. Sun Yatsen said 70 years ago: "The world trend goes forcefully. It will demolish everyone who tries to stop it, and only one who reconciles can survive!" That historic statement is an exact prophecy for China's future.

Notes

1. "List of Events of PRC's Economy in Fifty Years" (in Chinese), *China Business Monthly/Hong Kong and Macao,* October 1999, p. 72.

2. "Spoken PRC's History (First Half)" (in Chinese), *Zhonghua Readers' Digest,* October 13, 1999, p. 4.

3. In 1953, the first year of the First Five Year Plan, China began large-scale construction. On May 15, China and the USSR signed a contract titled "USSR to Help China Develop Its Economy." There were to be 141 projects (the final number came to 156 in 1954).

4. Zhu Zongyu et al., *Outline of the History of the PRC* (in Chinese) (Fujian: People's Press of Fujian, 1993).

5. Jin Dexing et al., *History of the PRC* (in Chinese) (Changsha: Henan University Press, 1993).

6. The figure of the death toll is determined by the definition of "death due to starvation." If the total accounts for unborn children, the figure may reach between 30 and 40 million. There are detailed discussions on the Great Famine in a special issue of *China Economic Review* (9, no. 2 [Fall 1998]) titled "China's Great Famine." See also Jasper Becker, *Hungry Ghosts: China's Secret Famine* (London: John Murray, 1996), pp. 266–74.

7. See Dali L. Yang, *Calamity and Reform in China* (Stanford, Calif.: Stanford University Press, 1966), p. 64. Yang confirmed the relationship between level of party membership and relative severity of famine. He writes, "It highlights the fact that the Great Leap Famine was rooted in politics rather than nature."

8. For an insightful analysis on the institutional changes in the Chinese economy, see Yingyi Qian, "The Institutional Foundation of China's Market Transition," Annual Bank Conference on Development Economics, The World Bank, April 28–30, 1999.

9. Until the mid-1990s, township industry, taking advantage of incomplete market competition, grew by more than 20 percent, but after the mid-1990s, the growth rate declined because of the industry's primitive technology and environmental impact. The countryside has been the center of China's dramatic changes over the last 20 years. See Jean C. Oi, "Peasants and Rural Changes in China," Paper delivered at U.S.-China Relations, Second Conference, Aspen Institute, Aspen, Colorado, March 30–April 4, 1999.

10. On March 24, 1980, the State Council announced the establishment of the Special Economic Zones. The most outstanding example of an SEZ is Shenzhen, which is now the most vigorous and prosperous city in China.

11. *Statistical Yearbook of China, 1998* (Chinese and English) (Beijing: China Statistical Publishing House, 1998).

12. There have been a number of stories published in China describing the miserable life of those who have faced such persecutions. The authors of these stories are intellectuals, army officials, students, workers, and peasants. However, the government does not encourage serious academic study about those persecutions.

13. James Wen, "Food Availability versus Consumption Efficiency: Causes of the Chinese Famine," *China Economic Review* 9, no. 2 (Fall 1998): 157–65. The author concluded that "the Famine was a man-made catastrophe with unique characteristics."

14. Ronald A. Edwards, "How Many Countries Is China?" Discussion paper, University of Minnesota, March 1997. Edwards has found that the disparities of per capita GDP across China's provinces are huge compared with disparities both within other countries and across groups of countries around the world.

15. In most transition economies, the equality of income has been worsening because of elimination of government subsidies, difference in past investment in human capital, and access to foreign markets. The inequality problem is especially difficult in a recession. Recent moderate recession in China since 1997 has caused rather serious problems in income inequality. See Grzegorz W. Kolodko, "Income Policy, Equity Issues, and Poverty Reduction in Transition Economies," *Finance and Development* 36, no. 3 (September 1999): 32–34.

16. The party approved "rule by law" in the recent change in the constitution, which should mean that the party's decision on policy must be in line with the law. The large-scale crushing of the Falung Gong since the summer of 1999 obviously violates freedom of religious belief. However, as a response to the party's decision, the People's Congress and Highest Court made a policy on October 30, 1999, on what kind of law can be adopted for crushing the Falung Gong. That decision shows that the legal system, even the constitution, is not independent.

17. By the definition of communism, a person earning a capital gain is prohibited from being a party member. The party, the ruling body of the nation, therefore, does not accept any investor, and the capital class cannot enter the ruling body. There has been a lot of debate about whether party members should be allowed to buy shares and whether CEOs and investors should be accepted as party members.

2. From Political Society to Economic Society: The Evolution of Civil Rights in China

Kate Xiao Zhou

This chapter discusses the development of civil rights in China during the past 50 years. Civil rights are defined as the right of free speech, the right to own property, the right of free movement, and the right to change occupations. The main argument suggests that the transformation from a political to an economic society has laid foundations that will support the emergence of civil rights. The Chinese civil rights movement differs from other social movements in that it is a spontaneous, unorganized, leaderless, nonideological, and apolitical movement (SULNAM).[1] Although most of the rights listed above are primarily economic, they have far-reaching political and social consequences.

China scholars who study state-society relations tend to focus on civil society, and although some of those scholars are optimistic about the future of civil society in China, others are pessimistic. For example, Roger Des Forges describes the longevity of Chinese civil society, whereas Minxin Pei sees the elite's tolerance of civil society and the rule of law as a result of market influence.[2] There has been a tendency for the state to play a greater role in the development of civil society. B. Michael Frolic credits the state with the rise of civil society in China.[3] The continued importance of the Chinese authoritarian tradition and the state's role in building civil society suggest that civil rights can be only given to, not won by, the people.

On the other hand, if one defines civil society as confrontational with the state, China does not have a civil society. Kenneth Dean refuses to use the term "civil society" to describe Chinese rural society, yet he recognizes the power of local resistance.[4] No one would deny that the Chinese people have more freedom than they have had since the founding of the People's Republic of China by

29

the Communists in 1949. Following Dean's analysis, I acknowledge the importance of the people's resistance and empowerment, but, unlike Dean, I recognize the importance of the people's popular movement, which deserves the credit for winning greater freedom in China. Thus, more specifically, this chapter focuses on how the evolution of civil rights could lead to the rise of civil society.

The Absence of Civil Rights between 1953 and 1978

Before explaining the civil rights movement in contemporary China, it is necessary to discuss the absence of civil rights between 1953 and 1978. Like those in other communist states, leaders in China had an encompassing and closed grand vision of the future communist state that gave them the justification for depriving people of their liberties without hesitation. Despite the differences among Chinese leaders, almost all of them after 1949 advocated social justice, equality, and national solidarity. To realize this grand vision, the Chinese people had to be transformed. To build a communist paradise, politics took precedence over the interests of people. In trying to attain its political goals, the Chinese Communist Party took away people's civil rights.

Abolition of Private Property

The first step was to take away private property. This Marxist tradition dated from Rousseau, who attributed the origin of inequality to the rise of private property. The Chinese Communists and their leader, Mao Zedong, were Marxist loyalists. For them, the abolition of private property was just and progressive. It was the only way to achieve equality for all.

In 1949, the year the Communists took over, private activity dominated the Chinese economy. More than 63 percent of industrial production, 85 percent of commercial retail value, and 98 percent of commercial entities belonged to the private sector.[5] In rural China, private cultivators and craftsmen were the majority, more than 90 percent. In China as a whole, even in 1952, the private sector accounted for 71.8 percent of gross national product. This private sphere laid the foundation for relative local autonomy. For many generations, under various regimes, the Chinese people had tried their best to dodge, deflect, and blunt the impact of demands that were detrimental to local interests and values, and those efforts put a limit on the reach of the state. The Chinese government launched three major political movements, described below, to eliminate the private sphere, which was the economic base of the social shield that protected civil society against the state.

1. The *zhengya fageming* (suppressing the anti-revolutionaries) movement took place in 1950. During that movement, at least 1 million "reactionaries" (mostly landlords and former government officials) were killed.[6]
2. The land reform movement in 1950–53 mobilized the rural poor against the rich, leading to the redistribution of land. As soon as the land reform was completed, in 1953, the state cleared the way for collectivization by nationalizing markets. By 1956, 88 percent of rural households were forced to join collectives, an action that eliminated the base of civil society in the countryside.
3. The state's collectivization movement had by 1956 collectivized 93 percent of the private handicraft industry and 99 percent of private industrial enterprises.

These so-called three great socialist changes effectively ended private-sector activities within five years of the Communist takeover. The private sector fell from 80 percent of GNP in 1949 to 7 percent in 1956 and 2.8 percent in 1957.[7] This socialist big bang had a devastating effect on Chinese civil society.

Danwei: Workplace Control System in the City

When private jobs (handicraft, industry, and commerce) disappeared, the state became the only source of jobs for the urban people. In the urban sector, most adult workers worked in a *danwei* (work unit), and their life and work were controlled by the state and their danwei. Work was assigned to each urban individual without regard to his wishes. The danwei would keep a *danan* (secret personal file) for each worker. Most Chinese people lived and worked in an environment that constrained or even denied individual rights.

In exchange for the loyalty and the compliance of urban workers, the danwei provided them with their basic needs, which included health care, pensions, education, and housing. As long as those commitments were met, workers submitted themselves to the authority of the state. Thus, in exchange for limited welfare, urban people lost their right to challenge authority. Such economic and welfare dependence under Mao resulted in an "extraordinary ability to prevent organized political activities even from reaching the stage of collective action."[8] The deprivation of civil rights ended any meaningful challenge to the state. Not many people dared to break the only rice bowl.

Rural Bondage: The Rise of Communist Serfs in China

In the countryside, the collectivization of private farmland was also linked to the loss of civil rights for the farmers. Because the state had become the only supplier of resources, farmers on the collectives lost the right to move, the right to occupational choices, and the right to make decisions for their own households. The most effective state control over the rural population was the *hukou* system (the household registration system determining grain rationing to each individual), which bound rural people to the land. The state hukou forbade farmers to seek nonfarm employment, and food rationing made it impossible to migrate. Since farmers could not get food outside their communes, to leave the collectives meant starvation. Farmers lost not just private property but their freedom and rights as well.

After collectivization in 1956, the cadres controlled farmers and, acting as feudal lords, replaced family heads as decisionmakers. Once farmers lost their economic power base to bargain with the state, their fate became linked to the state economic plan. Since the goal was to boost industrialization, farmers had a heavy burden. As the only buyer in the market, the state set agricultural prices low and industrial prices high to extract capital from the majority to support the socialist industrial plan.

Worse, the state did not provide farmers with a social safety net comparable to that available to the urban workers. Farmers had to rely on themselves for education, retirement, medical care, and other basic necessities. When the state-initiated famine occurred, from 1959 to 1961, most famine victims (between 25 million to 45 million) were farmers.[9] Although there were different estimates of the number of deaths, even the lowest estimate would make the so-called Great Leap Famine the worst famine and the worst case of human rights abuse in human history. When private ownership was taken away, famine spread nationwide. Before communism, when natural disasters caused famine, people could seek food in other places. But nationalization of farmers' land meant that one bad policy could cause a disaster throughout the country. In addition, mobility was banned; thus, people died in their local communities, helpless to seek outside relief.

When the state controlled nearly all goods and mobility, it also controlled individuals, who became vulnerable because their material well-being was under the state's control.

Collectivization in China provided the institutional basis for state control of a substantial rural surplus and of restriction of population movement, markets, and consumption. Annual growth rates in grain of 2.3 percent between 1952 and 1978 enabled China to slightly surpass the inexorable growth of its rural population and to feed close to 1 billion people by the end of the period. However, the growing disparity in income and opportunity between city and countryside, and between rising agricultural productivity and stagnant rural income and consumption, fueled rural discontent. Thus, the communist regime that took over China to help alleviate rural poverty actually made things much worse and betrayed those who had placed their trust in the party.

Class Struggle and Political Terror

By taking away private property and by eliminating private jobs, the state made people economically dependent. The dominance of state power led to arbitrary rule, which caused fear among the people. China's constitutions of 1954, 1972, and 1978 were all based on the principle of *yi jieji douzheng weigang* (class struggle), under which "class enemies" were to be eliminated. From 1949 to 1983, there were more than 20 political campaigns in which millions were victimized. The constant political struggles against the "enemies" of the state, the miserable fate of the enemies and their families, combined with their material dependence on the state, effectively silenced dissent. Even Liu Shaoqi, the head of state, could not escape the arbitrary persecution; he was tortured and died naked on a cement floor in a detention house. In 1984 when the government tried to "rehabilitate" the 20 million *di fu fan huai* (Four Bad Elements), which included landlords, rich peasants, counterrevolutionaries, and "rotten elements," only 709,504, about 4 percent, were given "political rehabilitation," while the rest simply vanished.[10]

When the majority of the people participated in Mao's land reform against the rich, most Chinese saw such revolutionary redistribution as harsh but just, thus willingly strengthening the power of the state. But when the rights of a small percentage of people are easily taken away, the rights of the rest become vulnerable.

No Freedom of the Press or Freedom of Speech

Political control was not limited to economic life. When private property was banned, independent writers, private schools, and independent publishers ceased to exist. Since the artists and the writers could work only for the state, they were not allowed to be critical of the state. As an old Chinese saying goes, "If one eats someone's food, one's voice becomes soft." In the United States, there is a similar saying, "Do not bite the hand that feeds you." In exchange for a lifelong salary and other basic necessities, writers and artists lost their freedom.

Furthermore, the Anti-rightist movement in 1957 destroyed 552,877 intellectuals. The movement labeled more than 10 percent of all Chinese educated elites as rightists and deprived them of their basic rights until 1978.[11] The silence of intellectuals and the nationalization of all presses led to total state control of the media and made intellectuals and writers the tools of the CCP.

As a result, art and literature and political propaganda served the same purpose: to indoctrinate people. Public entertainment was eliminated for many years. The political intimidation reached its peak during the Cultural Revolution (1966–76), in which Mao called on people to destroy the four "olds" (old ideas, old cultures, old customs, and old habits). Private collections of Chinese traditional art became the targets. In Beijing, between August and September 1966, 4,922 priceless private art collections were destroyed.[12]

Mao's Failed Utopia

On May 7, 1966, Mao wrote a letter to Lin Biao, his chosen successor, in which he stated that his goal in launching the Cultural Revolution was to get rid of all ideas and cultures of capitalist exploitation. But when the state attempted to level all differences between the poor and the more prosperous, when it eliminated private property and markets, the effort boomeranged. The gap between better-off and destitute regions and between communities and families grew. Mao's utopian dream, the Cultural Revolution, brought disaster to the nation. Even Ye Jianying, a veteran Chinese Communist leader, admitted on December 13, 1978, that more than 100 million people had been afflicted by the Cultural Revolution. There were at least 2 million false accusations, and several million innocent people were prosecuted.[13] Given that family members of those wrongly accused suffered too, the figure was actually much higher.

In short, to secure its power, the Chinese state under Mao eliminated private property, banned mobility, and used arbitrary terror and routine violence to force people to accept his vision of society. In so doing, he destroyed personal identity and disrupted the very ideas of social time and space, ending civil society in China. The Chinese case shows that, as Justice Louis Brandeis said, "the greatest dangers to liberty lurk in insidious encroachment by men of zeal, well meaning but without understanding"[14]—or, as Samuel Johnson said, "The road to hell is paved with good intentions."

We will never know exactly how many people were killed in China's violent political campaigns during the CCP's first 30 years of power. Those campaigns included the Three-antis and the Five-antis movements, the Anti-rightist movement, the Great Leap Forward, the Commune, the Anti-right Wind campaign, the Socialist Education and Four Clean Ups, the Cultural Revolution, the Clean Up Ranks campaign, and the Going Up to the Mountains and Settle Down in the Countryside movement. In all those political movements, individual liberty was taken away. The party itself calls the 10-year-long Cultural Revolution *"Haojie"* (roughly, holocaust, or gigantic catastrophe). The state's total control over society created social alienation from the system.

The Civil Rights Movement in Contemporary China

Gradually people began an attempt to avoid the power of the state, and in that attempt they created social space. When millions participated in civil disobedience, a civil rights movement was born. But unlike other civil rights movements, the Chinese movement is a SULNAM.

The Right to Be Left Alone

The first phase of the civil rights movement was called *"baochan daohu"* (turning production over to the household). In the late 1970s, farmers began to make deals with the local party bosses to farm on their own. The baochan daohu movement was a means of avoidance: farmers in poor areas tried to make deals out of range of the government leaders. Also, the death of Mao in 1976 created a political power vacuum that allowed the people's avoidance movement to spread. When this illegal practice spread throughout the country, the central government gave in, which led to a rapid increase in agricultural productivity. Once the state gave baochan daohu formal recognition in 1982, farmers were liberated from the daily control by the party-state. The new policy satisfied a long-standing desire of every rural household to acquire a piece of land to farm. The strong incentives from the new family system led to the rapid increase in agricultural productivity and the rapid growth of markets, first agricultural markets and then retail and industrial markets. Resources (primarily labor but also capital in the form of farmers' savings) were released from agriculture, stimulating both long-distance and local commercial activities and trade.

Deng Xiaoping and his associates tried to take credit for the economic takeoff brought about by the farmers. The farmers, although grateful that Deng had formalized the family farm system, wanted to be left alone to make their own decisions. Neither Deng nor Chinese farmers had anticipated the social and political impact of this massive, spontaneous movement toward economic freedom.

The Right to Own Property: The Rise of Independent, Individual Proprietorships

The second phase saw the evolution of property rights under two different patterns: (1) indigenous, springing from the family economy; and (2) foreign, adopting strategies from abroad (e.g., stock exchanges and foreign-funded enterprises). The government played a decisive role in developing stock markets and joint ventures. But indigenous property rights evolved through a weakening of the old planned system. Thus, the development of indigenous property rights weakened the power of the state.

The baochan daohu movement did not lead to privatization of land, but it did grant farmers temporary use rights. Even such limited rights enabled farm households to regain private initiative and other freedoms as well. By 1985 the average household was worth 3,812.77 yuan (assets included private housing, fixed production capital, cash, grain, and savings).[15] This limited ownership of private goods led to independence.

Although in 1981 the state allowed only jobless people in the city to become a *getihu* (a self-employed person), the baochan daohu movement enabled everyone in China to be self-employed, and 80 percent of Chinese people became self-employed. This reservoir of independent, self-employed entrepreneurs became the cornerstone for the rise of private enterprises. As millions of people began to own factories and service firms, public belief in private property gradually reemerged. The boom in private homebuilding in the 1980s was an indication of public interest in private property.

The public interest in private ownership effectively weakened communist ideology. Few in China today still believe in communism, and the desire to become independent has become a national obsession. Private entrepreneurs have mushroomed across China, and this swarm of entrepreneurial effort has not only revived interest in private ownership but also changed the rigidity of social stratification. Under Mao, political power and residential status determined one's social standing in the society. However, possession of material goods (money and property) has become a more important identity. Many former members of the lower classes have gained social mobility despite their disadvantage in the system.

The rise of private enterprises is a direct cause of the rise of private philanthropy. Many private businesspeople have donated large sums of money to schools, hospitals, projects for helping the poor, tree-planting programs, and environmental groups. Other businesspeople have provided jobs or free goods and services to poor families or trained young, unskilled poor persons. Susan Young points out that it has become the norm for private businesspeople in the countryside to donate some of their earnings to the local communities.[16] Although there may be community pressure for businesspeople to make donations, the rise of private charity in itself is an important part of the transition from the state to civil society. The nonstate sector is taking on more and more of the functions that had been monopolized by the state.

Freedom of Movement and Occupational Choices

The return of private economic activity brought about a massive flow of migration. When rural people gained goods of their own, they wanted to trade them in for cash and other goods. That led to the reemergence of professional traders and the growth of markets. Moreover, many people, especially the young, began to look for job opportunities. The new freedom of movement enabled massive numbers of individuals to pursue economic opportunities.

China's economic developments have had profound implications for rights consciousness in China. First, independent economic decisionmaking effectively killed the old rationing system, because in the new market economy migrants could buy food in the markets without food coupons. The food coupon, which was given only to urban residents, had been used not only to control people's movement but also to differentiate between rural and urban identities. For the majority of farmers, the death of the coupon was a liberation.

Second, the newly acquired freedom of movement broke the closed job system in which the state determined people's lives. Increasingly, people are changing their jobs according to market demand instead of staying at their government-assigned jobs. That change has been most profound in the countryside, where the majority of farmers' children no longer do farm work. By mid-1985, more than one-fifth of rural people had changed their occupation and residence. The geographical and occupational mobility varies from region to region, but in some rural areas like Zhejiang, more than 70 percent of the population experienced both geographical and occupational mobility, while in other places the percentage is much lower (as low as 10 to 20 percent).[17] An increasing number of Chinese people have been able to buy "the right to live where they want," thus weakening the government's control over their lives.

The formal recognition of freedom of movement occurred in 1984, when the state permitted farmers to settle down only in the townships, but that restriction could not constrain millions from moving into bigger cities. Every day across China, 100 million migrants are defying the state control over mobility. Within each province, there are another 100 million migrants either looking for jobs or working. Although those migrants are not organized, they have produced the largest coordinated movement of civil disobedience in the history of mankind. This massive migration pattern illustrates the relative gains ordinary people have made in their right to live and to work where they choose—in spite of the government's formal regulations and the hukou system. This change has had both economic and political consequences.

Rural migrants who were formerly denied the right to work in the city and in industrial jobs have become the most mobile workforce in China. One recent survey suggests that the turnover rate of jobs among migrant workers in Guangdong Province, the most developed industrial area in China, is very high, with 66 percent of migrant workers changing jobs.[18] This relative freedom of occupational choice would not have been possible without the rise of non-state-sector jobs.

The free flow of rural migrants gradually induced the elite to change its attitude. Wherever migrants went, the economic boom followed. The richest cities were the migrant cities. More and more people, including some members of the elite, began to doubt the old assumption that the control over mobility was good for political stability. The leaders soon realized that such restrictions were not good for economic prosperity in China.

What is most amazing about China's freedom of movement is its unorganized and apolitical nature. Most migrants found jobs and set up their own businesses by informal networks of friends and kin. Few migrants openly challenge the hukou system because what they desire most is to avoid the eyes of government officials.

Since China's economic miracle, more and more people are accepting the idea that loosening control over labor mobility is good for China's economy. Yet most Chinese still think that state control over mobility is not an offense against the liberty of the people. In 1998 China signed the U.N. Universal Rights Convention, which grants citizens the right to move.[19] Although the hukou system still exists and is a menace to liberty in China, an increasing number of people have gained the freedom to move and the freedom to choose their occupation. Let us hope that it will not be long before ordinary Chinese people will use the U.N. document to challenge the hukou system.

Private Publication

The link between private property and a freer flow of information is very strong in China because the rise of private enterprises and the nonstate sector (mainly rural industry) has led to the publication of politically incorrect materials. Many underground publications have been produced by nonstate rural factories, away from the city bureaucrats who control censorship. Those factories have been churning out tens of millions of unauthorized copies of books. The state's ban on "unhealthy content," such as love and desire, reserved for the underground firms a lucrative market in which they faced no competition from state-owned industry. Rural factories in Guangdong also produced massive numbers of tape recorders. When millions of Chinese households could buy tape recorders, it became virtually impossible to control what people listened to at home. The rapid rise of nonstate industry gave the Chinese people greater access to cultural artifacts (almanacs, accounts of crime, and pornography) that were officially forbidden by the state.

Publishers, who now had strong commercial motivations, were stimulated by the needs of their audience. After 30 years of high politics, people were ready for apolitical entertainment ranging from pornography to legendary stories. Publishers tried to satisfy consumers by producing books that were interesting, which in itself violated the state's principle for publication—political correctness. As the informal market became the mass market, formal state control over information weakened.

The spread of unofficial and illegal printing is also linked to the growth of the market distribution system. Street vendors, people who have booths in night markets, people who sell door to door, and even storefront businesses make up the swarm of entrepreneurs that has engulfed the official censorship. It is in this context that relative freedom of publication has accompanied the rise of the nonstate sector in both production (rural industry) and consumption (a parallel society). In most urban *jishi* (farmers' markets), books of all kinds (politically incorrect, pornographic, mystery, kung fu, fortunetelling) have been on sale. In fact, the informal sale of books has become so popular that the market has become specialized. Some merchants sell only detective stories, some only romance novels, and some only classical Chinese literature. Specialists are able to get books in their specialty from both international and national sources.

To a great extent, long-term government censorship of all sorts of information and artistic expression helped create an urge to have access to unofficial and uncensored material. But like mischievous teenagers, many Chinese found such publications interesting primarily because they were forbidden. Government bans on material often converted works into instant bestsellers. Ambitious writers hoped that they would be criticized by the government because the subsequent state ban often did more for the writers than did the best advertisement.

One reason that nonstate publications could escape the eye of the state was because of their apolitical content. Private-sector publication focused on mass demand, and since relatively few people in China were interested in politics, in the beginning, most private-sector publications were apolitical. When the state officials focused their attention on the dissident publications, the popular genres slipped right through their hands.

The sizable market demand led to the rise of professional writers to meet popular demand. Instead of writing party-state propaganda, these new writers paid attention to the diversified tastes of people. The publishers of cultural products used commissions to attract famous writers. Very quickly informal contracts between informal publishers and writers grew. Thus, the violation of state censorship and marketization added monetary value to their intellectual creations. As long as there is money to be made, it is hard for the government to enforce its ban on private publications. While the Chinese government focused manpower on dissident intellectuals and other organized political entities, private-sector publication, apolitical and unorganized, escaped official attention.

Nowadays private publishers have begun to publish materials that the government tries hardest to suppress (works on democracy, human rights, violence, kung fu, and sexuality). The illegal printing of *The Private Life of Chairman Mao* is a case in point.

The Rise of Publication Pluralism

The competition in publications from the nonstate sector has altered the game of publication in China and made it difficult for the state to continue total censorship. Because so many people are trying to make money to improve their lives, they have opened social space and won limited freedoms. When farmers and other private businesses were making money in the 1980s, they changed the social reference group. In the beginning, the state poured money into urban state enterprises to buy the workers' support, because few Chinese believed the communist ideology. The only way to achieve legitimacy was to provide (or at least not squelch) economic prosperity. But the state budget was running into serious trouble, which forced the state to reduce the size of subsidies. To keep the workers happy, the government acquiesced to many informal moneymaking schemes like "moonlighting" and "marketing."

From the Xinhua News Agency (the biggest and most influential news organization) to provincial news and presses, making money by using government property and influence (i.e., the name of the state presses) for private gains (i.e., members of the government organizations) has become a norm. This means that the state media

41

organizations have become the source of extra income for its workers. As a result, even the state presses pay attention to market demand, publishing books and articles that interest readers.

The more the state media organizations reduced their financial dependence on the state, the more they gained in discretion over content. Although a free press is a long way off, the nature of the state presses has changed and the public has acquired some freedom.

In China, if one is willing to pay, one can get hold of any book, film, video, or journal. In the summer of 1998, I was able to find on the streets of Beijing books about the Tiananmen incident and a copy of *The Private Life of Mao Zedong*, all banned by the state. As noted above, the availability of those materials undermines the party's ideology by offering alternative voices in music, films, and books and by providing an avenue for self-reflection. Self-reflection has become subversive—a threat to the state's political domination.

Because private channels provide interesting movies and games for mass entertainment, the state television stations have realized that they have to change to keep their audience. To compete, the state stations have begun to make programs that satisfy the consumers. In addition, they have also discovered the power of advertisements. As a substantial amount of money comes from advertising, the state TV stations have changed their strategy from getting money from the state to produce what the state wants to making programs to get money from advertisers. State television became bolder, producing programs to compete with other nonbroadcast entertainment such as illegally copied foreign films. To keep their traditional audience, the state news media (newspapers and television) began to experiment with news that pushed the limits of orthodox party propaganda. It is against such a background that the Chinese equivalents of *60 Minutes* and *20/20* have appeared. Since no foreign companies can compete directly with the state media, these news magazine programs enjoy great success in China. As a result, Chinese media have been de-politicized to some degree.

Facing competition from the market, the editor of *China Youth* (the party youth journal), Peng Bo, has two strategies to survive: (1) change the content and format of the journal to produce what the market most wants and (2) move the god (readers) by sincerity.

Competition also influenced the thinking of the Chinese publishing elite. The publication of the controversial book *Feidu* (Decadence of the Capital) is an example. When the government banned the book and fined the Beijing publisher, Arts Press, for publishing the "corrupt book," the editor in chief, Xie Dajun, paid the fine of 810,000 yuan (U.S.$75,000). But, at the same time, he also paid 270,000 yuan in royalties to Jia Pingao, the author. When the incident became known in China in 1996, the subscription of the Art Press's main journal *Shiyue* (The October) increased. The editor's act shows that he cared for both his company's reputation and his loyalty to the party leadership. Xie has also gained respect among many Chinese intellectuals who take pride in his bold behavior.

The government propaganda agencies, radio, newspapers, and TV stations used to get money from the state to make programs. But, in a consumer-dominated economy, those same agencies make programs to get money. This change has tremendous social and political implications. Driven by material incentives, entrepreneurs and book dealers have helped spread "politically incorrect" material in public, which has helped the Chinese people achieve limited freedom of the press. Entrepreneurs would usurp the name of the legal publishers to produce illegal or unofficial publications. To achieve that result, entrepreneurs would buy *shuhao* (ISBN numbers) from former publishing houses. The shuhao were in fact the official approval for book publication. Since shuhao are a free good from the state, any state publisher could make money by selling them. Now most ISBN numbers in China have a monetary value, ranging from 8,000 yuan to 10,000 yuan. This practice has enabled the public to have access to many "illegal" books.

To avoid political persecution, a state publisher would issue an announcement claiming that it would not be responsible for illegal publications that have usurped its name. The purpose of the statement is to avoid a governmental investigation or a copyright dispute.

The rise of nonstate publication brought about competition, ending the state's monopoly over information, which at the same time enabled people to gain a certain degree of freedom of information. A silent revolution from below was carried out by the everyday practice of violating the rules of the state.

Growth of the Legal Profession

The rise of private businesses also led to the growth of professional men and women, including those in the legal profession. As private business boomed, demand for legal professionals increased. Under Mao, there were no lawyers or judges. Now law has become one of the more highly paid professions, and supply has followed demand. Between 1985 and 1997, the number of law offices increased by 177 percent, the number of lawyers increased by 721 percent, the number of notaries increased by 18 percent, and the number of people working for notaries increased by 68 percent.[20] As more and more lawyers live a life that is economically independent of the state, they show more concern for their clients. As a result, individuals can sue government officials or a state-owned enterprise and often win the case. Cases won by ordinary individuals will encourage people to use the courts. As more lawyers represent more people in this diversified environment, people are learning and understanding more about the law, despite the corruption and intervention of the state.

Increase of Religious Freedom

Private economic activities have also opened public space for noneconomic activities. First, various religious activities have always existed with the local marketplace, which has served as a cultural meeting place in China. Thus, with so many people involved in nonstate economic exchange, different kinds of religious activities also boomed. Second, major religious holidays have become the biggest market-gathering occasions. Third, to attract tourists, thousands of religious temples have been rebuilt. Most of the money has come from private donations. Fourth, home churches of every variety have spread. As more people could make a living on their own, they could afford to "come out of the religious closet." They were no longer afraid of losing their only rice bowl.

The rise of the Falun Gong is a case in point. The Falun Gong sect grew fast during the peak of market development and at first tried to avoid the scrutiny of the state. However, the state discovered the sect when more than 10,000 members of the Falun Gong surrounded Zhong Naihai, the headquarters of the CCP, demanding that the government recognize their sect. The fierce reaction of CCP leaders to the Falun Gong is an indication of their nervousness in confronting competing ideas.

Conclusion

The Chinese civil rights movement has resulted in a parallel society, a social reality separate from the state, with a different belief system (pluralism versus communism), a different information distribution system, and a different economy. The parallel society provides the foundation for the creation of a civil society.

The evolution of a civil rights movement in China has several important implications. First, there is a direct link between the abolition of private property and the gradual erosion of people's rights. When the state was the only source of jobs, food, supplies, and art, individual rights became arbitrary—the CCP could take them away at whim. The Chinese people have paid a heavy price—the lives of millions of people. The rise of private and other forms of nonstate enterprises has created a base for key civil rights to evolve. The limited freedom of the press and information came as the direct result of private enterprises, especially in rural areas.

Second, when discussing human rights, many scholars tend to ignore some important aspects of civil rights of individuals: the right to move, the right of occupational choice, and the right to be left alone. Some would simply use the terms "economic" or "materialist" to describe the social phenomenon of the Chinese people. Behind the daily struggle to make a living, Chinese people, especially the poorest, are trying to create a private space that is independent of the state. As the result of the economic liberalization that began in 1978, most people today can live independently of the state. From work to pension, from housing to medical care, from education to mobility, people have, for the most part, depended on themselves or their networks (families and friends). This lack of state dependence has created social space.

Although the state continues to use force to intimidate people, they can still live a relatively free life without intervention from the state—so long as they do not openly challenge the party-state.

In the beginning, civil rights do not confront the state directly but add to economic development. Some members of the elite may even support the civil rights movement. From the institutionalization of baochan daohu in 1982 to the legalization of private enterprise in 1987 to formal acceptance of protection for property rights into China's constitution in 1999, we can see that some aspects of this movement were accepted by the regime.

The grassroots rise of civil rights in China suggests a new way to look at social movements. Too many theories of social movements stress the important role of ideology and leaders, like Mao's peasant movement in late 1940s. Given that Mao used the rural masses to achieve his revolutionary dream, it is ironic that the interests and concerns of people never mattered much to the intellectual leadership. In that aspect Mao's revolution was never a people's movement. The civil rights movement in China has been mainly a SULNAM.

Both the Chinese government and the international community emphasize the top-down approach to develop legal and civil rights in China. In the United States, the Ford Foundation is leading the way in China to help establish a system based on civil liberties and the presumption of innocence. In October 1998, China even hosted a human rights conference. However, for a formal system of legal and civil rights to take hold, there must be a civil basis for people's acceptance of individual rights. Our cases show that a consciousness of civil rights has been developing at the grassroots. Private property rights, market development, mobility of individuals, and freedom of the press happen together or not at all. The SULNAM civil rights movement, built on the spontaneous, unorganized participation of millions of individuals, has led to a massive movement of civil disobedience, the largest in human history.

What is interesting about the Chinese civil rights movement is that it is apolitical. People who participate in the movement follow no leaders and formulate no explicit credo or doctrine. But as the Chinese people increasingly pursue life, liberty, property, and happiness, they are spontaneously creating a civil rights movement.

Finally, the success of the civil rights movement in China suggests that there are certain universal human rights that all people should enjoy.

Notes

1. See Kate Xiao Zhou, *How the Farmers Changed China: Power of the People* (Boulder, Colo.: Westview, 1996).

2. See Roger Des Forges, "States, Societies, and Civil Societies in Chinese History," in *Civil Society in China*, ed. T. Brook and B. M. Frolic (Armonk, N.Y.: M. E. Sharpe, 1997); and Minxin Pei, "Is China Democratizing?" *Foreign Affairs* 77, no. 1 (January–February 1998).

3. B. Michael Frolic, "State-Led Civil Society," in *Civil Society in China*.

4. Kenneth Dean, "Ritual and Space: Civil Society or Popular Religion?" in ibid.

5. Zhang Zuo and Jiesi Yishen, *Jiu si yi sheng* (Nine Deaths and One Life) (Beijing: Zhongguo shehui kexue chubanshe, 1992), p. 225.

6. Editorial in *Xinghua Yuebao*, October 1950.

7. Zhang and Yishen, p. 234.

8. Andrew G. Walder, *Communist Neo-Traditionalism: Work and Authority in the Chinese Factory* (Berkeley: University of California Press, 1986). p. 19.

9. Dali Yang, *Calamity and Reform* (Stanford, Calif.: Stanford University Press, 1996).

10. News group discussion on the Internet, June 12, 1996.

11. Li Weihan, *Huiyi yu yanjiu* (Memory and Research) (Beijing: Zhonggong dangshi ciliao chubanshe, 1986), p. 480.

12. Wang Nienyi, *Dadong luan di niendai* (The Era of Upheavals) (Zhengzhou: Henan renming chubanshe, 1990), p. 100.

13. Editorial, *Beijing wanbao*, November 21, 1980, p. 1.

14. Quoted in F. A. Hayek, *The Constitution of Liberty* (Chicago: University of Chicago Press, 1960), p. 253.

15. Fazhan Yanjiusuo, *Gaige mianlin zhidu chuangxin* (Reform and System Innovation) (Shanghai: Sanlian chubanshe, 1988), pp. 9–10.

16. Susan Young, "Private Entrepreneurs and Evolutionary Change," in *China's Quiet Revolution*, ed. D. S. G. Goodman and B. Hooper (New York: St. Martin's, 1994).

17. Lei Jieqiong et al., *Gaige yilai zhongguo nongcun hunyan jiating de xingbianhua* (The Change of the Marriage and the Family in the Chinese Countryside since the Reform of the Economic System) (Beijing: Beijing University, 1994).

18. Nongcun Jingji and Yanjiu Zhongxin, "Zhongguo nongcun laodongli liudong yu renkou qianyi yanjiu zhongshu" (Summary of the Studies on China's Rural Labor Mobility and Population Migration), Working paper, Nongcun jingji yanjiu zhongxin (Rural Economy Research Center), Beijing, 1995.

19. Eric Eckholm, "China Hosts Human Rights Conference," *New York Times*, October 21, 1998.

20. Chinese Statistical Bureau, *Zhongguo tongji nianjian 1995* (Chinese Statistical Yearbook 1995) (Beijing: China Statistical Publishing House, 1996).

3. The Intellectual Turn: The Emergence of Liberalism in Contemporary China

Liu Junning

Beijing Spring and the Rise of Liberalism

In 1998 one of the most fantastic phenomena in China was the "Beijing Spring." In the *Far Eastern Economic Review*, Matt Forney described the atmosphere: "Emboldened by signs of tolerance, intellectuals [were] arguing for political reform more loudly than at any time since 1989."[1] There were two closely associated but distinct voices heard that spring. The first called for political reform in China; the second called for liberalism as an alternative to the established ideology. The latter voice received less attention from the outside world than did the former but survived the former, which was effectively silenced in 1999. The second voice, that of the "new school of thinkers [calling] itself 'the liberals,' or *ziyou pai*,"[2] made an appearance during the Beijing Spring and declared that liberalism was making a comeback after having been absent for almost 40 years.

In China's intellectual circles, liberalism is attracting more and more attention. Liberalism's reemergence, a watershed that divides the Chinese intelligentsia of the 1990s from that of the 1980s, has brought Chinese intellectual life into a new realm. A leading figure in the liberal revival, Li Shenzhi, asserted in his preface to *Peking University and the Liberalism in Modern China*, "After China's largest scale totalitarian experiment ever made in human history, after more than three centuries' comparison and selection, liberalism has been convincingly proved to be the most desirable, and universal system of values."[3]

The Western media have been able to get some candid glimpses of the effects of liberalism in China. According to a report in the *New York Times*, some Chinese intellectuals have claimed that liberal political ideas and discussions are quietly making a comeback. Changes in China have been slow but substantial. More and more newspapers and journals are inviting frank talks about politics, and

49

Chinese leaders are learning that liberalism is a byproduct of China's emerging market economy.[4]

In a *Newsweek* article, Jonathan Alter wrote: "Chicago School economists are 'hot,' especially the late Friedrich von Hayek. Hayek says that because man's reason is limited, we can never design a society that works—so let's have the market and society organize itself. Other Hayek acolytes say he's popular because he's the most antisocialist economist around. Even Prime Minister Zhu Rongji has Hayek on his bookshelf."[5] In addition, an online newsletter, *Hayek Currents — Recent & Noteworthy*, reported: "All 20,000 copies of the first printing of the new Beijing translation of Hayek's *The Constitution of Liberty* have sold out. Originally published in February, the book is currently in its second printing."[6]

The *Far Eastern Economic Review* reported a seminar on Hayek's *The Constitution of Liberty*:

> On February 27 [1998], the leading reformers and liberals in Beijing got together to discuss Hayek's *Constitution of Liberty*. This might sound arcane, but it is not. *The Constitution of Liberty* was banned in China when it was published in 1960. The conference concluded that "the things Hayek talked about are exactly what China is going through now.[7]

The momentum of China's emerging liberalism is evidenced by the responses of its adversaries, too. A neoleftist intellectual lamented recently, "It is natural for liberalism to be in the ascendant. And I deeply understand that its prosperity will endure for the long run. In this respect, I feel even more optimistic about the 'prospects' of liberalism than all the liberals. Therefore, I am more pessimistic about the future of the [neoleftist] critical theory than the estimation of the liberals."

Although the Beijing Spring has come to an end, liberalism has survived and is steadily moving forward.

Background and Dynamics

The return of liberalism is not accidental. Before the Communist triumph in 1949, a group of liberal intellectuals was caught in the two-way squeeze between the authoritarian Nationalist Party and the rising totalitarian Chinese Communist Party. The situation went from bad to worse when, in 1957, those intellectuals, as well as their liberal ideas, were rooted out by the Anti-rightist movement, which also outlawed private property, abolished free enterprise, and established a planned command economy.

The recent rebirth of liberalism in China is indicative both of the Chinese intelligentsia's post-Tiananmen soul-searching for freedom—which continues China's ongoing struggle for a free and democratic society—and of the profound transformation that China has been undergoing in the post-Mao, post-Deng period.

China today is witnessing a period of gradual withering of communist ideology and the totalitarian regime coupled with social and cultural disintegration. Above all, the era has seen an emergence of a well-educated, active liberal intelligentsia—both academic and public intellectuals who are strongly committed to a free society of responsible individuals. That commitment—rooted in Chinese liberals' anti-repression temperament, their respect for individual worth and freedom, and their belief in promoting liberal democratic institutions in China—could sustain and extend the influence of liberalism in China.

A lot of subtle but evident changes have allowed liberalism to reemerge. China is shifting from a planned command economy to a heavily state-regulated market economy—that is, from a Leninist political system to a one-party authoritarian system. Rapid economic growth gives rise to an increasingly large middle class, which is the most promising carrier of liberal ideas. That middle class is, implicitly, demanding participation in political decisionmaking and a more limited government to protect its newfound economic gains. The middle class expects to have sufficient analytical and theoretical information to examine the political scenario and initiate coordinated action. Also, the past decade witnessed a nascent civil society in China.

Although the people in China live in a spiritual vacuum and succumb to crass materialism, the intelligentsia simultaneously demonstrates its interest in liberal values. While government is shrinking, society and the market are expanding. The populace is increasingly diversified in lifestyles, avocations, and aspirations. Voluntary associations are forming, even without a license, and the number of licensed nongovernment organizations is increasing rapidly. The populace enjoys a greater variety of cultural choices. Furthermore, the number of magazines, newspapers, and books being published is increasing dramatically.

The established ideology has been withering away both as a practice and as an ideal—if not as a regime. That ideology has lost almost all of its "true believers." There is an unbridgeable cleavage between the official ideology and the practice of market economy in China. The two conflicting systems cannot coexist harmoniously. However, the mere displacement of the old system does not guarantee China's political liberalization and transition to democracy. On the contrary, to promote the transition, some unusual efforts must be made to steer China through the waters charted by liberalism. Although the ruling ideology is declining because of inherent contradictions in its political and economic systems, liberalism will not automatically grow up in its stead. Fortunately, the retreat of Red totalitarianism in China has left room for the growth of liberalism and provided a greenhouse for the growth of a liberal Zeitgeist.

Since 1990, liberalism has become a powerful intellectual movement in Chinese society. In today's China, most of the popular and influential people in all fields are liberals. Liberalism is much more intellectually appealing than the official ideology. Among Chinese intellectuals, the pride of being a leftist is being replaced by the pride of being a liberal.

Exodus of Mind

Before 1978, Chinese intellectuals had to fumble their way around in a totally closed society. Ideas and theories that were different from the dominant ideology had been shut out of China. After China began to open up to the West, in the late 1970s, intellectuals were gradually exposed to the various ideas and political thoughts of the outside world. Because of a close-minded mentality, and the superficial vitality of the Red ideology, during most of the 20th century Chinese intellectuals remained preoccupied with improving the established system. They were concerned with how to "perfect" the system by initiating reform proposals and with how to make it more "democratic" under one-party rule. Therefore, a majority of the intellectuals in the 1980s called themselves "democrats"; a few of them called themselves "humanist Marxists," as distinct from "Stalinist Marxists." None of them called themselves "liberals."

All liberal ideas were considered by the authorities to be "liberalization ideas" instead of "liberal thinking." Democrats are different from liberals, since democrats put (socialist) democracy above (individual) liberty and put government and regulation above the free market. Although some democrats have been very critical of some of the practices and policies of the regime, they have not been critical of the ideology behind the regime. Furthermore, some intellectuals ceased to "commit themselves" to the communist ideology. However, even though they had been pro-democratic, demanding freedom of thought and the press and an end to corruption, they failed to find an alternative to the orthodox ideology.

After the Tiananmen incident in 1989, some of the intellectuals in China were greatly shocked and awakened. They gave up the hope of transforming "the untransformable" and decided to search for a better and more a feasible alternative. As a result of the epoch-making "exodus of mind" from the orthodox ideology triggered by Tiananmen, some of the intellectuals recognized liberalism as the best way for China.

An eminent dissident reflected on his intellectual turn in this way: "Before [Tiananmen], I was only sympathetic to some of the liberal ideas. The most important thing that I learned from the Incident is that I came to realize that I will not only stick to the liberalism as a theoretical value, but I will also put liberal values into practice."[8]

Another dissident, one of the founders, in 1998, of the China Democratic Party, described his understanding of individual liberty and liberalism compared with democracy: "Sometimes, democracy is not a sharp weapon in slashing tyranny, instead it sometimes becomes a slogan abused and paid lip service to by those tyrants. Only individual freedom and liberalism are the genuine antidotes against tyranny. What all the tyrants dread most is freedom, which is the cornerstone of all other human values and the real motivation that promotes the development of society, science and technology, culture, and commerce. Therefore, to cure the chronic and stubborn disease of tyranny in China, liberalism and individual worth are the most effective remedies."[9]

Since 1989 the international environment has been very favorable for the growth of liberalism in China. The collapse of the Berlin Wall and the wave of democratization and liberalization throughout the world have elicited both shock and enlightenment from Chinese intellectuals. Since the defeat of its main rival, communism, liberalism has been experiencing a renaissance. Chinese intellectuals are realizing that China is lagging behind. The history of China in the 20th century was characterized by efforts to parallel trends in other parts of the world. In the early 20th century, China caught the tide of communism, which was on the rise worldwide. In the late 1980s, China attempted in vain to catch the third wave of democratization. Because the worldwide trend today is the decline of totalitarianism and authoritarianism and the rebirth of liberalism, China has no reason at all to miss the opportunity to join the mainstream of human civilization.

In the domestic environment in China, the initial development of a market economy has laid a solid foundation for liberal ideas and liberal social forces. Economic freedom and private property, although very much limited, have triggered aspiration for other civil and political liberties. The case of China shows that a free market of commodities will result in a free market of ideas and in the demand for liberal ideas. So long as people are free to choose, liberty and liberalism will certainly be the preference of most people.

What will make the rise of liberalism in China irresistible and irreversible? The answer is the market economy—"the system of natural liberty," in the words of Adam Smith.

The market mechanism in China promotes not only economic freedom but other freedoms as well. Take freedom of the press, for example. In the 1980s, the democrats argued that a free press should come before all other freedoms, even economic freedom. However, if there is no economic freedom and no private property, there can be no freedom of the press. Since the Chinese government stopped giving subsidies to most of the newspapers, magazines, presses, and TV stations after the market-oriented reform, all those media have had to publish primarily with the interests of their readers and audience in mind. Since more and more people in China are interested in liberal ideas, the media have been very enthusiastic about publishing such ideas to meet the demand in the market, despite censorship and harassment. I have found that people in the media publish liberal ideas not just for survival but because more and more of them are developing their own interest in liberalism. It is those editors and people in the media who are pushing the intellectuals to produce various kinds of liberal publications. In China, the only effective way to stop liberalization would be to resume full-scale subsidies to all the media. But that is beyond the capability of the government.

One crucial factor makes the spread of liberal ideas in China possible: the Internet. China is now making a great leap forward into the "information age" and a "network society." Internet use is rapidly growing in China, particularly in universities and academic institutions. In 1997 there were about 640,000 Internet users in China, today there are more than 4 million. According to the latest report by the China Internet Information Center, it is estimated that, with the cut in the prices of personal computers and Internet access, the number of Internet users will grow to more than 33 million in 2003.

E-mail is already Chinese intellectuals' preferred mode of communicating among themselves and with the West. The Internet could have a "revolutionary" impact on China both economically and politically. Access to economic information through the Internet is essential not only to attract investment but also to create an economic system that is fair, open, transparent, and competitive. The problem is that access to economic information is a very political issue. Information flows have been loosened considerably in China over last several years, less because of a conscious government policy than because of increased contact with the outside world and the rise of electronic media, which are much harder to police than are print media.[10]

The popularization of the Internet makes monopoly of and control over information resources more and more difficult. Together with the mechanism of the market, the Internet will promote the free flow of information into and out of China. That new freedom will in turn make it more convenient for Chinese intellectuals to use liberal resources outside China and to communicate and spread liberal ideas in a much more effective way. No library is bigger and handier than the Internet. It was on the Internet that I first learned of the Cato Institute and many other market liberal think tanks and read their online publications. In 1999 several Web sites on liberalism were set up in China. Fidel Castro once said, "Socialism in Central European [countries] failed because people received more information than was necessary."[11] He understood very well the power of information. With the assistance of the Internet, information can be even more powerful.

A Matter of Version

There are many different strains in the genealogy of contemporary liberalism. Chinese liberals today must draw experiences and lessons

55

from the intellectual movement that took place before the Communist takeover in 1949 and reflect on the causes of that earlier movement's failure in China. There have been some serious faults and deviations in the tradition of the liberal intellectual movement in modern China. Most pre-1949 Chinese liberals started their pilgrimage not from the fountainhead of classical liberalism but instead from a more socialistic interpretation of liberalism. Although calling themselves "liberal," most of them were either Deweyian pragmatic liberals or Laskian democratic socialists. None of them committed themselves to classical liberal doctrines. What those liberals had in common was their disregard for the market economy, free enterprise, and private property rights and their preference for a centrally planned, heavily regulated, and egalitarian economic order. In their writings, no citations to John Locke, David Hume, Adam Smith, Edmund Burke, Lord Acton, the Federalists, Montesquieu, Benjamin Constant, or Alexis de Tocqueville can be found. Rousseau's political writings were the main source of their intellectual inspirations. Their favorite contemporaries were John Dewey and Harold J. Lasky instead of Karl Popper and Hayek. They were collectivists rather than individualists. They claimed to be the descendants of the French Enlightenment rather than the Scottish Enlightenment. They favored the French Revolution over the Glorious Revolution and the American Revolution. The label of liberalism was, as Hayek had discovered in other parts of the world, "seized" by liberal-minded democratic socialists and quasi-liberals.

Thus, liberalism in post-1949 China was heavily stained by constructivist rationalism, perfectionism, scientism, and socialism. Chinese liberals' road to freedom was in fact "the road to serfdom."

Hayek's judgment proved sound in most respects. That is the main reason why today he is even more popular in China than in the West. His 1930s predictions about socialism and the command economy have proven exactly correct. His ideas encourage today's Chinese liberals and make them steadfast believers in free enterprise and individual liberty. From Hayek and other contemporary classical liberals, Chinese liberals have learned about the importance of economic freedom and private property rights and about the often-ignored conceptual difference between liberalism and democracy.

It has become the consensus among most contemporary Chinese liberals that it is important to distinguish themselves as classical liberals—in the tradition of Locke, Smith, and Hayek—since that distinction affects the destiny of liberalism in China and even the future of China itself.

The 1990s witnessed the prosperity and popularity of classical liberalism in China. More and more authors of books on classical liberalism have been translated into Chinese: Wilhelm von Humboldt, Thomas Jefferson, Alexis de Tocqueville, Herbert Spencer, Frederic Bastiat, Ludwig von Mises, Karl Popper, F. A. Hayek, Milton Friedman, James Buchanan, Robert Nozick, Douglass C. North, Michael Novak, Isaiah Berlin, and Ayn Rand, among others. Most of Hayek's important works have been translated into Chinese, including *The Road to Serfdom*; *Individualism and Economic Order*; *The Constitution of Liberty*; *Law, Legislation and Liberty*; and *The Fatal Conceit*. Some voluntary, unofficial study groups and readers' societies have been established in China's universities to study classical liberalism. One of those groups, the Austrian Group at Beijing University, is composed of undergraduate, postgraduate, and Ph.D. students in the disciplines of politics, economics, law, sociology, language, and even natural sciences. The works of the classical liberals have been widely and frequently quoted not only in the theses and dissertations of those graduate students but also in newspaper articles and academic papers. The demand for liberal ideas is so great that the supply lags behind.

Another distinction of today's liberalism in China is its special attention to several specific aspects of liberalism: economic liberalism, property rights, and economic freedom; constitutionalism, the rule of law, and limited government; and individualism, toleration, pluralism, and open society. *Res Publica*, founded in 1994 and the first academic journal to concentrate on (classical) liberalism since 1949, has initiated a lot of discussion of these topics in China.

Liberal Enterprise for Freedom

China's civil intellectual landscape was dominated by classical liberalism throughout the 1990s. No other political thoughts enjoy more enduring popularity than do the emerging classical liberal ideas among the intellectual community in China.

Some skeptics regard liberalism in China as premature and superfluous, since the country has existed for thousands of years without liberalism. Liberalism is also considered alien to the Chinese people, since it originated in the West. Indeed, China has its own cultural traditions that in many respects are at odds with the concept of liberalism. But I have confidence that liberalism will prevail in China; for liberalism, based on the common nature of humankind, is universal. If Chinese people hate for their property to be taken away arbitrarily by the government, if they want to enjoy freedom of speech and association without fear of being thrown into prison, if they want to express their own views about public policies without being accused of subversion, and if they want to freely choose their religion without intolerance, then they have every reason to embrace liberalism. In the West, liberalism has been the natural companion of a market economy. In China, as a market economy becomes inevitable, liberalism cannot be shut out any longer. Since the process of marketization in China is irrevocable, the prevalence of liberalism is irreversible.

Freedom to write on nonpolitical issues and to have private discussions of political issues is far greater than before. A growing range of activities is outside the scope of central and ideological control. For the most part, people are no longer mobilized in an endless series of political purges and campaigns. They need not affirm communism as their ideal. They enjoy much greater occupational choice and geographic mobility. Individuals can withdraw from political life and pursue private interests, so long as they do not directly challenge the right of the leaders to rule.

The atmosphere in China has greatly improved since the Cultural Revolution, which crushed all intellectual activities. Of course, there are still substantial restraints on the growth of liberalism in China. Chinese citizens cannot yet freely express their political beliefs publicly nor openly challenge the official ideology. However, it is silent sympathizers and supporters who make it possible for liberalism to grow in China. If people don't buy and read publications about liberalism, there will be no supply. If the editors do not risk their positions, houses, and promotions to get great books about liberalism published, there will be no prosperity of liberalism in China. Furthermore, liberal intellectuals have changed their strategy. They look to the general public rather than to those in power to develop a commitment to liberal values. Because they are teaching the Chinese people what to do when they have a chance to choose, the people should be ready to make good choices when a democratic breakthrough comes. The intellectuals' platform is this: "China's current government was designed to administer a command economy that no longer exists. Officialdom is too big and too corrupt, and must shrink. Officials must respond to the needs of citizens, not to orders from above. This will require elections, a strong legal system, and respect for individual rights."[12]

It is reasonable to be optimistic about the future of liberalism; however, the obstacles and the tasks ahead remain huge. It should be noted that, for a variety of cultural and political reasons, liberalism in China has never been fully developed and localized and therefore has historically failed to dominate China's political agenda. Even today, the liberal intellectuals in China have a lot of thorny questions to answer. For instance, since liberalism is defined much in terms of individual freedom, how will Chinese liberalism deal with China's traditional ethos and legacy of collectivism? Is Chinese liberalism an expression of the quest for answers to moral and cultural perplexities, for ideal moral norms, and for an ideal social establishment? It is quite clear that the process is not an even one and its progress cannot be taken for granted. Liberalism is now under attack from both old and new leftists. The idea of liberalism is limited and criticized by the old-fashioned leftists. And the young leftists, trained in the West and armed with "new" theories, such as neo-Marxism, postmodernism, communitarianism, nationalism, and populism, also attack liberalism. Fortunately, it is much easier for the common Chinese people to understand the value of property rights and economic freedom than to understand the obscure concepts of high-minded leftist "discourses."

Today demand for a society based on liberal principles is building incrementally. It would be a mistake to confine liberalism to the intellectual sphere. As Hayek said, "Freedom of action, even in humble things, is as important as freedom of thought."[13] The task of liberal intellectuals in China is to do everything they can to make a case for individual freedom. This new bottom-up strategy of the liberals will eventually make a difference.

The opportunity for China to finally get on the liberal democratic track is not slim. Moreover, the opening of China in the reform period, the eclipse of the regimes in the former Soviet Union and Eastern and Central Europe, and the expansion of global markets have all provided favorable conditions for democratization and liberalization in China.

Liberals in China now are trying to build consensus and to shape the following political reforms: securing greater individual freedom and property rights, strengthening legislative bodies, placing the military and police more firmly under civilian control, relaxing the controls on nongovernmental organizations, strengthening the judiciary, and granting the populace more meaningful avenues of political participation.

Whether China will be a constructive partner or an emerging threat will depend, to a very great extent, on the fate of liberalism in China: a liberal China will be a constructive partner; a nationalistic and authoritarian China will be an emerging threat. According to the theory of "democratic peace"—that liberal democracies won't fight against one another—the future role of China in the world and its relations with the West are very closely intertwined with the liberalization and democratization of China. So it is in the greatest interests of the established democracies to encourage the emerging liberal enterprise in China as the driving force for a new democracy based on liberalism.

Notes

1. Matt Forney, "Beijing Spring," *Far Eastern Economic Review*, April 2, 1998, p. 20.
2. Ibid.
3. Liu Junning, ed., *Peking University and the Liberalism in Modern China* (Beijing: China Renshi, 1998), pp. 4–5.
4. Elisabeth Rosenthal, "China's Leading University Celebrates and Ponders," *New York Times*, May 5, 1998.
5. Jonathan Alter, "On the Road in China," *Newsweek*, June 29, 1998, http://newsweek.com/nw-srv/issue/26_98a/printed/us/sr0826.htm.
6. *Hayek Currents — Recent & Noteworthy*, http://members.aol.com/grgransom/hayekpage.htm.
7. Forney, p. 21.
8. Liu Xiaobo, eminent Chinese dissident, report on the Internet, 1997.
9. Wang Youcai, "Liberalism, Constitutionalism and China's Democracy," September 1998, http://www.asiademo.org/19980917b.htm.
10. John Sullivan, "How the Internet Promises Free Market Philosophies and Democratic Principles Overseas," Statement before the House Committee on Commerce, July 29, 1998, http://www.cipe.org/jds7-98.htm.
11. Quoted in ibid.
12. Forney, p. 21.
13. F. A. Hayek, *The Constitution of Liberty* (Chicago: University of Chicago Press, 1976), p. 35.

4. The Gang of Three: Mao, Jesus, and Hayek

William McGurn

High atop the red Ming walls overlooking Tiananmen Square, the air is pregnant with China's past. One-half century ago, from the same rostrum where emperors once handed down their edicts, a triumphant Chairman Mao proclaimed the birth of a People's Republic. Also filled with history is the square below, which has become a focal point for Chinese student protest, from the May 4 Movement of 1919 to the pro-democracy demonstrators cut down so tragically 70 years later.

But in one of those delightful ironies peculiar to surviving communist societies, the portrait of Chairman Mao today stares out at the Golden Arches of a McDonald's looming up from the opposite side of the square. Now, no less a historian than Samuel Huntington has snickered about confusing the Magna Carta with "the Magna Mac." And certainly it is true that the opening of markets, which China has been doing incrementally since 1979, does not lead, hesto presto, to Westminster democracy. Yet it is no less true that the presence of McDonald's here both reflects and contributes to the awesome changes transforming the Chinese landscape.

A prominent conservative once dismissed the view that markets can open up totalitarian countries as "reverse Marxism." But the evidence, as even the U.S. Department of State reports concede, inclines to a Friedmanite view of things. Asian Communists no longer boast, à la Khrushchev, of "burying" capitalism. To the contrary, they recognize that development has forced them into a damned if they do, damned if they don't situation: the risk of becoming a South Korea if they open up and the certainty of becoming a North Korea if they don't. And as much as intellectuals would like to believe otherwise, it is not just the *Wall Street Journal* and the BBC that have their salutary effects. A Chinese man I met in Guangzhou once confided to me that the most revolutionary things he ever saw ón TV were the reruns of the American cop shows like *Hawaii Five-O* and *N.Y.P.D. Blue* beamed in from neighboring Hong Kong. Watching those shows, millions of ordinary mainlanders saw American police officers reading the Miranda warning to those they arrest—rather a revolutionary concept in the People's Republic.

My own views here have been slow to evolve. In my first incarnation in China, in the mid-1980s, I was suspicious of the laurels being heaped on Deng Xiaoping for his "pragmatism." It did not appear that anything dramatic was in the offing from the limited openings to trade and investment that Deng had helped make possible. And my visits to China generally confirmed suspicions about a dreary country mired in poverty and stuck with a totalitarian government.

Over the years, however, the slow accretion of experiences has persuaded me that the transformations we see in China are real, not because its leaders want such change but because those openings as they have created constitute cracks in a system that people are quick to exploit. In the grossest terms, the bankruptcy of the socialist system, as much as real market openings, means that much of what was once provided by the state—housing, health care, retirement, livelihood—has become something the Chinese people are doing for themselves. It is inconceivable that even on this level such a shift would be without social and political consequences.

In trying to communicate how I see these changes, I thought I would use three handy foils: what I call the Gang of Three: Mao, Jesus, and Hayek.

Mao

For Americans the image of Mao is inseparable from that of the Chinese government. Though Mao was downplayed for a time, his persistence on the wall overlooking Tiananmen, not to mention the corporal remains that rest in state on the square itself, signals his continuing importance to the regime in Beijing. This is true notwithstanding that Mao's successors have moved fast and hard in the direction opposite from which Mao had laid out, that the phrases used to justify this shift—for example, "a socialist market economy with Chinese characteristics"—are in fact rhetorical devices to get around the awkward facts of jettisoning the Maoist principles that wreaked such damage on China.

Yet the need to not take Mao head-on points to a genuine dilemma for those of us who understand that China's future freedom (not to mention morals) ultimately depends on its embrace of the market. The difficulty is that in the transition from totalitarian rule to what we hope will be a more liberal form of government, the middle is not pretty. In this stage the government retains considerable control over the resources while allowing for personal profit, which is not capitalism but fascism. Up and down the line, for example, Chinese ministries own their own business conglomerates. Next is the provincial level, right down to the town level; if the People's Liberation Army were considered as a business, to name but one example, it would be a Fortune 500 company. So what you have is a people who now know what they've been deprived of, are presided over by an increasingly ineffectual but brutish government, and are lorded over by well-connected nouveau riche—not infrequently high state officials themselves!

Jesus

Mao, who thought he was God, leads me to my second topic: Jesus, who *was* God. More specifically, I mean Christianity. Christianity is not the only religion to run up against the vestiges of Maoist control in today's China—look at the ongoing crackdowns on the Falun Gong—but it is among the more prominent. But here China has a problem. Because as it opens up, its crackdowns on Christian Chinese engender understandable outrage in America, not only from Christians such as Gary Bauer but also from non-Christians such as Abe Rosenthal of the *New York Times* and Bill Kristol of the *Weekly Standard*. Many of those people now demand that we cease trading with China until it begins respecting religious freedom.

My own experience teaches me that to pit religious freedom against trade is not only wrong, but it generally hurts those whom it aims to help. My first foray into a Chinese church was in 1988, when I visited the Nantang, or South Church, in Beijing with my brother.

After the Mass the congregation dispersed quickly, reluctant to be seen talking to foreigners. Today, however, up to three-quarters of the Catholic bishops in the government's patriotic association have secretly reconciled themselves with the Vatican. Of course, there remain many Christians harassed for their faith. On the World Wide Web, one can tune into www.freechurchforchina.org to see a video clip of a Catholic church in Fujian Province being destroyed. Again, whatever the intended outcome, market openings have increased the de facto freedom of the churches and opened the possibility for communication with their brothers in faith overseas.

Clearly, U.S. policy will always be crucial in promoting religious freedom in China. The pro-market side, on which I include myself, needs to concede that the situation in China remains far from good and that it is only the threat of sanctions that persuades Beijing to move on some things. But the pro-sanctions side needs to recognize that the world has not stood still waiting for the perfect piece of U.S. legislation. China's critics have no shortage of real violations to point to—the arrest of bishops, the sentencing of evangelicals, and the harassment of churches—but they are wrong about the context. As bad as it can be today, this is not 1966.

Specifically, by opening their doors to trade and investment, the Chinese people have set off a chain of events that each day expands the margins of opportunity. One example: In August 1997 the *New York Times* carried an article about a Sichuan village where couples can now pay a fine instead of having their second babies forcibly aborted. Is this freedom? Of course not. Is it better? Yes. As the *Times* noted, "Economic growth is eroding the old system of control over ordinary people's lives, creating loopholes large and small."[1]

How different this is from the atmosphere that prevails in societies in which the United States has played the embargo card for decades: North Korea, Cuba, and, until very recently, Vietnam. In many ways, what we see now is classic Marx: The rise of a merchant society created a power base that tempered that of the monarchs. What would be the effect on religious freedom if, for example, instead of trying to cut off trade, American Christians went into China to make business deals with their coreligionists? If U.S. Catholic universities sponsored more scholarships for Chinese clergy? If instead of cursing the darkness, conservative Christians began lighting a few more candles—by, say, pushing their congregations to adopt sister parishes in China?

Hayek

I don't think F. A. Hayek could have put it any better than that *Times* story on forced abortion in Sichuan. Central to Hayek's thought was his notion of "spontaneous order." At a time when intellectuals across the world associated progress with planning, Hayek posited a theory of spontaneous order emerging from the bottom up, as people made their own arrangements and developed institutions accordingly, taking into account not only goals but also culture, traditions, and values. That was too messy for most intellectuals, who preferred the crisp rationality of, say, a five-year plan. But Hayek argued that a workable messiness was the price of freedom, just as force was the inevitable conclusion of socialism. Small wonder that an internal Chinese Communist Party translation in 1962 of *The Road to Serfdom* characterized Hayek's works as "full of poison."

As my friend Mao Yushi will tell you—his think tank two years ago caused a stir by publishing a Chinese version of Hayek's *The Constitution of Liberty* and holding a conference on it—even though Hayek never wrote about China, his writings are immediately understandable because the Chinese people have firsthand experience in living without property rights. Even the man who doesn't own a printing press, Mao Yushi's associate told me, has a stake in seeing that someone else does—or else he will have no access to independent information. On the streets of Beijing the vivid improvements in housing, diet, transportation, and fashion illustrate the point: Other people's property rights give us options. And that explains why even a colonial Hong Kong with no democracy was still arguably the freest place in Asia.

It is hard to look at today's China and not see early signs of the spontaneous order Hayek so celebrated. The unevenness of this process can be frustrating. But in China liberals understand that the government cannot just decree freedom, even were it so inclined. Far better to expand the boundaries of the possible and allow nature to take its course.

Conclusion

None of this is to say that America should not be firm with China, since the hard old men in Beijing are acutely sensitive to criticism. But we should also recognize that a country where the Golden Arches now look across Tiananmen Square from the balcony whence Mao once addressed throngs of Red Guards, where millions of Chinese now have e-mail and access to foreign Web pages, and where Christianity can no longer be dismissed as a foreign import—that such a China exhibits possibilities lacking only a few years ago and that ought to be encouraged and pushed. In April 1999, Communist officials were taken completely by surprise when more than 10,000 adherents of a quasi-Buddhist movement of breathing and healing exercise, the Falun Gong, surrounded the compound where party leaders live and work, demanding that the government recognize their sect. The truth is something the party has to fear, not those of us who believe in more freedom. That is why the party has been sentencing them in secret one-day trials that it dare not report to its own people. Perhaps 30 years ago an isolated China might simply have given to dissenters its traditional answer: the club on the head. But today, the advance of communications plus China's own efforts to reach out to the world economy will make it exceedingly more difficult to crack down as effectively as it once did.

The delusion of both the right and the left is the notion that we can come up with some legal blueprint for China and sell it to China or bully Beijing into adopting it and—voilà!—China will be free. Stirring declarations of rights and justice will always enjoy the dramatic advantage, but people who have to live under repressive regimes typically have different priorities. The left dislikes China today because people are making money. But the right's delusion is that you can't have full freedom until it is enshrined in the law. During China's commemoration of the 50th anniversary of the founding of the People's Republic, the papers were full of op-eds and editorials telling us of a Chinese leadership whose spots have not changed much in the 20 years since Deng opened China's door. The papers may well be right. For it is not clear that China's leaders fully comprehend where the market is taking them. If Hayek is right, it may be better that they don't.

Notes
1. Seth Faison, "Chinese Are Happily Breaking the 'One Child' Rule," *New York Times*, August 17, 1997.

PART II

FRIENDLY NEIGHBOR OR EXPANSIONIST POWER?

5. Confusion and Stereotypes: U.S. Policy toward the PRC at the Dawn of the 21st Century

Ted Galen Carpenter

Washington's policy toward the People's Republic of China is increasingly notable for a lack of consistency and clarity. The Clinton administration officially pursues a policy of constructive engagement with the PRC and has even flirted on occasion with a full-blown strategic partnership. Yet whenever the administration's "accommodationist" approach comes under fire from domestic critics, U.S. officials take other actions that suggest a more wary, if not confrontational, posture. Thus, the administration has conveyed mixed messages about Washington's intentions and interests, thereby exacerbating Beijing's suspicions that the United States is being duplicitous about its goals.

Even more troubling than the lack of consistency in U.S. policy is the growing absence of a domestic consensus about what that policy should be. The Clinton administration mouths tired clichés about the virtues of engagement without really defining the substance of that concept or recognizing that skeptics are demanding a discussion of its specific features. The same is true of the administration's rote adherence to the one-China formula regarding the status of Taiwan. U.S. officials seem to cling to that policy with increasing tenacity as it becomes less and less appealing to both Taiwan and members of the opinion elite in the United States.

That does not bode well for the prospects of a prudent and sustainable China policy in the coming decade. A struggle is now under way between those who want to perpetuate the cooperative U.S.-Chinese relationship of the 1970s and 1980s (with a few modest modifications) and those who see China as a repressive dictatorship and an emerging adversary of the United States and, therefore, favor a more hard-line approach in dealing with the PRC.[1] The most prominent members of the first faction are the Clinton administration, representatives of the American business community with its multi-billion-dollar economic stake in friendly relations with China, and strategic analysts who fear that a confrontational policy will needlessly create an enemy for the United States. The second faction includes many ideological conservatives (who are repulsed by Beijing's brutal treatment of political and religious dissidents and see China as an embryonic military superpower), liberal human rights activists, and economic nationalists who are upset about the flood of low-cost goods from the PRC into the American market. It is increasingly apparent that the first faction is experiencing a slow but inexorable decline in strength while the second faction grows stronger and bolder.

If those trends do not change, it is likely that there will be a crisis in America's relations with the PRC as advocates of a containment strategy—treating China as Washington treated the Soviet Union during the Cold War—wrest control of policy from proponents of the status quo. Advocates of engagement will not likely prevail over the long term if the debate is framed (as is now largely the case) as a choice between appeasing Beijing to preserve the profits of American corporations and standing up for fundamental American values.[2]

A third faction that would articulate a more balanced and realistic policy is badly needed.[3] Members of such a faction would see formulation of U.S. policy toward the PRC as a complex but not an impossible task. They would move beyond the competing stereotypes of the PRC as either a "China card" that can be played against (now nonexistent) adversaries, as Washington played it against the Soviet Union during the final two decades of the Cold War, or as an East Asian version of the Soviet empire that must be contained by U.S.-led alliances. Both are false models and ought to be rejected.

Instead, U.S. policymakers should view the PRC as a normal great power with which we have both some common interests and some serious areas of disagreement. The challenge for an effective foreign policy is to seek avenues of cooperation in the former and ameliorate tensions in the latter.

The Rise and Fall of a Strategic Partnership

The early years of the Clinton presidency were marked by a frosty relationship between the United States and the PRC. Clinton had excoriated George Bush during the 1992 presidential campaign for being "soft" on Beijing and pledged that his administration would take a firm stand on human rights and other issues, if necessary linking China's most favored nation (MFN) trade status to improvements in Beijing's behavior. Although the new president backed away from such linkage a little more than a year after taking office, the U.S.-PRC relationship remained tense in other ways. Beijing reacted harshly to Washington's decision in the summer of 1995 to grant a visa to Taiwanese president Lee Teng-hui to deliver a speech at Cornell University. Matters grew worse in early 1996 when the PRC conducted a series of military exercises, including several missile tests, in the Taiwan Strait and the United States dispatched two U.S. aircraft carrier battle groups to waters near Taiwan.

Indeed, there are indications that the two countries may have come closer to armed conflict during that crisis than either the public or Congress realized at the time.[4] The episode apparently unnerved administration officials enough for them to seek a rapprochement with the PRC, and relations improved noticeably thereafter. In fact, critics in Asia and the United States concluded that Washington overshot the mark in its attempt to dampen tensions with China. The increasingly cozy U.S.-PRC relationship—with Clinton and Secretary of State Madeleine Albright using terms such as "cooperative partnership," "strategic cooperation," and "strategic partnership"— sent political tremors throughout East and South Asia. That rapprochement alarmed Taiwan, unsettled long-time U.S. allies Japan and South Korea, and provided India with a reason to take the wraps off its covert nuclear-weapons program.[5]

President Clinton's trip to China in the summer of 1998, and the summit meeting with China's president, Jiang Zemin, proved to be the high-water mark in U.S.-PRC relations in the initial post–Cold War decade.[6] During the course of the visit, the two leaders issued a joint statement pledging to cooperate to stem proliferation of nuclear weapons and ballistic missiles and to generally take responsibility for promoting peace and stability in South Asia—a manifestation of the new strategic partnership that New Delhi strongly condemned. Secretary of the Treasury Robert Rubin and his PRC counterpart stunned the government and people of Japan with a joint statement praising the PRC's role in containing the East Asian financial crisis and chastising Tokyo for its lack of action. Then, following the summit, Clinton journeyed to Shanghai where he issued a brief but crucial statement outlining the "three noes" of U.S. policy regarding Taiwan. Although the president stopped short of embracing the PRC's formulation, he affirmed that "we don't support independence for Taiwan, or two Chinas, or one Taiwan, one China. And we don't believe that Taiwan should be a member in any organization for which statehood is a requirement."[7]

U.S. policymakers apparently not only saw China as a major player in Asian affairs—and were willing to accord Beijing that status—but they implicitly assumed that Japan's star might be fading as China's was rising. That logic caused the administration to regard China as the inevitable leading power in Asia and, at least on economic issues, both a more capable and a more cooperative partner than Japan. The resulting policy course was not one of appeasement, but it was exceedingly accommodating of Beijing's preferences.

The attempt to construct a strategic partnership between the United States and the PRC, however, began to collapse almost as soon as Clinton returned from his trip in July 1998. A cascade of criticism in Congress, and among major portions of the opinion elite, about Clinton's "three noes" announcement in Shanghai and the accommodationist policy toward the PRC generally, caused the president and his advisers to beat a hasty retreat. Administration spokesmen rushed to assure critics that there was no substantive change in U.S. policy on the Taiwan issue, and within weeks the president dispatched to Taipei Secretary of Energy Bill Richardson—the highest-ranking U.S. official to visit Taiwan in years. Those actions, in turn, irritated PRC leaders, who suspected that Washington was once again implying that it was committed to one policy in discussions with Beijing while it presented another, entirely different policy to domestic audiences.

Other U.S. "trial balloons" deepened the chill in U.S.-PRC relations. Revised defense guidelines for the U.S.-Japanese alliance provoked speculation that Washington was attempting to facilitate a more robust military role for Japan and make the alliance into an instrument of a containment policy directed against China. Chinese leaders fretted that, since the new guidelines did not specify any geographic limitations to joint military actions, they might apply to U.S.-Japanese efforts to defend Taiwan. PRC anger and apprehension also were aroused in early 1999 when U.S. officials spoke of creating a regional shield to defend against ballistic missiles.[8] Again, there was speculation that this was another component of an anti-China containment policy being put together by Washington. More and more official and "semiofficial" articles, studies, reports, and speeches emanating from the PRC warned that the United States was using its power to achieve global domination, and that such hegemony posed a threat to important Chinese interests.

The release of the Cox committee report alleging systematic PRC espionage designed to steal information on America's nuclear-weapons program further poisoned relations.[9] Beijing vehemently denied the allegations and charged that the report was part of a plot by the PRC's political enemies in the United States to build the foundation of a comprehensive anti-China policy. As if the flap over the Cox committee report was not enough to exacerbate tensions, the U.S.-led military intervention in the Balkans intensified China's suspicions about America's global intentions and caused U.S.-PRC relations to decline to their lowest point since the Tiananmen Square massacre in 1989. The deterioration reached a crest following the U.S. bombing of the Chinese embassy in Belgrade on May 7 and the wave of violent, anti-American demonstrations that erupted in cities throughout China.[10]

The Clinton administration has gone to great lengths to foster the impression that relations with China are now back on track.[11] The resumption of high-level meetings between officials of the two countries in the summer of 1999 is touted as proof of a rapprochement, and it is true that both Washington and Beijing have made an effort to prevent a complete breach in their relationship.[12] Tensions delayed negotiations on China's accession to the World Trade Organization, for example, but did not preclude an eventual U.S.-PRC accord. The value of bilateral trade ties alone—now in excess of $80 billion annually—provides a significant incentive for both sides not to let the animosity get out of hand.

Nevertheless, it would be naive to assume that the Balkan episode and the other problems since the summer of 1998 have not left scars. The overall tone of statements and articles coming out of Beijing regarding relations with the United States has become noticeably more negative and hostile in the past year or so. One need look no further than the pages of *Foreign Affairs Journal*, published by the Chinese People's Institute of Foreign Affairs, an affiliate of the foreign ministry. In marked contrast to most earlier issues, recent issues of the journal have featured numerous strongly anti-U.S. articles. That was especially true of the June 1999 issue.[13]

Beijing fears that an increasingly assertive U.S.-led network of alliances might use Bosnia and Kosovo as precedents for intervening in similar problems of direct interest to China. In particular, Chinese officials fret that NATO's Balkan policy is the harbinger of a global humanitarian interventionist doctrine that someday might be applied to such problems as Taiwan and Tibet. Indeed, President Jiang specifically underlined his government's determination never to let Taiwan become "an Asian Kosovo."[14]

The chill in Beijing's attitude toward the United States is apparent in subtle but important policy changes as well. For example, the PRC had previously been helpful in attempting to discourage North Korea from pursuing a nuclear-weapons program or improving its ballistic missile capabilities.[15] In the aftermath of the Balkan war, Beijing has been somewhat less helpful. China's ambassador to Seoul defended North Korea's "sovereign right" to conduct launch tests of its new Taepodong 2 missile—a three-stage missile with a range that would enable it to strike U.S. territory. The ambassador further accused the United States of exaggerating the threat posed by such a missile.[16] Even more troubling, there is evidence that Chinese companies have recently transferred sophisticated missile components to North Korea.[17]

The conventional wisdom holds that Washington's strong support of Beijing's position on the one-China issue following Lee's assertion that relations between Taiwan and the mainland henceforth would be conducted on a state-to-state basis has repaired much of the damage to the U.S.-PRC relationship.[18] There may be some truth to that argument, but comments and actions by Beijing in the summer of 1999 conveyed, at best, a mixed message. Although Chinese leaders expressed appreciation for Washington's strong adherence to the one-China policy, they also gave unusually blunt warnings not to deviate from that policy. PRC foreign minister Tang Jiaxuan told Secretary of State Albright that the United States "should say little and act with great caution."[19] Moreover, any softening of Beijing's attitude certainly did not carry over to other political and security issues. In an address to a meeting of the Association of Southeast Asian Nations, Tang condemned countries that bypass the United Nations and "bully" others in the name of human rights. In an unmistakable swipe at the United States and its NATO allies, he stated that "claims such as 'the supremacy of human rights over sovereignty' and 'there is no national boundary in safeguarding human rights' are in essence excuses for strong countries to bully weak ones."[20] A few weeks later, Jiang explicitly denounced U.S. "gunboat diplomacy."[21]

Gone are the expressions of exuberant good feelings that led Clinton and Albright in 1997 and 1998 to speak of a strategic partnership. The relationship is now characterized by a wariness on Beijing's part that not even the Clinton administration's continuing determined efforts to be accommodating can seem to overcome.

The Duel between Two Misguided U.S. Policy Options

Beijing's rebuffs raise the question of why the Clinton administration flirted with the goal of a strategic partnership in the first place. There appears to be a complex array of motives. Certainly, the 1996 crisis created a powerful incentive within the administration to minimize the likelihood of a repetition. Clinton's post-spring 1996 policy contained echoes of the reasons for Washington's policy of détente with the Soviet Union during the 1970s. An important objective in the latter case was to defuse tensions and reduce the danger that the U.S.-Soviet rivalry might spiral out of control. University of Pennsylvania professor Walter McDougall emphasizes that possible motive in the case of the U.S.-PRC rapprochement, contending that Clinton "engages China in hopes of avoiding a Cold War."[22]

There may be some truth to the thesis that the administration is trying to entangle the PRC in such an elaborate web of diplomatic and economic ties with the United States that rogue behavior by Beijing is no longer an option. In a speech delivered just before his departure for China in June 1998, Clinton rebuked those who advocated isolating the PRC and warned that such a course could have extremely negative consequences. On other occasions, the president and his advisers have cautioned that treating China as an enemy may cause China to become an enemy.

Whatever the specific mix of motives, the administration's policy is misguided. It is correct to insist, as Clinton does, that it would be foolish and counterproductive to attempt to isolate China. But engaging the PRC and maintaining a cordial relationship is one thing; forming a strategic partnership is quite another.

Yet the Clinton approach is both practical and enlightened compared with the course favored by some conservative critics. They advocate terminating normal trade relations with the PRC, or at least conditioning economic ties on Beijing's willingness to capitulate on issues ranging from the treatment of political opponents to the PRC's technology transfer policies. Conservative intellectuals as well as GOP politicians Steve Forbes, Gary Bauer, and John McCain openly accuse the administration of "appeasing" China's communist dictatorship.[23] Rep. Dana Rohrabacher (R-Calif.) even argued that China was "the greatest threat in our Nation's history."[24] In the past three years there has been an outpouring of books denouncing the administration's conduct of policy toward China.[25]

Many of the critics openly consider China an enemy of the United States—a view that reached new intensity with the release of the Cox committee report. In addition to wanting to curtail trade with the PRC, they advocate greatly upgrading military ties to Taiwan and even offering an explicit defense guarantee to the island.[26] Some of them even fret about manifestly far-fetched security threats allegedly posed by the PRC. For example, several conservative analysts became agitated about the presence of Hutchinson Whampoa Ltd., a Chinese (actually, a Hong Kong-based) shipping and construction company in Panama. Overheated rhetoric soon described that firm and its operations as a People's Liberation Army "beachhead" that could menace the Panama Canal.[27] In a letter to Secretary of Defense William Cohen, Senate Majority Leader Trent Lott (R-Miss.) accused the administration of "allowing a scenario to develop where U.S. national security interests could not be protected without confronting the Chinese communists in the Americas. U.S. naval ships will be at the mercy of Chinese-controlled pilots and could even be denied passage through the Panama Canal by Hutchinson, an arm of the People's Liberation Army."[28]

There are legitimate reasons to be concerned about some aspects of Beijing's international behavior, but a plot to take over the Panama Canal would not seem to be among them. It makes little sense to establish a strategic beachhead thousands of miles from home with no credible air and naval forces to sustain it. And the PRC clearly lacks such a capability. American air and naval power could eradicate such a "beachhead" in a matter of hours in the event of a crisis.

Advocates of a hard-line policy toward China are wrong on multiple levels. Imposing trade sanctions would injure primarily those sectors of Chinese society that have the most extensive connections to the outside world and the greatest incentive to push for additional economic and political reforms. A military containment strategy would be even worse. The Clinton administration's confused and vacillating policy might well cause the United States to stumble into war with the PRC, but the right-wing alternative would virtually guarantee that outcome.

A Sober View of the Chinese "Threat"

Advocates of a containment policy misconstrue the nature of the challenge that Beijing poses for American diplomacy. Despite its many faults, the PRC is not a messianic political force in world affairs. In marked contrast to such powers as Nazi Germany and (even more so) the Soviet Union, China does not aim for global domination. Nor, in contrast to the Soviets, do Chinese leaders seriously expect that the entire world will someday embrace communism. Indeed, there is ample evidence that even the party cadres are not exactly communist ideologues any longer, however much they may officially express loyalty to Marxist-Leninist doctrine. Certainly, China's increasingly capitalistic economic system bears little resemblance to the rigid state-directed economies of the Soviet empire. Less noticed but equally important, the Chinese people already enjoy more latitude in directing their personal lives than their Soviet counterparts ever did.

China is a rising conventional great power, not a malignantly expansionist totalitarian state. It resembles Wilhelmine Germany far more than it does Nazi Germany. That being said, accommodating rising great powers —with their often abrasive demands for respect and their attempts to expand their power and influence—is not an easy task. Indeed, the last time the club of great powers faced that challenge, with the rise of Germany and Japan in the early 20th century, it failed miserably. That is why it is imperative for the United States to assess the challenge posed by the PRC in a balanced and rational manner rather than mindlessly apply stale analogies from the 1930s or the Cold War.

The PRC's recent record on relations with neighboring states— indeed, its overall strategic behavior—is mixed. In late 1996 and early 1997, the Chinese government pursued initiatives to defuse tensions with several adjacent countries, including India, Russia, and

Vietnam. One agreement outlined troop reductions along China's borders with Russia, Kyrgystan, Tajikistan, and Kazakstan and was hailed by President Jiang as "a model of security differing from the Cold War mentality."[29] Beijing made additional efforts in the summer of 1999 to resolve remaining border controversies and lessen other sources of friction.[30] Such actions lend credence to the view that the PRC harbors no expansionist ambitions and is serious about playing a peaceful and constructive role in international affairs.

China's apparently conciliatory moves may be less benign than they appear, however. Skeptics note that the PRC's peaceful gestures are largely confined to relations with its principal land neighbors. Especially intriguing in that regard is the marked improvement in relations between China and India since the spring of 1999. One of the least noticed but extremely significant side stories to the Indo-Pakistani skirmish over Kashmir in May and June 1999 was the surprising lack of support by the PRC for Pakistan's position. China's posture was in striking contrast to Beijing's behavior in previous armed conflicts between India and Pakistan. The PRC's restraint was followed by a flurry of diplomatic progress by Beijing and New Delhi on an array of issues.

The divergence between Beijing's conciliatory policies toward its major land neighbors and its decidedly less friendly behavior toward other states could be the result of many factors. One unsettling possibility, however, is that Chinese leaders may simply be securing their country's northern, western, and southern flanks so as to be able to more assertively pursue objectives on the eastern and southeastern (oceanic) sides.

Several important arms deals with Russia have also fostered such suspicions. A new agreement to pool resources in the development of military-related high technology was concluded in late June 1999, and preparations were made in August for the sale of 40 advanced SU-30 Sukhoi fighter aircraft to the PRC.[31] More alarming still were reports leaked to two Hong Kong newspapers in September that Jiang and Russian president Boris Yeltsin had discussed the sale of two of Russia's Typhoon-class nuclear-powered submarines to the PRC. Those submarines carry SSN-20 ballistic missiles capable of reaching the United States from the western Pacific.[32] Such a purchase would make the PRC a serious nuclear-weapons power overnight. Indeed, the gain to China's strategic arsenal would exceed any gain the PRC might achieve from the espionage alleged in the Cox committee report.

It is not China's mere acquisition of sophisticated military hardware over the past few years that troubles U.S. officials and many outside policy experts; rather, it is the nature of the systems that Beijing seems so determined to acquire. "The weapons China is buying or building have a clear anti-U.S. intention, as opposed to using them against Vietnam or places in the South China sea," charged one Pentagon official who insisted on anonymity.[33] Even allowing for the fact that Pentagon officials may have an institutional incentive to hype the Chinese military threat, it is difficult to deny that the pattern appears worrisome.

The arms deals are merely the most tangible manifestation of a growing Chinese "security partnership" with Russia, expressed succinctly in the April 1997 joint declaration issued by Jiang and Yeltsin and reiterated by them following their summit meeting in August 1999.[34] That partnership clearly seems directed against the United States. Indeed, there are increasing concerns about the emergence of a "Moscow-Beijing axis" that could support aggressive Chinese moves in East Asia as well as Russian efforts to counter the enlargement of NATO.

That may be an excessively suspicious and alarmist interpretation—at least with respect to China's motives. Until proven false, Beijing's ostensibly constructive and peaceful initiatives to improve relations with neighboring states should be viewed as genuine. Nevertheless, it is troubling that the PRC's conciliatory policies toward its major land neighbors have not been matched by similar conduct toward its neighbors in the western Pacific. Beijing's belligerent actions regarding Taiwan in late 1995 and early 1996 attracted a considerable amount of attention in the United States. So, too, have the more recent explicit and implicit threats directed against Taiwan in the aftermath of Taipei's comments that Taiwan and the PRC should conduct relations as equally legitimate states.[35] But belligerence regarding Taiwan is not the only problem; the PRC has also engaged in a distressing amount of saber-rattling on other issues in the western Pacific.

The PRC has shown a willingness to use its growing naval power to press territorial claims to the Spratly islands in the South China Sea,[36] which has led to friction with the Philippines, another claimant, on several occasions. To be sure, China's claims to the Spratlys are nothing new, and, as is often the case with territorial disputes, the historical and legal record is murky.[37] When it comes to territorial disputes, however, international law is a far less important factor than is military power. The PRC has repeatedly sought to assert its position, even when the country was far weaker economically and militarily than it is today. In 1974, several years before Beijing embarked on its economic reform program, China sent its naval forces to consolidate control over the Paracels—a smaller group of islands some 350 miles north of the Spratlys. The PRC constructed a sizable airfield on Woody Island in the Paracel chain in the early 1990s, fueling speculation that Chinese leaders intend to use the Paracels as a military stepping stone to the Spratlys.[38]

China's neighbors continue to resist its claims in the South China Sea. (Indeed, both Taiwan and Vietnam contest Beijing's legal right to the Paracels, although those islands have been under exclusive PRC control since 1974.) How seriously they would resist a Chinese military campaign to seize control is an open question.[39] The Spratlys are an important economic prize for all of the rival claimants—especially since there are indications of substantial oil reserves. The chain is also strategically significant. If the PRC successfully established its claim, the Chinese navy could construct bases and bring its presence well out into the South China Sea. That presence would be more than a little intimidating to other nations in the region and would give Beijing the ability to disrupt important shipping lanes, if it chose to do so.[40]

As China's economic base expands, and the PRC's military modernization proceeds, the balance of military power in the South China Sea seems likely to shift decisively in China's favor—unless more distant regional powers such as Japan, South Korea, and Australia help bolster the anti-PRC coalition. Or unless the United States intervenes militarily in the event of a crisis. U.S. intervention, however, would entail very serious risks to the American people.

The South China Sea is not the only arena in which the PRC has become increasingly assertive with regard to territorial disputes. Chinese officials also made inflammatory statements and gestures because of the territorial dispute with Japan over eight islands—known as the Diaoyu islands in China and the Senkaku islands in Japan. Beijing's actions included some pointed military exercises conducted in September 1996.[41]

The point is not that the United States has important interests at stake in such disputes. Whose claim to islands in the South China Sea is most valid ought to be a matter of indifference to Washington, and under no circumstances should the United States allow itself to be drawn into that multisided dispute if armed conflict erupts. Even keeping the sea-lanes open, while undoubtedly beneficial to American interests, should be far more important to the nations of East Asia. Similarly, whether China or Japan has the better claim to the Diaoyu (Senkaku) islands should have little relevance to the United States.

Unfortunately, because of its bilateral security treaties, the United States incurs significant risk exposure in the various territorial spats. Washington has a mutual defense treaty with the Philippines, one of the countries involved in the Spratlys dispute. U.S.-Philippine military cooperation has been strengthened by the recent signing of a new Visiting Forces Agreement. During the ratification debate by the Philippine senate in May 1999, ruling party senators openly contended that the joint exercises authorized by the VFA would discourage China from pursuing expansionist aims in the South China Sea.[42] The United States would be in a difficult position if a clash occurred between PRC and Philippine naval units and Manila invoked the treaty.

A similar problem exists with the U.S.-Japanese alliance. It is doubtful that U.S. policymakers anticipated possible entanglement in such a petty squabble as the Diaoyu-Senkaku dispute when they negotiated the mutual defense pact with Japan. Nevertheless, Tokyo considers the islands Japanese territory and would very likely call on the United States for assistance in the event of an armed clash with the PRC. That possibility provides another reason (among many) why the United States should phase out the mutual defense pact.[43]

Taiwan's continued economic and political autonomy is a more important American interest. Taiwan is now America's eighth largest trading partner, and a development that brought Taiwan's economic assets under Beijing's control would represent a major shift of power in East Asia, increasing the PRC's overall GDP by more than one-fourth. Americans are also understandably impressed with Taiwan's political transition to democracy, and they would dislike seeing that system extinguished by absorption (particularly if it were forcibly

81

absorbed) into the dictatorial PRC. That is not only a moral consideration; reunification achieved through intimidation or armed conquest could whet Beijing's appetite for aggressive revisionist conduct elsewhere in the region.

Nevertheless, while the goal of continued Taiwanese autonomy is certainly desirable, it still does not constitute an interest sufficient to justify America's willingness to risk war with a nuclear-armed great power. A risk of that magnitude should be incurred only for the defense of core American security interests.

The pertinent point for the United States is not simply the intrinsic merits of the various issues. What matters more is what Beijing's actions may be signaling about China's future behavior as a great power. If the PRC intends to pursue hegemonic ambitions in East Asia, that is a matter of concern to America.

China's intentions become all the more important because of the concerted effort in recent years to build up the PRC's military power. Beijing is clearly attempting to modernize its forces and seems determined to have a more potent strategic deterrent, a first-class air force, and a blue-water navy.[44] On the last point, two Chinese scholars have candidly summarized the PRC's goal. "The PLAN [People's Liberation Army Navy] is embarking on a massive modernization program and transition to a blue-water power. Its objective is to become a new world-class Pacific power in the twenty-first century."[45]

One should not overstate the magnitude and implications of the PRC's military improvements, as advocates of a hard-line U.S. policy toward China tend to do.[46] China has encountered more than a few obstacles and outright failures in its effort to create a first-class military force. Moreover, as political scientists Andrew J. Nathan and Robert S. Ross correctly point out, China is still, for all its recent economic progress, a poor country, and there are likely to be significant limits on its ability to sustain a military buildup. China's geostrategic position is not enviable either, as it must deal with multiple neighbors—including several actual or potential rivals—along lengthy frontiers.[47]

It is also pertinent that the PRC's expansion of military spending started from a low base and is still, by most estimates, relatively modest. Coming up with an accurate estimate of Chinese military expenditures is a challenge in itself. The official PRC defense budget was a mere $12.6 billion in 1999.[48] There is almost universal agreement among Western experts that the official figure greatly understates actual expenditures, and most credible estimates of overall PRC military spending fall in the range of $30 billion to $50 billion a year.[49] That is a significant but not unduly alarming figure; it is, for example, comparable to the expenditures of such midsized powers as Japan, Britain, France, and Germany.

Nevertheless, the trend bears watching. China is already a significant military player with a nuclear arsenal and ICBMs (albeit fewer than two dozen) capable of reaching American territory.[50] Washington, therefore, cannot be indifferent to Beijing's conduct in the security realm.

The PRC can help allay American concerns by matching its conciliatory initiatives toward its major land neighbors with similar moves in the western Pacific. Beijing's acceptance of proposals from other claimants to submit the various island disputes to international arbitration would provide compelling evidence of China's peaceful intentions.[51] A statement renouncing the use of force to resolve the Taiwan issue would defuse that dangerous situation and offer even stronger evidence that worries about possible aggressive behavior by the PRC in East Asia are unfounded. Unfortunately, Beijing's policy toward Taiwan seems to be moving in the opposite direction. A major policy statement issued in February 2000 indicated that the PRC might use force against Taiwan if the Taiwanese continued to decline to negotiate about reunification. Previous PRC statements had threatened force only if Taiwan declared independence.[52]

Toward a Prudent and Sustainable U.S. Policy

If conciliatory initiatives are not forthcoming, the dilemma facing the United States will be how to avoid becoming embroiled in China's disputes with its neighbors without creating an East Asian power vacuum that might prove irresistibly tempting to Beijing. That could lead eventually to China's domination of the region and the emergence of a serious security threat to the United States.

Nowhere is the dilemma more acute than with regard to the chief flash point in U.S.-Chinese relations: Taiwan. Beijing's missile tests and military exercises in the Taiwan Strait in early 1996 and the recent upsurge in tensions between Beijing and Taipei over Lee's comments and the PRC's February 2000 military policy statement underscore the danger that the United States may someday be pressured to defend Taiwan, at considerable peril to the American people. That may not be an immediate danger; given the extent of Beijing's military limitations, a full-scale assault on Taiwan is improbable—although more limited action against one or more small offshore islands remains a possibility.[53] The risk is likely to increase in the future, however.

Taiwan's de facto security dependence on the United States is dangerous for all concerned. The Clinton administration's policy of "strategic ambiguity" (that the United States would regard an attack on Taiwan as an extremely serious breach of the peace and might defend the island, depending on the circumstances) is risky enough. Even worse is the approach, advocated by many of Taipei's friends in the United States, that would include an explicit U.S. pledge to protect Taiwan.

A defense guarantee would have dubious credibility and virtually invite a challenge. The absence of a treaty obligation raises from the outset questions about Washington's probable response. The binding obligations in the mutual defense treaty signed in the 1950s were replaced by the vague provisions of the 1979 Taiwan Relations Act when the United States transferred diplomatic recognition from the Taipei government to the PRC.[54] Equally important, there are no U.S. troops stationed on Taiwan to guarantee U.S. entanglement in a conflict that might erupt—in contrast to the situation in such places as Japan and South Korea.

Lessons drawn from America's Cold War experience with the Soviet Union may lead U.S. policymakers (and bombastic members of Congress) to make overly optimistic assumptions about the ability to the United States to deter Beijing from coercing Taiwan.[55] The credibility of a promise to defend an ally or client from a nuclear-armed adversary does not depend merely on the balance of forces—although that factor is certainly important. An equally crucial consideration is the relative importance of the issue at stake to the guarantor power and to the challenging power—what might be termed the "balance of fervor." And that balance is decidedly in Beijing's favor.

The Kremlin considered it reasonably credible that the United States would risk nuclear war to keep such strategically and economically important prizes as Western Europe and Northeast Asia out of the orbit of a totalitarian superpower rival. A threat to incur the same grave risk merely to keep the PRC from absorbing Taiwan—a political entity the United States does not even officially recognize—is far less credible.

Instead of creating a stronger and more explicit commitment, Washington should reduce America's risk exposure by making it clear that the United States would *not* intervene in an armed conflict between the PRC and Taiwan. The only politically feasible way of doing that, however, would be for Washington to liberalize its arms export policy and allow Taiwan to buy the weapons needed to become and remain militarily self-sufficient.[56] Such an initiative would undoubtedly cause serious friction in U.S.-PRC relations. Chinese officials point to U.S. promises in the August 17, 1982, communiqué and other agreements to gradually curtail arms exports to Taiwan.[57] But both U.S. and PRC leaders need to recognize that the alternative to Taiwan's military self-reliance will be growing public and congressional pressure to have the United States shield the island from attack. Beijing would undoubtedly prefer the termination of U.S. arms sales to Taiwan combined with a nonintervention pledge. That option, though, is a nonstarter, given the realities of domestic American politics.

A promise to risk the lives of millions of Americans to defend Taiwan is a promise that rational Americans should not want their government to fulfill in any case. A better option is to let Taiwan buy all the weapons it needs for its own defense. A Taiwan with robust military capabilities would maximize the chances that Beijing would use only peaceful measures in its campaign to achieve reunification. Conversely, a militarily inferior Taiwan might tempt PRC leaders to consider using force and thereby precipitate an East Asian crisis.

The Taiwan issue underscores a more general problem for American foreign policy. It is simply not clear whether the PRC will be a status quo power or a revisionist power.[58] Significant factors push Beijing in both directions. Precisely because of that uncertainty, the United States must not lock itself into a strategy based on expectations of either friendship or an adversarial relationship. Instead, Washington should adopt a hedging strategy—a set of principles that are likely to work reasonably well no matter what kind of great power the PRC turns out to be.

Although Beijing's extensive economic ties with its Asian neighbors (and with the United States) are an important incentive for status quo behavior, there are other factors that produce incentives for aggressive revisionism. Most important, China is still nursing grievances about the humiliations and territorial amputations that occurred during its period of weakness in the 19th century and the first half of the 20th century.[59] That is why the return of Hong Kong acquired an importance that transcended the territory's economic value; it was a symbol of China's restored national pride. The return of Macao is another step, but it is far from certain that China's leaders and population will consider the process complete until Taiwan is regained, the land taken by the Russian empire is recovered, and Beijing's claims in the South China and East China seas are vindicated.

Some experts argue that the PRC does not harbor expansionist ambitions and wants to concentrate on internal economic progress.[60] That may be true, at least at the moment, but the existence of such an array of unresolved problems points to less sanguine possibilities. Moreover, the history of international relations shows that rising great powers, especially those with territorial claims, typically pursue assertive, if not abrasive, policies. One need only recall the behavior of the United States throughout the 19th century and the early years of the 20th century.

There is no way to know yet whether China will replicate such behavior, but it is unduly optimistic to assume that American and Chinese security interests are so compatible as to warrant a strategic partnership. Moreover, if those policy experts and political leaders who contend that the interests of the two countries are likely to conflict are correct, choosing the PRC as a strategic partner would be an act of folly. Indeed, if the concerns about China's future strategic behavior have even the slightest merit, the United States should be pursuing precisely the opposite course: creating an incentive structure for other regional powers or groups of powers to counterbalance the PRC.

UCLA political science professor Deepak Lal notes the potential arenas in which U.S. and Chinese interests are likely to clash—as well as Beijing's ongoing effort to increase the capabilities of its ballistic missile forces, which he concludes is aimed at securing an effective deterrent against the United States—and argues that Washington's behavior toward India makes no strategic sense. "If the strategic interests of China and the U.S. are so clearly at odds, it would seem bizarre to penalise the one country in the region that might provide a strategic counterweight."[61] Even if one does not fully agree with Lal's assessment of China's behavior, his observation about India's potential as a partial strategic counterweight has merit. Other analysts note that Japan could likewise play a counterbalancing role—indeed Japan would probably be an even more important factor in Asia's strategic equation.[62] Russia, Vietnam, Korea, and other powers would also likely be relevant players in the overall balance of power.

Although it is important for the United States to avoid the extremes of containment or strategic partnership in its relations with China, it is even more important for the United States to adjust its overall Asian policy. That requires new thinking, something that has not been in abundance among policymakers.[63] The best course from the standpoint of American interests would be to encourage the emergence of multiple centers of power in Asia. The existence of several significant security actors would complicate the calculations of the PRC—or any other power that might have hegemonic ambitions. Otherwise, Washington is creating the blueprint for a brittle bipolar security environment in which the only security actors that will matter a decade or two from now are the United States and the PRC. The likely outcome would be either a war between China and the United States or China's emergence as the new regional hegemon.

Encouraging the evolution of a multipolar strategic environment is not the same as adopting a U.S.-led containment policy against China. Washington does not have to be the godfather of a vast anti-PRC alliance. If U.S. officials stop smothering Japan and other allies in an effort to perpetuate their security dependence on the United States, and refrain from berating India for wanting to be a first-class military power, China's neighbors will draw their own conclusions about Beijing's probable strategic behavior and adopt policies based on those conclusions. Washington merely needs to get out of the way of that most normal of processes in the international system.[64]

Encouraging—or at least accepting—the evolution of a balance of power designed to contain any PRC expansionist ambitions is also distinct from regarding China as an implacable foe of the United States. Washington ought to treat China as simply another great power and cultivate a normal relationship, recognizing that the interests of the two countries will sometimes coincide and sometimes conflict. Cooperation needs to be fostered in the first case, and an effort to contain adverse effects must be made in the latter. A normal relationship is inconsistent with attempts to isolate the PRC economically or to adopt an overt containment policy. Such an approach would be especially unwise. A policy based on the assumption that China will inevitably become an aggressor and a mortal enemy of the United States could easily become a tragic, self-fulfilling prophecy.

Embracing the goal of multipolarity, of course, would mean relinquishing America's own hegemony in East Asia. Washington would have to be content with the status of "first among equals" in the region, and that would entail some loss of control. But a hegemonic role is probably not sustainable over the long term in any case. It is a manifestation of national hubris to think that the United States can forever dominate a region that contains nearly a third of the world's population and that, despite a brief stumble, is becoming an increasingly sophisticated locus of economic and technological output. Only an unusual convergence of circumstances following World War II—the eradication of Japan as a political and military player, China's exceptional weakness, and the final stages of decay of the various European colonial empires—enabled the United States to establish a hegemonic position in the first place and maintain it for more than a half-century.[65] It defies both logic and history to assume that U.S. hegemony can be maintained for another half-century.

U.S. leaders can adjust gracefully to the emergence of a more normal configuration of power in the region, or they can resist change to the bitter end. If they choose the former course, the United States will be able to influence the nature of the new multipolar strategic environment in Asia and seek the maximum advantage for American interests. The U.S.-PRC relationship would then be merely one component of a complex mosaic of relationships throughout the region, and there would be a significant opportunity for the United States to pursue a policy that avoided the extremes of viewing the PRC as a strategic partner or a new enemy. The danger of a U.S.-PRC military clash would substantially decline, and Washington would be able to develop a policy toward China that was prudent, sustainable, and beneficial to American interests.

If U.S. leaders choose the course of prolonged resistance to change, the United States will either end up in an armed struggle with the

PRC for dominance in East Asia or be compelled to relinquish power to the region's new hegemon. The opportunity to facilitate the emergence of a relatively stable regional balance of power involving several major players will have been lost, and America's strategic and economic interests will be less rather than more secure. Washington's current erratic and muddled China policy may enable the United States to avoid making the hard choices for a while longer, but the day of reckoning is coming.

Notes

1. For a discussion of these competing approaches and Beijing's probable reaction to them, see David Shambaugh, "Containment or Engagement of China? Calculating Beijing's Responses," *International Security* 21, no. 2 (Fall 1996): 180–209.

2. That is precisely how conservative China bashers want the debate to be framed. See Bruce Herschensohn, "Dollars or Liberty?" *Washington Times,* August 19, 1999, p. A17.

3. For criticism of the engagement versus containment framework from a somewhat different perspective, see Phillip C. Saunders, "A Virtual Alliance for Asian Security," *Orbis* 43, no. 2 (Spring 1999): 237–56. Saunders advocates a "virtual" (informal) alliance of friendly East Asian countries and the United States—with the East Asian powers doing far more in the security arena than is currently the case—to limit Beijing's expansionist options.

4. Barton Gellman, "U.S. and China Nearly Came to Blows in 1996," *Washington Post,* June 21, 1998, p. A1.

5. Clinton also declared that the United States and China "have a special responsibility to the future of the world." Quoted in John F. Harris and Michael Laris, "Clinton Calls for Closer U.S.-China Cooperation," *Washington Post,* June 26, 1998, p. A1. For a discussion of the reaction of China's neighbors to talk of a U.S.-PRC strategic partnership, see Ted Galen Carpenter, "Roiling Asia: U.S. Coziness with China Upsets the Neighbors," *Foreign Affairs* 77, no. 6 (November–December 1998): 1–6.

6. The rapprochement also spawned a brief flurry of journal articles by foreign policy experts who sought to examine the substance, implications, and prospects of the U.S.-PRC strategic partnership. Examples include Harry Harding, "The Uncertain Future of U.S.-China Relations," *Asia-Pacific Review* 6, no. 1 (1999): 7–24; and Sheng Lijun, "China and the United States: Asymmetrical Strategic Partners," *Washington Quarterly* 22, no. 3 (Summer 1999): 147–64.

7. White House, Office of the Press Secretary, "Remarks by the President and First Lady in Discussion on Shaping China for the 21st Century." "Remarks" text appears in Press release, Shanghai Library, Shanghai, People's Republic of China, June 30, 1998, p. 12.

8. Jane Perlez, "Hopes for Improved Ties with China Fade," *New York Times,* February 12, 1999, p. A6.

9. U.S. House of Representatives, *Report of the Select Committee on U.S. National Security and Military/Commercial Concerns with the People's Republic of China,* 3 vols., 105th Cong., 2d sess., 1999, H. Rept. 105-851. The allegations in the report have themselves come under criticism. William J. Broad, "Spies versus Sweat: The Debate

over China's Nuclear Advance," *New York Times*, September 7, 1999, p. A1; and Robert Scheer, "Time to Say Farewell to Spy Scandal," *Los Angeles Times*, September 14, 1999, p. A17.

10. For a more detailed description, see Ted Galen Carpenter, "Damage to Relations with Russia and China," in *NATO's Empty Victory: A Postmortem on the Balkan War*, ed. Ted Galen Carpenter (Washington: Cato Institute, 2000), pp. 83–84.

11. Carol Giacomo, "Albright Says Talks Ease U.S.-China Tensions," Reuters, July 25, 1999; Leslie Lopez, "Albright Welcomes Eased Tension with China and Chastises Taiwan," *Wall Street Journal*, July 26, 1999, p. A19; John Pomfret, "Albright, Chinese Foreign Minister Hold 'Very Friendly Lunch,'" *Washington Post*, July 26, 1999, p. A1; and Jane Perlez, "U.S. and China Say They Are Mending Post-Bombing Rift," *New York Times*, July 26, 1999, p. A1.

12. Perlez, "U.S. and China Say They Are Mending Post-Bombing Rift," p. A1. Washington and Beijing also reached an agreement on financial compensation for the damage to the PRC's embassy in Belgrade and the damage to the U.S. embassy in Beijing caused by the mob violence. Elisabeth Rosenthal, "U.S. Agrees to Pay China $28 Million for Bombing," *New York Times*, December 16, 1999, p. A8.

13. Note especially the following articles in *Foreign Affairs Journal* 52 (June 1999): Zhu Muzhi, "NATO Lifts Its Mask of Humanitarianism," pp. 48–49; Zhao Qizheng, "The U.S.-Concocted 'Cox Report': A Farce to Instigate Anti-China Feelings and Undermine Sino-U.S. Relations," pp. 11–15; Xin Hua, "'Fighting for Values' an Excuse for War," pp. 50–51; and Liu Jiang, "NATO's New Strategic Concept Threatens World Peace," pp. 52–53. Wang Naicheng, "New NATO in the 21st Century," pp. 1–10, provides a more comprehensive but equally hostile overview of NATO's role.

14. Quoted in "Jiang Calls for Action on 'Taipei Conspiracy,'" *South China Morning Post*, July 14, 1999.

15. Georgetown University professor Victor Cha noted a "remarkable détente between China and South Korea" and argued that engaging China further was a promising factor in reducing tensions on the Korean Peninsula, although Beijing was unlikely to completely abandon its support of North Korea. Victor D. Cha, "Engaging China: Seoul-Beijing Détente and Korean Security," *Survival* 41, no. 1 (Spring 1999): 73–98.

16. John Burton, "China Defends N. Korea Rocket Launches," *Financial Times*, July 23, 1999, p. 4.

17. Bill Gertz, "Missile Parts Sent to North Korea by Chinese Companies," *Washington Times*, July 20, 1999, p. A1.

18. For an example of that conventional wisdom, see Helene Cooper and Ian Johnson, "Taiwan Flap Brings China Closer to U.S.," *Wall Street Journal*, July 28, 1999, p. A18.

19. Quoted in James Kynge, Sheila McNulty, and Mure Dickie, "China Warns U.S. Not to Interfere over Taiwan," *Financial Times*, July 26, 1999, p. A1.

20. Quoted in Laurinda Keys, "China Minister Criticizes Nations," Associated Press, July 27, 1999.

21. Quoted in Thaksina Khaikaew, "Chinese Leader Criticizes U.S.," Associated Press, September 4, 1999.

22. Walter A. McDougall, "Nixon, Clinton, and the Baby Boom Rising," Foreign Policy Research Institute E-Notes, August 3, 1998, FPRI@aol.com.

23. "Forbes, Bauer Take Aim at Clinton," Associated Press, September 10, 1999; Ron Fournier, "McCain Urges Toughness on China," Associated Press, September

8, 1999; and Charles Krauthammer, "Appeasing China Doesn't Work," *Washington Post,* August 8, 1999.

24. U.S. House of Representatives, "Disapproving Extension of Nondiscriminatory Treatment to Products of the People's Republic of China," *Congressional Record,* July 27, 1999, p. H6439.

25. Examples include Richard Bernstein and Ross H. Munro, *The Coming Conflict with China* (New York: Knopf, 1997); Bill Gertz, *Betrayal: How the Clinton Administration Undermined American Security* (Washington: Regnery, 1999); and Edward Timperlake and William C. Triplett II, *Year of the Rat: How Bill Clinton Compromised U.S. Security for Chinese Cash* (Washington: Regnery, 1998).

26. Harvey J. Feldman, "How Washington Can Defuse Escalating Tensions in the Taiwan Strait," Heritage Foundation Executive Memorandum no. 620, August 19, 1999; and "Dole Says She Would Use Force to Defend Taiwan," Reuters, August 15, 1999. In the summer of 1999, Sen. Jesse Helms (R-N.C.) introduced legislation, the Taiwan Security Enhancement Act, that would mandate wide U.S.-Taiwanese military cooperation and virtually re-create the defunct mutual defense pact. In February 2000, the House of Representatives passed a somewhat diluted version of such legislation by a 340-71 vote. Art Pine, "House Votes to Strengthen Military Ties with Taiwan," *Los Angeles Times,* February 2, 2000, p. A7.

27. J. Michael Waller, "China's Beachhead at the Panama Canal," *Insight,* August 16, 1999, p. 20; Rowan Scarborough, "China Company Grabs Power over Panama Canal," *Washington Times,* August 12, 1999, p. A1; and G. Russell Evans, "China's Strategic Beachhead," *Washington Times,* August 24, 1999, p. A12. For a critique that punctures much of the alarmism, see Frank Ching, "Hutchinson: Arm of the PLA?" *Far Eastern Economic Review* 16, no. 35 (September 2, 1999): 30.

28. Quoted in Scarborough, p. A1.

29. Quoted in David Hoffman, "Border Pact Signed by Asian Powers," *Washington Post,* April 25, 1997, p. A31.

30. "Kyrgyz, Chinese Leaders Sign Key Border Agreement," Reuters, August 26, 1999; and Vladimir Isachenkov, "Russia, China Discuss Border Stability," *Washington Times,* August 25, 1999, p. A11.

31. Benjamin Kang Lim, "China Preparing to Buy SU-30 Fighters—Russia," Reuters, August 26, 1999; and John Pomfret, "China Plans for Stronger Air Force," *Washington Post,* November 9, 1999, p. A17. Russia and China also conducted their first joint naval exercises in the autumn of 1999. "Russia, China Plan Naval Exercises," Associated Press, September 27, 1999.

32. Willy Wo-Lap Lam, "Beijing and Moscow in High-Tech Arms Pact," *South China Morning Post,* June 26, 1999; and "Russia May Sell Nuke Subs to China," Associated Press, September 1, 1999. For a discussion of earlier Russian-PRC arms deals, see Ted Galen Carpenter, "Managing a Great Power Relationship: The United States, China and East Asian Security," *Journal of Strategic Studies* 21, no. 1 (March 1998): 4–7.

33. Quoted in Bill Gertz, "Russia Sells China High-Tech Artillery," *Washington Times,* July 3, 1997, p. A1.

34. Vladimir Isachenkov, "Russia, China Seek Closer Alliance," Associated Press, August 25, 1999.

35. Benjamin Kang Lim, "China Tells Clinton That Force on Taiwan an Option," Reuters, July 19, 1999; Matt Forney, "China Raises Hints of War with Taiwan on Autonomy," *Wall Street Journal,* July 27, 1999, p. A14; Benjamin Kang Lim, "China

Says Force Still an Option with Taiwan," Reuters, July 24, 1999; James Kynge, "China Boosts Military Presence Near Taiwan," *Financial Times*, August 13, 1999, p. 1; and Tom Raum, "Envoy Threatens Force to Resolve Row with Taiwan," *Washington Times*, August 20, 1999, p. A13.

36. Patrick E. Tyler, "China Revamps Forces with Eye to Sea Claims," *New York Times*, January 2, 1995, p. A2. For an example of a fairly sanguine conclusion about Beijing's military capabilities and intentions in the region, see Michael G. Gallagher, "China's Illusory Threat to the South China Sea," *International Security* 19, no. 1 (Summer 1994): 169-94.

37. For an excellent, concise discussion of the history of the Spratlys controversy, see Michael Leifer, "Chinese Economic Reform and Security Policy: The South China Sea Connection," *Survival* 37, no. 2 (Summer 1995): 46–48.

38. Denny Roy, "Hegemon on the Horizon? China's Threat to East Asian Security," *International Security* 19, no. 1 (Summer 1994): 149–68; and Esmond D. Smith Jr., "China's Aspirations in the Spratly Islands," *Contemporary Southeast Asia* 16, no. 3 (December 1994): 274–94.

39. Felix K. Chang, "Beijing's Reach in the South China Sea," *Orbis* 40, no. 3 (Summer 1996): 353–75.

40. John H. Noer with David Gregory, *Chokepoints: Maritime Economic Concerns in Southeast Asia* (Washington: National Defense University Institute for National Strategic Studies, 1996), pp. 31–33, 35.

41. Steven Mufson, "Chinese Warnings Heighten Tension over Island Dispute with Japan," *Washington Post*, September 25, 1996, p. A26; and Steven Mufson, "Premier of China Joins Fray," *Washington Post*, October 1, 1996, p. A15.

42. "U.S. Military Pact Denounced," *Financial Times*, May 6, 1999, p. 8; and Jim Gomez, "Senate Oks Troops Deal with U.S. Amid Protests," *Washington Times*, May 28, 1999, p. A13.

43. For detailed discussions of the pitfalls of the alliance, see Ted Galen Carpenter, "Paternalism and Dependence: The U.S.-Japanese Security Relationship," Cato Institute Policy Analysis no. 244, November 1, 1995; and Ted Galen Carpenter, "Unjust and Unsustainable: The U.S.-Japan Security Relationship," *NIRA Review* (Winter 1996): 8–11.

44. For discussions of the PRC's military modernization goals, the progress made toward achieving those goals, and the obstacles encountered, see Kenneth W. Allen, Glenn Krumel, and Jonathan D. Pollack, *China's Air Force Enters the 21st Century* (Santa Monica, Calif.: RAND Corporation, 1995); Zhan Jun, "China Goes to the Blue Waters: The Navy, Seapower Mentality and the South China Sea," *Journal of Strategic Studies* 17, no. 3 (September 1994): 180–208; John Wilson Lewis and Xue Litai, *China's Strategic Seapower: The Politics of Force Modernization in the Nuclear Age* (Stanford, Calif.: Stanford University Press, 1994); John Wilson Lewis and Xue Litai, "China's Search for a Modern Air Force," *International Security* 24, no. 1 (Summer 1999): 64–94; Evan A. Figenbaum, "Who's behind China's High-Technology 'Revolution'? How Bomb Makers Remade Beijing's Priorities, Policies and Institutions," *International Security* 24, no. 1 (Summer 1999): 95–126; and James Kynge and Mure Dickie, "China Gives Air Force Offensive Role," *Financial Times*, November 11, 1999, p. 1.

45. You Xi and You Xu, "In Search of Blue Water Power: The PLA Navy's Maritime Strategy in the 1990s," *Pacific Review* 4, no. 2 (1991): 147–48.

46. See, for example, Edward Timperlake and William C. Triplett II, *Red Dragon Rising: Communist China's Military Threat to America* (Washington: Regnery, 1999). For

an analysis that emphasizes the limitations of the PRC's military progress, see Bates Gill and Michael O'Hanlon, "China's Hollow Military," *National Interest* 56 (Summer 1999): 55–61. For a reasoned rebuttal, see James R. Lilley and Carl Ford, "China's Military: A Second Opinion," *National Interest* 57 (Fall 1999): 71–77.

47. Andrew J. Nathan and Robert S. Ross, *The Great Wall and the Empty Fortress: China's Search for Security* (New York: W.W. Norton, 1997). For a slightly less sanguine view that still fully appreciates the daunting obstacles faced by China, see Harry Harding, "A Chinese Colossus?" *Journal of Strategic Studies* 18, no. 3 (September 1995): 104–22.

48. International Institute for Strategic Studies, *The Military Balance, 1999–2000* (London: Oxford University Press, 1999), pp. 175, 186.

49. The only serious study that has placed PRC military expenditures outside the $30 billion to $50 billion range is a Pentagon-commissioned study by the RAND Corporation, *Long-Term Economic and Military Trends* (Santa Monica, Calif.: RAND Corporation, 1995), which used a "purchasing parity" standard to peg China's military spending at a whopping $140 billion. The International Institute for Strategic Studies concludes that China's military outlays in 1998 were the equivalent of $37 billion. International Institute for Strategic Studies, *The Military Balance, 1999–2000*, p. 175.

For discussions of the various estimates of PRC military spending, and the military capabilities such outlays can purchase, see David Shambaugh, "China's Military: Real or Paper Tiger?" *Washington Quarterly* 19, no. 2 (Spring 1996): 19–36; and Charles W. Freeman Jr., "China, Taiwan, and the United States," in *Asia after the Miracle: Redefining U.S. Economic and Security Priorities*, ed. Selig S. Harrison and Clyde V. Prestowitz Jr. (Washington: Economic Strategy Institute, 1998), pp. 170–71, 180–81.

50. Both the number and the sophistication of such missiles and their warheads may increase in the coming years. James Risen, "New Chinese Missiles Seen as Threat to U.S.," *New York Times*, September 10, 1999, p. A12.

51. Beijing's November 1999 proposal for a "code of conduct" for joint exploitation of resources in the Spratlys is mildly encouraging. Jamie Tarabay, "China Makes Proposal in Island Fight," Associated Press, November 29, 1999.

52. Benjamin Kang Lim, "China Says Reunification with Taiwan Urgent," Reuters, February 22, 2000; and Jeremy Page, "Army Paper Hails China's Threat to Taiwan," Reuters, February 23, 2000.

53. Richard Halloran, "China a Long Shot in Taiwan Attack," *Washington Times*, September 3, 1999, p. A12; Matt Forney, "With Bark Worse Than Its Bite, China Lacks Ships, Jets to Take Taiwan," *Wall Street Journal*, September 8, 1999, p. A22; and Philip Finnegan, "Isolated Taiwan Islands May Tempt Chinese," *Defense News*, August 30, 1999, p. 1.

54. For a detailed discussion of the Taiwan Relations Act, see *Legislative History of the Taiwan Relations Act: An Analytic Compilation with Documents on Subsequent Developments*, ed. Lester L. Wolff and David L. Simon (Jamaica, N.Y.: American Association for Chinese Studies, 1982). The text of the act is on pp. 288–95. For a comparison of the provisions of the TRA and those of the defunct mutual defense treaty, see Ted Galen Carpenter, "Let Taiwan Defend Itself," Cato Institute Policy Analysis no. 313, August 24, 1998, pp. 10–12.

55. Ted Galen Carpenter, "Move beyond Cold War Theories," *Los Angeles Times*, March 3, 1996.

56. Doug Bandow, "Taiwan: Not Worth War but Well Worth Arming," *Christian Science Monitor*, October 2, 1996; and Carpenter, "Let Taiwan Defend Itself." That option was unfortunately missing from Nancy Bernkopf Tucker's otherwise interesting and far-ranging assessment of the debate on U.S. policy toward Taiwan. Nancy Bernkopf Tucker, "China-Taiwan: U.S. Debates and Policy Choices," *Survival* 40, no. 4 (Winter 1998–99): 150–67.

57. "China Warns U.S. to Stop Selling Arms to Taiwan," *Inside China Today*, December 12, 1996, http://www.insidechina.com/china/news/02.html.

58. For a discussion of the nuances and tensions in Chinese thinking about what kind of great power the PRC can become, see Gilbert Rozman, "China's Quest for Great Power Identity," *Orbis* 43, no. 3 (Summer 1999): 383–401.

59. Leslie Chang, "In China, History Class Means an 'Education in National Shame,'" *Wall Street Journal*, June 23, 1999, p. A1.

60. Examples of the argument that China's objectives are defensive rather than offensive include Freeman; Nathan and Ross; and Patrick Tyler, "Who's Afraid of China?" *New York Times Magazine*, August 1, 1999, pp 46–49.

61. Deepak Lal, "Hypocrisy and the Bomb," *Financial Times*, May 18, 1998, p. 14. United Press International foreign correspondent Martin Sieff makes a similar point. Martin Sieff, "Passage to India," *National Review*, June 22, 1998, pp. 36–38.

62. See, for example, Christopher Layne, "Less Is More: Minimal Realism in East Asia," *National Interest* 43 (Spring 1996): 64–77.

63. See Doug Bandow, "Old Wine in New Bottles: The Pentagon's East Asia Security Strategy Report," Cato Institute Policy Analysis no. 344, May 18, 1999.

64. Scholars have noted that major powers tend to resist encroachments by other major powers, frequently joining together to balance against such a power rather than tamely submitting to or "bandwagoning" with it. See Stephen M. Walt, *The Origins of Alliances* (Ithaca, N.Y.: Cornell University Press, 1987); and Christopher Layne, "From Preponderance to Offshore Balancing: America's Future Grand Strategy," *International Security* 22, no. 1 (Summer 1997): 86–124.

65. See Ted Galen Carpenter, "Washington's Smothering Strategy: American Interests in East Asia," *World Policy Journal* (Winter 1997–98): 20–32.

6. China and the United States in Asia: The "Threat" in Perspective

Selig S. Harrison

The central challenge that China has faced historically, and still faces today, is the need to manage powerful centrifugal forces. In addition to the significant ethnic minorities on its periphery, the vast Han heartland encompasses eight separate spoken languages that define distinct provincial identities. During periods of weak central authority, these ancient identities have been the basis for recurrent warlordism. Mao Zedong imposed unprecedented Chinese unity: first, in the name of combating Japanese aggression and later, under the banner of modernization and eradication of poverty. As the memory of his leadership fades, however, Mao's successors are facing a resurgence of regional and social divisions that are accentuated by rapidly growing economic expectations.

The current debate over whether the People's Republic of China poses an expansionist threat to its neighbors and to the United States rarely takes into account the domestic factors that condition China's external role. Yet the starting point for a balanced approach to this debate should be a clear recognition of the staggering challenges in domestic management that face Beijing. Food and energy shortages threaten the high growth rates of recent years as China experiences falling prices, lower corporate earnings, growing unemployment, and a collapse of consumer demand that leads to further price declines.

Fearful that economic failure could soon lead to political disarray, Chinese leaders have become preoccupied with resolving their economic problems at home and with building foreign relationships that will make that task easier. *New York Times* Beijing bureau chief Patrick E. Tyler, who has lived in China for five years, observed: "If any generalization is to be made about 1.3 billion people, it would be that the Chinese want nothing more than to have a long period of peace and stability in which to develop their economy. Prosperity at home and military expansionism abroad are fundamentally incompatible in China today."[1]

To understand that China is preoccupied with its domestic problems does not assuage the anxieties of alarmists who point to Beijing's growing military capabilities as evidence of expansionist goals. This chapter begins, accordingly, by assessing China's military strength and intentions in the context of the U.S. military presence in Asia and Japan's growing military power, including Japan's potential for nuclear weapons and long-range ballistic missiles. My conclusion is that China's conventional force posture and nuclear-weapons deployments are defensive and are likely to remain so in the absence of grave provocation, such as foreign military intervention in Taiwan.

I show why Taiwan is an internecine Chinese matter that has no bearing on the debate about whether China will be expansionist. In one case, that of India, my analysis acknowledges understandable concern about Beijing's ambitions. I underline the nascent strategic rivalry between New Delhi and Beijing in the Indian Ocean and the legitimate Indian concern that China could, through a combination of subversion and military pressure, pursue historically based border claims in northeastern India. In three other areas, the South China Sea, the Senkaku (Diaoyu) islands, and Kazakhstan, I discuss economic conflicts in which China has been jockeying for position but has shown a readiness for compromise not shown toward India. Finally, I conclude with a warning that U.S. efforts to decide the terms of the balance of power between Beijing and its neighbors would strengthen ultranationalist forces in China and inflame regional tensions.

The PRC's Modest Conventional Military Capabilities

In alarmist assessments of Chinese military power, it is argued that China's official defense budget figures are understated and that substantial defense spending is hidden in other budget categories, including military purchases abroad that will enhance China's ability to project power. Although there is an element of truth in that argument, extremely misleading numbers are frequently advanced.

Ross H. Munro and Richard Bernstein, authors of *The Coming Conflict with China*, for example, contend that a "conservative" estimate of Chinese military spending would be at least $87 billion per year, not the $8.7 billion figure reported in 1996.[2] A more widely accepted consensus of government and academic experts suggests an annual figure of $30 billion to $35 billion, which is about 1.5 percent of gross domestic product, in contrast with U.S. expenditures, which are 3 to 4 percent of gross domestic product. The highest figure for Chinese military spending cited in expert debates is $65 billion.[3] Moreover, when Munro and Bernstein point to increases during recent years in China's announced defense-spending levels, they ignore or minimize the extent to which those increases reflect higher outlays for pay raises and other benefits for the armed forces as well as for defensive systems such as air defense radar and anti-aircraft systems on ships. CIA China specialist John Culver, reviewing Beijing's defense spending, concludes that "if one focuses on the resources being dedicated to the Chinese military as a measure of change in intentions or difference in capability over time, changes in orders of magnitude are not apparent over the last decade."[4]

Recent reports of projected Chinese weapons acquisitions from Russia impart an element of uncertainty to assessments of Chinese military capabilities. However, those acquisitions should be evaluated in relation to the overall decrease in most aspects of Chinese military power that has taken place in recent years.

Military modernization is slower in China than in Japan, South Korea, or Taiwan. Chinese military capabilities are declining in personnel and hardware, and Chinese plans for projecting power are still largely at the drawing-board stage. The most striking example of China's military decline is the drop in combat aircraft from 6,000 in 1980 to some 5,000 today; most of those aircraft are obsolescent MiG-17s, MiG-19s, MiG-21s, and their Chinese clones. It is because almost all of those fighters are retiring or will be retiring soon that China has purchased 74 SU-27s from Russia and obtained a license to produce another 200.[5] Dwight Perkins, an expert on the Chinese economy, observed that the number of military aircraft and submarines purchased from Russia to date has been "modest" because China "distrusts dependence on the outside world."[6] A Russian defense analyst complains that China limits its annual military imports from all sources to $1 billion.[7]

Bates Gill of the Brookings Institution emphasizes in a recent study that Beijing has "only a few dozen top-line fighters and no intercontinental bombers."[8] He cites a Defense Intelligence Agency

97

estimate that only 10 percent of China's armed forces will have even "late cold war equivalent" weaponry by 2010.[9] Significantly, China had to import SU-27s after its failure to develop its own F-10 supersonic fighter. Its domestically produced fighter plane, the F8-2, is comparable to military aircraft produced in the United States three decades ago. With Japan now producing the U.S. F-2 fighter jet, equipped with air-to-air missiles more advanced than those deployed by Beijing, Tokyo will enjoy air superiority for the next decade in areas within reach of Japan, including the East China Sea.

Furthermore, although China is buying four diesel submarines and two destroyers from Russia, the PRC's naval capabilities are still limited. The Chinese surface fleet, with 58 major surface combatants, is not growing numerically, and Chinese submarines, which numbered more than 100 a decade ago, are now down to 60 at most—and almost 40 of those are Romeo-class boats based on obsolete German-model U-boats.

China is expected to acquire, within five to seven years, the amphibious and airlift capability that would be needed to invade Taiwan. The PRC is capable even now of short-range missile attacks and of blockading Taiwan's ports, which would inflict crippling economic damage. Most observers agree, however, that Beijing wants to avoid a military conflict with Taiwan and is likely to risk one only if faced with a declaration of independence or irrevocable steps foreshadowing such a declaration.

In addition to the overwhelming U.S. superiority over China in air and naval power projection, some other Asian countries already have or soon will have air and naval capabilities that in the foreseeable future will equal or surpass China's capabilities. South Korea has six German-designed diesel submarines that are more advanced than the Romeo-class Chinese fleet, and Malaysia has several MiG-29 fighters. Japan has acquired Aegis-class destroyers that will permit maritime operations beyond land-based air cover and is developing airborne refueling technology that will greatly increase its power projection capabilities. Faced with those challenges, the commander of the Chinese air force announced plans in late 1999 for a shift in air strategy "from territorial defense to a combination of defense and offense"[10] that would lead to new aircraft acquisitions.

The projected SSM-IB missile will give the Japanese Maritime Self-Defense Forces (MSDF) a significant anti-ship capability. China has watched warily as the mission of the MSDF has evolved from one of limited coastal defense two decades ago to one now encompassing a 1,000-nautical-mile defense perimeter reaching close to Guam and the Philippines. Japan's National Defense Program Outline authorizes the MSDF to build up to 60 surface combatant ships, 16 submarines, and 200 combat aircraft. At present, the Japanese naval forces number 34 surface combatant ships in operation or under construction. But with its new ocean-going replenishment ships, one for each of its four flotillas, the MSDF will have a much greater ability than will the Chinese navy to operate on the high seas for sustained periods.[11]

During the next two decades, China will be able to project conventional military power effectively only in areas reachable by its land-based aircraft—notably, the South China Sea. Thus, the PRC will be able to defend its territorial claims to the Paracel islands and to the petroleum-rich seabed areas contested by Vietnam. To project power over greater distances, to areas where it might come into conflict with U.S. interests, Beijing would have to acquire aircraft carriers. Although one carrier could conceivably be purchased or built within a decade, a rotating fleet of three carriers would be necessary so that one could be kept regularly on station. That would require another decade, assuming that Beijing would decide to sacrifice civilian economic needs for a carrier program—an assumption that many experts consider unlikely.

Hypothetically, China could pose a conventional threat in future decades that it does not pose today, but only if one makes assumptions that are highly questionable. One assumption is that the PRC will be able to sustain indefinitely such high levels of economic development that it will be free to channel more resources into defense spending. Another assumption is that China will make much more rapid progress in developing its defense industries than it has done so far and thus will be able to produce advanced weapons systems that it does not now possess or has been reluctant to purchase from others. Still another questionable assumption is that China will shift from its present inward-oriented posture, with its focus on economic development, to an expansionist posture.

The Chinese goals most often cited as evidence of expansionist intentions are the reincorporation of Taiwan into a one-China framework and the restoration of sovereignty over the Spratly, Paracel, and Senkaku islands. But those goals do not reflect a desire to expand beyond what China sees as its historic borders.

On the basis of his contacts with the Chinese armed forces and his access to U.S. intelligence as U.S. deputy chief of mission in Beijing and later as assistant secretary of defense for International Security Affairs, former ambassador Charles W. Freeman Jr. writes that the People's Liberation Army has a sevenfold mission:

1. to defend the borders and territories currently controlled by China against further efforts by foreign nations to alter or detach those territories;
2. to back up Chinese diplomatic efforts to avoid permanent separation from and ultimately achieve the recovery of territories wrested from China by great-power intervention: the European seizures of Hong Kong and Macao, the Japanese annexation of Taiwan and the Senkaku (Diaoyu) archipelago, and Cold War efforts by the United States to foster a rival Chinese regime on Taiwan;
3. to establish for the Chinese state secure and recognized maritime boundaries where long-standing Chinese claims are now subject to challenge, as in the case of postindependence claims by the Philippines, Malaysia, Brunei, and Vietnam to islets and reefs in the South China Sea and by North Korea, South Korea, and Indonesia to continental-shelf and other seabed resources;
4. to retake Taiwan by force if Chinese diplomacy fails (unlike the cases of Hong Kong and Macao, in which diplomacy has succeeded);
5. to protect other borders if they are subjected to military challenge (e.g., by Russia, India, Vietnam, or other member states of the Association of Southeast Asian Nations);
6. to safeguard the Chinese state against external intervention, coercion, or dictation by other great powers; and
7. to support China's emergence as a world power with comprehensive strength.

"Notably absent from this list," Freeman concludes,

> are many of the aspirations and objectives that made the rise of other great powers, such as the United States, Japan, Germany, or the Soviet Union, so disruptive of international peace and security. China asserts no doctrine of "manifest

destiny" or hemispheric exclusion. It has no ideology of Lebensraum to motivate territorial expansion. Its revanchism does not extend to areas inhabited and claimed by non-Chinese. China does not seek to bring additional minorities (non-Han peoples) within its borders. China appears to believe that access to distant resources is best guaranteed by an open international trading system, rather than by power projection. It has no colonies or satellites and no apparent impulse to establish them.[12]

China's Nuclear Capabilities

To make a balanced assessment of China's military capabilities in relation to those of its neighbors, it is necessary to distinguish sharply between its conventional and nuclear capabilities.

In contrast with the limitations of its domestic capability to produce conventional weaponry, Beijing already possesses the ability to make its own nuclear weapons as well as short-range ballistic and cruise missiles, which are viewed as a potential threat by neighboring countries. China's nuclear arsenal includes not only intercontinental ballistic missiles but also DF-3 intermediate-range ballistic missiles (IRBMs) and DF-21 mobile IRBMs capable of reaching nearby targets in Asia. According to Western intelligence reports shared with Japan, most of the DF-3s, with a range of 1,689 miles, are deployed in northern China—some near Tianjin opposite Korea and the rest at Xuanhua west of Beijing, Liujihou south of Tianjin, Yidu in Shangdong Province, and Dalong in Hubei Province—all close to Japan.[13]

China argues that those deployments are not directed at its neighbors but are necessary to have a balanced deterrent posture in the face of U.S. and Russian nuclear deployments that are still maintained in Asia despite the end of the Cold War. Beijing has repeatedly offered to join in regional nuclear arms control negotiations if the United States and Russia would also participate. Moreover, Beijing correctly points out that Japan's sophisticated civilian nuclear and space capabilities could be transformed quickly into a formidable nuclear-weapons program, complete with missiles comparable in thrust and range to the most advanced U.S. missiles.[14] Beijing would likely intensify its nuclear buildup if Tokyo were to undertake the major expansion of its conventional military capabilities urged by Munro and Bernstein, commit itself under the revised Japan-U.S.

101

Defense Guidelines to support intervention in Taiwan, and continue to accumulate stockpiles of nuclear materials in its civilian nuclear program. In particular, if Japan and the United States create the Theater Missile Defense system now under discussion, China would conclude that Tokyo does indeed intend to develop a nuclear-weapons program using the projected missile defense system as a shield behind which it could mount a first strike.

The danger of a Sino-Japanese nuclear arms race is directly linked to whether the United States and Russia take meaningful steps toward a process of global disarmament that embraces China. In a world moving toward de-nuclearization, however gradually, Japan's anti-nuclear consensus is likely to hold firm, and China is likely to join in de-nuclearization measures. With a frozen power structure in which Washington and Moscow seek to keep a margin of overwhelming nuclear superiority, China will undoubtedly attempt to catch up with them, and the pro-nuclear hawks in Japan will become progressively stronger as China's nuclear capabilities grow.

China is acutely aware that the U.S. nuclear umbrella over Japan will not, in itself, ensure a non-nuclear Japan. Would the United States actually risk a nuclear exchange with China to defend Japan against nuclear blackmail or a nuclear attack? Most Japanese do not really expect nuclear protection from Washington. Even during the Cold War, a panel of Japanese security experts convened by the *Yomiuri Shimbun* in 1966 declared that it would be "highly unthinkable" for the United States to use nuclear weapons or any other form of military pressure to protect Japan from nuclear blackmail by the Soviet Union or China. The communist powers could use Japan as a hostage to deter a U.S. attack, the panel concluded, and there would be "little practical meaning" in the destruction of communist cities after "Tokyo and Osaka had been turned into a second Hiroshima and Nagasaki."[15]

Although its credibility is questionable, the U.S. pledge of nuclear protection for Japan contained in the Mutual Security Treaty serves a useful purpose by making it difficult for pro-nuclear hawks in Japan to justify a Japanese nuclear capability. But the danger of a nuclear Japan will persist unless Washington and Moscow negotiate global nuclear arms control limitations that go far enough to draw in China. Significantly, many of the opponents of nuclear weapons in Japan, while welcoming a symbolic U.S. nuclear umbrella, also call for the reduction or complete removal of U.S. conventional combat forces. Their argument is that a U.S. combat force presence exacerbates tensions with China, especially in the context of the U.S.-Japan Defense Guidelines. The language of the guidelines leaves open the possibility of U.S.-Japanese cooperation in the defense of Taiwan in a war with China. Beijing has repeatedly, but to no avail, called on Tokyo to disavow such a possibility.

Like other neighbors of Japan, China has until recently been ambivalent about the U.S. military presence. While opposed in principle to foreign forces in Asia, China has been tolerant of the U.S. role as insurance against a Japanese conventional and nuclear military buildup. But the revised guidelines have radically changed Chinese attitudes. In Chinese eyes, Japan's repeated refusal to rule out the application of the guidelines to Taiwan foreshadows eventual Japanese support for U.S. military intervention in any future war between China and Taiwan over the future of the island.

The Taiwan Issue as a Special Case

Beijing's determination to reincorporate Taiwan into some form of one-China framework is not relevant to the debate over whether the PRC poses an expansionist threat to its Asian neighbors or to the United States. To understand why that is so, it is necessary to remember that Taiwan has historically been a part of China and is a symbol today of the humiliations suffered by China in past centuries when it was weak, disunited, and vulnerable to foreign incursions. The Ming Dynasty was unable to stop Spanish and Dutch adventurers from occupying Taiwan during the 14th and 15th centuries. The Ching Dynasty incorporated the island into the realm for 212 years and initiated economic development programs there during the 19th century. Then Japan started the Sino-Japanese war in 1895. China lost that war ignominiously and the Ching emperor had to cede Taiwan to Japan as the price for getting Japanese forces to leave the mainland. That act is remembered by all Chinese as one of the most shameful chapters in Chinese history.

At the end of World War II, Japan was forced to relinquish Taiwan, but the United States immediately stepped in to build up Chiang Kai-Shek's power on the island. Taiwan became a pawn in the unfinished Chinese civil war, and once again the island was a beachhead of foreign influence in Chinese territory. After Chiang's forces retreated to Taiwan in 1949, the United States poured in massive economic and military aid to make the island a forward bastion against the new communist regime on the mainland. American and Japanese investors followed. With hard work and dynamic enterprise, Taiwan made the most of the Cold War dollars and technology flowing its way. Economically, Taiwan prospered, and, politically, despite the de facto independence of the island, Chiang's Nationalist regime remained committed to reunification with the mainland.

As Taiwan's prosperity grew, so did the aspirations of some of its leaders for de jure independence. Those aspirations were encouraged by Japanese rightists such as former prime minister Nobosuke Kishi, who dreamed of reestablishing Japanese hegemony on the island. To the newly resurgent Chinese regime in Beijing, however, the consolidation of the one-China framework in some form is a historically patriotic mission of transcendent importance. Past humiliations in Taiwan symbolize the impotence of earlier Chinese regimes. Reunification in some form is seen as necessary to demonstrate that a strong, unified China has now emerged on the world stage.

In refusing to treat the Taiwan issue as an internecine Chinese affair, many observers distinguish between "Taiwanese" and "Chinese" as if they were ethnically different. In reality, however, 16 million of the 19 million residents of Taiwan are ethnically and culturally Han Chinese. Thirteen million are the descendants of settlers who came from Fukien Province in the 17th, 18th, and 19th centuries. They speak the Fukienese dialect of Chinese. Another 3 million are immigrants from a variety of Chinese provinces who came with Chiang when he fled the mainland in 1945. The remaining 3 million are immigrants from China of the Hakka minority, and those immigrants are still treated in Taiwan, as they are in China, as an ethnic minority.

Advocates of Taiwan's independence, both on the island and in the United States, dismiss the importance of ethnic identity, arguing that the island has evolved a separate character during five decades of Japanese colonial rule and five Cold War decades under the wing of the United States. China, sensitive to that argument, insists that it is not seeking the direct incorporation of Taiwan, given the island's system of private enterprise and democratic institutions. Pointing to its "one country, two systems" policy in Hong Kong, Beijing pledges that it would respect Taiwan's autonomy within some form of one-China framework.

The United States professes to be neutral in the struggle for advantage between Beijing and Taipei over the future of the island. In recognizing Beijing and in ending the U.S. security treaty with Taipei in 1979, the Carter administration formally accepted the one-China principle. But the continuance of large-scale sales of weaponry and military technology to Taiwan in direct violation of the 1982 U.S.-China Second Shanghai Communiqué, which explicitly pledged a gradual phasing out of such sales, places Washington squarely on Taipei's side. So long as the United States fails to honor the 1982 accord, pro-independence advocates in Taiwan will feel emboldened to press their case, confident that Washington will come to their aid in any war with Beijing over the island.

Under the Taiwan Relations Act, American presidents are empowered to limit arms sales to Taiwan to those judged "sufficient" for the defense of the island. In contrast with this carefully qualified language in the Taiwan Relations Act, the Taiwan lobby in Congress is pressing for upgraded arms sales that would commit the United States to an increasingly flagrant disregard of the 1982 accord.

It is beyond the scope of this chapter to discuss in detail American policy toward Taiwan. In assessing whether China poses an expansionist threat, however, it is necessary to underline the sensitivity of the Taiwan issue as a potential source of U.S.-Chinese military conflict. That conflict, in turn, could draw in other Asian powers, notably Japan, thus creating the possibility of severe tensions between China and neighboring powers that might otherwise not arise.

Sino-Indian Rivalry

Although the image of China bent on territorial aggrandizement at the expense of its neighbors is clearly inaccurate, it does not follow that Beijing is uniformly benign in its posture toward all of the states on its periphery. In the case of India, Asia's other nuclear giant, China has pursued policies that reflect a strong sense of strategic rivalry for leadership in the region.

This Sino-Indian rivalry differs from the more complex Sino-Japanese competition for influence. Economically, Tokyo has set a faster

pace than has Beijing, but ingrained feelings of cultural subordination to China make it impossible for Japan to look on China as a
junior power. Powerful psychological bonds, summed up in the
Japanese expression *dobun dosyu* (same race, same letters), coupled
with mutualities of economic interest, temper military tensions and
offset China's memories of past Japanese aggression.[16] India, by
contrast, has historically regarded itself, as has China, as the "Middle
Kingdom." Thus, New Delhi's ambitions for a global superpower
status comparable to that of Beijing are a constant affront to the PRC.

The 1962 Chinese border incursion in the Himalayas was, apart
from China's desire to show its displeasure with India's close Cold
War ties with the Soviet Union, an attempt to put India in its place.
More important, China and India have a serious incipient conflict
of military ambitions in the eastern Indian Ocean and the adjacent
areas of the South China Sea. The substantial Indian naval base in
the Andaman islands is insurance against China's possible development of blue-water naval forces capable of operating close to India.
Indian suspicions of Chinese intentions have been aroused in recent
years by the establishment of Chinese-built radar facilities, ostensibly
operated by the Burmese armed forces, on the Cocos islands, off the
west coast of Burma near the Andamans. New Delhi is also concerned by the Chinese manipulation of ethnic rivalries in the tribal
regions of India's northeast frontier bordering Burma. The PRC's
actions are linked to pressures for the redemarcation of India's
boundaries with Burma and China—boundaries that are regarded
by Beijing as unjust legacies of colonialism. Perhaps the most menac-
ing aspect of Chinese behavior in Indian eyes was the construction
of railroad and highway links running north to south through Burma
that are big enough to accommodate tanks and heavy trucks.
Although the construction is officially part of China's economic aid
program to Burma, the military implications of these north-south
transportation arteries deeply disturb Indian military planners.

China's Quest for Petroleum

Much has been made of China's establishment of military aviation
facilities on Mischief Reef in the Spratly islands and on Woody
Island in the Paracels. But, as I have explained in my book *China,
Oil and Asia: Conflict Ahead?*[17] China's objectives in the South China
Sea relate primarily to the petroleum potential there. The purpose

of the minor military facilities that Beijing set up there is not to prepare the way for military expansion or to interfere with freedom of navigation but rather to back up Chinese seabed demarcation claims in Law of the Sea disputes over petroleum rights. All of the potential rival claimants to such rights have made military moves of some sort to bolster their base-line claims. Moreover, China has repeatedly offered to join in cooperative arrangements for petroleum development.

Although it has not set up military facilities in contested areas, as it has in the case of the South China Sea, China is actively exploring the petroleum potential of the East China Sea as well. Beijing claims full jurisdiction over the East China Sea continental shelf, including the portions of the shelf on the Japanese side of a hypothetical median line. So far, however, China has not attempted to extract petroleum on the Japanese side and has repeatedly offered to work out a joint program to develop the promising and readily accessible shallow-water petroleum deposits surrounding the disputed Senkaku islands. Tokyo is reluctant to suspend its claims to sovereignty over the Senkakus to make joint development possible lest such an action set a precedent that could complicate Tokyo's negotiations with Russia over the future of the Kurile islands.[18]

Petroleum and lebensraum are both factors that have contributed to the growth of tensions between China and Kazakhstan. China recently concluded a $10 billion agreement with Kazakhstan to develop two oil fields there and to build a pipeline connecting them to China. As the *Financial Times* observed, however, the oil fields are not large enough to justify such a big pipeline, "which indicates that China is planning on obtaining additional volumes of oil in Central Asia."[19] The push for oil might not in itself alarm the Kazakhs, but it is coupled with the aggressive pursuit of territorial claims in border disputes and with signs that Beijing is looking westward to find outlets for its burgeoning population. A massive program to settle ethnic Chinese in the PRC's Xinjiang Province has aroused Kazakh fears of large-scale Chinese migration into its territory. Chinese archaeologists point to new evidence allegedly showing that China's lost province of Xi Yu (northwest province), cited in ancient lore, extended almost to the Caspian Sea, embracing most of Kazakhstan.

A Rising China and America's Preeminence

What underlies the alarmist view of a Chinese menace is not concern that Beijing might threaten its neighbors but rather fear of a Chinese threat to American influence in Asia. Thus the bottom line of the Munro-Bernstein indictment of Beijing is that "China's goal is to become the paramount power in Asia and to supplant the United States in that role."[20]

The assumption that the United States, as the "only superpower," is destined and entitled to be the paramount power in all parts of the world betrays a parochial insensitivity to the nature of the emerging global environment. For all its worldwide reach as the pacesetter in economic globalization, Washington will increasingly face a multipolar geopolitical environment. As China grows in strength, Beijing will expect to end the paramount role asserted by the United States in Asia in the aftermath of World War II. Beijing will also consider a permanent U.S. combat force presence in Korea and Japan increasingly unacceptable. But an end to U.S. paramountcy would not, for the reasons stated in this chapter, lead to a Chinese effort to assert its own paramountcy through military power.

Although China and the United States have an unavoidable conflict of interest, that conflict is not limited to Asia and it is economic, not military. As Beijing intensifies its global export offensive, Washington should insist on equity in bilateral trade and investment relations. China's membership in the World Trade Organization should strengthen the ability of the United States to pursue equitable relations; however, China will also have to make the institutional changes, especially in its legal system, necessary for carrying out its WTO obligations. Conflicts of economic interest will lead to continual contention between the two countries; that tension should not be exacerbated by needless conflict in the security realm.

By virtue of its size and its nuclear capabilities, China is likely to consolidate its position as first among equals in an evolving Asian balance of power in which India, Japan, Indonesia, and a unified Korea will all make claims for recognition. To seek to determine the terms of this power balance and, worse still, to interfere in the final stages of the Chinese civil war by backing Taiwan could well embroil the United States in recurrent military quagmires and make prophecies of an adversarial China self-fulfilling.

Notes

1. Patrick E. Tyler, "Who's Afraid of China?" *New York Times Magazine*, August 1, 1999, p. 48.

2. Ross H. Munro and Richard Bernstein, *The Coming Conflict with China* (New York: Knopf, 1997).

3. Bates Gill and Michael O'Hanlon, "There's Less to the Chinese Threat Than Meets the Eye," *Washington Post*, June 20, 1999, p. B1.

4. Hans Binnendijk and Ronald N. Montaperto, eds., *Strategic Trends in China* (Washington: Institute for National Strategic Studies, National Defense University Press, 1998).

5. Clyde Prestowitz and Selig S. Harrison, eds., *Asia after the "Miracle"* (Washington: Economic Strategy Institute, 1998), p. 18; see also Georgy Bovt, "'Hi' from the Heavenly Empire to Clinton" (in Russian), *Izvestia* (Moscow), December 10, 1999, p. 1.

6. Dwight Perkins, "Trade and Foreign Direct Investment in China's Development Strategies," in *Trade, Security, and National Strategy in the Asia-Pacific*, NBR Analysis, vol. 7, no. 3 (Seattle, Wash.: National Bureau of Asian Research, October 1996), p. 19.

7. Pavel Felgenhauer, "The Arms Market Is a Cynical Matter" (in Russian), *Segodnya* (Moscow), July 21, 1999, p. 2.

8. Gill and O'Hanlon.

9. Ibid.

10. Quoted in John Pomfret, "China Plans for a Stronger Air Force," *Washington Post*, November 9, 1999, p. 8.

11. *The United States, Japan and the Future of Nuclear Weapons*, Report of the U.S.-Japan Study Group on Arms Control and Non-Proliferation after the Cold War (Washington: Carnegie Endowment for International Peace, 1995), p. 47.

12. Charles F. Freeman, "China, Taiwan, and the United States," in Prestowitz and Harrison, pp. 172–73.

13. See Prestowitz and Harrison, p. 21.

14. Selig S. Harrison, *Japan's Nuclear Future: The Plutonium Debate and East Asia Security* (Washington: Carnegie Endowment for International Peace, 1996).

15. Kobayashi Yosaji, ed., *An Approach to the Revision of the Security Treaty* (Tokyo: Yomiuri Shimbun, 1970), pp. 109–10.

16. Selig S. Harrison, *The Widening Gulf: Asian Nationalism and American Policy* (New York: Free Press, 1978).

17. Selig S. Harrison, *China, Oil and Asia: Conflict Ahead?* (New York: Columbia University Press, 1977).

18. Ibid., pp. 89–125 and 213–31.

19. Charles Clover, "Kazakhs Tread Softly in the Shadow of Giant Neighbor," *Financial Times*, July 3, 1999, p. 4.

20. Munro and Bernstein, p. 64.

7. The Dragon's Reach: China and Southeast Asia

Marvin C. Ott

Southeast Asia has arguably been the global region most neglected by American foreign policy and strategic analysts. As a corollary to that proposition, the relationship between China and Southeast Asia is the most disregarded of the major regional relationships that will shape international security in the early 21st century. That indifference is puzzling because Southeast Asia is likely to be the principal geographic arena in which the strategic competition of the future, that between the United States and China, will be played out.

The rationale for that proposition is deceptively simple. China is emerging as a regional great power—diplomatically, economically, and militarily. As such, it is the one potential peer competitor of the United States in world affairs. Moreover, China for the first time in at least two centuries is unimpeded by its two traditional security preoccupations: Russia and Japan. Beijing is strategically free to pursue its natural inclination to assert influence and interests to the south. China is unlikely to seriously challenge the status quo in Northeast Asia; it is too tough a neighborhood. China's strategic posture in that region will be inherently defensive, for example, in a possible reassertion of Japanese military capability and the reunification of the Korean Peninsula.

But Southeast Asia is another story. From China's perspective, Southeast Asia is attractive, vulnerable, and nearby. There are many phrases in Chinese that characterize the *Nanyang* (South Seas) as golden lands of opportunity. For three decades Southeast Asia has been a region of rapidly growing wealth, much of it generated and owned by large Chinese populations in major urban centers. Even after wholesale despoliation of tropical forests and other natural

The views in this chapter are those of the author alone, not the National War College or the U.S. Department of Defense.

111

endowments, the physical resources of Southeast Asia remain impressive and the world's busiest sea-lanes traverse the region. With the exception of Indonesia, individual states that compose the political map of Southeast Asia are only a fraction the size of China. The southern border of China abuts Southeast Asia along the northern borders of Burma, Laos, and Vietnam.

Historically, China's presence and influence in Southeast Asia have waxed and waned over two millennia. During China's long imperial epoch, strong dynasties asserted a kind of cultural-political suzerainty through the "tribute system." Southeast Asian monarchs, chieftains, and sultans gave symbolic deference to the Celestial Throne as the apogee of human civilization. But as a general rule China did not attempt to exert physical control on the ground. The principal exception was in northern Vietnam, which was long treated by China as a province of the Middle Kingdom. After a struggle waged episodically for 1,000 years, the Vietnamese finally wrested their political independence from China in A.D. 939. However, China's long presence left its cultural mark, and Vietnam today is the one predominantly Confucian nation in the region.

With the communist conquest of China an unsettling new era dawned. Initially, the People's Republic of China embraced the Comintern policy of support for communist insurrections in the Third World. China provided political, moral, and sometimes material backing to communist guerrillas and urban revolutionaries seeking to topple noncommunist regimes throughout Southeast Asia. However, as colonial rule gave way to new independent governments, communist movements increasingly found themselves in opposition not to European colonialists but to indigenous nationalists. The definitive signal of a change in Beijing's policy came at the Afro-Asian Nonaligned Conference in Bandung, Indonesia, in April 1955. China's urbane diplomatic genius, Chou En-lai, unveiled a new "peaceful coexistence" policy under which Beijing shifted its priority to improving relations with the newly independent regimes of Southeast Asia, implicit allies in a contest between Afro-Asia and the West. The broad outline of that policy is in place to this day. But the memory of Beijing's effort to overthrow and replace local governments also remains alive with varying degrees of intensity throughout Southeast Asia.

The Emergence of a Southeast Asian Identity

The relationship between China and Southeast Asia is shaped to a considerable degree by geographic proximity, disparities in size and power, the presence of "overseas Chinese" populations in Southeast Asia, and historical experience. The major new variable over the last 20 years has been economics. In the postcolonial race for Third World economic modernization, Southeast Asia has been the big winner. In a little more than a generation, aggregate per capita incomes have quintupled in much of the region. Major urban centers like Bangkok, Kuala Lumpur, and Jakarta have been utterly transformed; such terms as "Asian tigers" and "Mini-dragons" have become familiar. In 1993 the World Bank produced a much-cited study, the *East Asian Miracle*, that held up Southeast Asia as a model for other developing countries.[1]

However, in late 1997 the entire Southeast Asian economic edifice was shaken to its foundations. Beginning with a bank failure in Thailand, a financial crisis that soon took on the dimensions of a major economic nosedive rolled across East Asia. Indonesia was particularly hard hit, but Malaysia and South Korea were also seriously affected. None of the region (even the vaunted economies of Singapore and Hong Kong) fully escaped the effects. In some of the more insulated economies like Vietnam and China, the consequences will probably not be fully evident for several years.

Nevertheless, the picture in early 2000 is broadly upbeat, as signs of recovery seem increasingly widespread. A cautiously optimistic prophet might conclude that the "crash of '97" will prove to be a perturbation in the overall secular trend of Asian economic growth and modernization. Indonesia remains the largest question. Not only was the crash more severe (amounting to a real depression), but the economic problems precipitated long overdue, but still wrenching, political changes. Yet even in the political sphere there are solid grounds for hope. Under very difficult circumstances, Indonesia held its first nationwide democratic election since 1955. In a surprise outcome, a moderate Muslim cleric, Abdul Rahman Wahid, emerged as president. Wahid's record and instincts are as a man of tolerance and inclusion—a healer. Indonesia will need all of his skills as key regions continue to be wracked by ethnic and religious strife. The most immediate and serious threat is a militant secessionist movement in the Aceh region of Sumatra. The secession, under U.N.

auspices, of East Timor after horrific abuses by pro-Indonesian "militias" was made official by the Indonesian parliament. But the issues raised by the apparent complicity of the Indonesian army in militia killings—and demands that senior officers be held accountable—have not gone away.

Accompanying the economic metamorphosis of the region has come a less dramatic but important psychological change. The term "Southeast Asia" entered the international affairs lexicon during World War II when Lord Mountbatten was given the "Southeast Asia Command," comprising the region between India and China south of the Tropic of Cancer. As a geographic designator the term stuck. But to borrow a phrase from Gertrude Stein, "There was no there, there." There was almost no regional consciousness—few, if any, of the inhabitants thought of themselves as "Southeast Asians." But against the backdrop of rapid economic modernization, that picture has changed. A real sense of regional identity has emerged, underpinned by growing intraregional transactions and communications and by the emergence of regional institutions. The most prominent expression of this trend was the advent of the Association of Southeast Asian Nations (ASEAN), established in 1967 and expanded over the years until today it includes all 10 countries that make up the region. Jakarta's insistence that the East Timor peacekeeping force include substantial participation by Southeast Asian countries is a kind of bellwether in the regionalization process. It is hard to imagine the Indonesian government under any circumstances accepting the presence of uniformed military forces from Singapore, Malaysia, Thailand, the Philippines, and Australia on its territory a decade or two ago.

Southeast Asia's Concerns about a Resurgent China

About a decade after Southeast Asia entered its era of rapid economic growth, China set out on a similar path. As a consequence, the contemporary relationship between Southeast Asia and China plays out against the common setting of dramatic economic transformation. For China that means increasing capabilities as economic growth provides the sinews of national power. No longer the "sick man of Asia," China is an emerging regional great power with a widely acknowledged potential to become, in time, a global superpower. For Southeast Asia it is a development pregnant with implications and uncertainties. An economically vibrant China provides obvious opportunities for investment, particularly by ethnic Chinese business interests in Southeast Asia. China's growing presence in international trade is less benign because the nation's growing exports compete fiercely with those from Southeast Asia. In the area of security, the emergence of China as a powerful "colossus of the north" has obvious implications. For the Southeast Asian countries, the optimal circumstances with regard to China existed in the 1980s and early 1990s. China's economy was expanding but China remained, overall, poor, relatively weak, and preoccupied with·a daunting array of domestic problems. A stronger, more confident, and more outward-looking China can be expected to do what all major powers have done—assert its interests with growing effect in adjacent regions.

Whether China becomes a "threat" to the region depends not only on capabilities but also on intentions. The public posture of the ASEAN governments on that score has been to repeatedly express confidence that China's intentions are benign—that it will prove to be a politically and economically conservative power in Asia. The basic argument in defense of that stance is that China does not have a history of imperial expansion and that it stands to gain economically from a stable, peaceful Southeast Asia. As more than one Southeast Asian official has put it, "We can all get rich together." The ASEAN governments have supported that proposition with what might be termed a "Gulliver" strategy of lashing China to Southeast Asia with myriad ties of mutual interest. Those include investments, trade, cultural exchanges, visits by senior leaders and officials, and a far-ranging discourse with China on economic and security issues in a variety of regional forums, including the ASEAN Dialogue, the ASEAN Regional Forum, the Asia-Pacific Economic Cooperation meetings, and numerous semiofficial "track-two" contacts among officials, scholars, and analysts. The expectation is that an increasingly prosperous China will see its interests and future tied to an economically successful and peaceful Southeast Asia. If that expectation is fulfilled, China will complete its transformation from revolutionary firebrand to guardian of the status quo.

Any worthy strategy cannot simply assume favorable outcomes, however. The most important task for strategists and policymakers is to prepare for the failure of optimistic assumptions. Southeast Asian governments have tried to do that in two principal ways: by strengthening their national military capabilities and by maintaining a cooperative relationship with the U.S. military presence in the region.

There is no shortage of both off- and on-the-record worries among Southeast Asian officials about China's intentions—particularly as manifested recently in very assertive Chinese claims to sovereignty over the South China Sea. Flare-ups between China and the Philippines over Mischief Reef occasioned a rare instance of ASEAN's publicly rebuking China.[2] Southeast Asia's economic boom throughout the 1980s and most of the 1990s was accompanied by growing defense budgets. Southeast Asia became the most active regional market for the world's major arms manufacturers and exporters. That arms investment was aimed at transforming militaries designed for domestic counterguerrilla and security missions into more robust armed forces, including naval and air defenses, capable of responding to foreign threats. Malaysia, the Philippines, and Vietnam, countries with claims to territory in the South China Sea, worked to establish and strengthen military outposts on selected reefs and islets. But if the Gulliver strategy fails, no Southeast Asian military officer is under the illusion that the countries of the region could alone, or even together, stand up to a determined Chinese incursion in the future.

However, the more general Southeast Asian concern is not a Chinese attempt to conquer territory but a progressive subordination of the region to Beijing's strategic interests. Perhaps the closest analogy would be the assertion, in time, of a Chinese Monroe Doctrine for Southeast Asia. Such a strategy would seek to expel any non-Asian (and Japanese) military presence from the region and create a strategic environment in which Southeast Asian governments understood that they were not to make any major decisions affecting Chinese interests without first consulting, and obtaining the approval of, Beijing. It is with that scenario in mind that several ASEAN governments have watched with increasing concern China's growing influence in Burma and, to a lesser extent, in Laos and Cambodia.

The general concern about China's influence in the region applies with varying degrees of accuracy to specific Southeast Asian countries. In formulating policy toward China, each responds to its own geographic, economic, political, demographic, historical, and security considerations. Four examples illustrate the point.

At one end of the spectrum is Vietnam, with a long history of uneasy and often conflictive relations with China. As recently as 1979, China and Vietnam fought a major border war. China still occupies some former Vietnamese territory seized during that conflict, and the two countries have unresolved border disputes on land and offshore. Both have claims to the same territory in the South China Sea—a dispute that has produced a significant naval clash and a number of Vietnamese casualties.[3] However, Vietnam is still a communist state, as is China. For orthodox hard-liners in Hanoi, Beijing is an ideological ally in the continuing contest with a West that seeks communism's destruction.

Indonesia is deeply suspicious of China for historical, demographic, and geopolitical reasons. Because it has long dominated the Indonesian economy, the Chinese minority (only 3 percent of the population) has engendered widespread resentment manifested in periodic outbreaks of anti-Chinese violence. Even more serious, most Indonesians seriously implicate China in the communist-inspired coup attempt in 1965 that touched off a social and political cataclysm in Indonesia. Finally, some Chinese maps show China's boundary encompassing Indonesia's Natuna islands—the site of important natural gas fields.

Toward the other end of the spectrum are Thailand and Malaysia, whose respective relationships with China have historically been cooperative. In Thailand, unlike in Indonesia, the Chinese minority, while economically ascendant, has been largely integrated into mainstream Thai society. Thailand has no territorial disputes with China and has generally enjoyed a smooth diplomatic relationship with Beijing—attributable in part to the Thai talent for artfully bending to the prevailing winds of great-power interests. It is indicative that China's president, Jiang Zemin, visited Thailand on his way to the summer 1999 Asia-Pacific Economic Cooperation meetings in New Zealand. Nevertheless, the Thais view growing Chinese influence and presence in neighboring Burma with considerable disquiet.

Malaysia is a peculiar case. Malaysia has the largest Chinese community of the Southeast Asian countries. The community is so large that peaceful cooperation between the ethnic Chinese minority and the Malay majority has been a political and societal imperative since before independence. Malaysia, like Vietnam, has territorial claims in the South China Sea that conflict with those of China, but so far

117

those disputes have not produced a significant physical confrontation. Malaysian Chinese are important investors in China, and Malaysian prime minister Mohammed Mahathir, who almost single-handedly determines Malaysian foreign policy, has made clear his commitment to a cooperative relationship with China. In part that cooperative attitude derives from the commercial importance of Malaysian-Chinese ties, and in part it reflects the prime minister's visceral distrust of the West, in general, and the United States, in particular.

The U.S. Role as Regional Balancer

America's place in the China–Southeast Asia strategic picture is extremely important. If Southeast Asian security is to rest on a stable balance of power vis-à-vis China, the balancer must come from outside the region. Put another way, the Gulliver strategy is most likely to be successful if China is deterred by regional strength rather than tempted by regional weakness. Deterrence is more likely to be credible and effective if buttressed by the United States. If the strategy ultimately fails and China seeks to assert dominance through military means, the military response will have to come in large part from outside the region. The United States, and, more particularly, the Seventh Fleet, is Southeast Asia's insurance against adverse outcomes.

U.S. national interests at stake in Southeast Asia are more substantial than is generally appreciated. Economically, ASEAN is America's fourth largest trading partner after Canada, Mexico, and Japan. U.S. private direct investment in the ASEAN countries totals nearly $40 billion.[4] The sea-lanes through the Strait of Malacca and the South China Sea are among the most heavily traveled in the world.

The region is no less important in security terms. Twice in the 20th century U.S. forces were engaged in large-scale combat in Southeast Asia. The region was a major theater in the Cold War, and, as recently as the end of the 1980s, the United States was actively engaged in supporting noncommunist guerrillas opposed to Vietnam's military occupation of Cambodia. As previously noted, Southeast Asia, along with neighboring Taiwan, will be the most likely region in which U.S.-Chinese rivalry will be focused.

Thus it is disturbing that Southeast Asia has received so little serious attention from U.S. security analysts and practitioners outside the headquarters of the Pacific Command (PACOM) in Hawaii.

A senior Australian foreign affairs official observed recently that, from Canberra's vantage point, Washington appears to have its strategic ducks firmly in line in Northeast Asia but that Southeast Asia seems to be suffering from benign neglect.[5]

A shortlist of American strategic objectives in the region can be easily formulated: (1) ready access for U.S. commerce and defense assets, (2) unimpeded transit through major sea-lanes used by both commercial and military vessels, (3) political stability, (4) economic viability and prosperity, and (5) a security environment free from hegemonic domination. China's possible (but as yet ambiguous) ambition to reestablish the historic preeminence of the Middle Kingdom potentially jeopardizes several of those objectives.

Clear strategic thinking is the bedrock on which effective foreign policy and security policy must be built. But today, U.S. foreign policy toward Southeast Asia is being made in something disturbingly—even dangerously—close to a strategic vacuum. A retrospective look at American strategy toward this region is a bit like looking at a movie in which the picture keeps going in and out of focus. There have been periods of strategic acuity, but they have been episodic, and, occasionally, while parts of the picture have been in focus, others have not.

During World War II and the early stages of the Cold War, Washington did think strategically and clearly about Southeast Asia. It was an important theater in World War II and quickly became significant in the Cold War. Communist and communist-inspired insurgencies and revolutionary movements roiled the waters of Southeast Asia. Beginning in the early 1950s in the Philippines, the United States became engaged in a considerable effort to buttress counterinsurgency programs by noncommunist governments. For the next decade the American objective was clear—the defeat of communist insurgencies as part of a global containment strategy—and the means and costs were roughly proportionate to that goal.

The efforts to achieve that objective culminated in Vietnam, where, by the mid-1960s, Washington had lost its strategic moorings. The commitments made, the resources expended, and the costs incurred all vastly exceeded any reasonable assessment of U.S. interests. That is not to say there was no strategic rationale for the defense of an independent South Vietnam. It is to say that the essence of strategy is to identify real national interests and determine whether a proposed course of action serves those interests at an affordable and proportionate cost. It is easy to produce a wish list of desirable policy outcomes; it is hard to prune that list to include only those that can be achieved within budget and to abandon those whose costs in blood and treasure prove greater than anticipated.

Following the Vietnam War, U.S. strategy erred in the opposite direction. After investing over 50,000 lives in support of the proposition that Southeast Asia was strategically vital, Washington then treated the region as if it had no strategic significance whatsoever. In the strategy maps of the National Security Council and the Pentagon, Southeast Asia became terra incognita.

The grip of the Vietnam syndrome on Washington policymakers was partially broken when the Vietnamese army invaded and occupied Cambodia at the end of 1978. In response to quiet but urgent requests from Thailand and other ASEAN governments, the United States joined with them and China in semicovert support for a Cambodian guerrilla resistance against the Vietnamese occupation. That military effort was complemented by an international diplomatic campaign led by ASEAN to deny international recognition to the Vietnamese-installed regime in Phnom Penh—and by international economic sanctions, led by the United States, against Vietnam. It was, in short, a real strategy, thoughtfully conceived and skillfully implemented.[6]

From the U.S. standpoint, the strategy was also low cost. The military effort was inexpensive (as those things go), the economic opportunity costs were minimal, and the domestic political costs within the United States were contained by the covert nature of much of the program. ASEAN's leadership of the public diplomacy dimension of the strategy provided further cover for Washington. Finally, the Cambodian program coincided positively with a much higher-priority effort to strengthen U.S.-Chinese relations.

For all the positives, however, the Cambodia policy did not constitute a U.S. strategy for all Southeast Asia—and was even incomplete with regard to Cambodia. That became evident in September 1989 when, to the surprise of Washington, Vietnam withdrew its army from Cambodia. Having not anticipated or planned for the success of its Cambodia strategy, Washington soon became enmeshed in a policy dispute between the White House and Capitol Hill over what to do next. The Bush White House, represented primarily by

National Security Council staff, argued that the Hun Sen regime—still in power in Phnom Penh—had been installed by the Vietnamese. As a communist dictatorship, the regime was not acceptable to the United States or to the noncommunist Khmer. Therefore, the Bush administration believed that U.S. assistance to the anti-Vietnamese guerrillas should continue until Hun Sen was removed. The predominant view in Congress, represented by the Democratic leadership, was that continued assistance to the guerrillas would benefit the strongest element in the coalition—the Khmer Rouge. For the United States to pursue a policy that might bring the architects of the killing fields back into power was viewed as morally abhorrent and politically unacceptable. That debate was concluded only with the signing in October 1991 of the Paris Accords, an international settlement involving interested states (including the United States and China) and the contending factions in Cambodia (the Hun Sen regime, the noncommunist resistance, and the Khmer Rouge). Under the agreement the United Nations established a transitional administration in Cambodia and conducted nationwide elections in 1993. Those elections produced a new government for Cambodia that included Hun Sen and the noncommunists but excluded the Khmer Rouge.

The next shock to U.S. policy was the rejection by the Philippine Senate in 1991 of a renewal of U.S. basing rights at Subic Bay Naval Base. (U.S. Air Force facilities at Clark Field had already been taken off the negotiating table by the dramatic volcanic eruption of Mount Pinatubo, which covered the installation in mud and ash.) Suddenly, the southern anchor of the U.S. military presence in East Asia had disappeared.

In response Washington formulated the closest thing to a region-wide strategy since the 1950s. A collaborative effort by the Pentagon, the Senate Armed Services Committee, and the headquarters of PACOM in Honolulu produced what Adm. Charles Larson labeled a "places-not-bases" cooperative-engagement approach.[7] Receptive and cooperative officials in Southeast Asia, notably in Singapore, made implementation of that initiative possible. The initiative involved dispersing the U.S. military presence through access arrangements (ship repair, shore visits, training exercises, joint consultations, etc.) and by having an administrative facility in Singapore rather than large permanent bases around the region. It was a well-conceived and superbly implemented design for preserving the viability of the U.S. military presence in the face of a major adverse development. It was only part of a strategy, however; it dealt with the instruments of security but not with the purposes for which they would be used.

That element of the strategy was addressed in a succession of public documents produced by the Pentagon under congressional mandate. The 1995 edition of the Pentagon's *East Asia Strategy Report* came the closest to articulating a strategy that included interests, objectives, threats, capabilities, and policy.

That document contained anomalous elements, however. Most notably, it committed the United States to the continued forward deployment of approximately 100,000 uniformed personnel, without providing a clear mission-based rationale for that number. To its credit, the document did cautiously address security issues involving China and Southeast Asia.

> [The] United States military presence in the region . . . guarantees the security of sea-lanes vital to the flow of Middle East oil, serves to deter armed conflict in the region, and promotes regional cooperation. It also denies political or economic control of the Asia-Pacific region by a rival, hostile power. . . . Contested claims to islands and territorial waters in the South China Sea are a source of tension in Southeast Asia that could carry serious consequences for regional stability. . . . It is worth noting in this context that the United States regards the high seas as an international commons. Our strategic interest in maintaining the lines of communication linking Southeast Asia, Northeast Asia and the Indian Ocean make it essential that we resist any maritime claims beyond those permitted by the Law of the Sea Convention.[8]

Beyond issues raised by the *EASR*, U.S. strategy was weakened by a mismatch between means and ends. With the new access agreements, PACOM could maintain a presence adequate for peacetime reassurance, despite the loss of Clark and Subic. But if a major military contingency would require a substantial operational commitment of U.S. forces, the supporting infrastructure in the region would be inadequate.

The *EASRs*, through 1995, at least presented a progressive sharpening of U.S. security thinking about Southeast Asia. That progress has apparently ceased. The recently released (December 1998) iteration of the *EASR* is a remarkably anodyne product.[9] The core strategic issues posed by emerging Chinese power go essentially unmentioned. The commitment of 100,000 U.S. troops is still there, but it is detached from any specific mission requirement. The casual reader would get the impression that in the entire sweep of East Asia, not to mention Southeast Asia, those security challenges that remain are muted and controlled. To the lay reader it is clear that America is carrying a big stick in Asia but is not at all clear why. The 1998 *EASR* reads like a document designed to avoid controversy or offense—and in that it is successful. That would be of less concern if one were confident that a real, comprehensive strategy document, of which the public is unaware, guided U.S. policy. One suspects, however, that no such document exists.

Apparently, responding to the financial-economic crisis that has afflicted the region has become the near total of U.S. strategy. But an economic strategy, however well conceived and executed, is not a security strategy.

None of that would matter greatly if Southeast Asia were free of serious security issues. But the strategic challenges—and with them the need for strategy—are growing. China is emerging as a regional great power—diplomatically, economically, and militarily—which is hardly a trivial development because China is the one potential peer competitor to the United States in world affairs. That is not to presume that China will be an adversary, but the PRC will surely be a competitor in all the dimensions that great powers interact.

The rise of China currently coincides with the Asian economic crisis and the consequent loss of cohesion, confidence, and capacity of the Southeast Asian states. The crippling of Indonesia alone greatly alters the balance of capabilities between ASEAN and China. Japan's apparent loss of stature in the wake of an arguably ineffective response to Asia's economic difficulties and its own persistent recession have further accentuated China's rise. The logical outcome of those developments is to push Southeast Asia, however reluctantly, back toward greater reliance on the United States as a strategic counterweight to China.

The Causes of America's Strategic Drift

Why is the United States so prone to strategic drift in Asia, especially Southeast Asia? This is a significant question that warrants a considered answer. One factor, easily identified, is that the current roster of key decisionmakers in U.S. foreign policy is bereft of anyone with sustained, in-depth expertise on Asia. The incumbent secretary of defense comes the closest to being an exception. The paucity of senior executive branch officials who have experience in Asian affairs is more than matched on Capitol Hill, where very few members of Congress have made Asia a focus of their interest. It is difficult to watch contemporary American foreign policy without concluding that most planning, thinking, and effort go into policy toward Europe, Russia, and the Middle East—not Asia.

A second factor is the inbuilt emphasis within PACOM on Northeast Asia. The loss of Clark and Subic simply reinforced a natural tendency to focus attention on the northern portion of the command's area of responsibility.

A third factor goes beyond Asia and speaks to a fundamental tendency in American thinking about international affairs. Since the earliest days of the Republic, U.S. foreign policy has exhibited two, often conflicting, tendencies. One is a normative, "idealist" impulse to use foreign policy to further deeply held American political values—notably, democracy and human rights. The other is a geopolitical, "realist" approach that stresses the pursuit of national interests—generally defined in terms of power and economic advantage. Nowhere has the tension between those two propensities been more evident than in policy toward China. Each year, for example, the president and Congress wrestle over the question of whether to grant most favored nation (MFN)—now normal trade relations (NTR)—status with China. Proponents of conditioning NTR on Beijing's adherence to basic human rights standards clash with those who see NTR as economic self-interest. It is difficult to maintain a steady strategic vision when policy is being whipsawed by ideals and self-interest.

A fourth, related factor is the uniquely emotive quality in American perceptions of China. To a remarkable degree, U.S.-Chinese relations have oscillated between extremes of amity and enmity. As in a bad love affair, Americans have been either uncritically enamored of all things Chinese or convinced that China is deeply hostile and threatening toward U.S. interests and values.[10]

The explanation for such dramatic swings in public (and elite) attitudes is found in the peculiar emotional investment Americans have made in China. The origins of that investment go back over a century to the Christian missionary effort initiated in China by American churches in the late 19th century. That factor, coupled with Washington's "Open Door" policy, designed to prevent the colonial dismemberment of China (and thereby preserve U.S. access to the Chinese market), gave a particular coloration to American perceptions of the Middle Kingdom. In that perception, China became America's protégé. The United States would protect, foster, and ultimately convert China into America's mirror image in Asia. That outlook received a powerful boost when postimperial China came under the leadership of President and Madame Chiang Kaishek, both Christians. During World War II, U.S. and Nationalist Chinese soldiers fought as allies. After the war, the United States pressed for the inclusion of China as a permanent member of the newly established U.N. Security Council.

Then, suddenly, it all went terribly wrong. An anti-American communist regime overthrew the Christian president. That shock was followed shortly by a brutal war in Korea that pitted U.S. forces against the People's Liberation Army. American views of China swung 180 degrees: the PRC had become the incarnation of evil, the citadel of the "blue ants," the new "yellow peril." The American foreign policy establishment self-immolated over the question of who lost China. The subsequent radical excesses of China's Cultural Revolution in the 1960s solidified the U.S. view of China as beyond the pale of civilized behavior.

Again, suddenly, everything changed. Almost overnight, ping-pong diplomacy and President Richard Nixon's 1972 trip to China revived America's infatuation. Television logged long hours not only chronicling the visits but also presenting sympathetic portrayals of Chinese life and society. Deng Xiaoping's return visit in 1978 was a virtual love fest. By the early 1980s, Washington and Beijing had become quasi-allies in the global Cold War contest with Moscow. That common strategic interest seemed, finally, to have stabilized relations.

But then came the end of the Cold War and the June 4 "incident" in Tiananmen Square, which played out on the television screens of America. The pendulum swung again. Today, 57 percent of the American public identifies China as a "critical threat" to U.S. interests.[11] Congress has become a hotbed of criticism of China on everything from abortion to satellite launches. Conservative Christian organizations have adopted oppressed Chinese Christians as a foreign policy crusade. Republicans have attacked the White House over alleged Chinese efforts to buy influence (and perhaps national security secrets) with campaign contributions. Without the anchor of a common strategic concern, U.S. policy toward China has become a magnet for seemingly every domestic group with a foreign policy agenda.

A final factor concerns the profound ambiguities of the Southeast Asian strategic environment. In Southeast Asia, there is no clear threat, no defined adversary, and no specific territorial boundaries to defend. A major objective of U.S. policy is to avoid words and actions that might seem to prejudge whether any country (i.e., China) will become an adversary. Not too long ago, China was a quasi-ally of the United States. Washington's allies today also occupy an ambiguous status. America has two declared defense commitments in the region—with the Philippines and Thailand. But neither is clear-cut. The alliance with the Philippines has been attenuated by the decision of the Philippine Senate to terminate the U.S. lease on Subic Bay, a disagreement over whether the Mutual Security Treaty covers Philippine-claimed outcroppings in the South China Sea (the United States says it does not) and by continued high-decibel political criticism in the Philippines of any U.S. military presence. The recent ratification of a Visiting Forces Agreement between the two countries may be the first step in rebuilding the defense relationship. Security ties with Thailand rest on executive understandings rather than a formal treaty. As a consequence, U.S. use of Thai military facilities (as was the case in the Persian Gulf War) is dependent on a Thai government decision at the time of the request for use of the facilities.

The U.S. relationship with Taiwan, on the periphery of the region, is extraordinarily ambiguous. The island state has the status of an unofficial and unrecognized, but de facto, ally. The Tripartite Security Treaty between the Governments of Australia, New Zealand, and the United States was once a model of clarity, but that situation ended in the mid-1980s with the dispute between the United States and New Zealand over the latter's opposition to nuclear-armed or nuclear-powered U.S. naval vessels in its territorial waters. The disagreement led to the suspension of formal U.S. security obligations to Wellington.

126

The Need for U.S. Strategic Clarity

One could conclude that the ambiguities in the strategic environment are being matched by ambiguities in U.S. policy. In certain circumstances ambiguity is a valuable, even essential, element of policy. U.S. policy toward Taiwan is a prominent example.[12] But ambiguity can become a comfortable substitute for clear thinking—the policy equivalent of "See no evil, hear no evil, speak no evil."

The South China Sea is a case in point. Serious analysts can (and will) differ about Chinese intentions there. However, one would have to discount official Chinese statements—and actions taken in support of them—to conclude that China poses no serious challenge to the status quo in the Spratlys and surrounding waters.[13] For the ASEAN governments, several of which have competing (though less far-reaching) claims, Beijing's assertion that the entire sea is Chinese territory is a very serious matter. It is the more so because China has buttressed its claims with "facts on the ground" in the form of permanent installations. As for the United States, the South China Sea encompasses important sea-lanes traversed by both commercial and naval shipping. Keeping those sea-lanes of communication secure and unencumbered is an important American economic and security interest. For Japan those same interests are even more pronounced.

Any statement of U.S. strategy should make such interests explicit. The stakes are potentially far too high for muddled messages. Southeast Asia needs reliable cues about what to expect, or not to expect, from the U.S. security presence. China needs the same. America has a disconcerting history of becoming engaged in major military confrontations after potential adversaries thought they had received indications of U.S. disinterest or noninvolvement. The Korean War, the Persian Gulf War, and the 1996 confrontation over Taiwan offer similar cautionary tales.

Recent Chinese actions and statements about Southeast Asia make it clear that the strategic acumen of leaders in the region, as well as in Washington, will be tested in the months and years ahead. China's determination to be recognized as Asia's premier power is unmistakable. As China's ambassador to the Philippines rather primly put it, "There is no denying that China is getting stronger and will have a growing role to play in the region."[14] Despite calls for easing tensions and peaceful negotiations, Beijing's claim to complete sovereignty over the entire South China Sea remains undiluted. As the ambassador noted, "We can never compromise our sovereignty over our own territory."[15] China recently buttressed its claims in the form of "renovated" structures on Mischief Reef, less than 200 miles from the Philippine coast.

At the same time, China has demonstrated a smoother, more sophisticated, and more ingratiating diplomatic style than it has at any time since the days of Chou. Chinese diplomats have become active participants in the almost nonstop round of diplomatic negotiations that characterize contemporary Southeast Asia. China has already established its right to a seat at the table when issues of significant strategic import are being addressed. China's decision to contribute a contingent of police to the U.N. peacekeeping mission in East Timor represents a logical extension of that tendency.

Paradoxically, perhaps, the Asian economic crisis has strengthened China's diplomatic hand in the region. Beijing made two astute moves in that regard. First, China was quick to come to Thailand's assistance in the early days of the financial meltdown with an offer of $1 billion in aid. Second, China pledged not to devalue its currency—thus providing a firebreak against a round of competitive devaluations across Asia. Those initiatives, coupled with the growing importance of China as a site for substantial investments by Southeast Asian Chinese businesses, have fostered a growing appreciation in the region of the importance of economic ties with China—particularly in hard economic times. In some Southeast Asian countries, notably, Burma, Laos, and Cambodia, China is becoming an increasingly important trading partner and a source of foreign investment, as well. In northern Burma, large numbers of Chinese have effectively immigrated and taken up residence. Today, travelers report that Mandalay has taken the look and feel of a Chinese city. There is an irony here because it is the Gulliver strategy in reverse—growing interactions that tend to bind Southeast Asia to China.

None of this yet adds up to Chinese primacy over Southeast Asia, and some important obstacles stand in the way of that outcome. Regional suspicions about China's intentions are deeply ingrained. Not only is China simply too big and too close, but there are too many economically powerful Chinese in the region for those sentiments to be otherwise. As the Southeast Asian states have modernized, their sense of national and regional identity has grown apace. Nationalism everywhere stands as a barrier to would-be hegemons. President Jiang Zemin risked stirring up that nationalism when during his recent trip to Thailand he appealed to Thai Chinese to support Beijing's claim to Taiwan.[16] The implicit message that the Sino-Thai are more Chinese than Thai undercuts three decades of diplomatic assurances by Beijing that it had no claim on the loyalty of ethnic Chinese living in Southeast Asia. As Southeast Asia's economic recovery gathers momentum—and the region gathers self-confidence—the resistance to Chinese strategic ambitions can be expected to grow.

The other principal impediment to Beijing's design is, of course, the United States. The success of China's strategy will be measured by its success in supplanting the United States—diplomatically and militarily—in Southeast Asia. For the foreseeable future China will lack the military power to compel the United States to accede to China's regional preeminence. Furthermore, the Southeast Asian states are not likely to align themselves, even loosely and implicitly, against Washington. The American presence is not universally welcomed, and regional irritation with U.S. actions can run high, but the United States enjoys two critical advantages. First, because it is far away and without territorial ambitions, it is perceived as strategically benign. Second, the American market remains by far the largest available to Southeast Asian exports, and the United States ranks with Japan as one of the two largest sources of foreign direct investment in the region. As a consequence, most Southeast Asian countries continue to welcome (however cautiously) U.S. military deployments in the region. Singapore is upgrading its port facilities so they can accommodate U.S. aircraft carriers; the Philippines will again receive visits of U.S. naval ships; and Thailand annually hosts the largest U.S. military exercise in Asia.

The far-flung elements of PACOM constitute a third, unique, American asset in Southeast Asia. If the thinking behind U.S. strategy in Southeast Asia has been soft, its implementation has not. The ambiguities of the strategic environment confronting U.S. forces have already been noted. Ambiguity is reinforced by a complex human and geopolitical landscape. The 10 nations of the region comprise a rich cultural tapestry of innumerable ethnicities and languages, plus all the world's major religions. The extraordinarily rapid modernization of the region has added further complexity, with traditional villages next to ultramodern office towers. Geopolitically, the region encompasses virtually every regime type from military authoritarian (Burma) to feudal monarchy (Brunei) to pluralist democracy (Philippines). The political orientation of those regimes ranges from conservative-traditional (Thailand) to communist (Vietnam).

For U.S. security policy in that environment, any distinction between security policy and foreign policy largely disappears. U.S. armed forces in Southeast Asia must be adept in the political, diplomatic, and even cultural dimensions of policy. In many respects, the commander in chief of PACOM is the most influential and prominent representative of U.S. foreign policy in East Asia on a continuing basis. The commander in chief must be as much a diplomat as a warrior, he must be capable of playing a sophisticated and nuanced policy game. As U.S. economic assistance programs wind down in an increasingly wealthy region, American influence rests on two pillars: (1) trade and investment and (2) security provided by U.S. military forces. But to be effective, those forces must be used with subtlety and full knowledge of the complexities of the regional environment. To date, U.S. PACOM commanders have demonstrated a remarkable skill in doing just that.

Notes

1. The World Bank, *The East Asian Miracle: Economic Growth and Public Policy* (Washington: The World Bank, 1993).

2. See W. M. Carpenter and D. C. Wiencek, *Asian Security Handbook* (Armonk, N.Y.: M. E. Sharpe, 1996), p. 27; and Larry A. Niksch, "The South China Sea Dispute," Congressional Research Service, August 29, 1995.

3. Carpenter and Wiencek, p. 35.

4. The US-ASEAN Business Council, *The US-ASEAN Business Council Report—1999*, Washington, 1999.

5. Confidential interview with author, October 9, 1997.

6. The author was personally engaged in this effort as a professional staff member of the Senate Select Committee on Intelligence, working closely with the CIA and the U.S. Department of State.

7. Howard J. Wiarda, ed., *U.S. Foreign and Strategic Policy in the Post–Cold War Era: A Geopolitical Perspective* (Westport, Conn.: Greenwood, 1996), pp. 167–68.

8. Office of the Secretary of Defense, *U.S. Security Strategy for the East Asia-Pacific Region*, February 1995, pp. 7 and 20.

9. Office of the Secretary of Defense, *U.S. Security Strategy for the East Asia-Pacific Region*, November 1998.

10. See James Mann, *About Face: A History of the Curious Relationship with China, from Nixon to Clinton* (New York: Knopf, 1999); and Harry Harding, *Fragile Relationship: The United States and China since 1972* (Washington: Brookings Institution, 1992).

11. John E. Rielly, ed., *American Public Opinion and U.S. Foreign Policy 1999* (Chicago: Chicago Council on Foreign Relations, 1999), p. 32.

12. The unequivocal clarification of Washington's position to either defend or not defend Taiwan against Chinese attack could have dangerously destabilizing effects. China would regard a statement from Washington pledging to defend Taiwan as akin to a formal declaration that the United States was an enemy of China. Cooperation between the two countries on a range of diplomatic, economic, and security issues would become very difficult and perhaps impossible. If the United States declared that it would not defend Taiwan, it might be taken by China as an invitation to attack the island. The government of Taiwan could be expected to resort to extreme measures, including the acquisition or development of missiles and nuclear weapons, to protect itself.

13. See John W. Garver, "China's Push through the South China Sea: The Interaction of Bureaucratic and National Interests," *China Quarterly*, no. 132 (December 1992): 998–1028; and "The Law of the People's Republic of China on Its Territorial Waters and Their Contiguous Areas," FBIS-OW2602112192, February 25, 1992. For a recent and typical restatement of the Chinese position, see "Spokesman Urges PI Stop Creating 'Disturbances'" (in Chinese), FBIS-FTS20000127000944, January 27, 2000. Foreign Broadcast Information Service material can be found at http://wnc.fedworld.gov.

14. Ben Dolven and Lorien Holland, "Softly, Softly," *Far Eastern Economic Review* 162, no. 3 (June 10, 1999): 28–30.

15. Ibid.

16. "Intelligence: Streetwise Thais," *Far Eastern Economic Review* 162, no. 37 (September 16, 1999): 8.

8. Between Friendship and Rivalry

Peter W. Rodman

Some developments in world politics have an objective quality; they occur regardless of anyone's preferences. There may be some people in America—probably not many—who are content if not eager to see a new enemy emerge to galvanize this country to maintain its international position. There are others—probably many more—who are not at all eager for a new danger that would require a renewal of our international exertion. The inexorable emergence of the People's Republic of China as a great power is occurring in a manner that will not satisfy either group.

The Structural Problem

The present tension in Sino-American relations is, most notably, the symptom of a *structural* problem—a series of significant changes in the international system that have occurred since the heyday of Sino-American partnership in the early 1970s.

First, the collapse of the Soviet Union removed the common threat that did so much to bring China and America together. Indeed, China and Russia have patched up the strategic quarrels that fueled their bitter antagonism in during the 1960s, 1970s, and 1980s. Those quarrels, which were declared by Deng Xiaoping to be the "three obstacles" to Sino-Soviet normalization, included the Soviet occupation of Afghanistan, the Vietnamese occupation of Cambodia, and the tense military confrontation along the disputed 6,000-kilometer Sino-Soviet border.[1] Much of the patching up, symbolized by Mikhail Gorbachev's historic visit to Beijing in May 1989, was accomplished while the Soviet Union still existed and Gorbachev was in power. Rapprochement has only accelerated under Gorbachev's and Deng's successors, who regularly hail their new "strategic partnership."

The second major change was the repression at Tiananmen Square in June 1989, which undercut the U.S.-Chinese relationship in two

133

ways. The Tiananmen episode shattered the broad domestic constituency in America that had supported the Sino-American partnership since the Nixon administration. Simultaneously, the Chinese Communist leadership came to see Western democratic ideas (and American promotion of them) as a subversive threat to the survival of the regime. In both those respects, the Tiananmen incident struck the Sino-American relationship a blow from which it has not yet recovered.

The third change was Taiwan's democratization. In 1987 the Kuomintang regime, which had ruled the island since fleeing the mainland, lifted martial law and legalized opposition political parties. In 1992 a new parliament was elected. Chosen only by the people of Taiwan, the new parliament ended the phantom representation of mainland constituencies. In March 1996, a president was popularly elected for the first time. Taiwan's democratic evolution has won broad bipartisan sympathy in the United States, especially in contrast with the "people's dictatorship" on the mainland, and has sharpened our domestic debate over policy toward Beijing. Meanwhile, the interest of Taiwan's population in reunification fades with time, and the Taiwanese people are tempted more and more to assert Taiwan's separate existence. Thus the Taiwan matter becomes more crisis prone, just as the international conditions that led Washington and Beijing to put that issue on ice throughout the 1970s and 1980s have vanished.

The fourth change is that the Soviet Union's collapse left the United States as the sole remaining superpower. Even in the early 1980s, as Soviet power waned, China, stressing its "independent" foreign policy, began distancing itself from its strategic partnership with the United States. When the USSR finally collapsed, this Chinese distancing from the United States accelerated to the point of becoming a systematic opposition to alleged U.S. "hegemony." Postcommunist Russia has now joined China in that position. In the "unipolar" world celebrated by many Americans,[2] China and Russia now agree on the need to restore some "multipolarity" to the global system. When Chinese premier Li Peng met with Boris Yeltsin in Moscow at the end of December 1996, for example, their joint communiqué declared: "The sides are unanimous that . . . a partnership of equal rights and trust between Russia and China aimed at strategic cooperation in the 21st century . . . promotes the formation of a multipolar world."[3]

Earlier, when Yeltsin visited Beijing in April 1996, the rhetoric on both the Russian and Chinese sides had been extraordinary in its bluntness. The joint communiqué of that visit, signed by Yeltsin and President Jiang Zemin, came close to branding the United States a threat to peace: "The world is far from being tranquil. Hegemonism, power politics and repeated imposition of pressures on other countries have continued to occur. Bloc politics has taken up new manifestations."[4]

More recently, the rhetoric of the Russians and the Chinese has calmed down somewhat. Their joint statements assure us that their partnership is not directed at any third country; nonetheless, they continue to stress the imperative of multipolarity in the world and criticize certain (unnamed) "big countries" unilaterally exerting political and economic leverage.[5] When Yeltsin visited Beijing in December 1999, he and Jiang repeated the catalogue of complaints against American impositions and stressed again their "strategic partnership" and foreign policy "coordination."[6]

Finally, there is the rise of China as a potential superpower in its own right. Its rapid economic growth since Deng's market reforms began in 1979—averaging 10 percent a year until a few years ago—has raised the possibility of a China whose gross domestic product could match America's in the early decades of this century. It has been almost 100 years since we Americans have had to even imagine the existence of another country whose economy was the same size as ours. For China's neighbors in the Asia-Pacific region, China's new economic strength represents an even more fundamental development. That new strength has obvious security implications, and the PRC's recent military buildup emphasizes naval, air, and missile capabilities that pose problems for its neighbors. If its economic growth continues, China will soon be, for the first time in centuries, the strongest power in the region.

The problem for the United States is that—as natural as it may be for China to grow strong in its own neighborhood—on China's periphery are millions of people who have relied on the United States as the guarantor of their independence. China's increasing power inevitably impinges on America's present forward strategic position and commitments in the region. China does not accept the legitimacy of the present U.S. global and regional dominance; therefore, China's foreign policy is, to one degree or another, necessarily "revisionist."

If one takes the point of view expressed by analysts at the Cato Institute—let nature take its course—there is no strategic problem for the United States. China is not really a threat, its neighbors can handle it, and America can safely jettison its alliances in the region.[7] Since U.S. policy is *not* disposed to following such a course of abdication, however (and this is an important premise), something has to give. Some degree of strategic competition is now inevitable, although the outcome is not foreordained; that competition could end in conflict or in some mutual adjustment.

It is clear that U.S.-Chinese relations are today suspended somewhere between friendship and rivalry. Cooperation, including on economic matters, is threatened by the emergence of issues on which both countries see their interests as increasingly competitive.

Competing Interests

A number of examples can be cited in which Chinese and American interests, or perceptions of interests, used to be compatible but are now more competitive.

One such example—indeed a barometer of the entire U.S.-Chinese relationship—is the U.S. alliance system and forward presence in the Pacific. Japan, the Republic of Korea, Australia, and New Zealand are formal treaty allies; the Association of Southeast Asian Nations (ASEAN) is a group of countries whose independence and security we have considered important. In the 1970s and 1980s, during the period of the U.S.-Chinese strategic partnership, China had a benign view of the U.S. forward presence, regarding it as a bulwark against the Soviets, not as a threat. Now, with the Soviets gone, the Chinese clearly no longer welcome that presence. They have not yet declared war on it in the manner of the 1949–71 period, but their eagerness to de-legitimize our military alliances in the post–Cold War era is palpable. The views expressed in *China's National Defense* in July 1998 are indicative of that attitude:

> Hegemonism and power politics remain the main source of threats to world peace and stability; Cold War mentality and its influence still have a certain currency, and the enlargement of military blocs and the strengthening of military alliances have added factors of instability to international security.
>
> History has proved that the concepts and systems of security with military alliances as the basis and increasing military might as the means could not be conducive to peace

during the Cold War. Under the new situation, especially, enlarging military blocs and strengthening military alliances run counter to the tide of the times. Security cannot be guaranteed by an increase in arms, nor by military alliances. Security should be based on mutual trust and common interests. We should promote trust through dialogue, seek security through cooperation, respect each other's sovereignty, solve disputes through peaceful means and strive for common development. To obtain lasting peace, it is imperative to abandon the Cold War mentality, cultivate a new concept of security and seek a new way to safeguard peace.[8]

China's "new concept of security," in which the U.S. alliance system is gone from the region, would of course leave China as the dominant power. The Chinese often express confidence that the trend of history is such that in the long run the United States will indeed be gone from its forward presence in the Pacific.

China's position on theater missile defense (TMD) is similarly self-serving. The Chinese are eloquent on the subject of "keeping outer space weapon free," for example, especially if anyone should be contemplating basing missile defenses there.[9] Chinese foreign ministers, in their presentations to the U.N. General Assembly, have been known to criticize missile defenses as a danger to "strategic security and stability."[10] The Chinese repeat familiar arguments of strategic doctrine that were always invoked by Soviet spokesmen when denouncing U.S. missile-defense programs (but never Soviet missile-defense programs). The comments by the director of the Arms Control Department of the PRC's foreign ministry are typical:

> Attack and defense can both be changed around, however, and as soon as this development plan is implemented and the defense system is deployed, it may give the countries concerned more of a false "sense of security," and make them more adventurist for attack. This move may also stimulate a regional arms race in space and force other countries to resort to corresponding measures, thus affecting regional peace and security.[11]

The fact that China has recently been expanding its arsenal of ballistic missiles, both short and longer range, is probably not coincidental. China already has hundreds of such weapons, of various

137

ranges, and is developing more sophisticated versions in every category; in 10 years, its missiles may also have multiple warheads. Ballistic missiles thus can provide a kind of poor man's power projection. In the absence of an effective amphibious capability with which to invade Taiwan, for example, China's ballistic missiles are useful weapons of intimidation (as the March 1996 crisis showed). Basing such missiles at various locations near China's borders places Japan, Korea, India, the Philippines, Vietnam, and Russia, as well as Taiwan, all within range of the warheads.[12] China's unhappiness with American plans for sharing missile defenses with its Asian allies and friends could be interpreted as an admission that those allies and friends are the targets of the Chinese missiles.

Another source of policy disagreement between Washington and Beijing has been nuclear proliferation. China's transfers of missiles, nuclear know-how, and other advanced technologies to Iran, Pakistan, and other nations are a source of concern. China's purposes in doing so are many. Pakistan is a long-standing Chinese (and American) ally and has faced the strategic problem of India's military superiority in conventional weapons. In the case of Saudi Arabia, the benefit to Beijing may be mainly commercial or a means of ensuring energy supplies.

China's nuclear assistance to Iran, however, is another matter, given that the United States has considered Iran one of its most serious strategic problems. The most important concern raised by China's nuclear links with Iran is, not that they may violate international agreements such as the Nuclear Nonproliferation Treaty (which they may not) or bilateral promises the Chinese may or may not have given to us (the legalistic Wilsonian criteria by which the Clinton administration seems to judge such things), but that China does not see its strategic interests in the same way we see ours. Beijing may think that it is gaining commercial benefits and energy security, but, given the disadvantages of appeasing a radical state in the Persian Gulf, that attitude seems short-sighted. China's policy here may be, at bottom, another exercise in multipolarity (based on a Gaullist assumption that America's motive in trying to deny other states these capabilities rests on a desire to preserve its own dominance).[13]

NATO's recent humanitarian intervention in Kosovo is another topic on which China's and America's perceptions seem fundamentally to diverge. The problem goes far deeper than just the accidental bombing of the Chinese embassy in Belgrade. The United States and its allies seem to believe that, in the post–Cold War era, one of the most important functions of our military power is to prevent "humanitarian catastrophes." In the Kosovo crisis, moreover, the moral urgency of intervention trumped the need for a vote in the U.N. Security Council. Russia and China, convinced that this new theory of humanitarian interventionism would provide a blank check for the United States to exploit its dominance, would certainly have vetoed any resolution to authorize the use of force against Yugoslavia. "The so-called 'new interventionism' which is now raising its head," Jiang has complained, "is the new manifestation of hegemonism and power politics."[14] China also has the particular concern that outside intervention on moral grounds to assist a "breakaway province" has clear implications for Taiwan, Tibet, and even Xinjiang.

All of those issues point to a divergence of Chinese and American geopolitical perceptions. The Taiwan question—the most dangerous potential flash point—reflects the same phenomenon in a different way.

For the first two decades of the U.S.-Chinese rapprochement, Beijing and Washington put the Taiwan dispute aside because of their overriding common interest in resisting Soviet hegemony. Mao Zedong told President Nixon in February 1972 that China was in no hurry to reclaim Taiwan; it could "do without them [the Taiwanese] for the time being"—even for "100 years." The Taiwan issue was "not an important one," said Mao; the important issue was "the international situation"—namely, the Soviet threat.[15]

Now, of course, the Soviet threat no longer provides this buffer or excuse. And, as noted previously, Taiwan's democratization means a Taiwan more assertive of its separateness. Thus the issue is much more volatile today. But in large part it is a structural problem—a *symptom* of the more competitive quality that has come into the U.S.-Chinese relationship.

The Security Problem

It is important to understand with some precision what the military problem that China poses is, and what it isn't.

China is modernizing its military but is proceeding gradually; also, the modernization starts from a very low base. China's defense expenditure in 1998, as calculated by the International Institute for Strategic Studies, was the purchasing-power equivalent of $37.5 billion.[16] By comparison, the U.S. defense budget is around $270 billion. By almost all serious assessments, the People's Liberation Army remains decades away from being a modern all-around force capable of sustained power projection, especially when matched against the more modern and better-equipped capabilities of its neighbors in the region, let alone those of the United States. China's recent procurement effort—concentrated in naval, air, and missile forces—is perhaps to be expected after a generation of maintaining a large army to face the principal threat from a contiguous land power to the north. In any case, China lacks a long-range sealift or airlift capability, as well as the ability to protect an amphibious force or to operate aircraft at extended ranges.

The U.S. Pacific Command (PACOM) takes a fairly relaxed view of the situation. In fact, it seems to feel that China's expressions of concern are a reflection of how well PACOM is doing its job. In interviews in the spring of 1998, PACOM Adm. Joseph W. Prueher (since appointed by President Clinton as U.S. ambassador in Beijing) expressed his firm conviction that Chinese military leaders were "smart, pragmatic" officers who understood that the PLA did not compare with U.S. forces "in any way."[17]

All that being said, there are reasons to pay attention to China's military modernization. Although a direct threat to the United States is clearly a long way off, a challenge to our effectiveness as defender of allies and friends in the region is not so remote.

One reason for concern is the pattern of Chinese military procurement. Not only do some Chinese military strategists explicitly identify the United States as "the opponent,"[18] but much of China's procurement seems to proceed on the same premise. For example, the Chinese are purchasing SS-N-22, "Sunburn," supersonic anti-ship cruise missiles, which were designed by their Russian manufacturers as a counter to the Aegis-class cruisers and destroyers that are the "brain" of American naval power projection. The modern diesel Kilo-class submarines that China is also purchasing from Russia will be equipped with 53-65KE wake-homing torpedoes—an advanced torpedo that is more difficult to detect and is particularly well suited to attacking U.S. aircraft carriers.[19] (U.S. carriers are well armored on the deck and sides but are vulnerable to torpedoes that home in on the rear and underside.)

In more exotic areas that the Pentagon calls the "Revolution in Military Affairs"—the supercomputers, microelectronics, and telecommunications that are revolutionizing American weapons systems and battle management—the Chinese are decades behind. Yet they have begun work on ways to cripple an opponent's computers, to defeat stealth systems, and to attack satellites. In other words, in the best spirit of Sun Tzu, they are zeroing in on the vulnerabilities of a superpower that relies heavily on advanced technology.[20]

It is clear to any rational observer that the U.S. Seventh Fleet remains the dominant naval force in the western Pacific and that the United States, with its allies, forward bases, and technology, remains overwhelmingly superior. But there is another standard by which the impact of the Chinese buildup can be judged. The implicit challenge to our allies and friends in the region is also an implicit challenge to a U.S. policy that has the mission of protecting them. The ability to blow the entire U.S. Navy out of the Pacific is not the standard that the Chinese military must meet; rather, it is the ability to raise the costs to the United States of coming to the aid of those allies and friends. With "missile diplomacy," advanced anti-ship missiles and torpedoes, China will soon be able to increase the risks of casualties. That scenario will add substantially to an American president's inhibitions about getting involved in some future crisis, such as one over Taiwan. America's ability to deter Chinese misconduct remains high. But China's ability to *deter us* in a future crisis is increasing, and the balance of deterrence is less unequal than it used to be.

Chinese probing for our Achilles' heel in advanced technology should be enough to make us work harder at preserving our dominance. China views its nuclear capabilities, which are certainly rudimentary compared with ours, as a means not of defeating us but of doing enough to complicate our decisions. The Chinese see nuclear weapons as a "great equalizer"—as another way of giving us pause as we contemplate intervention in a future crisis. During the August 1999 tension over Taiwan, an authoritative Chinese journal brandished China's putative neutron-bomb capability as a deterrent to U.S. intervention: "China's neutron bombs are more than enough to handle aircraft carriers," it boasted.[21]

Thus, there is indeed a *near-term* security problem. China may not match our overall military power in 50 years, if ever, but Beijing's ability to complicate U.S. strategy and policy in the Asia-Pacific region is rapidly increasing. If that is the case, then China's military buildup, even if slow, will have changed the psychological balance in the region, an accomplishment that will have considerable geopolitical consequences.

This analysis also sheds some light on the problem of technology transfer investigated by the Cox committee, whose report not only documented accounts of Chinese theft of advanced military technology but also criticized the laxity of U.S. government procedures for vetting transfers of commercial technology.[22] Even this episode is, in a sense, another symptom of the changing perception of the compatibility—or the incompatibility—of Chinese and American interests.

In the 1970s and 1980s, when Chinese and American strategic interests were seen as convergent, or at least parallel, the United States had an interest in helping China build up its military strength. Technology transfers were gradually liberalized as an act of policy (until Tiananmen). It is conceivable that U.S. officials, to the extent that they were conscious of Chinese acquisition efforts that slipped into a gray area of legality, or worse, looked the other way. They did not view technology transfers as a top-priority problem because China was perceived as a virtual ally. (This is pure speculation on my part.)

It is clear now that, as the strategic context shifted during the 1990s and as the element of rivalry entered into the U.S.-Chinese relationship, the U.S. government should have been more vigilant about technology transfers to China. We no longer had the same stake, to put it mildly, in helping China build up its military strength. Yet the Clinton administration chose to liberalize the tech-transfer regime as never before, in part as a feature of the administration's philosophy of export promotion. History will record that change as a lapse of strategic judgment at the very highest level, regardless of whatever particular violations of law may have been committed at lower levels.

Policy Conclusions

The emergence of China as a great power is not a novel problem but a classical one, which the United States is in a strong enough position to handle if it remains vigilant and engaged. The policy prescription for the United States should be strategic firmness and patience to maintain the solidarity of our alliances and our forward presence and to preserve our naval and military primacy in the Asia-Pacific region. The present bipartisan commitment to keeping 100,000 troops in the region is wise and well within our means to sustain. It is possible for us to shape the international environment into which China is emerging.

A path of cooperation is open to both countries. Contrasts with the Soviet case are instructive. First, China's foreign policy is not ideologically driven; not for 30 years has China attempted to exploit radical movements in East or Southeast Asia to subvert pro-Western governments as the Soviets did to undermine Western positions globally until near the end of the Cold War. There are a number of issues—Korea, South Asia, the Persian Gulf—on which a strategic dialogue could be productive. China's conflicts with its neighbors today—such as offshore territorial disputes based on historical claims and exacerbated by competition for energy resources—are classically geopolitical, not ideological. If there is an ideological impetus behind the growing sense of confrontation, it comes from *American* discomfort with coexistence with the last great communist dictatorship.

A second contrast is that, unlike the Soviets, China has an economic stake in the existing international system. The Soviets attempted autarchy and clung, until near the end, to the socialist-statist economic model in its most extreme form. The Chinese have based their economic policy—and their economic success—on market reforms that presuppose a continuing and increasing integration into the free world economy. Chinese membership in the World Trade Organization will only deepen that tendency. As communist ideology erodes as a belief system at home, the regime's very legitimacy is tied to its economic performance, which depends more and more on its international economic integration.

The Chinese may view all this as a temporary expedient while they build up their "comprehensive national strength." Chinese officials, such as National Security Adviser Liu Huaqiu, are fond of quoting a maxim of Deng's that is not altogether reassuring to outsiders: "We should hide our capacity and bide our time, quietly immerse ourselves in work, wave no loud banner and champion no cause, and say nothing that is exaggerated, and do nothing that is excessive."[23]

The Chinese are entitled to their dreams of future supremacy. But, again, it is in large part up to us to determine whether their dreams will be realized. Former assistant secretary of defense Joseph Nye described the constraints that will operate on China's ambitions:

> Every country has a wish-list that reads like a menu without prices. But defining national interests in concrete situations involves understanding constraints and costs. Left to itself, China would probably like to force the return of Taiwan, ensure dominance of the South China Sea and be recognised as the primary state in the East Asian region. But Chinese leaders have to contend with the constraints imposed by other countries and by the trade-offs among their own objectives. Given the priority accorded to economic modernisation and the reliance on external markets and resources, China faces a constraint of its own making. It also faces the constraints placed on it by U.S. power, which are unlikely to vanish. Finally, it faces constraints in terms of its relations with other countries in the region. In the real world, countries need to redefine their interests.[24]

Thus, there is an ultimate reassurance. There can be no doubt of China's aspiration—and ability—to be a major power in the Asia-Pacific region. Yet the controversial Chinese military actions of 1995 and 1996—and the responses to them—suggest that a certain corrective mechanism is at work. Almost as a law of Newtonian physics, overreaching by China is likely to produce a reaction by China's neighbors, who are already hypersensitive to any flexing of its military muscles. For example, the expansion of ASEAN; the consolidation of U.S. military ties with Japan, ASEAN (especially Singapore and the Philippines), Australia, and New Zealand; the moves toward Russo-Japanese rapprochement; and the Indian nuclear tests were responses that cannot have been entirely anticipated by Beijing.

It will not be so easy for the emerging China to "hide its capacities." Indeed, the anticipation of Chinese power may already be outrunning its reality.

China is vulnerable in another sense—namely, the fragility of its discredited internal system. The recent slowdown in its economic growth, attributable in part to the Asian financial crisis, plus the intractability of the remaining challenges to economic reform, are placing new strains on the political system. The regime could face a serious political crisis in the coming decade.[25]

However, the effect of a change of regime on China's foreign policy may not be as profound as some think. Although a Taiwan settlement will likely be easier with a postcommunist government on the mainland, and the friction with the United States over human rights will be eased, the main motivating force of Beijing's foreign policy today is classical Chinese nationalism. A China that finally sheds its "socialist" shackles decisively is likely to be economically stronger; it is not self-evident that it will renounce its newfound military strength or its claim to regional leadership.

Thus, the challenge of China is more complex than either those who fear it as an ideological menace or those who see no problem at all seem to realize. On the one hand, alarmism about China—particularly the notion that China is hell-bent on domination—is overblown. The United States is well positioned to set objective limits that require China to adapt to an international environment that presents clear incentives for cooperation and disincentives for mischief.

There is no place for complacency, however, about China's military modernization and its near-term impact on the regional balance of power. Corrective mechanisms will operate only if the United States and its allies remain vigilant. A happy ending is not automatic. Without American strength and deterrence, the risks of conflict are too high for comfort. It is not surprising, then, that China is the most complex and serious challenge to American global strategy as we enter the 21st century.

Notes

1. See Richard Evans, *Deng Xiaoping and the Making of Modern China* (London: Penguin, 1995), pp. 262, 288–89.
2. See, for example, Charles Krauthammer, "The Unipolar Moment," *Foreign Affairs* 70, no. 1 (1990–91): 29–32.
3. Russian-Chinese Joint Statement on Premier Li Peng's visit to Moscow, December 28, 1996, FBIS-SOV-96-251, December 28, 1996. Foreign Broadcast Information Service material can be found at http://wnc.fedworld.gov.
4. Russian-Chinese Joint Statement on President Boris Yeltsin's visit to Beijing, April 25, 1996, FBIS-CHI-96-081, April 25, 1996.
5. See, for example, Russian-Chinese Joint Statement on President Jiang Zemin's visit to Moscow, November 23, 1998, and coverage of the Yeltsin-Jiang meeting in Bishkek, Kyrgyzstan, August 24–25, 1999, FBIS-CHI-99-0824, August 24, 1999.
6. Joint Russian-Chinese communiqué of President Yeltsin's visit to Beijing, December 10, 1999, FBIS-CHI-1999-1210, December 10, 1999.

7. See, for example, Doug Bandow, "Old Wine in New Bottles: The Pentagon's East Asia Security Strategy Report," Cato Institute Policy Analysis no. 344, May 18, 1999.

8. *China's National Defense* (Beijing: Information Office of the State Council, July 1998), part 1.

9. Ibid., part 5.

10. See, for example, Vice Minister and Minister of Foreign Affairs Qian Qichen, Statement at the 51st Session of the United Nations General Assembly, New York, September 25, 1996, Embassy of the People's Republic of China Press release no. 1, September 26, 1996, p. 5.

11. Sha Zukang, director of the Arms Control Department of the Ministry of Foreign Affairs, interview in *Wen Wei Po* (Hong Kong), November 17, 1998, FBIS-CHI-98-321, November 17, 1998.

12. Bill Gertz, "China Targets Nukes at U.S.," *Washington Times*, May 1, 1998, p. 1.

13. See, for example, Hu Yomin, "The United States Post–Cold War Nonproliferation Policy," *International Strategic Studies*, no. 3 (July 1999): 50–53.

14. Jiang Zemin, Speech at Bishkek on August 25, 1999, during the meeting of the heads of state of China, Kyrgyzstan, Russia, Kazakhstan and Tajikistan, Xinhua Domestic Service, FBIS-CHI-1999-0825, August 25, 1999.

15. Quoted in Henry Kissinger, *White House Years* (Boston: Little, Brown, 1979), p. 1062.

16. International Institute for Strategic Studies, *The Military Balance, 1999–2000* (London: Oxford University Press, October 1999), p. 186.

17. Quoted in Richard Halloran, "Which Path Will China Leaders Follow?" *Washington Times*, March 27, 1998, p. A16; and Richard Halloran, "Muscle Display," *Far Eastern Economic Review* 161, no. 12 (March 19, 1998): 26–28.

18. See, for example, Fu Liqun, "Several Basic Ideas in U.S. Strategic Thinking," *China Military Science*, no. 1 (1997), FBIS-CHI-97-108, February 20, 1997.

19. See sources in Peter W. Rodman, *Between Friendship and Rivalry: China and America in the 21st Century* (Washington: Nixon Center, June 1998), pp. 24–26.

20. See, for example, the compilation of Chinese military writings in Michael Pillsbury, ed., *Chinese Views of Future Warfare* (Washington: National Defense University Press, 1997), part 4.

21. "USA, Do Not Mix In," *Global Times*, August 19, 1999, reported by Agence France Presse, FBIS-CHI-1999-0819, August 19, 1999.

22. U.S. House of Representatives, *Report of the Select Committee on U.S. National Security and Military/Commercial Concerns with the People's Republic of China*, 3 vols., 105th Cong., 2d sess., 1999, H. Rept. 105-851.

23. Deng Xiaoping, quoted in Liu Huaqiu, "China Will Always Pursue a Peaceful Foreign Policy of Independence and Self-determination," *Qiushi*, no. 23 (December 1, 1997), FBIS-CHI-98-078, March 19, 1998; and also in Liu Huaqiu, "Strive for a Peaceful International Environment," *Jiefang Ribao* (November 3, 1997): 5, FBIS-CHI-97-321, November 17, 1997. For the original Deng quote, see *BBC Summary of World Broadcasts*, FE/1346, April 3, 1992, p. B2/2, cited in Evans, pp. 304–5.

24. Joseph S. Nye, "China's Re-emergence and the Future of the Asia-Pacific," *Survival* 39, no. 4 (Winter 1997–98): 73.

25. Rodman, chap. 4.

PART III

TRADE, SECURITY, AND HUMAN RIGHTS

9. The Tao of Trade

James A. Dorn

When the world is governed according to Tao,
Horses are used to work on the farm.
When the world is not governed according to Tao,
Horses and weapons are produced for the frontier.

—Lao-tzu, *Tao Te Ching*

Whither China?

Whether China becomes a friend or an enemy will depend, in large part, on whether U.S.-Chinese trade ties strengthen or weaken. The transition from a state-controlled trade sector to a market-driven economy has transformed the People's Republic of China. Although the Chinese Communist Party is celebrating 50 years of the socialist state, the Chinese people, in their hearts and minds, must be celebrating two decades of capitalist prosperity.

Since 1978, real per capita incomes have more than quadrupled, and China is now the 10th largest trading nation in the world. By opening to the outside world, China's leaders, especially the late Deng Xiaoping, have increased the scope of the market and diminished the scope of government—increasing individual autonomy in the process. Millions of Chinese now work outside the state sector, own their own homes and businesses, travel freely, and have access to a wide variety of books and cultural experiences. Intellectuals are now reading Hayek and Friedman rather than Marx and Engels.

The mushrooming of the nonstate sector and the dismal condition of state-owned enterprises (SOEs) have adversely affected government revenues and forced the CCP to search for alternatives to state-provided social welfare services in urban areas. Meanwhile, in rural areas the end of communal farming and the rise of the household responsibility system have created a new class of entrepreneurs and made possible the rebirth of civil society, which was destroyed during the Cultural Revolution (1966–76).

149

Although China has a long way to go toward a free society, there is ample evidence that the PRC is moving in the right direction and that economic liberalization has lessened the danger of war and enhanced the prospect for peace. That said, one should not be under the illusion that free trade will solve all problems—trade is a necessary but not a sufficient condition for global stability and peace.

The Republic of China (Taiwan) is one of the PRC's largest trading partners, but no one is naive enough to believe that the mainland would not go to war with the ROC if that country declared independence. Yet one could argue that the threat of conflict has been diminished by cross-strait trade and investment, as well as by the strength of Taiwan's national defense and an implicit guarantee of U.S. intervention.

The sufficient condition for peace is that China change its political regime to one based on the rule of law and limited government, so that liberty prevails rather than a system that spawns corruption. Whether that change occurs will ultimately depend on the Chinese people, but the probability that it will occur can be increased by strengthening commercial ties, spreading the use of information technology, and allowing China to enter the World Trade Organization on mutually beneficial terms. Commercial diplomacy, not gunboat diplomacy, is the key to China's future as a constructive partner rather than an emerging threat.

It would be a mistake to diverge from the path of liberalization—indeed, human rights in China are best secured by openness to the West. Isolating China could turn it into another North Korea or Cuba. Trade is a constructive way to change China. But trade is a two-way street, and the West must remove its restrictions as well.

Finally, in deciding on its future path—whether liberal or illiberal—China should look back to its own heritage and grasp the principle of noninterference and recognize the importance of spontaneous order, if it is to achieve economic and social harmony.

The Principle of Noninterference

Writing more than 2,000 years before Adam Smith, the great Chinese philosopher Lao-tzu, in the *Tao Te Ching*, advocated the principle of *wu wei* (noninterference) as the basis for good government and a harmonious social order. Although he did not provide a detailed theory of the "invisible hand" of the free market, he did recognize that there is a natural tendency for mutually beneficial trade if people are left alone.

Peace and prosperity follow naturally when the government safeguards property rights, rules justly, and lets markets operate freely. The idea of spontaneous order is central to Lao-tzu's way of thinking. He clearly recognized that overregulation can upset the spontaneous market order and destroy the wealth of a nation: "The more restrictions and limitations there are, the more impoverished men will be." The wise ruler therefore knows that, "Through my noninterfering, men spontaneously increase their wealth."[1]

If Lao-tzu had read *The Wealth of Nations*, he certainly would have understood Smith's central argument that, if "all systems either of preference or of restraint" were "completely taken away," a "simple system of natural liberty" would evolve "of its own accord."[2]

The principle of wu wei is consistent with an individual's natural rights to life, liberty, and property and implies that the proper function of government is to protect, not deny, those rights. The private space of each individual is protected to bring about peace and prosperity.

Thus, "when the world is governed according to Tao," individuals will pursue their happiness through markets, and resources will be used to satisfy consumers' preferences. Trade is the natural way for individuals and nations to increase their wealth. But "when the world is not governed according to Tao," conflicts will result, and resources will be diverted from more productive uses.

The principle of noninterference applies to all government action—in the private, social, economic, and cultural spheres. Limited government is the norm for natural order, unlimited government the norm for disorder.

The Market, Spontaneous Order, and Security

In his essay "The Principles of a Liberal Social Order," F. A. Hayek wrote, "The central concept of liberalism is that under the enforcement of universal rules of just conduct, protecting a recognizable private domain of individuals, a spontaneous order of human activities of much greater complexity will form itself than could ever be produced by deliberate arrangement."[3] He warned against trying to plan the market, which is a complex system dependent on the

151

decisions of millions of individuals, each of whom has unique information.

The "market order" is a "catallaxy," or "spontaneous order produced by the market through people acting within the rules of the law of property, tort, and contract," argued Hayek.[4] By its very nature, the market order is based on consent and openness, not on force and protectionism—free trade is the friend of peace and civility. Indeed, Hayek reminds us that "the term 'catallactics' was derived from the Greek verb *katallattein* (or *katallassein*) which meant, significantly, not only 'to exchange' but also 'to admit into the community' and 'to change from enemy into friend.'"[5] A respect for the rule of law and a spirit of independence are important byproducts of commercial society. Adam Smith tells us how the development of commercial life in Europe "gradually introduced order and good government, and with them, the liberty and security of individuals."[6] And, in his classic book *Democracy in America*, Alexis de Tocqueville wrote, "Trade makes men independent of one another and gives them a high idea of their personal importance; it leads them to want to manage their own affairs and teaches them how to succeed therein."[7]

It is no accident that during the 19th century the "voluntary principle" became the norm in the United States as free trade became widespread. Writing in the *United States Magazine and Democratic Review* in 1837, John O'Sullivan stated, "This is the fundamental principle of the philosophy of democracy, to furnish a system of the administration of justice, and then to leave all the business and interests of society to themselves, to free competition and association—in a word, to the voluntary principle."[8] Constitutional democracy, not unlimited government, is the natural ally of free markets.

There is increasing evidence that greater reliance on markets, rather than on central planning, leads to growing pressure for political liberalization as a rising middle class demands the right to participate in the political process in order to protect newly acquired wealth. Harvard economist Robert Barro, for example, found "that improvements in the standard of living . . . substantially raise the probability that political institutions will become more democratic over time."[9] He concluded:

> The advanced Western countries would contribute more to the welfare of poor nations by exporting their economic systems, notably property rights and free markets, rather than

their political systems, which typically developed after reasonable standards of living had been attained. If economic freedom can be established in a poor country, then growth would be encouraged, and the country would tend eventually to become more democratic on its own.[10]

The dynamic gains from international trade—in the form of new ideas, new technology, the expansion of consumer choice, the spread of culture, the development of a commercial code, the strengthening of property rights, and the growth of civil society—should not be lost sight of. As each nation moves toward the market and away from state planning and mercantilism, a liberal international order develops—increasing the chance for peace and prosperity. That was true in the 18th and 19th centuries, and it is true today.[11]

Trade and Human Rights in China

The right to trade freely is an important human right—it is a natural right and an integral component of our property rights.

As James Madison, the chief architect of the U.S. Constitution, wrote in 1829:

> It is sufficiently obvious, that persons and property are the two great subjects on which Governments are to act; and that the rights of persons, and the rights of property, are the objects, for the protection of which Government was instituted. These rights cannot well be separated. The personal right to acquire property [and therefore to trade], which is a natural right, gives to property, when acquired, a right to protection as a social right.[12]

Although human rights are precarious in China, the growth of the market has strengthened economic liberties, weakened the monopoly power of the CCP, and given civil society new life. In contrast to the Cultural Revolution, the post-Mao era has seen a substantial increase in economic, social, and personal freedom but little change in political freedom. And that is one reason the CCP has lost "the mandate of heaven."

Under state ownership and central planning, the individual is simply part of the machinery of government. From 1953 to 1978, China relied on Soviet-style economic planning and shunned the market. Economic life was fully politicized—individuals were totally

153

dependent on the state and had to bow before the CCP. As Kate Zhou notes, "When the state controlled nearly all goods and mobility, it also controlled individuals."[13]

The relaxation of economic controls after 1978 and the liberalization of foreign trade have had a dramatic effect, as any visitor to China can attest. Commenting on China's transformation, Jianying Zha writes in her book *China Pop:*

> The economic reforms have created new opportunities, new dreams, and to some extent, a new atmosphere and new mindsets. The old control system has weakened in many areas, especially in the spheres of economy and lifestyle. There is a growing sense of increased space for personal freedom.[14]

Although economic reform has not brought about a political transformation or a significant increase in civil liberties, those shortcomings should not lead one to deny the important changes that have made individuals substantially better off than they were in the pre-1978 period. As William McGurn, a former senior editor of the *Far Eastern Economic Review*, recently stated, "Repression and corruption continue, yet China grows freer, more prosperous, and more modern each day."[15] That is why he thinks the United States should continue its policy of engagement.

Critics of engagement should also consider the words of former student rights activist Li Lu. According to Li, "Politically, China suppresses its people, but because the government allows some freedom in economic matters, business has become the ultimate expression of individuality." In his view, the annual debate over China's trade status "has become an utterly ineffective showcase for channelling all of the truly serious issues."[16]

A more constructive way to change China, says Li, is to involve private enterprise in the process of bringing about greater personal freedom. Modern business enterprise depends on ready access to information, labor mobility, and human capital—and most important, on a sound legal system that protects property and contractual rights.

Foreign-funded enterprises, and other firms in the nonstate sector, have an incentive to create an institutional infrastructure that enhances opportunities for profitable exchange. "If companies push for a credible legal system—the rule of law—they will create conditions for competition and revitalize the private economy," argues Li.[17]

As the private sector grows and the state sector shrinks, individuals will become less dependent on the state and eventually call for political change. That is exactly what happened in Taiwan—and there is evidence that Beijing is slowly moving toward the rule of law.

In March 1999 the National People's Congress (NPC) amended China's constitution to provide for "building a socialist country of law" and recognized nonstate enterprises—including private firms—as "major components of the socialist market economy."[18] As a result, the All-China Federation of Industry and Commerce has proposed that the NPC adopt "new policies and laws" in accordance with "the principle of equal protection embodied in the amended Constitution"—the goal being "to promote the healthy development of the non-public economy."[19] Those changes, influenced by commercial contacts with the West, are another step toward limiting the power of the CCP and recognizing the sanctity of private property.

Liberalism is on the rise in China. Intellectuals who were once hostile to private property and free markets are beginning to understand their importance for economic and social harmony and human well-being.[20] Mao Yushi, director of the Unirule Institute, a private, market-oriented think tank in Beijing, states: "The market means plural ownership. It creates a community with many individual groups. [Before] we had only one owner—the state—and now we have many. Their independence comes from property rights. This is the crucial point."[21]

Although the CCP still adheres to the primacy of state ownership, the massive failure of SOEs—in the face of competition from the nonstate sector—and rampant corruption have driven a stake into the heart of Marxist-Leninist ideology. The party is rapidly losing its credibility as more and more people experience the freedom of the marketplace.

The government is finding it difficult to contain the market as people gain income and demand a greater variety of goods and services, including Western literature. Elisabeth Rosenthal of the *New York Times* has provided a fascinating account of the changes taking place in China's publishing world as a result of market reforms. She writes:

> It is free market economics that is spawning liberalization and eroding Government control: Having lost their once hefty subsidies in the move to a market economy, the state publishers have become increasingly willing to print controversial material, looking to make money by catering to consumer demand.[22]

Liu Junning and Kate Zhou both present striking evidence to support Rosenthal's claim.[23] The fact that Hayek's *Constitution of Liberty* is now in its second printing indicates that consumer demand for classical liberal ideas is being met.[24]

The problem, argues Rosenthal, is that there is still no clear line between what is permissible and what is not: "Publishers and editors risk official criticism and even their jobs if they aid and abet projects that stray too far over the invisible and ever changing line."[25]

That problem is pervasive and not limited to publishing. Without clearly defined and enforced private property rights, no one is safe from government intervention. Policies can change at any moment, causing substantial losses to investors—both domestic and foreign. That is why it is so important to move toward the rule of law and to adopt a "constitution of liberty" for China. As my colleague Roger Pilon, director of Cato's Center for Constitutional Studies, has emphasized, "If China is to preserve and expand upon its recent achievements, it will need a constitution that institutionalizes, not simply tolerates, the forces that have led to improvements there."[26]

Minxin Pei, a scholar at the Carnegie Endowment for International Peace, views the slow evolution of the NPC as a legislative body as an encouraging sign, along with the increase in the number of laws enacted to protect persons and property, including laws of contract. He also points to the spread of elections for rural officials, not all party members, as a sign of "creeping democratization."[27]

Even though the CCP continues to crack down on dissidents, Pei finds that "the level of political repression (defined as physical persecution of the regime's opponents) has fallen dramatically from the Mao era to the post-Mao era."[28] By current international standards, China's human rights record is still horrendous, but that should not blind one to the improvements that have taken place.

Kate Zhou refers to "a silent revolution from below" that is being "carried out by the everyday practice of violating the rules of the state."[29] In her book *How the Farmers Changed China*, she shows how brave peasants confronted the state and independently moved toward market exchange before it was legal. Only afterward, when the success of those efforts was clearly visible, did the party bosses in Beijing officially sanction the farmers' spontaneous, nonpolitical movement to a *baochan daohu* (household responsibility system).[30]

What the leaders failed to see was that the opening of rural areas to nonstate enterprises would undercut the CCP's power. According to Pei:

> Pro-market reforms have seriously eroded the broad social base of the CCP. This change has come about, ironically, precisely because of the relative success of the economic reform under Deng Xiaoping. For the peasantry, market-oriented reforms have resulted not only in direct economic benefits and independence from the state; they have fundamentally eroded the Communist Party's political control in rural areas and left the regime without means of mobilizing political support there.[31]

Since 1978, civil rights have advanced in China, but at a slow and uneven pace. As Zhou indicates in her study of the evolution of civil rights in the PRC, the economic reforms have increased freedom of movement and occupational choice, reduced dependence on the *danwei* (work unit), downsized government, increased the number of law schools and lawyers, spurred private charity, and increased people's willingness to openly practice their religions.[32]

In his pioneering study "The Growth of Civil Society in China," Pei also provides strong evidence of the expanding private, nonpolitical sphere. He traces the numerous civic associations that have sprung up since 1978, such as associations of private entrepreneurs, associations of lawyers, and associations of consumers. He concludes that, "as the state continues to withdraw its influence in economic and social activities, Chinese society has gradually gained more space previously claimed and controlled by the state under the pre-reform regime."[33]

Millions of people are beginning to question the current political system, as they depend more and more on the market than on the state for their livelihoods. Self-reliance is the enemy of the state. Economic independence is spilling over into the call for greater civil liberty, including more religious freedom. "As more people could make a living on their own," notes Zhou, "they could afford to 'come out of the religious closet.' They were no longer afraid of losing their only rice bowl."[34]

Ned Graham, president of East Gates International, a nonprofit Christian organization, has said that the U.S. policy of engagement and new information technology have made it possible for numerous mission groups to work in China. According to Graham, "Because of this engagement, we have been able to legally distribute over 2.5 million Bibles to nonregistered religious practitioners since 1992." In his view, "China's opening to the West through the gates of trade and the economic reforms initiated by Deng Xiaoping" have allowed us to witness "one of the most remarkable changes in history." Graham and his associates now "routinely communicate with thousands of friends all over China via fax, cell phones, and e-mail."[35]

The same openness and use of information technology recently allowed practitioners of Falun Gong to stage a massive, but silent, protest at the CCP compound in Beijing. The protest drew more than 10,000 practitioners and was a total surprise to China's leaders. The demonstrators, who were protesting the government's interference with their beliefs and practices, "said they had been brought together by secret mobile phone numbers and faxes."[36] The subsequent crackdown on this sect is a reminder of the authorities' intolerance of any person or group that is seen as a threat to the power of the Communist Party.

It is getting more difficult, however, to keep track of all the people who differ with official dogma. Even though Beijing has set up firewalls to control the Internet, individuals typically learn how to circumvent those barriers. With the rapid growth of personal computers in the PRC and even more sophisticated ways of entering the Internet, the government will not be able to prevent the flow of most information into and out of China.[37]

Lawrence Kudlow, chief economist at Schroders, has correctly described the Internet as "an economic-freedom metaphor for our time. The Internet empowers ordinary people and disempowers government. The Internet creates wealth, expands growth, produces jobs and spreads prosperity."[38] That is why hard-liners are nervous.

Now that the United States has reached an accord with China for the latter's accession to the WTO, America should work with other industrialized countries to help China develop the rule of law and to further expand its nascent market economy. Most important,

Congress should not let protectionism and politics destroy the chances for a freer future by denying the world's 10th largest trading nation permanent normal trade relations and keeping it out of the WTO—a move that would decrease economic freedom and erode, not advance, human rights in China.

That is not to say that the United States should ignore the plight of dissidents or the use of slave labor, or tolerate technology transfers that jeopardize our security. Those issues are important, but they should be dealt with separately. Normalizing trade relations is still the best way to teach the Chinese people that the voluntary market offers a better chance for happiness, peace, and prosperity than does the heavy hand of the state.

Market Socialism or Market Taoism?

China has made much progress since 1978 in ridding itself of Soviet-style planning and moving toward the free market. The non-state sector now accounts for over 70 percent of industrial output value, and only about 5 percent of industrial product prices are determined by the government. Denying China greater opportunities for free trade harms its emerging market economy and strengthens SOEs.

Serious institutional incompatibilities still exist in China's market-socialist economy, reflecting the uneasy mix of plan and market. Those inconsistencies must be resolved in favor of the free market if China is to achieve stable long-run growth and prosperity.[39] The crux of the problem is that hard-liners still cling to state ownership in order to protect their power base, while the market requires clearly defined and enforced private property rights. To resolve that tension requires constitutional and political reform. As Beijing University economist Justin Lin and his coauthors Fang Cai and Zhou Li of the Chinese Academy of Social Sciences point out, "It is essential for the continuous growth of the Chinese economy to establish a transparent legal system that protects property rights so as to encourage innovations, technological progress, and domestic as well as foreign investment in China."[40]

The Soviet system failed because it disregarded reality—namely, the reality that the way of the market (the tao of trade), not the plan, is most consistent with human nature and, thus, with individual rights to life, liberty, and property. What China needs is not market socialism but market liberalism—or what could be appropriately called "market taoism."[41]

The reformers in the CCP, such as Premier Zhu Rongji, recognize the importance of competition in turning China into a modern market economy. But Zhu and others are pitted against a stubborn coalition of hard-liners whose primary concern is to stay in power and to eliminate competition. If China enters the WTO and significantly opens its markets to foreign competition, that will substantially increase the chances for a true market economy to develop and for eventual political liberalization. On the other hand, if the party, rather than the market, leads the economy, the Chinese people will never realize their full potential.

As Lao-tzu and Adam Smith pointed out, people have a natural propensity to trade and a natural right to be left alone to pursue their happiness—whether in the West or in the East. The Chinese people, when allowed to choose, favor the market over the plan and private over state ownership. In the booming coastal regions, individuals have freely opted for the nonstate sector, and millions of people have voluntarily left their homes in the countryside to search for a better life. The new urban centers, such as Shishi in the province of Fujian, are characterized by vibrant private market activity. Their model of development, writes Kathy Chen of the *Wall Street Journal,* is *"xiao zhenfu, da shehui*—small government, big society—which advocates less involvement by cash-strapped governments and more by society."[42]

When 5,455 people in six provinces were asked to express their view on private ownership, "78 percent agreed with the statement, 'Private property is sacred and must not be violated'"—and that was in 1993.[43] In 1999, on the 10th anniversary of the so-called Tiananmen Incident, a lone protestor opened his umbrella to reveal in Chinese characters the slogan: "Privatize. Give all state property to the people." His courage and boldness reveal what China may become in the next several decades, if the party gets out of the way of the market revolution that is sweeping the global economy.

China's leaders know they must allow alternatives to state ownership if the economy is to be efficient. But if the nonstate sector continues to grow, the party will continue to shrink in influence. So there is a natural clash between the party and the market, with the result being a regulated socialist market, not a free, private market.

As Milton Friedman said at his lecture in Beijing on September 30, 1980, what China needs are "free private markets"—in a word, "privatization."[44] Eventually a decision will have to be made to either allow full privatization of state assets or continue to suffer the inefficiencies of state control.

The division within the CCP on the question of how best to deal with SOEs is reflected in the following slogan, which was approved for the PRC's 50th anniversary celebration: "Adhere to the basic economic system with public ownership dominant and diverse forms of ownership developing side-by-side, and 'to each according to his work' as the main distribution form and with other forms as well"—a prime example of socialism with Chinese characteristics![45]

Marx and Engels, in 1888, recognized the popularity of private property due to the benefits it generates. In their "Manifesto of the Communist Party," they wrote:

> The bourgeoisie [i.e., private owners of capital], by the rapid improvement of all instruments of production, by the immensely facilitated means of communication, draws all, even the most barbarian, nations into civilization. The cheap prices of its commodities are the heavy artillery with which it batters down all Chinese walls, with which it forces the barbarians' intensely obstinate hatred of foreigners to capitulate.[46]

But it is not "force" that is the secret of the success of private property and trade, it is consent. Voluntary exchange always leads to mutual gain, and specialization according to comparative cost advantage benefits the global economy. The abolition of private property under Marxist regimes and the limitation of voluntary exchange have impoverished millions of people during the 20th century. Communism has been tried and has failed.

There are not many young communists left—in China or elsewhere. The CCP has lost much of its credibility and is no longer the major route to success.[47] People are now free to trade and to travel, and to see for themselves the benefits of the spontaneous market order. So, the answer to the question of China's future is clear: If China adopts the principles of market liberalism and practices market taoism, the people themselves will prosper; if it sticks with market socialism and fails to be integrated into the global economy, the Chinese people—and those of the West—will be poorer.

Notes

1. Lao-tzu, *Tao Te Ching*, trans. Chang Chung-yuan, in *Tao: A New Way of Thinking* (New York: Harper & Row, 1975), chap. 57.

2. Adam Smith, *The Wealth of Nations* (1776), ed. Edwin Cannan (New York: Modern Library, Random House, 1937), p. 651.

3. F. A. Hayek, "The Principles of a Liberal Social Order," in *Studies in Philosophy, Politics, and Economics* (Chicago: University of Chicago Press, 1967), p. 162.

4. F. A. Hayek, *Law, Legislation, and Liberty*, vol. 2, *The Mirage of Social Justice* (Chicago: University of Chicago Press, 1976), pp. 108–9.

5. Ibid., p. 108.

6. Smith, p. 385.

7. Alexis de Tocqueville, *Democracy in America* (1835), ed. J. P. Mayer (Garden City, N.Y.: Anchor Books, Doubleday, 1969), p. 637.

8. Quoted in Richard Vernier, "Interpreting the American Republic: Civic Humanism vs. Liberalism," *Humane Studies Review* 4 (Summer 1987): 12–13.

9. Robert J. Barro, *Getting It Right: Markets and Choices in a Free Society* (Cambridge, Mass.: MIT Press, 1996), p. 11.

10. Ibid.

11. On the dynamic gains from trade and the views of Smith and David Hume, see Razeen Sally, *Classical Liberalism and International Economic Order* (London: Routledge, 1998), pp. 40–50.

12. James Madison, "Speech in the Virginia State Convention of 1829–30, on the Question of the Ratio of Representation in the Two Branches of the Legislature," in *Letters and Other Writings of James Madison*, vol. 4, *1829–1836* (Philadelphia: J. B. Lippincott, published by Order of Congress, 1865), p. 51. See also James A. Dorn, "Madison's Constitutional Political Economy: Principles for a Liberal Order," *Constitutional Political Economy* 2, no. 2 (1991): 171.

13. Kate Xiao Zhou, "From Political Society to Economic Society: The Evolution of Civil Rights in China," in *China's Future: Constructive Partner or Emerging Threat?* ed. Ted Galen Carpenter and James A. Dorn (Washington: Cato Institute, 2000), chap. 2, p. 33.

14. Jianying Zha, *China Pop* (New York: New Press, 1995), p. 202.

15. William McGurn, "The Other China," *American Spectator*, July 1999, p. 37.

16. Quoted in Stephan Somogyi, "He's the Voice of the Tiananmen Generation," *Fast Company* 10 (August 1997): 32, http://www.fastcompany.com/online/10/lilu.html.

17. Ibid.

18. "Amendments to the Constitution of the People's Republic of China, Adopted at the Second Session of the Ninth National People's Congress on March 15, 1999," *Beijing Review*, May 3–9, 1999, pp. 14–15.

19. "Out-Dated Laws and Regulations Should Be Duly and Timely Removed," *China Financial Quarterly* (Summer 1999): 73.

20. See Liu Junning, "The Intellectual Turn: The Emergence of Liberalism in Contemporary China," in *China's Future*, chap. 3.

21. Quoted in an interview with William McGurn, "China Rediscovers Hayek," *Asian Wall Street Journal*, June 12, 1998.

22. Elisabeth Rosenthal, "New Gray Market in China Loosens Grip on Publishing," *New York Times*, June 27, 1999, p. 6.

23. See Liu, pp. 54–60; and Zhou, "From Political Society to Economic Society," pp. 39–43.

24. See Matt Forney, "Beijing Spring," *Far Eastern Economic Review*, April 2, 1998; and "Hayek's Children," *Far Eastern Economic Review*, May 14, 1998.

25. Rosenthal, p. 6.

26. Roger Pilon, "A Constitution of Liberty for China," in *China in the New Millennium*, ed. James A. Dorn (Washington: Cato Institute, 1998), p. 333.

27. Minxin Pei, "Creeping Democratization in China," *Journal of Democracy* 6, no. 4 (1995): 65–79. See also Minxin Pei, "Political Change in Post-Mao China: Progress and Challenges," in *China's Future*, chap. 17.

28. Ibid., p. 296.

29. Zhou, "From Political Society to Economic Society," p. 43.

30. Kate Xiao Zhou, *How the Farmers Changed China* (Boulder, Colo.: Westview, 1996).

31. Minxin Pei, "Is China Unstable?" Foreign Policy Research Institute *WIRE* 7, no. 8 (July 1999): 2.

32. Zhou, "From Political Society to Economic Society."

33. Minxin Pei, "The Growth of Civil Society in China," in *China in the New Millennium*, p. 245.

34. Zhou, "From Political Society to Economic Society," p. 44.

35. Ned Graham, "Engagement Opens Opportunities for Christian Service," in "Trade and the Transformation of China: The Case for Normal Trade Relations," Cato Institute Trade Briefing Paper no. 5, July 19, 1999, pp. 3–4.

36. James Kynge and James Harding, "Cult's Thousands Voice Beijing Protest," *Financial Times*, April 26, 1999, p. 1.

37. For a discussion of the different ways to get around the Chinese firewalls, see Zhang Weiguo, "Evading State Censorship: From the Bible to New Century Net," *China Rights Forum* (Fall 1998): 22–25. The number of Web sites covering China is growing by leaps and bounds. For a partial listing, see the Fall 1998 issue of *China Rights Forum*, especially the list compiled by Kris Torgeson, p. 31. A useful discussion of the chilling effect of PRC regulations on Internet use can be found in Judy M. Chen, "China On-Line: Surfing into the Future," *China Rights Forum* (Fall 1998): 26–31.

38. Lawrence Kudlow, "What's More Important Than the Fed?" *Wall Street Journal*, August 27, 1999, p. A8.

39. On the "institutional incompatibilities" between the old system of planning and the new market realities, see Justin Yifu Lin, Fang Cai, and Zhou Li, "The Lessons of China's Transition to a Market Economy," *Cato Journal* 16, no. 2 (1996): 226.

40. Ibid.

41. See James A. Dorn, "China's Future: Market Socialism or Market Taoism?" *Cato Journal* 18, no. 1 (Spring–Summer 1998): 131–46.

42. Kathy Chen, "Chinese Are Going to Town As Growth of Cities Takes Off," *Wall Street Journal*, January 4, 1996, pp. A1, A12.

43. Minxin Pei, "Is China Democratizing?" *Foreign Affairs* 77, no. 1 (January–February 1998): 76.

44. Milton Friedman, "Using the Market for Social Development," in *Economic Reform in China: Problems and Prospects*, ed. James A. Dorn and Wang Xi (Chicago: University of Chicago Press, 1990), p. 5.

45. Quoted in "Verbatim," *Time*, September 27, 1999, p. 25.

46. Karl Marx and Friedrich Engels, "Manifesto of the Communist Party," in *Social and Political Philosophy: Readings from Plato to Gandhi,* ed. John Somerville and Ronald E. Santoni (Garden City, N.Y.: Anchor Books, Doubleday, 1963), p. 348.

47. See James A. Dorn, "Trade and Human Rights: The Case of China," *Cato Journal* 16, no. 1 (Spring–Summer 1996): 82–83.

10. China's Accession to the World Trade Organization: Costs and Benefits

Mark A. Groombridge

For over 13 years, the People's Republic China has been seeking entry to the World Trade Organization, the multilateral institution governing international trade in goods and services. With the successful completion of most of the bilateral Accession Protocols necessary for membership, China is now poised to enter the WTO. For many people, China's entry to the WTO is a source of consternation, sparking fears of job losses in domestic markets. Others worry that such a large, still highly state-regulated economy will disrupt the WTO, an institution committed (by and large) to the principles of free trade.[1]

Although such fears are understandable, particularly in the short-term, the argument of this chapter is that consumers and the world trading community will benefit from China's accession to the WTO. Short-term economic losses will be incurred in certain sectors in some countries because of the inherent redistributive nature of a change in trading patterns. The dynamic benefits of China's WTO accession, however, will outweigh those economic dislocation costs, particularly over the long-term. None will gain greater advantage, however, than the citizens of China, who will benefit from the pressure the WTO will keep on China's leadership to stay the course of reforming the country's economy in a market-oriented direction.

While impossible to predict, the historical evidence to support the claim that freeing one's economy improves human well-being is overwhelming. James Gwartney, Robert Lawson, and Dexter Samida, in the most recent and comprehensive analysis on this subject, find that "greater economic freedom is strongly related with higher levels of income" and that the "general pattern repeats itself when looking at economic growth."[2] More specifically, countries that have been brought into the multilateral trading system have been well served by the GATT, formed in 1947 and the treaty on which the WTO (formed in 1995) is based. As Anne Krueger observes:

> Under the GATT, trade was greatly liberalized, and the world economy grew at unprecedented rates in the quarter century after the war. . . . While real world GNP [gross national product] had grown at rates never before realized over such a long period of time, the growth of world trade had proceeded almost twice as rapidly. By any standard, therefore, the open multilateral trading system served the world well.[3]

After discussing briefly the history of China's long march to enter the WTO, this chapter will analyze the costs and benefits of China's accession to that organization. These costs and benefits are evaluated largely from the perspective of China and the United States, not only because the U.S.-Chinese bilateral Accession Protocol is the most far-reaching in concessions made by China, but also because it is the only bilateral agreement that has been made quasi-public.[4]

China's Long March to the WTO

History of the Negotiations

In July 1986 the PRC sent a delegation to Geneva to submit a formal request to join the GATT.[5] Six years previously, in 1980, the PRC did express some interest in the multilateral trading system, as shown by its sending officials to economic, trade, and commercial policy courses conducted by the GATT. Those early signs of interest in joining the GATT were formalized in July 1981, when the PRC requested and received permission to serve as an observer at a GATT meeting on the renewal of the Multifibre Arrangement (MFA), which established rules governing trade in textiles. In addition to joining the MFA in December 1983, the PRC was also granted formal observer status to GATT proceedings at large in 1984. It was not until May 1987, however, that a formal working party was established to determine the exact terms and conditions under which the PRC would be allowed to enter the GATT.[6]

Thirteen years later, China is poised to enter the GATT's successor, the WTO. The official process of accession is somewhat complex. Specifically, three documents make up the accession instrument: the "Protocol," which sets out the terms and conditions for compliance with the general agreement; the report of the working party; and the tariff schedule and market-access schedules, which consist of the bound items of the new member's tariff schedule and individual market-access agreements.

The first substantive step toward membership consists of a memorandum from the applicant describing all laws, regulations, and policies affecting trade and investment. At that point the process divides into two tracks. The WTO General Council appoints a working party composed of trade negotiators from WTO members to bargain with the applicant over bringing its domestic laws and regulations into compliance with the WTO. At the end of the process, the working party produces a report that includes "commitment paragraphs" that track the Protocol and are enforceable through the WTO dispute settlement process. The report also contains a description of the applicant's trade regime, an amplification of the applicant's plan for implementation, and views of working-party members about their understanding of the applicant's commitments. As explained by Jeffrey Gertler, a member of the U.S. working party on China's accession, this aspect of the Protocol is multilateral in that it establishes how China and WTO members can ensure that China "will have the capacity to observe the rules and obligations of the WTO and also to enforce these rules domestically in a uniform and predictable manner, so that foreign businesses and traders are not discriminated against in their operations in China."[7]

At the same time, the potential new member-state undertakes a series of bilateral negotiations with individual WTO members on reciprocal tariff reductions and—of equal importance in recent years—other market-access issues covering agriculture, industrial goods, and services. After the successful conclusion of the bilateral discussions, the working party may submit an Accession Protocol for approval by the WTO's top governing body, the Ministerial Conference. As Gertler continues, "Once China accedes, the results of these bilateral negotiations will be 'multilateralized,' or in other words, they will be extended to all WTO Members on a most-favored-nation basis."[8] At this final stage, a vote will take place among WTO members, two-thirds of whom must vote in favor of China's accession.

Two Barriers

There are still two barriers to China's WTO accession. The first is that China has yet to conclude bilateral negotiations with the European Union, Brazil, and India. While China's negotiations with the

EU are expected to be somewhat difficult, the bilateral agreements with Brazil and India are expected to be concluded with relative ease. It is widely acknowledged that the primary hurdle to China's accession to the WTO had been the lack of an Accession Protocol between the United States and China, an obstacle that was removed in November 1999. It is also widely acknowledged that China will have little difficulty securing the necessary two-thirds support among WTO members.

The second barrier to China's accession is Congress, which must cast a vote to reconcile U.S. domestic law with the rules of the WTO. Specifically, Congress must revoke or amend Title IV, popularly known as the Jackson-Vanik Amendment, of the Trade Act of 1974. That law reaffirmed the 1951 ban on granting *unconditional* most favored nation (MFN) status to all countries characterized as "nonmarket economies" (with the exception of Poland and Yugoslavia). At present Congress can, on the basis of certain criteria, vote annually on whether to grant *conditional* MFN status, now called normal trade relations (NTR), to a nonmarket economy.[9] Jackson-Vanik, however, violates the unconditional MFN clause (in Article I, Section I, of the GATT treaty to reflect MFN's importance to the WTO).[10]

Every year since 1980, even in the aftermath of the Tiananmen Square incident in 1989, the United States has extended China MFN, now NTR, tariff status, on a reciprocal basis. (The United States currently applies NTR status to over 160 nations, including Iran, Iraq, and Libya. Only Afghanistan, Cuba, Laos, North Korea, Serbia, Montenegro, and Vietnam do not have NTR under U.S. law.)

Now that China is poised to enter the WTO, Congress must decide whether to extend permanent normal trade relations (PNTR) to China by repealing or amending Jackson-Vanik in some way. While China has indicated that, for political reasons, a congressional vote on PNTR is a prerequisite for China's accession to the WTO, this need not be the case legally. Congress could decide not to extend PNTR and forgo (pursuant to Article XIII of the GATT) the trade-liberalizing benefits and market-access concessions that China will be granting to other countries. Recall that China needs only two-thirds of the WTO members to support its entry.

Outline of the Agreement

While the exact terms under which China will accede are not known, the broad outlines of the agreement are well-known. Most analysts agree that China has committed to a number of sweeping reforms. According to the Office of the United States Trade Representative, China has committed to some market-access concessions.[11] A summary of those concessions follows.

- Agriculture: Significant cuts in tariffs will be completed by January 2004. The overall average tariff for agricultural products will be 17 percent. For U.S. priority products such as beef, grapes, wine, cheese, poultry, and pork, the average will be 14.5 percent, down from a preagreement level of 31.5 percent. China will also eliminate export subsidies and for the first time permit private trade between importers and exporters. Finally, China has agreed to base health restrictions of agricultural imports on stricter scientific evidence.

- Industry: China will lower industrial tariffs from an overall average of 24.6 percent to 9.4 percent by 2005; the rate will fall to 7.1 percent for U.S. priority products such as wood, paper, chemicals, capital, and medical equipment. China will also participate in the Information Technology Agreement, which eliminates all tariffs on such products as computers, telecommunications equipment, semiconductors, and other high-tech products. On automobiles, China will cut tariffs from the current 100 or 80 percent to 25 percent by 2006.

- Telecommunications: China will become a member and adopt the regulatory principles of the Basic Telecommunications Agreement, which include cost-based pricing, interconnection rights, and independent regulatory authority. China will also phase out all geographic restrictions for value-added paging services in two years, mobile-cellular in five years, and domestic wireline services in six years. Finally, in two years China will allow a 49 percent foreign ownership share in all telecommunications services and a 50 percent share in value-added paging services. China will also allow foreigners to invest in its growing Internet service provider industry.

- Insurance: Currently China allows foreign companies to operate only in Guangzhou and Shanghai. Under the new agreement, China will permit foreign property and casualty firms to insure large-scale risks nationwide immediately and will eliminate all geographic restrictions in three years. China will also expand the scope of activities for foreign insurers to include group, health, and pension insurance, which represent about 85 percent of total premiums. China has agreed to allow 50 percent foreign ownership for life insurance; for other types of insurance, China will allow branching and 51 percent foreign ownership on accession and will form wholly owned subsidiaries in two years.

- Banking: At this time, foreign banks are not permitted to conduct business in local currency with Chinese clients, and China imposes severe geographic restrictions on the establishment of foreign banks. Under the agreement, on accession China will allow full market access for foreign banks in five years, and foreign banks will be able to conduct business in local currency with Chinese businesses in two years and with Chinese citizens in five years.
- Trading: Foreign firms will, for the first time, have trading and distribution rights for most products. Those rights will be phased in over three years.
- Services: China will eliminate most foreign equity restrictions and allow greater access to the market for professional services such as foreign law and accounting firms. In travel and tourism, China will allow unrestricted access to its market for hotel operators, with the ability to set up totally foreign-owned hotels in three years. Foreign-travel operators will be able to provide the full range of travel agency services.
- Movies: Prior to the agreement, China permitted a maximum of 10 foreign films annually. After accession, China will allow 40 foreign films annually.
- State-Owned Enterprises: China has agreed that state-owned and state-invested enterprises will make purchases and sales solely on the basis of commercial considerations. The Chinese government has agreed that it will not influence commercial decisions except in a manner consistent with WTO protocol.

In addition to those concessions on market access, China has also reached agreement with the United States on mechanisms to control import surges through the application of anti-dumping laws and special safeguard provisions, including specific provisions for textiles (discussed below). As a cautionary aside, there is a danger that the United States (and eventually the EU once it reaches an agreement with China) will use those mechanisms to restrict Chinese imports. Such an action would serve neither the world trading community nor China.[12]

Although the above summary is based on the bilateral Accession Protocol signed between the United States and China, the Protocol will likely serve as a basis for any final document. The following section on the costs and benefits of China's accession to the WTO will thus be based on the U.S.-Chinese deal.

Costs of China's Accession to the WTO

Costs to the United States

Protectionist trade policies are inherently redistributive. When governments impose tariffs or other trade barriers to protect a particular sector, they raise costs to consumers of that product and redistribute the wealth generated from the tariff to a particular sector. By definition then, the removal of a protectionist trade barrier will cause some sectors to "lose out," at least in the short run. Long-term dynamic effects, however, are likely to be positive. It is well known, for example, that the removal of automobile protections in the 1980s forced U.S. automakers to improve the quality of their automobiles. Consequently, the U.S. auto industry is among the most competitive in the world.

Very few import-sensitive sectors will be affected by China's accession to the WTO. The reason is straightforward: the U.S. market is already quite open to China's imports. No changes are required for U.S. tariff levels in the agreement. Nevertheless, some sectors will face increased competition, particularly over the long-term. Specifically, the U.S. International Trade Commission (ITC) concluded, "Sectors that are to be negatively affected are footwear, wearing apparel, wood products, and other light manufactures."[13] And, overall, the ITC did predict "an increase in the U.S. trade deficit with China."[14]

The case of textiles and apparel is illustrative. Currently trade in textiles and clothing is subject to the WTO Agreement on Textiles and Clothing (ATC). Under the ATC, all countries are required to eliminate quotas by 2005. The United States, however, negotiated in the bilateral Accession Protocol a provision that would enable the United States to invoke additional protection against import surges in this sector by means of a textile safeguard provision that expires at the end of 2008. Despite this additional protection, the ITC is likely correct that "although much of this increase in China's

171

exports of textiles and apparel comes at the expense of other suppliers to the U.S. market, the U.S. textile and apparel industries could also be affected, with U.S. apparel producers and workers experiencing the more adverse effects."[15]

Costs to China

As China has agreed to a number of sweeping concessions on market access, it should come as little surprise that many sectors in China will feel the bite. One top Chinese official put it this way, "The blow will not be light . . . [and] pain is unavoidable."[16] The Chinese government has acknowledged that China's accession to the WTO will cost more than 10 million jobs and force over 9 million farmers out of work.

The automobile, machinery, and banking sectors are likely to take big hits as well.[17] In the automobile industry, for example, it is widely recognized that there will be consolidation of China's 120 auto producers. Chinese markets were quick to feel the bite as well, with automotive listings plummeting on the Shanghai and Shenzhen stock exchanges the day after the signing of the U.S.-Chinese bilateral agreement.[18] Top executives in China's state-owned banking system (of which four banks dominate) are considering ownership changes to help brace the industry for increased competition from foreign banks, particularly two years after accession, at which time all banks will be permitted to do business with Chinese companies in local currency.[19]

Quite clearly, China's costs will be much greater than those of the United States. Despite 20 years of reform, China still has far to go to redress the problems caused by decades of following inefficient socialist policies. It should also be noted that the social instability in China caused by unemployment poses risks to the regime, one still dominated by the Chinese Communist Party. It is widely cited, and acknowledged by Chinese government officials, that some 35 percent of China's 140 million workers in state and collective enterprises are superfluous and that urban areas will need to absorb some 150 million agricultural workers who will be seeking work in urban areas.[20] Undoubtedly, this will create potential for social, perhaps even political, instability.

Benefits of China's Accession to the WTO for the United States

Benefits to the U.S. Economy

China is the United States' 13th largest market abroad for U.S. goods, and since 1990, U.S. exports to China have increased by 167 percent. In 1998, U.S. merchandise exports to China totaled over $14 billion (up 10.9 percent from 1997), and another $5.3 billion worth of U.S. goods sold to Hong Kong was reexported to China.[21] Those exports support high-quality jobs in sectors of the American economy that have been driving U.S. economic growth in recent years. Notable among those sectors are power-generating equipment, telecommunications equipment, and medical equipment, as well as aircraft, computers, fertilizers, and organic chemicals.

Over the past 20 years American consumers and the U.S. economy have benefited from the expanding trade relationship with China. In 1978, when the PRC launched its "Open Door" policy and abandoned its largely autarkic past, trade between the two countries stood at an inconsequential $2 billion. Today China is the United States' fourth largest trading partner, trading goods worth some $85 billion. Table 10.1 documents this growing relationship in the past decade.

There is strong reason to believe that this beneficial trading relationship would expand if China becomes a member of the WTO. Although the United States would incur short-term losses in some sectors, such as footwear and textiles, other sectors would benefit greatly. As noted above, China has agreed to undertake a number of liberalizing reforms to satisfy WTO rules and obligations. U.S. firms would have unprecedented access to China's burgeoning market economy. Opportunities in important sectors such as agriculture would expand remarkably—for example, tariffs on beef products would be lowered to 12 percent by 2004 in comparison with the current 45 percent.

It is difficult, of course, to quantify gains to U.S. firms, but estimates suggest that the gains would be significant. One study by the Institute for International Economics estimates that "the induced increase in world exports of goods and services to China can be estimated at $21.3 billion. The immediate increase in U.S. exports of goods and services to China can be estimated at $3.1 billion."[22] Other estimates predict even higher benefits, taking into account the potential dynamic gains of increased competition. Fred Hu of Goldman Sachs, for example, estimates that China's accession to the WTO would lead to an additional $13 billion in U.S. exports by 2005.[23]

Even the ITC, which acknowledged losses in the textile and apparel industry, concluded that China's participation in the ATC,

Table 10.1
TRADE BETWEEN THE UNITED STATES AND CHINA
(BILLIONS OF U.S. DOLLARS)

	1990	1991	1992	1993	1994	1995	1996	1997	1998
U.S. imports from China	15.2	19.0	25.7	31.5	38.8	45.6	51.5	62.5	71.2
U.S. exports to China	4.8	6.2	7.5	8.8	9.3	11.8	12.0	12.8	14.3

SOURCE: United States International Trade Administration, http://www.ita.doc.gov/industry/otea/usfth/aggregate/HI98t10.txt.

which would eliminate quotas, would benefit the U.S. economy. In the first place, China would primarily be displacing other textile producers from foreign countries. More important, however,

> the overall impact on the U.S. economy of China's participation in the ATC would be positive. The economy-wide welfare gains for the United States would amount to about $2.4 billion in 2006, while GDP would increase by about $1.9 billion from the elimination of quotas in the same year. This occurs as a result of efficiency gains from factor reallocation in the U.S. economy, as well as from lower-priced goods imported into the United States.[24]

It is important to consider the benefits to U.S. consumers who have access to inexpensive imports. Put differently, *imports are good*, and China's entry to the WTO will help U.S. consumers. If China is a member of the WTO and has PNTR, the tariffs imposed on goods will be far lower than if it did not have that status. If the two countries revoked NTR reciprocally, the economic implications would be significant. Average tariff rates on Chinese goods would rise from 4 to 40 percent, a number comparable to the highly protectionist and deleterious Smoot-Hawley tariffs of 1930. Tariff rates for some items would increase more than 100 percent. Who would be hit hardest by those increased rates? U.S. consumers who enjoy low prices for top Chinese imports such as toys, sporting goods, footwear, clothes, plastic goods, suitcases, and furniture.[25]

A number of honorable critics of China's entry to the WTO point out that these benefits to U.S. consumers and firms will occur only if China abides by the agreement. Moreover, they point out the possibility of severe disruptions to the WTO process should China become a member and not play by the rules. Even if China's leaders are intent on implementing the agreement, it is not lost on the world trading community that some local bureaucrats in China will be resistant to change. Moreover, there is a lack of transparency in the rule-making process in China, a problem that hinders foreign access to China's market.

These are legitimate concerns; however, two mitigating factors should be noted. First, China is at least aware of the problem. Top trade and foreign investment officials forthrightly acknowledge that "laws that were made during the 1970s or 1980s did not take into consideration international regulations. There are even conflicts between them and some recently-made laws, such as the Contract Law and the Corporate Law."[26] Trade officials have also been more forceful in pushing through laws and regulations "to conform to the requirement of WTO rules" and in acknowledging that "the government's project-review and decisionmaking processes should be more transparent."[27]

The second factor mitigating concerns that China will not abide by the WTO agreement is the strength of the WTO dispute settlement process. Should China not live up to its WTO obligations, the United States and other member nations would have a better forum in which to air their grievances. China would be forced to blame the entire world trading community and the WTO should it lose a case—something China would find difficult to do if it is intent on becoming a respected global leader in its own right.

Currently, in the sometimes poisonous bilateral relationship, anti-reform elements in China invoke the argument that trade disputes with the United States stem either from the desire to protect failing U.S. industries or from a fear of China's emergence as a regional hegemon. China's accession to the WTO would blunt that argument and, in so doing, would allow U.S. policymakers to more effectively address non-trade-related aspects of the Sino-U.S. relationship.

Dispelling the Trade Deficit Myth

Fears of an increase in the U.S. bilateral trade deficit with China are also unwarranted. First, it is important to clarify that trade deficits reflect the flow of *capital*, not just the value of merchandise goods, across international borders. Given the health of the U.S. economy at this time, the United States provides an excellent destination for investment that the current level of savings by U.S. citizens cannot satisfy. Second, critics of the U.S. bilateral merchandise trade deficit with China mistakenly look at the trading relationship in isolation from trade with other countries. While the U.S. trade deficit with China has increased, the U.S. trade deficit with other countries has decreased. The reason is straightforward: investors in a number of countries, largely from East and Southeast Asia, have relocated production facilities to the PRC.

Consequently, the growth in the bilateral trade deficit with China is not nearly as dramatic as some might think, because job opportunities taken away by relocation of facilities in China were transferred to other countries one or two decades ago.[28] For that reason, as Nicholas Lardy concludes, "U.S. data on bilateral trade with China are seriously flawed," and "the argument that the growing deficit with China has caused a large loss of manufacturing jobs in the United States is wrong."[29]

Dispelling the "Trade as a Weapon" Myth

Some fear that China's entry to the WTO would be tantamount to rewarding a rogue nation for bad behavior. Critics of China's WTO membership point to a panoply of non-trade-related conduct by the Chinese government that offends core American values and runs counter to U.S. national interests. A shortlist of issues includes human rights abuses, technology transfers, nuclear espionage, missile proliferation, Asian security, campaign finance scandals, and China's handling of demonstrations in the aftermath of the accidental U.S. bombing of the Chinese embassy in Belgrade. It is important not to paint the opinions of those critics with a broad brush. Since their views span the political spectrum, they will interpret some aspects of the Sino-U.S. relationship differently.

Regardless of ideological stripe, these critics raise important concerns that should be addressed by both the United States and China. There are several reasons, though, why blocking China's entry to the WTO (which Congress could effectively do by not amending Jackson-Vanik and keeping NTR status for China conditional) is not the proper solution for resolving those outstanding issues.

First, conditional NTR is an "empty cannon." Some suggest that, "except for the post-Tiananmen sanctions, no policy has been as effective in achieving modifications of Chinese human rights policy as the threat of MFN (NTR) withdrawal."[30] It is true that, in the past, before the annual debates on the extension of NTR, China would engage in a widespread publicity campaign and sometimes release a high-profile dissident. These short-term gains, however, did little to change government attitudes or promote long-term change. Indeed, to some extent, the threat of NTR withdrawal might have actually weakened U.S. credibility. While speaking about the debates on MFN in the mid-1990s, James Lilley, former U.S. ambassador to China, aptly said: "The fundamental issue for China policy makers is that if the United States is to brandish MFN (NTR) as a weapon, we must be prepared to use it or our opponents will treat us with contempt. If we are not ready to revoke MFN for China, and clearly we are not, the president should . . . deemphasize the issue."[31] In 1999 Sino-U.S. relations were arguably at their lowest point in years. Thus it is reasonable to question why the House held annual debates on the floor despite Senate Majority Leader Trent Lott's announcement that the Senate would not even take up the issue of whether to revoke NTR. Moreover, in the same year, the House garnered a meager 170 votes in favor of revoking NTR for China.

The second reason that the annual debate on China's NTR status is not an appropriate weapon to influence China's behavior is that the unilateral sanctions would fail. It is true that the United States is the sole superpower in the world today, but that does not mean that the we live in a unipolar world where the United States can impose its will indiscriminately. If one looks at the history of using economic sanctions as a weapon (which not extending PNTR would be), there is a clear and consistent trend: multilateral sanctions sometimes work; unilateral sanctions almost never do.[32] The reason is straightforward: other countries will "free ride" on U.S. actions and continue to trade with China. Those countries against China's entry to the WTO for fear of Chinese access to high-tech products would find their efforts stymied as well. Other countries are quite explicit that they will continue to give China their most advanced technology. For example, Christian Pierret, the French junior industrial minister, publicly declared in Beijing in 1998 that "we [the French government] are playing to the fullest the game of technology transfers."[33]

Benefits of China's Accession to the WTO for China

The Historical Context: China's Transition to a Market-Oriented Economy

After decades of inefficient centralized planning and overemphasis of heavy industry at the expense of light industry, not to mention chaos unleashed by the Cultural Revolution, China's economy was in near ruins by 1978. While growth figures in a number of sectors such as industry and agriculture were positive at that time, numerous analysts have pointed out that those figures "masked increasingly serious structural problems," which led the government to conclude that the economy had been pushed to "the brink of disaster."[34]

In the 20 ensuing years, China has made impressive strides to move to a more market-oriented economy. That process is by no means complete. Centralized state planning continues to play a prominent role in some parts of the economy, and there is a pervasive statism to many elements of the reform program.[35] China is still best characterized as a "hybrid" economy, in which both the market and the state regulate various aspects of the economy.[36] Nevertheless, as the last 20 years of reform history unequivocally show, China is moving toward an economy based on market principles.

Today the most vibrant and dynamic sector in China is the burgeoning nonstate sector, consisting of a growing number of private-sector firms, as well joint ventures between foreign and Chinese firms. State-owned enterprises (SOEs) now account for about 25 percent of gross-value industrial output (GVIO) in China, down from some 80 percent in 1978. That contrasts with the trend in the private sector, which in 1978 accounted for a near-zero share of GVIO but now accounts for 18 percent.[37] A report by the Chinese Academy of Social Sciences notes that today some 70 percent of labor allocation, 62 percent of product pricing and distribution, 51 percent of enterprise management, 23 percent of land transfers, and 17 percent of capital distribution are market regulated—up from nearly zero percent.[38] In light of those developments, China has experienced impressive economic growth rates throughout the reform period. China's gross domestic product has nearly quadrupled since 1978 and now stands close to 8 trillion yuan ($960 billion).

China is also more deeply integrated into the world economy. In 1978 trade accounted for roughly 10 percent of the country's GDP; in the late-1990s trade accounted for closer to 36 percent of GDP.[39] Government officials in Beijing routinely note that export growth was responsible for about 20 percent of China's GDP growth in the 1990s.[40] Of particular relevance here is the fact that the nonstate sector has generated about three-quarters of total export growth since 1978.[41]

The Impact of Reform and Expanded Trade on the Chinese People

It would be disingenuous to suggest that China's primary goal or intent in reforming its moribund economy and opening to the outside world goes beyond maintaining the dominance of the CCP. Indeed, to this day there is a pervasive statism behind the reform

179

effort. As Dorothy Solinger argues, China's leadership views the economic reforms in China as largely "a means, a set of tools to be manipulated in the service of a few fundamental and overarching statist ends: the modernization, invigoration, and enhanced efficiency of the national economy and its consequently heightened capacity to boost both productivity and returns to the central state treasury."[42] Regardless of altruistic motives, however, the impact of China's centralized economy on the needs and comforts of the average Chinese citizen was not lost on the top leadership in Beijing in 1978. As Thomas Bernstein observes:

> What disturbed the leaders were immense imbalances, inefficiencies and poor results. These included disparities in growth rates among the three major sectors of heavy industry, light industry, and agriculture, and the neglect of services, which sharply lowered the quality of life. For instance, in a city such as Beijing, whose population moved about on bicycles, there were fewer bicycle repair shops in 1978 than there had been in 1957. . . . Living standards in both town and country had more or less stagnated since 1957. Rural poverty was an acute problem thirty years after the Chinese Communist Party had come to power with peasant support. According to the Central Committee, about 150 million peasants out of 800 million lived in dire poverty in 1978. . . . Socially, China was in a state of stunted or even frozen development, in which popular energies could not be fully unleashed and in which there was a great deal of suppressed frustration.[43]

Today the situation is quite different, and it is difficult to overstate how the reforms since 1978 have improved the life of the average Chinese citizen. According to China's Office on Poverty Alleviation and Development, well over 100 million individuals have risen out of destitution and now live above the official poverty line (annual per capita income below 640 yuan [U.S.$77]).[44] As the Chinese government itself acknowledges, much work remains to be done in that regard. Yu Shuning, minister-counselor of the Embassy of the People's Republic of China, conceded that "at present, 42 million Chinese still live below the poverty line."[45] In addition to helping alleviate poverty, the economic reforms in China have brought overall gains, as the gains in per capita income for both urban and rural residents suggest. While there is some question as to the accuracy

Table 10.2
PER CAPITA INCOME IN THE PEOPLE'S REPUBLIC OF CHINA
(IN 1990 YUAN)

	1978	1988	1998
Urban residents	316	1,119	5,454
Rural residents	134	545	2,150

SOURCES: Chinese Statistical Bureau, *Zhongguo tongji nianjian 1997, 1998* (China Statistical Yearbook 1997, 1998); and *China Monthly Statistics*. Related information can be found at http://www.state.gov/www/issues/economic/trade_reports/eastasia98/china98.pdf.

NOTE: U.S.$1 = 8.3 yuan. Figures from the United States correspond as well and are sometimes higher. For example, in its 1998 Country Reports on Economic Policy and Trade Practices for China, the U.S. Department of State reported that China had a per capita income of 6,465 yuan (U.S.$779).

of the data (macroeconomic data on China's GDP, particularly in the early reform period, are questionable), the trend is clear, as Table 10.2 suggests.

The overall quality of life for the average citizen in China has improved dramatically as well. Citizens now have access to better services in crucial areas such as health care and education. Millions more now have electricity (and consequently, refrigeration) and telephone service. The better lives that the Chinese people now lead are a direct result of the decision by China's leadership in 1978 to pursue economic reform in a more market-oriented direction. Undoubtedly, the internal rationalization of China's economy accounts for most of those gains. Astute observers wisely caution that although "trade is important to China . . . what goes on in the rest of its huge economy remains the critical factor."[46]

The Impact of WTO Accession

Despite the overall importance of the domestic economy in determining China's economic future, there still are two reasons why China's accession to the WTO will help that country's citizens lead better lives. First, as China's largest export market after Hong Kong, the United States plays a principal role in enriching Chinese companies, primarily non-state-owned ones. As noted above, government officials in China reported that roughly 20 percent of the increase in GDP during the 1990s was attributable to growth in exports.

However, since China already enjoys full market access to the United States, the expansion of exports from China will be limited.

Still, on accession, exports in some key sectors such as textiles and other labor-intensive industries would expand. Overall, in light of long-term dynamic effects, the Chinese government predicts that the PRC's accession to the WTO would increase GDP by 95.5 billion yuan (U.S.$23.64 billion), or 1.5 percent, by 2005.[47] And while acknowledging that some 10 million jobs will be lost in the agricultural, automobile, and machinery sectors, Chinese economists predict that WTO membership will create 12 million new jobs in other sectors such as textiles, toys, and footwear.[48] Chinese firms will also face a more stable export environment, one less subject to antidumping and special safeguard provisions (despite the WTO legality of such provisions). As Yang Donghui, secretary-general of the China National Federation of textile Industries, points out, one of the primary benefits of WTO membership, "especially in the long-run . . . is that the country will be able to enjoy stable multilateral preferential trade polices in a rules-based market."[49]

The second and more important reason that China's accession to the WTO will help the Chinese people is that it will strengthen the hand of pro-reform elements in the government. As noted above, China's transition to a market-oriented economy is not complete, and elements of centralized planning remain. And it is quite clear that despite the impressive economic gains China has made over the past 20 years, many intractable problems remain, such as the restructuring of SOEs, half of which are losing money.[50] China's industrial landscape is littered with *kongqiao qiye* (empty-shell enterprises), and state officials routinely argue that some 30 percent of the workforce in SOEs are superfluous. China's banking system is in a precarious position as well, given declining capital adequacy and the continued reliance of the state banking system on policy-based lending instead of the examination of market criteria.[51]

To a large extent these economic problems reflect the inherent difficulty of trying to recover from the 30 years of horribly misguided economic policies during Mao Zedong's reign. The recent Asian financial crisis has undoubtedly exacerbated those problems as well. The way out of this economic quagmire is for China to continue to deepen its reform effort. That will require China's leaders to exercise savvy economic and political policymaking. A primary reason that

182

China has not moved more quickly down the reform path is the divisive political battles currently fracturing the government. Different factions exist in China with markedly different attitudes toward economic reform.[52] Such leaders as Premier Zhu Rongji are widely credited for pushing China's reform effort and integrating more with the global trading community. Others, however, such as Li Peng, the former premier and now head of the National People's Congress, are fearful of the inherent instability that reforms entail and are a powerful force preventing China from reforming more quickly.

Although no panacea for China's economic problems, membership in the WTO would give political cover to pro-reformers, who could say that their hands were tied by international commitments. That would help legitimize the undoubtedly painful transition that China will have to undertake for it not only to live up to its WTO obligations but also to help continue lifting its remaining 42 million citizens out of poverty. It is well-known that there were heated debates at top WTO levels about China's accession after Clinton (foolishly) rejected Zhu's WTO offer in April 1999 (and after the accidental bombing of the Chinese embassy in Belgrade during the Kosovo crisis). There were also concerns about Zhu's influence. As Zhu is by far the most pro-reform leader of the top three leaders, the United States and the world trading community should do all they can to help strengthen his position.

There is some evidence to support the notion that China's accession to the WTO will help strengthen pro-reformers in Beijing. In preparation for increased competition after WTO entry, China's central bank governor, Dai Xianglong, announced a series of banking reforms, including gradual interest rate liberalization and expanding the band within which the bank allows its lending and deposit rates to fluctuate.[53] And while proving direct causality is, of course, impossible, it is noteworthy that after China signed the bilateral Accession Protocol with the United States, it took the unprecedented step of elevating the importance of the private-sector economy. State Development Planning Commission Chairman Zeng Peiyan acknowledged that China's multi-billion-dollar effort to resuscitate its moribund state-run sector had failed. Specifically, he announced that the government would "actively guide and encourage private investment" and would "eliminate all restrictive and discriminatory regulations that are not friendly toward private investment and private economic development in taxes, land use, business start-up and import and export."[54] Just as important, Zeng announced that more private firms would have access to China's fledgling stock markets in Shanghai and Shenzhen, which are currently restricted almost exclusively to SOEs.[55]

Conclusion

The most important beneficiaries of China's accession to the WTO will be the citizens of China. Keeping China out of the WTO will only hurt China's poorest communities. Strengthening the hand of pro-reform elements in Beijing by allowing China to accede to the WTO will only help China's leadership in its quest to lift its citizenry out of abject poverty. And, while beyond the scope of this chapter (see chapters by James A. Dorn and Kate Xiao Zhou in this volume), it bears mentioning that economic reform in China will likely help foster the growth of civil society as well. China's nascent civil society is still weak; however, as Gordon White points out, "This relative weakness of 'civil society' must be situated in the context of a semi-reformed command economy in which the state retains its dominant position in the economy."[56]

The world trading community, which has a strong interest in seeing China continue to reform its economy in a more market-oriented direction, will benefit as well from market access. China's commitments to open its market have been unprecedented since the country launched its Open Door policy in 1978. It is true that China will have difficulty living up to the agreement, but it is only a few narrow interest groups that have a stake in seeing China not integrated into the world's most important trading club. Most of those groups are interested in delaying the inevitable as they try to protect jobs in which they are longer competitive.

Societies will have to decide how to deal with the inevitable short-term dislocation costs that will stem from China's accession to the WTO. That applies not only to the United States but particularly to Southeast Asian nations, which are China's primary competitors in labor-intensive manufacturing. To balance the real concern that China will have difficulty abiding by WTO rules, it is important to bear in mind that as a member of the WTO, China will be subject to the WTO's multilateral dispute settlement process, a far more effective tool than unilateral sanctions stemming from bilateral trade disputes. Against the short-term dislocation costs the world trading community should weigh the long-term benefits, as countries rationalize their economies to more accurately reflect their respective comparative advantages. The historical record strongly suggests that this is the road to economic prosperity.

Notes

1. Both the General Agreements on Tariffs and Trade and the WTO were premised on the virtues of free trade. As noted in its preamble, the GATT attempted to achieve its goal of "raising standards of living" through "the substantial reduction of tariffs and other barriers to trade and to the elimination of discriminatory treatment in international commerce." See the "Preamble" to The General Agreement on Tariffs and Trade, 1947, http://pacific.commerce.ubc.ca/trade/GATT.html. Similarly, the main function of the stronger WTO is "to ensure that trade flows as smoothly, predictably and freely as possible" so that we all live in a "more prosperous, peaceful and accountable economic world." Quoted in World Trade Organization, http://www.wto.org. Neither the WTO nor the GATT, the treaty on which the it is based, operates wholly in accordance with free trade principles, and much work remains to be done in that regard, particularly in such sectors as agriculture.

2. James Gwartney, Robert Lawson, and Dexter Samida, *Economic Freedom of the World: 2000 Annual Report* (Vancouver, B.C.: Fraser Institute, 2000), p. 15.

3. Anne Krueger, *American Trade Policy*, (Washington: American Enterprise Institute, 1995), p. 7.

4. Largely to quell opposition in the United States, the Office of the United States Trade Representative made the document public. It should be pointed out that there remain some disagreements about the veracity of the office's press release, particularly from some Chinese observers. See Lester J. Gesteland, "Reports on WTO 'Inaccurate,'" *China Online*, November 19, 1999, http://www.chinaonline.com.

5. For a more detailed discussion on this point, see Harold K. Jacobson and Michael Oksenberg, *China's Participation in the IMF, the World Bank, and GATT* (Ann Arbor: University of Michigan Press, 1990).

6. This step would have been taken sooner but for an initial disagreement over the nature of the PRC's membership: would it be entering the GATT as a new contracting party, or would it be resuming a membership originally established in 1948? The PRC originally claimed that "the founding of the People's Republic of China in 1949 did not alter China's status as a subject of international law. The withdrawal from GATT in 1950 by the deposed regime in Taiwan was illegal and invalid. . . . Therefore, there is a sufficient political and legal basis for China's request for resumption of its status as a contracting party." Statement by Shen Jueren, deputy minister of foreign relations and trade, at the third session of the GATT working party on China, Geneva, Switzerland, April 26, 1988. See Ya Qin, "China and GATT: Accession instead of Resumption," *Journal of World Trade* 27 (1993): 77–98. Unfortunately, from the perspective of the Chinese, that option of joining the WTO as an original member of the GATT expired on January 1, 1997. Moreover, had China "resumed" its contracting status, even the Chinese acknowledged that the PRC would have had to enter into substantive negotiations based on contemporary conditions.

7. Jeffrey L. Gertler, "The Process of China's Accession to the World Trade Organization," in *China in the World Trading System: Defining Principles of Engagement,* ed. Frederick M. Abbott (The Hague: Kluwer Law International, 1998), p. 68.

8. Ibid.

9. First, in accordance with sect. 405 of the Jackson-Vanik Amendment the president must conclude a bilateral trade agreement with the subject country that provides for (1) reciprocal MFN treatment, (2) safeguard measures against disruptive import surges, and (3) the protection of intellectual property rights. This agreement is limited to an initial three-year period but subject to additional three-year renewals. And, second, as sect. 402(b) stipulates, the president must also determine that the subject country permits free and unrestricted emigration. The latter condition is subject to a waiver through sect. 402(c) for 12 months if the president determines that such a waiver will promote free emigration.

10. "With respect to customs duties and charges of any kind imposed on or in connection with importation or exportation or imposed on the international transfer of payments for imports or exports, and with respect to the method of levying such duties and charges, and with respect to all rules and formalities in connection with importation and exportation . . . any advantage, favour, privilege or immunity granted by any contracting party to any product originating in or destined for any other country shall be accorded immediately and unconditionally to the like product originating in or destined for the territories of all other contracting parties." GATT, Article I, Section I, 1947, http://pacific.commerce.ubc.ca/trade/GATT.html.

11. The next section is based on White House Office of Public Liaison, *Summary of U.S.-China Bilateral WTO Agreement,* November 17, 1999, http://www.uschina.org.

12. See Claude E. Barfield and Mark A. Groombridge, "The China WTO Deal: Sweet and Sour," *Asian Wall Street Journal,* November 17, 1999, p. 8. For a broader discussion of these issues, see Mark A. Groombridge and Claude E. Barfield, *Tiger by the Tail: China and the World Trade Organization* (Washington: American Enterprise Institute, 1999).

13. U.S. International Trade Commission, "Assessment of the Economic Effects on the United States of China's Accession to the WTO," *Publication 3229,* September 1999, p. xx. (Note that this assessment is based on the market-access package put forward by China during Zhu Rongji's visit to Washington in April 1999. While technically the agreements are not the same, the broad outlines are.)

14. Ibid.

15. Ibid., p. xv.

16. "China Bracing for Membership in WTO," Associated Press, January 11, 2000.

17. "China WTO Entry Could Spur Jobs," Associated Press, December 12, 1999.

18. See "GM, China and the WTO," *China Online,* December 8, 1999, http://www.chinaonline.com.

19. See James Kynge, "China: WTO Entry May Force Banks to Go Public," *Financial Times,* December 13, 1999.

20. See Li Jiange, "China: Big Boost for Economy Next Year," *Financial Times,* December 10, 1999.

21. For a thorough review of the Sino-U.S. trading relationship, see U.S.-China Business Council, http://www.uschina.org.

22. Daniel H. Rosen, "China and the World Trade Organization: An Economic Balance Sheet," *International Economic Policy Briefs, Number 99-6* (Washington: Institute for International Economics, June 1999), p. 2.

23. Fred Hu, Global Economics Paper no. 14, Goldman Sachs, New York, April 1999.

24. U.S. International Trade Commission, p. xv.

25. These are among the top goods listed by the United States International Trade Administration for 1998, http://www.ita.doc.gov/industry/otea/usfth/top80cty/china.cp.

26. Zhang Yan, "Shi: Trade Rules to Be Reviewed," *China Daily Business Weekly*, January 9, 2000, p. 2.

27. Ibid.

28. For a detailed documentation of this point, see Robert C. Feenstra et al., "The U.S.-China Bilateral Trade Balance: Its Size and Determinants," National Bureau of Economic Research, Working Paper no. 6598, June 1998. See also Ma Xiaoye and Zheng Han-Da, "China and the United States: 'Rules of Origin' and Trade Statistics Discrepancies," *Journal of World Trade* 30, no. 6 (December 1996).

29. Nicholas R. Lardy, "China and the WTO," Brookings Policy Brief no. 10, November 1996, pp. 2–3.

30. Andrew Nathan, "Influencing Human Rights in China," in *Beyond MFN: Trade with China and American Interests*, ed. James R. Lilley and Wendell L. Willkie (Washington: American Enterprise Institute, 1994), p. 88.

31. James R. Lilley, "Trade and the Waking Giant," in *Beyond MFN*, p. 54.

32. For a more thorough discussion on this point, see Claude E. Barfield and Mark A. Groombridge, "Unilateral Sanctions Undermine U.S. Interests," *The World & I*, December 1998, pp. 92–97.

33. "France Ready to Transfer Technology to China," Reuters, June 15, 1998.

34. Quoted in Carl Riskin, *China's Political Economy* (Oxford: Oxford University Press, 1987), p. 237. This evaluation had a political rationale as well. Newly established leaders often are quick to point out that the ancien régime performed miserably. China was no different.

35. See Dorothy Solinger, *China's Transition from Socialism* (Armonk, N.Y.: M. E. Sharpe, 1993).

36. See Victor Nee, "Organizational Dynamics of Market Transition: Hybrid Forms, Property Rights, and Mixed Economy in China," *Administrative Science Quarterly* 37 (1992). 1–27.

37. Chinese Statistical Bureau, *Zhongguo tongji nianjian 1998* (China Statistical Yearbook 1998).

38. "Unfinished Business," *Far Eastern Economic Review*, December 17, 1998, p. 22.

39. See Thomas W. Robinson, "Interdependence in China's Foreign Relations," in *China and the World*, 3d ed., ed. Samuel S. Kim (Boulder, Colo.: Westview, 1994), p. 193.

40. See Mark A. Groombridge, "Is the Asian Flu Still Infectious? The Case of China," *Looking Ahead*, August 1998, pp. 21–24.

41. East Asia Analytical Unit, Australian Department of Foreign Affairs and Trade, *China Embraces the Market* (Barton, Australia: Commonwealth of Australia, 1997), p. 10.

42. Solinger, p. 3.

43. Thomas P. Bernstein, "Change in a Marxist-Leninist State," in *Driven by Growth: Political Change in the Asia-Pacific Region*, ed. James W. Morley (Armonk, N.Y.: M. E. Sharpe, 1993), pp. 45–46.

44. The most dramatic improvements were made in the rural areas. Between 1986 and 1993, 45 million rural poor were officially removed from the poverty list, an average of about 6.4 million a year; from 1994 to 1996, another 5 million rose above

the poverty line. See Zhao Huanxin, "Poverty Relief Work to Intensify," *China Daily*, April 8, 1999.

45. Yu Shuning, "China's Poverty Program," Letter to the Editor, *Washington Post*, July 17, 1999, p. A18.

46. Peter Harrold, "China: Foreign Trade Reform—Now for the Hard Part," *Oxford Review of Economic Policy* 11 (1995): 135.

47. "China's WTO Entry to Boost GDP 1.5%," *China Online*, November 18, 1999, http://www.chinaonline.com.

48. "China WTO Entry Could Spur Jobs."

49. Quoted in Meng Yan, "Riding High on the WTO Wave," *China Daily Business Weekly*, December 26, 1999, p. 1.

50. For a more thorough discussion of this point, see Mark A. Groombridge, "Dragon Droop: Why China's Economic Future May Be Less Spectacular Than You Think," *American Enterprise*, July–August, 1998, pp. 34–39.

51. A thorough discussion of the banking situation is offered in Nicholas R. Lardy, *China's Unfinished Economic Revolution* (Washington: Brookings Institution, 1998).

52. See Andrew Nathan, "Factionalism and the Limits of Reform," in *China's Crisis* (New York: Columbia University Press, 1990), pp. 21–68.

53. See James Kynge, "China: Financial Reforms to Accelerate," *Financial Times*, January 21, 2000.

54. Quoted in John Pomfret, "China Gives Broad Rein to Economy's Private Sector," *Washington Post*, January 5, 2000, p. A1. There are some sectors that will be limited. As Zeng pointed out in the same article, "Except for the areas that are related to national security and those that must be monopolized by the state, all the rest of the areas should allow private capital to enter."

55. Ibid.

56. Gordon White, "Prospects for Civil Society in China," *Australian Journal of Chinese Affairs* 29 (January 1993): 86.

11. Living with Ambiguity? U.S.-China Relations in an Era of Transition

Robert A. Manning

F. Scott Fitzgerald wrote that the mark of a first-rate intellect is the ability to hold two opposing ideas in mind and still be able to function. In many respects, that sums up the challenge of establishing a stable, enduring U.S.-Chinese relationship during this period of transition both in the international system and in China's own gradual transformation. Can the United States protect its national interests while hedging against uncertainty about China's intentions? And what impact does economic interaction with China have on security and human rights? For the past decade, since the June 1989 brutal crackdown at Tiananmen Square and the fall of the Berlin Wall, U.S.-Chinese relations have lurched from crisis to crisis. Those two events served both to shatter the sense of purpose underpinning the Cold War bipartisan consensus for relations with China and to freeze in the American psyche the horrific image of tanks rolling over students.

Since the days of the missionaries 150 years ago, American views of China have tended to swing wildly from irrational exuberance, when we felt that China was becoming increasingly like the United States, to bitter disappointment and resentment, when we saw that it was not. Nevertheless, in the four decades preceding the 1990s, there was a clear strategic rationale underlying U.S. policy toward China: anti-communist enmity and containment from 1949 to 1971 and an anti-Soviet strategic partnership from 1971 to 1989. Amid growing American apprehension about China, U.S.-Chinese relations have become a political roller coaster whose final destination remains uncertain. Beyond Beijing's serious human rights failings, allegations of illegal campaign contributions by the People's Republic of China, of spying to obtain nuclear technology, and of episodic reports of PRC exports of missiles and other technologies of mass destruction have shaped a troubling pathology of mutual recrimination in Sino-American relations. While many in the United States see a huge authoritarian state challenging America's interests and values around the world, many in China fear that the U.S. goal in the new century is to stifle the PRC's emergence as a major power.

Although the China debate in the United States has varied in ferocity at different moments, accentuated by the annual ritual of renewing normal trade status with China, it has become a defining issue of—if not a metaphor for—American foreign policy in the 21st century. As China emerges as a major economic, military, and political power over the next half-century (along with the possible addition of a united Europe), it is one of the few likely peer competitors that could conceivably challenge American preeminence. The problem is that the three large and politically inseparable sets of issues—trade, security, and human rights—that subsume the multitude of irritants composing much of U.S.-Chinese relationship are ambiguous, while our debate seeks unambiguous categories and quick resolutions: Either China's markets are open or the Chinese are unfair traders. Either China cooperates on nonproliferation of missiles and weapons of mass destruction, regional security, and the status of Taiwan, or it goes into the "rogue state" adversarial column. Either China is becoming a tolerant democracy or it is a totalitarian Leninist state. In the quest for black or white, there is little room for the more ambiguous gray that is China in the midst of an unprecedented historic transformation.

America's Flawed Policy Debate

The inability to tolerate such ambiguity is reflected in a confused debate dominated by false categories. Since it de-linked human rights from the annual executive branch decision whether to grant China the once-misnamed most favored nation (MFN)—now normal trade relations (NTR)—trade status in 1994, the Clinton administration has defined the policy choice as one of engagement or containment, integration or isolation. The initial intent was to move beyond the post-Tiananmen stigma that prevented normal dealings with the world's largest country and forge a post–Cold War relationship. But over time that construct set up a false debate. The problem is that engagement is a tactic, not a policy or a strategy. Showing up for meetings is better than not talking at all; however, it is merely process. Engagement is policy as tautology: We meet, therefore we are. If policy is defined merely as process, then how can one judge success or failure? The real issue is the nature and purpose of engagement, not simply whether to engage. Framing the issue as one of process so contorted the debate that, for example, an otherwise sober RAND Corporation analysis recently concluded that U.S. policy should be "Congagement."[1]

Behind the engagement buzzword is the notion that such processes would integrate rather than isolate China, thus ensuring its role as a benign actor in the international system. In a June 1997 speech to the Council on Foreign Relations, National Security Advisor Samuel (Sandy) Berger posed the issue as whether China would move toward "inward-looking nationalism or outward-looking integration."[2] President Clinton elaborated in a major policy speech on the eve of his first summit with Chinese president Jiang Zemin: "China stands at a crossroads. The direction China takes toward cooperation or conflict will profoundly affect Asia, America, and the world for decades. The emergence of a China as a power that is stable, open, and non-aggressive, that embraces free markets, political pluralism, and the rule of law, that works with us to build a secure international order—that kind of China, rather than a China turned inward and confrontational, is deeply in the interests of the American people."[3]

The reality, however, is more complex. There is no reason why China cannot be both. It might be willing to integrate into regimes governing international behavior, such as the World Trade Organization; the hundreds of conventions on such matters as air travel and telecommunications; and security regimes such as the Nuclear Nonproliferation Treaty (NPT), the Comprehensive Test Ban Treaty, and the Chemical Weapons Convention. At the same time, however, the PRC might be nationalistic about issues it regards as vital questions of sovereignty (such as Taiwan), seek to expand its influence on the Korean Peninsula, and continue to modernize its military forces. None of those actions would necessarily lead one to conclude that China will be in the early 21st century what Germany was at the beginning of the 20th—a revisionist power seeking to overturn the existing order. Germany wanted the kind of power and influence that Britain had. There is little evidence that the same can now be said of China. The PRC clearly wants an appropriately sized seat at the table, and like all great powers, it seeks to shape the rules to best serve its interests. But the evidence suggests that beyond seeking a dominant role in the Asia-Pacific region, China wants to join the international system not overturn it. It is true, however, that China appears to have an expansive sense of the meaning of "sovereignty." For example, the February 1992 Law on National Sovereignty, passed by the National People's Congress, defines the entire South China Sea as Chinese territory. In theory, that law would contradict the Law of the Sea Treaty, to which Beijing is a party and to which it pledges to adhere. In practice, however, China's sovereignty claims to the South China Sea, which would contravene freedom of navigation, have never been enforced. Furthermore, China lacks a blue-water navy and the force projection capability to enforce such claims.

However, China is clearly an irredentist power, jealously seeking territories it defines as belonging under its sovereignty—notably, Taiwan, Hong Kong, and Macao—that were severed by foreign colonial intervention. Beyond that, China seeks to neutralize threats along its 5,000-mile border stretching from India to Vietnam and, over the long term, to establish a preeminent role in East Asia. In any case, one has to deal with a regime that controls 22 percent of the human race, has nuclear weapons and a veto at the U.N. Security Council, borders 15 countries, and is the 11th largest trading power and one of the nine largest economies. Unlike U.S. Cold War policy toward the Soviet Union, which was based on simple organizing principles, China—an emerging major power whose interests and those of the United States overlap in some areas and may conflict in others—is extremely complex. It is not an ideological adversary— few of the 50-plus million members of the Chinese Communist Party take its Marxist rhetoric seriously. Official rhetoric has become increasingly tortured, as China becomes a marketized economy with oxymoronic terms like "socialist market economy."

Even in the bad old days of the Cold War, a policy of containment did not preclude "engaging" Moscow as necessary to advance U.S. interests. Such engagements included regular summit meetings and arms control agreements. The issue is not whether to "engage" China in order to pursue American interests through the full range of diplomatic venues but rather to engage toward what results. Moreover, the issue is not simply whether China will be integrated into the international system of relations. Deng Xiaoping made the strategic choice in 1978 that, in order to achieve its highest objective (to modernize its economy), China had to reform and open its economy and integrate it into the global economy. By some estimates, 40 percent or more of China's economy is already in the private sector. In effect, China's Leninist leaders have made a huge bet on economic modernization—from which most of their legitimacy is derived. They are betting that they can ride the tiger of economic reform and dependence on the global economy while maintaining their political monopoly. In the interim, the issue is whether China, like all emerging great powers, will seek to bend the rules to its benefit in ways that run counter to U.S. interests or whether there is room for mutual accommodation. That is the China policy debate we have not really had.

From MFN Squabble to WTO Membership

The problem with the issue of MFN began with the unfortunate, misleading semantics that distorted the debate. MFN is not a trade concession or a type of foreign aid. Granting MFN to China does not mean that China is our favorite nation, that we are granting a special privilege, or that we are doing China a favor. It does not mean that we give "favorable tariff rates to Chinese exports," as a Senate Democratic Policy Committee report argued.[4] Instead, MFN simply means that China and the United States grant each other the same—no *less* favorable—tariff treatment that they provide to their other respective trading partners granted MFN. The United States grants that treatment to some 180 other countries, including Iran, Iraq, Libya, and Burma. To eliminate the semantic confusion, MFN is now more appropriately called NTR, as it is merely the basis on which international trade is typically conducted.

No other nation conditions trade with China, and no other country would likely follow the United States in removing NTR for China if the United States did so. Trade has been the one strand in the beleaguered U.S.-Chinese relationship that has not seriously frayed over the past decade, perhaps because it is a high-priority issue and one in which there is an overlap of mutual interests. Viewing commerce with a nation with which one is not at war—and that is not even considered an overt adversary—as a favor or a concession, or as conveying a moral judgment, is curious indeed. Withdrawing NTR from China would be an extraordinary act that would impose tariffs likely to destroy a burgeoning annual $70-plus billion commercial relationship with one of the world's largest and fastest-growing economies (and U.S. export markets). The United States does indeed grant more favorable treatment to exports from more than 100 countries through such agreements as the Generalized System of Preferences (GSP), the North American Free Trade Agreement, and the Caribbean Basin Initiative, to cite a few.

NTR became the vehicle for expressing American moral outrage at and concern for human rights in China largely by historical accident. In 1974 Congress attached to a major trade bill (the Trade Act of 1974) language known as the Jackson-Vanik Amendment. Jackson-Vanik was passed to ensure that President Nixon could proceed with his policy of détente, which included granting MFN treatment to the Soviet Union if the Soviets permitted Jewish emigration.[5] It is important to note that, at the time, U.S. trade with the largely autarkic Soviet economy was all but nonexistent. Jackson-Vanik barred MFN trade status for nonmarket economies unless the president certified annually that the country in question allowed free emigration of its citizens.

Emigration was not, and is not, a serious concern with regard to China. But Jackson-Vanik has become a classic example of the law of unintended consequences: it has remained on the books long after the issue that rightly generated it was resolved. MFN renewal for China became a Christmas tree on which single-issue activist groups can hang their frustration-ornaments, many often accompanied by stringent conditions for renewal. Grievances include forced abortion, religious persecution, human rights abuses, Taiwan, Tibet, maltreatment of orphans, prison-labor exports, environmental degradation, nuclear and ballistic missile proliferation, mercantilist trade practices, political repression, belligerent military actions violating international norms, increased military spending, and failure to honor international economic agreements. Those grievances may all be legitimate, but conditioning the bilateral trade relationship on PRC concessions on them would almost certainly be counterproductive. Granted, such myths as "oil for the lamps of China" and "if only each Chinese bought one yard of cloth" have fostered generations of unrealistic fantasies about the Chinese market. Nonetheless, no U.S. business is prepared to write off one of the world's fastest-growing markets. Beijing is very effective at the classic Chinese technique of "using the barbarians against the barbarians." In modern terms, that means canceling orders for Boeing airplanes and buying Airbus planes instead or giving Europeans or Japanese large contracts for infrastructure projects such as airport facilities or metro trains. Revoking NTR would not advance any of the multitude of U.S. interests in China, and it might even worsen the situation for some of them if, as is likely, China responded petulantly and became more uncooperative. Fears that imposing conditions on the right to trade were unlikely to alter Beijing's behavior and could even unravel the entire relationship led President Clinton in 1994 to delink MFN from human rights and other issues.

The issue of NTR status should never have become an annual affair. It is valid to ask *once* whether Americans should trade with and invest in China. If China reversed course and began to close off its markets and return to Maoism, basic questions about whether to trade should be revisited. However, there is no sign at present of any shift by China from its policy of widening and deepening economic reform. Moreover, that there is already a large, dynamic, two-way trade relationship of some $70 billion annually, and more than $12 billion in direct U.S. investment in China, suggests that the question has largely been answered. (Of course there are critical issues, such as export controls on militarily relevant products, that should be continually examined.)

China's success as an exporter—particularly of apparel, footwear, toys, and electronics—has led to a massive trade surplus with the United States that reached nearly $59 billion in 1999. China's trade surplus is a complex issue, in some respects more political than economic. It is the overall current account deficit, not the bilateral deficits or surpluses, that is of economic importance. However, in cases such as Japan, which also runs persistent large surpluses, such a gap can be an indicator of impediments to a nation's markets. Even the trade numbers are debatable, though. China computes only direct trade, while U.S. figures reflect reexports of PRC goods via Hong Kong but do not reflect Hong Kong's reexports of U.S. goods to China, thus understating U.S. sales. One can see a clear correlation between the growing U.S. trade deficit with China during the 1990s and a decline in the corresponding trade deficits with Taiwan and Hong Kong. That is the result of investment on the mainland by overseas Chinese from those locales using the mainland as an export platform. Thus, a kind of integrated "Greater China" economy has begun to take shape.[6] Prior to China's accession to the WTO, threats of unilateral action based on sect. 201 or sect. 301 of U.S. trade law and other bilateral mechanisms have been and continue to be important recourses to unfair Chinese trade practices. For example, concern about rampant pirating of intellectual property in the PRC resulted in a bilateral accord in 1994 that, while not totally effective, has substantially improved the protection of U.S. intellectual property.

Fortunately, that phase of the China trade debate is coming to an end. Now there is an opportunity to achieve an important, multilateral means of increasing pressure on China to play by the rules of international commerce, to better address unfair trade practices, and to fully test China's willingness and ability to do so. That opportunity is created by China's accession to the WTO, the locus of the current debate on trade with China. Most of the contentious issues in U.S.-Chinese trade relations are precisely the issues China must address to join the WTO. It is a historic anomaly that one of the world's largest economies, with more than $320 billion in annual trade, has been outside the official global trading system. Because China had sought special dispensation as a "developing nation," the United States has rightly insisted that any terms of accession be "commercially viable," not a political deal.

After a process of negotiations that floundered since 1988, U.S. and Chinese trade negotiators reached accord on an impressive set of provisions in April 1999, on the eve of the Washington visit by Premier Zhu Rongji, committing China to sweeping market openings. A document released by the Office of the U.S. Trade Representative boasted that the United States had achieved commitments that addressed the principal barriers to American products; were highly specific and fully enforceable; were phased in over a relatively short period of time, with increased market access in every area; did not offer China special treatment; and met or exceeded commitments made by many present WTO members. Those achievements included full market access for U.S. firms in distribution; deeper tariff cuts and elimination of quotas; phasing out quotas and reducing tariffs on its agricultural market; opening of service sectors, including insurance, telecommunications, and computer; and joining the International Telecommunications Agreement. One area in which the accord was legitimately open to criticism was finance and securities, in which phase-in time frames for market opening in certain areas and the limited extent of openings in others generated mixed response on Wall Street. Arguably, however, in the aftermath of the Asian financial crisis, there is a compelling case for cautious movement. That is particularly true in light of China's horrific banking system, in which bad loans amount to as much as 40 percent of gross domestic product and outstanding debt is in excess of 100 percent of GDP.[7]

Despite frantic 11th-hour efforts by negotiators and overwhelming support in the business community, President Clinton, fearing inadequate support in Congress, rejected the deal worked out by the USTR and its Chinese counterpart. In retrospect, it appears to have been a major blunder. Bejing's concessions were a remarkable shift from positions taken just weeks earlier. As the details of the agreement were analyzed, it appeared, according to well-placed sources, that Clinton had received wrong-headed advice. The support for the WTO accord in the business community was overwhelming, but White House political advisers underestimated the ability to obtain congressional approval for permanent NTR status, the de facto legislative referendum on the accord.

In the aftermath of the failure of Zhu's visit to produce an accord, and the resulting weakening of his political position inside China, negotiators sought to cobble together a mutually acceptable deal— an agreement that was formally reached in late September. The key point is that a deal was possible because Zhu and the Chinese leadership made difficult decisions that will inevitably involve short-term pain for state-owned Chinese industry in exchange for the longer-term goals of global competitiveness and boosting foreign direct investment by accelerating market reforms—with WTO disciplines as an additional prod.

Chinese accession to the WTO will be no panacea for U.S.-Chinese trade relations. Implementing China's new commitments and enforcing them will almost certainly be a constant struggle. One consequence of China's WTO accession, however, is that congressional critics will have to find other vehicles for anti-China legislation. But that has been a pattern since 1996: even as NTR was approved that year, Congress passed a package of anti-China legislation encompassing other myriad concerns. After the September 1997 summit,

Congress passed legislation, for example, seeking to ban trade with People's Liberation Army companies and calling for new arms sales to Taiwan. In the 105th Congress (1997–98), a number of House resolutions were introduced addressing everything from control of exports to China (H.R. 1942) to concerns over the human rights situation (H.R. 76) to prohibition of U.S. funds to sponsor Chinese officials for conferences if those officials were believed to have taken actions to limit free exercise of religion (H.R. 967).

There are various estimates of what China's WTO accession will mean for U.S.-Chinese economic relations, but by all accounts, it will be a net gain, as U.S. markets are already substantially open. The U.S. International Trade Commission, in a classified study for the USTR, concluded that China's accession to the WTO (on terms similar to those proposed in April) would result in a roughly $2.5 billion increase in U.S. exports to China. The Institute for International Economics argues that U.S. government projections are based on conservative modeling techniques and projects a $3.1 billion increase. A Goldman Sachs forecast estimates an additional $13 billion in U.S. exports by 2005.[8]

Strategic Trade

The area in which trade issues directly merge with larger security concerns about China as a rising military power—and is a central focus of recent controversy involving spying charges and the Cox report[9] is strategic trade. We live in a world in which high-tech items increasingly have military applications. That dual-use problem creates perpetual export-control dilemmas. It was concerns about knowledge that China had gained as a result of information from Loral and other U.S. space industry firms in connection with launching U.S. satellites that originally led to the creation of the Cox committee. Yet the committee's voluminous study added only incremental knowledge to what had been leaked to the press about the satellite issue. Although the Pentagon has a careful on-the-ground monitoring system for Chinese launches of U.S. payloads, the experience of launching what are actually ballistic missiles is almost certain to increase the PRC's knowledge about the accuracy of missiles. After a number of failed launches, at significant cost to Hughes, Loral, and other firms in the late 1980s and early 1990s, U.S. firms clearly had an interest in more reliable launching of their satellites. In the case of Loral, information was faxed to Chinese officials without a license from the U.S. Department of State.

But the larger point from the whole satellite affair is that if preventing greater PRC knowledge about satellites is a strategic U.S. goal, then avoiding dependence on relatively cheap Chinese launches may be a reasonable public policy goal. Perhaps a policy of government–private sector partnership involving some level of subsidized U.S. launches might be considered. The initial reason that the United States began approving Chinese launches in 1988 was a shortage of launch capacity (combined with the prospect of cheap Chinese launches).

Espionage is obviously an enduring feature of statecraft. The spate of disclosures about Chinese "extracurricular activities" is as much about the foibles of the U.S. political system as it is about China. It was the shift of licensing of satellite launches from the State Department to the U.S. Department of Commerce and of the pursuit of commercial interests by U.S. aerospace firms that helped enhance Chinese missile know-how. Likewise, it is the U.S. campaign finance system that created an opening for Chinese military officials to funnel money through Johnny Chung. It appears that it was inadequate security at U.S. labs, combined with the inherent nature of scientific exchange, that may have allowed China to make advances in its nuclear and other technology that would otherwise not have been possible.

It is too early to know with any certainty what gains China obtained for its nuclear modernization program.[10] An exhaustive investigation by the *New York Times* (whose reporting extensively chronicled the allegations) concluded that "the Congressional report [Cox report] went beyond the evidence in asserting that stolen secrets were the main reason for China's breakthrough."[11] Nonetheless, it appears that some measure of benefit many have been obtained—even if by licit means (e.g., unclassified scientific papers)—to increase the accuracy of the PRC's missiles; leapfrog an entire generation in nuclear technology to miniaturize nuclear warheads and place multiple warheads on a missile (MIRV); and acquire knowledge of the most advanced submarine-tracking radar and laser-weapons technology. China is in the process of modernizing its military in all those areas, and thus the question is the degree to which the alleged activities advanced the timetable for Beijing's obtaining those capabilities. Whatever technology it has gained has only begun to show up in new military capabilities. It is likely to be as much as two decades before the fruits of its efforts to acquire American technology are fully evident.

Regardless of the degree to which the Cox report may have reached conclusions based on conjecture and unproven assumptions, many of its recommendations make sense. Strengthening counterintelligence efforts and toughening export controls are two good illustrations. In regard to export controls, particularly on computers, dual-use technology creates a continually difficult problem, as the pace of change in the electronics industry far outpaces changes in government regulations.

The principle that has guided export controls since the Cold War ended and dual-use technology has become substantially more widespread and can be expressed as "higher fences around fewer goods." Because China is a major importer of U.S. computer equipment, high-end machine tools, and semiconductor manufacturing equipment, it has taken center stage in what is a long-standing debate. The steady increase in standard computing power has led the U.S. government to reduce the number of licenses required for exports. For example, from 1996 to 1998, of the 450 high-performance computers that China purchased from U.S. firms, most were purchased without any export licenses.[12]

At present, all U.S. sales to China of computers that operate at more than 7,000 million theoretical operations per second (MTOPS) require export licenses. Sales to the PRC military require an export license for computers in the 2,000–7,000 MTOPS range. Industry experts argue that the rate of change has overtaken government regulations. It has been an axiom in Silicon Valley that each generation of computer chips has a life span of about 18 months. Off-the-shelf PCs now use Pentium 3, and Apple's PC Powerchip already operates in the range of 2,000 MTOPS range; Intel's next-generation chip, likely on the market in 2000, will be around 2,600 MTOPS. Moreover, U.S. industry argues that there are 25 or more non-American firms that can now build advanced computers that compete for the high-end business in China.[13]

Setting export controls is a judgment that should be made with a bias toward national security by means of an interagency process in which military and commercial considerations are weighed and balanced. Ambiguity is a factor here as well. Export controls are more likely to be effective if they are multilateral. But the system of Cold War controls (COCOM), by which the United States could veto allies' exports, is gone, and China is not viewed as a security threat the way the Soviet Union was. Industrialized democracies have not been able to reach consensus on an effective replacement for COCOM. If there are advanced supercomputers or other technologies for which there are no alternative suppliers, Washington should deny the licenses for export to China. The diffusion of technology in an information age is something that can be deferred—albeit with increasing difficulty—but is unlikely to be ultimately denied. Nonetheless, buying time to maintain U.S. strategic advantage is a reasonable security objective. But the whole issue highlights the absurdity of President Clinton's talking of building a "strategic partnership" with China. If the message to the U.S. bureaucracy from the top is partnership, that hardly sends a message of caution on sharing science and technology with China.

Dilemmas of Modernization

The dilemmas of strategic trade highlight the ambiguity that necessarily characterizes Sino-American relations. There is a long list of positive developments in the daily lives of Chinese citizens. Yet there is an equally long list of political repression (crackdowns on such groups as the Daoist-Buddhist movement Falun Gong) and endemic corruption. The latter is so pervasive that approximately $14 billion, some 20 percent of China's national tax revenues, was unaccounted for in 1998. Some 1,000 local judges were dismissed in late 1999.[14] While the outcome of China's historic transformation is uncertain, and is likely to remain so for another generation, U.S. policy must be made on current perceptions of national interest. As Beijing is betting on reform and the global economy to secure its future, the Clinton administration, as did its predecessors, is also betting that the economic, social, and ultimately, political forces unleashed by China's reform and opening policies will have a positive impact on its international behavior. China will modernize regardless of U.S. policy. It is a process that Washington cannot control—or even influence—except at the margins.

The trajectory of China's reforms and the country's integration into the global economy have meant an unprecedented social and economic transformation. China has maintained its Leninist political system by striking a de facto new social bargain: the regime tolerates a modicum of individual freedom so long as it remains outside the political realm. There has been a steady trend toward shrinking the domain of the state in people's daily lives. The role of the *danwei* (work unit) in controlling the fate of many Chinese has radically diminished. Chinese can now choose where to go to school, where to work, and what music to listen to; they have access to many international publications and have formed hundreds of nongovernmental organizations; more than 13 million Chinese have mobile phones and some 10 million have access to the Internet. Internet use in China is projected to grow to 33 million by 2003.[15] Chinese citizens can and do sue the government. The new China is filled with talk radio, faxes, and a fledgling legal system—all of which are tolerated because they are necessary for economic modernization. Yet those developments also signify the beginnings of a civil society.

Former Chinese dissident Minxin Pei, now a senior fellow at the Carnegie Endowment for International Peace, has argued that economic and civil rights must be factored into the equation of human rights progress. Pei points out that, since 1979, internal travel, choice of residence, autonomous civic organizations, and perhaps, most important, access to information have expanded greatly. There are now almost seven times as many newspapers and magazines in China (over 8,000) as there were in 1978 (1,116), and whereas only one in 300 Chinese had a television in 1978, now it is one in five.[16] Some 100 million Chinese also have access to satellite dishes bringing in CNN, MTV, and other foreign stations.

Trade and Human Rights

Those developments are an inevitable consequence of China's modernization. Deng dismissed the dilemmas of economic reform for the CCP with his folksy line, "When you open the window, some flies come in." The implication was, of course, that the flies were merely a minor nuisance that could be tolerated. Nonetheless, the path China has chosen necessarily sets in motion new social forces, including new strata of entrepreneurs, technicians, professionals, and intellectuals—the beginnings of a Chinese middle class. Other East Asian countries—the Philippines, Thailand, South Korea, Taiwan—began to democratize when their middle classes reached a kind of critical mass and demanded more accountable government. One analyst argued that recent experience suggests that, when per capita annual income goes above $6,000, democratization tends to occur, and he predicts that China will become a democracy by 2015.[17]

Yet it is not enough to say that commerce produces openness, which leads to a middle class, which leads to democracy, which results in China's becoming a benign international actor. Repression—the absence of tolerance of any political parties or even dissident movements—continues alongside the greater personal freedoms in the new China. Moreover, one can even envision a democratic China invading Taiwan if the latter declared formal independence or a democratic China acting counter to U.S. interests in Korea or elsewhere in the world.

It is, however, plausible that expanding Western trade and investment in China opens up social space that might otherwise be occupied by the state. That could justify a more effective, if lower-profile, U.S. human rights policy. Instead of merely focusing on the pressure of summits and other events to obtain the release of celebrity dissidents, a less glamorous—but a more long-term—approach would be to concentrate on bolstering the new social forces from within rather than seeking to impose policies from without. For example, the International Republican Institute has quietly assisted China in holding village elections, which now occur in tens of thousands of villages across China. Other examples might include helping build legal curricula in Chinese universities, training lawyers and judges, and broadening the exposure of China's parliament, which has become increasingly less "rubber stamp" in recent years. Such measures, along with the usual quiet diplomacy, could pay long-term dividends. And while it would overstate the case to say that trade alone promotes human rights, the expansion of trade and investment is certainly a factor affecting social change in China. In addition, trade is improving China's grudging and inconsistent, yet gradually increasing, adherence to international norms of behavior. A group of scholars at Georgetown University Law Center compiled a scorecard of China's compliance with its obligations in a range of international regimes—economic, security, and environmental—and found a mixed record, but not one that would conclude that China dismisses agreements as mere sheets of paper.[18]

China is in the midst of unprecedented transformations in every respect except, thus far, that of its political system, which, unlike economic reform, demographic and social change, and cultural norms, has remained static, controlled by an elite. China faces enormous challenges as it seeks to consolidate a post-Deng leadership. Those challenges include redefining relations between Beijing and the regions of China, reforming state industries and the banking system, reducing the coastal-interior disparity in economic growth and incomes, and moving beyond widespread corruption to a rule of law system. How China meets those challenges will affect the legitimacy of the CCP, and that legitimacy issue will likely increase the role of nationalism in China's foreign relations.

There are at least four plausible futures for China, each with varying implications for East Asia. The best-case outcome is that China will continue its long march of reform toward some type of constitutionalism or rule-of-law-based system with Chinese characteristics. Another possible direction (in which some current trends point) is a renewed corporatist authoritarianism facilitated by nationalist appeal. A third scenario is a degeneration into a loose coalition of regional neo-warlords. The final possibility is a variant of the first two, what Robert Scalapino, dean of U.S. Asia scholars and professor emeritus at the University of California-Berkeley, has dubbed, "authoritarian pluralism," incorporating some aspects of rule of law with an authoritarian, collectivist state. Regardless of which future China embraces, there will be some measure of nationalism inherent in China's international behavior. Some analysts suggest that China may be evolving not toward the mechanistic free-market, middle-class, political pluralism model as seen elsewhere in East Asia but rather toward a corporatist rent-seeking economy that may gravitate toward an authoritarian posture.[19]

Even if it is democratic, popular nationalism can be an unwieldy force. One may recall a young democracy nearly 180 years ago, declaring its dominance over an entire hemisphere by proclaiming the Monroe Doctrine. But a more accountable regime in China would certainly have a significant impact on U.S. and Japanese policies toward Beijing. It is important to note that virtually all of the disputes that have triggered fears about Chinese behavior involve territory historically Chinese or part of a suzerainty system—Hong Kong, Taiwan, Tibet, for example—severed by Western imperial powers over the past 150 years—a brief moment in five thousand years of Chinese history.

Conclusion

Where does this leave U.S.-Chinese relations? It leaves them with significantly less common ground than the illusionary Clinton rhetoric about a "strategic partnership" would suggest but with enough to muddle through to a scaled-back relationship if both sides act on enlightened self-interest. The economic component of the relationship is a key factor. China's top priority is economic modernization. For that it needs U.S. markets (we consume 40 percent of China's exports), investment, and technology. It is no accident that what appears most active in the U.S.-Chinese relationship is the WTO talks. China needs to avoid conflict with the United States for the short- to medium-term, whatever its ultimate intentions. China is an important emerging market, a nuclear-weapons state, a permanent U.N. Security Council member, and a key power in Asia. It can and will play a spoiler role—whether on Kosovo or Korea—absent a modicum of cooperation.

Both sides are certain to be dissatisfied with a relationship in which each one's intentions remain ambiguous for the foreseeable future. The discomfiting reality is that China defies our comfortable stereotypes. It is in the midst of a social and economic transformation whose outcome remains uncertain. For every political opponent jailed, 100 more Chinese students may be gaining access to the Internet or getting degrees in business management. Beijing may be modernizing its arsenal, but it also joins the NPT and the CTBT. Its markets are opening, albeit grudgingly. We will likely have to live for a generation with an ambiguous China—a China that is neither ally nor enemy, that does not have a black or white hat but one with only shades of gray.

The challenge is to foster a new realism in which the minimal needs of both countries are met, expectations are lowered, and results, however modest, gradually build a more stable relationship. It is a relationship that must be rebuilt, brick by brick. Each side will measure the other's intentions by its respective behavior and the degree to which it meets the minimum necessary interests of both parties. That means avoiding the temptation on the Chinese side to fan the flames of aggrieved nationalism and on the U.S. side to minimize playing the "China card," as Clinton did to President Bush in 1992. The danger is that the many irritants on both sides outweigh the benefits, and we will then drift toward confrontation.

Whether the necessary degree of maturity and forbearance on both sides is possible remains an open question.

The three sets of issues—trade, security, and human rights—could, if understandings were reached on all, create the basis for a stable Sino-American relationship, which, in turn, consists of three pillars. The first pillar of that relationship is strategic, including nuclear weapons and missile defense. China is the only declared nuclear-weapons state increasing—and modernizing—its arsenal. While its arsenal of 350 to 400 weapons is modest compared with those of the United States and Russia, the trend is cause for concern. As the United States and Russia build down to 2,000 warheads, suggested in START 3—or still lower numbers suggested by Moscow—there must be a connection between the floor of our builddown and the ceiling of China's modernization. Whether China becomes an adversary or remains merely an ambiguous great power is the essence of a strategic relationship. Decisions taken by the United States and its allies on the deployment of missile defenses—particularly those capable of neutralizing Beijing's strategic weapons—now fewer than two dozen but possibly will be 200 or more by 2010–15, also will be important. The United States has yet to begin a serious discussion on testing China's willingness to limit its nuclear modernization program if the United States and Russia agree to continue their nuclear builddown and at least discuss missile defense.

The second pillar is the commercial and financial relationship, which is closest to an understanding. China's accession to the WTO will be a significant step forward in that area. The third pillar is our respective political and military postures in the Asia-Pacific region. That includes managing the Taiwan problem. China must accept that the United States will remain a Pacific power—whether from forward bases in Japan and Korea or from Guam and Hawaii—with emerging military technologies offering new ways to project force (e.g., arsenal ships, floating bases). At the same time, the United States will have to accommodate China's having a much larger geopolitical footprint in Asia. The visions of the future articulated by the United States in the Pentagon's *U.S. Security Strategy for the East Asia-Pacific Region* and by China in its 1998 *China's National Defense* are incompatible. Washington insists that U.S. alliances are the cornerstone of peace and stability; Beijing says they are sources of distrust and instability.[20] How the issues of Taiwan and the reunification of Korea are managed will likely determine the degree to which the United States and China can find a modus vivendi in the Pacific.

The importance of these three pillars is not intended to exclude human rights as important in the Sino-American relationship. However, progress in human rights is a matter for rhetoric and constant, if subtle, pressure. But in a complex, multifaceted relationship like the Sino-American bilateral relationship, understandings in those three broad areas would render the other elements of the relationship far more manageable.

The policy approach outlined above is one of sustained interaction, not efforts to isolate or halt China's inevitable modernization. It is one of patience, not instant gratification; one of subtlety, not unnecessary confrontation. It requires a businesslike stance, not demonization, condescension, or unreciprocated accommodation. As long as China maintains a one-party political monopoly and an authoritarian party-state, there will be tensions over human rights. But the approach outlined in this chapter reflects an underlying confidence that an information-age economy cannot be sustained without a comparably open political system. Political Leninism and economic *dirigisme* are not the waves of the future. The approach reflects a confidence in the universal aspects of Western values. That confidence grows out of the experience, noted above, of East Asia over the past quarter-century. East Asia is experiencing tremendous economic dynamism and multitiered growth. As Japan took off economically, it pulled along the four Newly Industrialized Economies: Hong Kong, Taiwan, South Korea, and Singapore. Japan and the NIEs are now pulling along the NIEs of the 21st century: Indonesia, Malaysia, and Thailand. That economic pattern of horizontal integration has fostered a burgeoning urban middle class, which, in turn, has led to political pluralism. Taiwan, South Korea, and Thailand have seen democracy triumph. In a sense, the demonstrations in Tiananmen Square were an effort by emerging social forces created by economic reform to assert themselves politically.

The driving force in shaping China's future is economics. In November 1997 the CCP's Central Committee Plenum decided to accelerate economic reforms by beginning to privatize the more than 300,000 state-owned industries, most of which are not profit making, and by adopting banking and tax reform. Roughly half of China's economy is already privatized. Political reform can not be deferred indefinitely. Indeed, the logic of the current wave of China's reforms—breaking the "iron rice bowl"—begins to raise the question in the minds of some Chinese of why a communist party is needed at all. The key questions are whether the forces of geoeconomics will shape geopolitics in China's international behavior and whether economic growth will foster a parallel political transformation. If China is seen as adversarial on certain issues, it should be seen that way not because of miscalculation and the law of unintended consequences but because all reasonable efforts to forge cooperative relations have been exhausted.

Notes

1. See Zalmay Khalilzad, *The United States and a Rising China* (Santa Monica, Calif.: RAND Corporation, 1999).

2. Samuel R. Berger, Assistant to the President for National Security Affairs, "Remarks to the Council on Foreign Relations," June 6, 1997, http://www.whitehouse.gov/WH/EOP/NSC/html/speeches/srb060697.html.

3. William Jefferson Clinton, "On China and the National Interest," Voice of America, White House Press Office, October 24, 1997.

4. Democratic Policy Committee, "Special Report: China MFN Status," U.S. Senate, May 3, 1994.

5. For a detailed history of the Jackson-Vanik Amendment, see Paula Stern, *Water's Edge: Domestic Politics and the Making of U.S. Foreign Policy* (New York: Greenwood, 1979).

6. See Nicholas Lardy, "Normalizing Economic Relations with China," in *Promoting U.S. Interests in China: Alternatives to the Annual MFN Review National*, NBR Analysis, vol. 8, no. 4 (Seattle, Wash.: National Bureau of Asian Research, July 1997), pp. 15–21.

7. See Nicholas Lardy, *China's Unfinished Revolution* (Washington: Brookings Institution, 1999), for a detailed assessment of China's financial foibles.

8. For a discussion of estimates of the impact of China's WTO accession on U.S.-Chinese trade, see Daniel H. Rosen, "China and the World Trade Organization: An Economic Balance Sheet," Briefing, Institute for International Economics Policy, June 1999; see also Mark W. Frasier, "Coming to Terms with the 'WTO Effect' on U.S.-China Trade," National Bureau of Asian Research, NBR Briefing, September 1999.

9. U.S. House of Representatives, *Report of the Select Committee on U.S. National Security and Military/Commercial Concerns with the People's Republic of China*, 3 vols., 105th Cong., 2d sess., 1999, H. Rept. 105-851.

10. See Lars-Erik Nelson, "Washington: The Yellow Peril," *New York Review of Books*, July 15, 1999, pp. 6-10, for a thoughtful, skeptical view of the spying episode.

11. William J. Broad, "Spies vs. Sweat: The Debate over China's Nuclear Advance," *New York Times*, September 7, 1999, p. A1.

12. See Bruce Stokes, "Lethal Exports," *National Journal* 31, no. 22 (May 29, 1999): 1473–75.

13. Ibid.

14. See "$14 Billion in Revenues Missing from Treasury," *Financial Times*, September 15, 1999; and "Beijing Fires 1,000 Judges," *South China Morning Post*, October 16, 1999, for item on judges.

15. Mark Landler," In China, Visions of Internet Riches in a PC Short Land," *New York Times*, December 23, 1999, p. C1.

16. See Minxin Pei, "Here's Evidence of a Kindler, Gentler China," *Asian Wall Street Journal*, March 30, 1994.

17. See Henry S. Rowan, "The Short March: China's Road to Democracy," *National Interest*, no. 57 (Fall 1996): 61–70.

18. Cited in Rosen.

19. See David Zweig, "China's Undemocratic Capitalism, *National Interest*, no. 56 (Summer 1999): 63–72.

20. *China's National Defense* (Beijing: Information Office of the State Council, July 1998); and Office of the Secretary of Defense, *U.S. Security Strategy for the East Asia-Pacific Region*, November 1998.

12. Trading with China? Balancing Free Trade with National Security

Stefan Halper

The end of the Cold War ushered in a decadelong slide in the public's interest in international affairs. Even the Clinton administration's rapid-fire deployments of U.S. troops in Haiti, Bosnia, and Kosovo failed to bring sustained, nationwide interest in international security. All that abruptly changed, however, in 1998–99 when China, espionage, money, trade and politics combined to spice an otherwise bland pudding.

In his new book, *A Great Wall: Six Presidents and China: An Investigative History*,[1] Patrick Tyler illustrates the complex interaction among various factors: perception and fact, domestic opinion and ideology, ethics and expedience, and the pull of China's market, which has characterized our China policy. Each postwar president has emphasized different aspects of the China relationship, but consistent throughout has been the view that if the security issues could be stabilized, China could be America's greatest potential market—a market insatiable for U.S. goods and services, especially technology and investment.

That vision seems to have entranced the Clinton administration, in particular, after a brief show of Sinophobia during the 1992 election campaign. While Chinese authorities were steadily pursuing their quarter-century-old strategy of acquiring the means—licitly or illicitly—to build a modern military force in order to become the dominant power in Asia, President Clinton and his advisers, disregarding warnings from more experienced analysts, relaxed the old standards of export controls and replaced them with a neo-laissez-faire regime that allowed Beijing to have what it wanted.

The consequences of that reckless approach to national security are only now becoming clear. Historically, trade and export policies were not seen through the national security lens. In fact, government officials and others concerned with those questions often found themselves on the periphery of both the trade and national security communities. But in the latter Cold War years, decisionmakers sharpened their focus on the military and strategic dimensions of technology transfer decisions and export policy. That set of issues, paired with several high-profile counterintelligence failures, has convulsed the U.S.-Chinese relationship from 1998 to the present.

This chapter explores how the damage was done, the extent of that damage, and the consequences to U.S. national security. How to approach trade with China in the future is also discussed. This is neither an anti-trade screed nor a portrayal of China as an evil empire intent on our destruction. But it does assert that the two nations have profound differences, that those differences will remain, and that China may use its newly acquired military muscle in ways that are not in this nation's interest.

Old and New Illusions about China

With the end of the Cold War and the demise of the Soviet Union, many, if not most, in the West felt that a new age had dawned in which nations would, at last, pursue their rational interests untainted by ideology and do so within an international architecture inclined to peace and economic growth. Unhappily, that blessed state of affairs is more elusive than had been expected; it has proven our complacency ill founded and the hoped-for new order a mirage. Thus, it is worthwhile to revisit the nexus where export policy and security join, particularly in relation to China—a country whose national ambitions remain large and unfulfilled.

If there has been a consensus over the last decade within the American foreign policy establishment—government officials, think tank experts, business leaders—it is this: China has abandoned Marxism-Leninism and is committed to market-driven growth as understood in the West. Moreover, it is also believed by those in U.S. foreign policy that trading with a former adversary bears little or no risk and that restrictions on free trade should be minimal if not absent. The scrapping in March 1994 of the Coordinating Committee (COCOM), the 16-nation association of NATO members plus Japan that decided which technology could not be safely traded to potential adversaries of the West, was eagerly sought and secured by U.S. commercial interests. They found a friend in the Clinton administration, which saw an opportunity to bolster its political coffers while promoting the umbrella idea that a liberalized trading system was the most effective engine for the global market and democratic growth.

For China, those developments were particularly significant. The China market, of course, has lured the West since caravans following the Silk Route reached Cathay and the Portuguese first found their way to Asia by sea early in the 16th century. Nineteenth-century investors in the British Midlands were animated by the notion that "adding an inch to each China man's smock would keep the mills of Leicester running forever." A century later, Yankee traders would follow the same will-o'-the-wisp. The "endless market" inspired America's first foreign policy doctrine in Asia: Secretary of State John Hay's "Open Door" policy, a high-minded statement that sought an American share of the China trade through diplomacy, just as the European powers through arms might have extracted concessions from China's tottering imperial government.

The Chinese market kept its allure for many Americans, despite Japanese military occupation of China, civil war, and, finally, the Communist conquest in 1949. With the death of Mao Zedong in 1976, four years after Richard Nixon's dramatic trip to Beijing, China's new leader, Deng Xiaoping, gradually returned the country to quasi-normality after nearly two decades of Mao-led economic and political insanity. Deng's announcement that "getting rich was glorious" signaled to many American business leaders that China was open for business on capitalist terms. The Middle Kingdom, with its 1.2 billion-person market, was ready and eager to absorb the outer world's goods and technology it so badly needed for rapid modernization. And no one was better placed or more eager than Americans to do just that.

Trading with China had bipartisan support during the Republican administrations of the 1980s. For many business, government, and academic elites, it was a unique—even serendipitous—moment. As the West prospered from the greatest pent-up demand in history, China would edge further toward capitalism. Its slowly emerging middle class would develop a taste for fashion, consumer goods, travel, and hitherto forbidden Western entertainment, along with the individual rights characteristic of the more mature bourgeois democracies. That such progress would be difficult and uneven was accepted—and brutally demonstrated by the events at Tiananmen

Square in June 1989. But Sinophiles looked to the silver lining, arguing that the demonstrations revealed Beijing's gerontocracy was fragile, its days numbered. The Sinophiles asserted that democracy almost always follows the market—that China's expanding market made democracy inevitable and that China should be seen as a "strategic partner," anchoring the region's stability. Meanwhile, among the high-tech exporting community—both government and corporate—the mantra was "on with the business of business."

China's Actions and America's Interests

In retrospect, the only amazing part about all this is how long it has taken for challenges to those facile assumptions to gain traction. Those challenges have happened only in the wake of China's sharp and calculated hostility toward Taiwan; its brutal and very public crackdown on religious groups, dissidents, and Internet users; its secret arms sales to Southwest Asia and the Middle East; and its not-so-secret espionage efforts in the United States.

Clearly, we have not entered a new era in which geopolitical rivalries no longer exist. Contrary to the naive expectations of some observers in the immediate post–Cold War era, certain former adversaries have not become allies or partners, strategic or otherwise. What has changed is the context of the U.S.-Chinese relationship. The collapse of the Soviet system lifted the restraints that kept less emotional but compelling issues—such as Taiwan's status, military modernization, and U.S. regional military presence—from driving the relationship. And so we can expect differences that had been drawn in pastels to emerge now in primary colors.

Although Marxism as an ideology is waning, it retains in China a strong functional role as both a "legitimizing" theory of state and an organizational tool. Indeed, many people within the Chinese hierarchy still profess loyalty to the Chinese Communist Party and cling grimly to its credo of class warfare and unyielding international struggle with the capitalist world. The party is also an easily understood bulwark against chaos, a widespread fear that many foreign observers feel unreasonably haunts the Chinese psyche. In fact, fear of dismemberment—for example, an independent Taiwan or Tibet, insurrection from Uighars (Muslim separatists), or disruption from sects like the Falun Gong—has stiffened the party and its conservative supporters. One result of such paranoia has been new questions about the wisdom of Premier Zhu Rongji's market-led growth policies and accompanying social liberalization—although likely normal trade relations (NTR) and World Trade Organization agreements with the United States and the People's Republic of China have dampened that danger for the time being.

As the remaining Mao-era leaders fade into history, the easy assumption is that China's growing market sector will bring political pluralism, with respect for freedoms, and lead to a benign China whose international behavior is rooted in rationality and cooperation. That assumption is simply not warranted. Even if the regime's Marxism-Leninism were to abate, it does not follow that all—or even most—differences with Washington would ameliorate with Western goodwill.[2]

Indeed, the Chinese leadership, increasingly confident in recent years, is apparently driven by a vision that, while seeking to avoid conflict with the West (over Taiwan or the Spratly islands, for example), does not rule out conflict. That vision will remain unchanged even if Marxism is repudiated. Chinese territorial ambitions led to military clashes with India, Russia, and Vietnam during the communist era. Those ambitions have also produced tensions with six other nations that claim the Spratly islands, on which the PRC has placed military units. Moreover, the clash of Chinese and Western interests extends beyond the obvious regional hot spots to include functional matters—intellectual property, missile and arms sales, human rights, and trade issues. Beijing's increased reliance on military technology, its renewed regional ambitions, the high cost of research and development (essential preconditions for military modernization), and strategic competition with the United States create a potent recipe for tension. There is little doubt that individuals associated with Chinese intelligence stole nuclear technology from the Los Alamos National Laboratory. Furthermore, according to the Central Intelligence Agency, most of China's major weapons systems now contain technology illicitly acquired from the United States. As a policy matter, it seems clear that China will steal what it chooses not to buy—often not a hard decision, as the economic cost of theft has been, until now, quite reasonable. Thus, the most pressing threat to the United States is not anything so crude as a decision by Beijing to foster world revolution under the banner of Mao henchman Lin Biao's old slogans about the Second and Third Worlds' eventually exterminating the First. Rather, the threat is that Beijing, reflecting Lenin's axiom that capitalists will sell the rope that will be used to hang them, will either steal or purchase militarily useful technology that will alter the balance of regional security in ways adverse to U.S. commercial and security interests.

Specific objectives in that category include China's goals of reclaiming its self-styled runaway province, Taiwan, by use of force if necessary, and of becoming Asia's hegemonic power. Although one might question the viability of those goals, and the extent of their impact on American interests, they are rational from Beijing's perspective. They also represent current Chinese foreign policy doctrine. That there are differences between China's calculations and U.S. requirements should come as no surprise, and the fact that the two nations have clearly diverging interests can no longer be ignored. That reality suggests that the Clinton administration's "strategic partnership" needs to be replaced with "strategic engagement" or something similar.

Does that mean China should be isolated—kept out of the WTO, for example? Certainly not. WTO membership will sustain China's market development and benefit American exporters, both legitimate objectives of U.S. policy. U.S. Trade Representative Charlene Barshefsky reached agreements in Beijing in the fall of 1999 that sustained the process of opening closed economic sectors, including finance and insurance, and of eliminating state subsidies that undercut foreign competition in other areas. These agreements are now before Congress for approval. More broadly, however, certain questions remain: What can we safely export to China and what can we not? How has U.S. technology now used in Chinese strategic systems (miniaturization, nuclear and satellite technology, missiles, and lenses) been deployed? How does such a development threaten the interests of the United States and its allies? How can export controls be reconstituted and applied?

Espionage always makes headlines, but shock at China's espionage efforts in the United States is naive at best and all too often leads to the wrong conclusions. Instead of expressing surprise at China's attempts to steal American military secrets, we should be concerned about the inadequate security at U.S. facilities—and the bungled investigation that followed the discovery of wrongdoing.

There is now little question that China painstakingly established in the United States an elaborate technology acquisition process focusing on strategic weapons systems, especially land- and sea-based intercontinental ballistic missiles (ICBMs). The Chinese effort is multidimensional and broad based, involving over 1,000 front companies registered in the United States and generally unknown to U.S. business leaders as Chinese owned.

Former U.S. ambassador to China James Lilley points out that Chinese "Ministry of State Security operatives, and others who became U.S. agents in recent years, stated that the penetration of the Labs and acquisition of nuclear and related military technologies were a top priority of their military and industrial intelligence apparatus."[3] Beijing's intelligence agents had been photographed pocketing videos of military technology at conferences, caught dipping their ties into chemical solutions so that secret formulas could be analyzed later, observed attempting to purchase classified spare parts, and stopped from exporting high-performance computers through U.S.-registered front companies to the People's Liberation Army.

That Beijing has penetrated our national weapons laboratories is now known thanks to the prodigious labor of the bipartisan Cox committee and other sources. One preliminary conclusion offered by the CIA is that the compromised warhead design data and satellite-based guidance technology systems could, within the next decade, increase China's strategic threat to the continental United States.[4]

While China's culpability is clear, the major responsibility for our laxness rests not on Beijing's shoulders but on ours, and, more precisely, with those government officials sworn to protect the nation's secrets. We have no final assessment of those guilty of dereliction, but it is increasingly apparent that the national weapons laboratories as well as the U.S. Department of Energy that monitors them, have been at fault. The most serious lapse, however, is found at the U.S. Department of Justice, whose senior officials have reacted to evidence of illegal Chinese activity in catatonic fashion—a pattern of response that has become familiar throughout the Clinton administration. At this point the highest priority should be a thorough investigation of what went wrong and why and what can be done about it. Punishing midlevel officials, the typical modus operandi in these situations (and something that is occurring at present), simply will not do.

The Clinton Administration's Approach to Trade with China

How did this serious breach of national security come about? Neither the answer nor the solution is simple. The problem did not arise simply with the advent of the Clinton presidency, which promised one policy on China during the 1992 campaign and delivered another once in office. But before exploring the switch in policy and its consequences, it would be useful to outline what had been trade policy with China before the Clinton administration.

Following the romanticism that characterized Sino-American policy in the Nixon and Carter years, during which full diplomatic relations were established and a sense of strategic partnership vis-à-vis the Soviet Union prevailed, the early years of the Reagan presidency reflected caution. Washington had more limited expectations in what the Sino-American relationship would yield in terms of progress on intellectual property rights, human rights, proliferation questions, arms sales, and market access for U.S. goods—although cooperation on intelligence, aimed entirely at Moscow, continued as before. In trade, there was general agreement among the Reaganites: commerce should be encouraged, but not all goods were for sale. James Mann, in his book *About Face*, makes the broader point that the economic relationship was sensitive to and largely conditional on China's good behavior—for example, toward Taiwan, whose prosperity and security were long an idée fixe of Ronald Reagan.[5]

Nevertheless, beginning in 1983, in response to pressure from such U.S. exporters as IBM and Boeing, some export controls were relaxed on high-tech products, including dual-use goods, items that were not available to the Soviet Union and its satellites. Despite Chinese pressure, however, decisions were made on a case-by-case basis, which meant that each sale was scrutinized by the U.S. Departments of State, Defense, and Commerce. Guidance was sought from the CIA on dual-use exports whose final destinations were questionable. Decisions could be, and often were, appealed to the National Security Council, which ensured that pressure from interest groups directed at one of the involved agencies was not decisive.

A year later, in 1984, the Reagan administration also allowed, for the first time, direct military sales of selected weapons systems to the Chinese. That materiel included torpedoes, artillery ammunition, radar, helicopters, and the equipment needed for the wholesale modernization of Chinese military jets. That project, code-named

Peace Pearl, ended when the F-8 upgrade kits failed to turn a "Model T" into a modern car—to the chagrin and frustration of both governments.

The purpose of all of this was perfectly clear: to upgrade China's military capability to help counter the Soviet threat. China may have been a looming giant in the eyes of some gazing at the 21st century, but in the early 1980s nearly all reputable geostrategic analysts considered Beijing, compared with both the United States and the USSR, a military Pygmy. This was also, of course, Moscow's view.

For Taiwan, however, Washington's longer-term intentions were not so clear. Although the United States remained faithful to its obligations under the Taiwan Relations Act to ensure Taiwan's capability to defend itself, it seemed at times—on both sides of the Pacific—that the United States was overly solicitous of its new "strategic partner" and less responsive to Taipei's expressed military needs. Throughout that decade a rough, often contentious military balance was maintained between the PRC and Taiwan.

Nineteen eighty-nine, however, was a fateful year: two events put an end to that geopolitically driven policy. While the accelerating collapse of the Soviet Union removed the strategic rationale that had anchored the Washington-Beijing relationship, the events on June 4 in Tiananmen Square triggered an immediate freeze on weapons sales. The freeze banned the purchase of two aircraft built by Hughes Electronics Corporation—a decision that would remain in place through the Bush presidency and the end of Clinton's first term. Bush imposed a further Tiananmen penalty: when the CIA uncovered evidence of Beijing's sale of M-11 rocket launchers to Pakistan, U.S. sales to China of supercomputers and satellite components were also forbidden.

President Bush would be criticized by many people as being too soft on China, especially after Tiananmen Square, but the record shows that he took a relatively cautious approach to Beijing when it came to the sale of goods that could potentially involve national security. In fact, President Bush's post-Tiananmen attempts to reenergize the U.S.-Chinese relationship brought little diplomatic progress but much controversy, rendering him vulnerable to Clinton's criticism in the 1992 campaign.

Clinton chose first to attack Bush's China policy of constructive engagement from the left. Clinton loudly denounced the Bush administration's alleged disinterest in human rights and its apparent willingness to conduct "business as usual" with Beijing. In his acceptance speech at the Democratic National Convention Clinton promised that he would never "coddle dictators from Baghdad to Beijing."[6] The alliteration was nice, but specifics were few. Clinton hinted at various times in public that China's most favored nation (MFN) trade status was in serious danger and said that Bush's extension of MFN to China in June 1992 was "unconscionable."

One would have concluded that, at a minimum, a Clinton-led government would attach severe conditions for continuing China's prized MFN status, conditions that would have included tough standards on human rights, as the Democratic candidate himself had suggested. As to the question of whether to sell goods with military applications to China, Clinton's public emphasis on nonproliferation seemed to make that answer a foregone conclusion, particularly after Governor Clinton's December 1991 foreign policy speech at Georgetown University in which he attacked Bush from the right, denouncing the administration's "irresponsible export of nuclear and missile technology."[7]

But as the nation would learn, all was not what it seemed when it came to Bill Clinton. In fact, Clinton, once in the Oval Office, would soon show that past policy pronouncements were designed largely for their political effect rather than for any real indication of what he would do in the future. From the record, it is now abundantly clear that U.S. national security interests were not a major priority, perhaps not a priority at all, in trade control decisions. The domestic political calculus, in fact, drove the entire foreign policy agenda.

Eight months after assuming office, President Clinton would spell out his real views on trade policy with China in a letter to Edward McCracken, CEO of Silicon Graphics, a high-tech firm in Silicon Valley. McCracken, like other New Age entrepreneurs, was a strong supporter of the Clinton campaign, and part of that support included giving the Democrats what they most needed (and because of their two-decade love affair with McGovernism long lacked): cash.

Reflecting the quid pro quo, the president outlined in his letter to McCracken what he was going to do about the problem of export controls. Although the president never mentions China by name, the thrust of his new policy is apparent. "We will continue to need strong controls to combat the growing threat of proliferation of weapons of mass destruction and dangerous conventional weapons, as well as to send a strong signal to countries that support international terrorism. *But* we also need to make long overdue reforms to ensure that we do not unfairly and unnecessarily burden our important commercial interests."[8]

This remarkable paragraph combines the lead sentence, which restates Clinton's public campaign stance, with a second, which says something entirely new. More important, as those who have crafted such statements know, the first serves as rhetorical cover for the second, operative statement—namely, that export controls would be lifted in the near future.

In fact, the president went on to outline his thoughts. He told McCracken, for example, that an interagency review of export controls would finish at the end of the month. Then Clinton, in effect, disclosed what would be recommended, and had already been accepted, by the White House. That was no feat of fortunetelling, since the interagency review was a precooked affair, supervised not by the Pentagon or the State Department but the Commerce Department and its export-promoting chief, Secretary of Commerce Ron Brown, who presided over the Trade Promotion Coordinating Committee. Clinton did mention a National Security Council role in developing these new sets of controls. The NSC, however, acted in this case largely as a rubber stamp for the politically active secretary of commerce. Moreover, the NSC is, as it always has been since its beginnings in the Truman years, a vehicle through which staff members reflect the president's views and serve at his pleasure. It's no wonder, then, that President Clinton could confidently tell his campaign supporter about trade control reforms that would soon be in place.

Clinton outlined those new changes in four broad categories. First, controls on computer and telecommunications would be liberalized. This meant that far more powerful computers could be sold to "free world" countries—a term that remained undefined. Second, time delays in handling export control licenses by the bureaucracy would be reduced. Third, the availability of distribution licenses would be expanded "significantly" for controlled computers so that business executives would not have to return repeatedly to the federal government for permission to export their products. Finally, Clinton promised, those controls that are imposed unilaterally by Washington—which often did result in lost opportunities for American businesses—would be pared back as far as possible.

In raising the question of unilateral controls, the president tipped his hand. Knowing full well that the United States had been virtually alone in guarding Western national security interests within and outside COCOM, any diminution in the willingness to impose restrictions unilaterally would leave the door wide open for selling the most sensitive, militarily relevant technologies to China. Seldom, if ever, have our allies, including Japan, raised concerns about the security implications of technology exports—a fact the president knew only too well.

But Clinton was not quite through. In the same letter to McCracken, he disclosed that the mentioned reforms were only part of the export scheme he had in mind. "Soon," he wrote, "we will complete our review of non-proliferation and export control policy, which will set guidelines for further steps we should take."[9] Further steps? The president continued, "I am also currently engaged in seeking major reforms to COCOM, which should lead to significant liberalization of controls on computers, telecommunications, and machine tools, while establishing a more effective structure for addressing the changing national security threats we will face in the years ahead."[10]

Clinton had more than "major reform" in mind for COCOM, which had during the Cold War served as the chief, albeit imperfect, barrier to the export of sensitive goods and technology to the Soviet Union and other communist countries. Instead of being reformed— or even declawed—COCOM was abolished entirely. That was implemented six months after Clinton had signed his letter to McCracken.

In COCOM's place, the Clinton administration has done little, allowing America's friends and allies in Europe and Japan to do largely as they please in trade with China and other high-risk trade partners—including Iran and Libya. Indeed, there is not even an obligation that the old COCOM members inform each other about what they are selling. That omission gave the Chinese and other high-risk trade partners the freedom to surreptitiously shop around and assemble the various bits and pieces—which separately may be innocent enough—into effective weapons systems.

Controlling Exports, Clinton Style

Naturally, the administration would not characterize its current export control policy as laissez faire on trade with China or other countries. And indeed, the administration's spokesmen have expressed concern about proliferation among rogue countries like Iraq, whose ongoing strategic threat to Israel and other countries brings an added political dimension. What then replaced the COCOM system that over the decades governed the export of militarily useful technology?

Beginning in 1993, the Clinton administration followed a policy of making one move at a time, a strategy that proved highly effective, since its very gradualism drew the least attention possible in an already arcane corner of the policy universe. Replacing COCOM, however, was the first order of the day. But instead of openly dropping the pretense of security controls on exports of arms and dual-use goods and technology, Washington opted for the so-called Wassenaar Agreement, which was signed in Wassenaar, Netherlands, in July 1996. More shadow than substance, and in direct contrast with COCOM, Wassenaar allows its members (33 nations at its birth) to decide individually what is and what is not to be sold on the open market under the "national discretion" clause. Wassenaar also permits its members to report technology transfers after they occur, instead of providing notice before the sale. There are no enforcement capabilities, thus avoiding the need to impose any penalties on those who violate the agreement's lax standards. In addition to the NATO countries plus Japan, Wassenaar members include the Russian Federation and Ukraine, plus a handful of such "neutral" states as Finland, Sweden, and Switzerland. One lone Latin American republic, Argentina, also signed the agreement. Wassenaar does not include such major arms-exporting nations as China and North Korea.

But Wassenaar was only the beginning of the radical undermining of export controls. Over the next three years, the Clinton administration turned its attention to loosening controls on high-performance computers, which have applications in the most sensitive areas of national security, including anti-submarine warfare; nuclear, biological, and chemical warfare; and the so-called C4I—the integrated command, control, communication, and intelligence system that is at the heart of any nation's military complex. During this period,

China received more than 100 high-performance computers, but because the administration eliminated critical reporting requirements and because China prohibits access to users, no one knows exactly how many went or who is using them.

Even before COCOM's demise, the Clinton administration's real, versus rhetorical, approach to trade with China had already become quite clear when William Perry, then secretary of defense, approved the sale of a fiber optics–based telecommunications system, which, in effect, made China's communications traffic secure from outside eavesdropping. That approval was given despite the robust objections of the Joint Chiefs of Staff and the National Security Agency, which is chartered to monitor foreign governments.[11]

In 1996, coincident with Wassenaar, Washington unilaterally lifted controls on the sale of supercomputers, leaving only the most advanced versions subject to licensing arrangements. Most critical of all, the responsibility for identifying the end user for the goods or technology exported switched from the government to the exporter, who often had neither the means for nor an interest in acquiring that information.

One year later, in 1997, telecommunications became the administration's next priority for export liberalization. The Commerce Department created a civil-licensing process, which explicitly declined to inform exporters of the criteria for determining when a civil entity is considered a military end user. During that same period, the administration also liberalized export procedures for satellites and their ground stations, C4I, encryption-manufacturing technology (including fiber optic and microelectronic), and communications-switching technology that allows military commanders to communicate when phone lines are jammed.

Abolishing COCOM allowed those rules to be modified, of course. But multilateral controls, most of which were instigated by the United States, were, in the end, of secondary importance. Of greater impact in gutting national security controls were the ascendancy of the Commerce Department in China trade decisions and the growing exclusion of what had been the lead agency. That instrument of national security was the Pentagon's Defense Technology Security Agency, which had the depth of expertise and the will to thoroughly vet proposed dual-use exports to questionable countries—expertise neither the State Department nor the Commerce Department has ever possessed.[12]

Stephen Bryen, director of the DTSA under Presidents Bush and Reagan, testifying before the Senate Banking Committee, Subcommittee on International Trade and Finance, said: "The export program is in chaos and . . . vital technology is being exported to rival countries, including China. This is leading to significant erosion in the balance of power in the Pacific, which I expect to get worse in the next few years as China converts acquired technology into weapons."[13] Moreover, the sentinels still serving in the DTSA have been pressured to conform to the new laissez-faire policy or face unpleasant bureaucratic consequences—including what appear to be politically motivated security investigations.

The struggles, however, are by no means over. Even as this administration enters its waning months, the battles over controls continue. One such dispute concerns the further liberalization of sales of encryption technology. Far from being a one-shot issue, as is often portrayed in the popular press, the controversy is ongoing because of advancing technology, a factor that, given the fertility of American engineering minds, is not likely to change in the near future.

What modern technology has made possible—far beyond the wildest dreams of code makers even as late as World War II—are computer-generated codes that are difficult, if not impossible, to break. Those codes are now provided on a commercial basis and thus are available to nearly everyone—foreign governments, criminals, and terrorists alike. However, that threat depends entirely on the capabilities of the encryption system, and its security, in turn, depends on the electronic key that decrypts the encoded data. That key, according to a staff memorandum prepared for members of the House Armed Services Committee, is determined by the number of data "bits" in the key. The memorandum continues, "Generally speaking, the longer the key (or number of key bits) the more secure the encryption program and the more difficult it is to 'break the code.'"[14]

The Clinton administration has allowed, again incrementally, sophisticated decryption programs to be made available while transferring supervision of these ultra-high-tech products once again from the State Department to the Commerce Department, where promoting foreign sales remains the overriding priority. Beginning in October 1996, keys of 56 bits were partly decontrolled; they were completely decontrolled two years later. Meanwhile, in June 1997, the sale of encryption software of up to 128 bits was approved provided the encryption was used only for banking and financial transactions. Although defense and law enforcement officials have publicly opposed some of those moves, the administration intends further liberalization.

It has thus become a familiar pattern: Liberalize trade controls while making assurances that there will be adequate safeguards connected to the new regime. Then, after a decent interval, those assurances are quietly shelved.

What Hath Clinton Wrought?

According to Michael Maloof, a highly regarded Defense Department analyst, decontrolled exports have enabled the Chinese military to develop a "nation-wide integrated command, control, communications, computers and intelligence (C4I) system . . . it could not have developed on its own."[15] The encrypted system provides the PLA with a potent instrument for domestic repression, dramatically enhanced military power in the region, and the ability to intercept messages for both military and economic purposes. Maloof adds that, by combining U.S. satellite and ground-station technology (much of it provided by Hughes Electronics Corporation), high-performance computers (many provided by Silicon Graphics), and telecommunications-switching technology (provided, in part, by AT&T), the PLA can now coordinate the movement of its army, navy, and air force by means of encrypted messages that are difficult, if not impossible, for the NSA to decipher.

Easing trade restrictions on high-tech and dual-use products destined for China and eviscerating safeguards that have been in place for a generation are not the only worrisome developments during the long Clinton years. The administration's relaxed view on national security in the post–Cold War era seems to have spread to issues other than technology exports. Recent headlines about Chinese espionage only underscore that point and make a broader one—namely, that there should be no surprise that China or any other country, including otherwise friendly allies such as France, Argentina, Germany, Brazil, India, and Israel, would target the United States for espionage. It should also come as no surprise that the specific targets for espionage these days are largely economic and industrial.

Chinese leaders, like their Soviet counterparts, were convinced that military power rested ultimately on acquiring high technology, most of which could not be produced at home—or if it could, it would come at too high a price. While the U.S. government over the last decade took an increasingly benign, if not lax, attitude about protecting its intellectual property, China and other nations have steadily built up an infrastructure, legally and illegally, to acquire that property.

How China has acquired that ability is now beginning to be understood only in outline. But even in outline, the results are impressive and disturbing. What is known publicly can in large part be attributed to the work of Rep. Curt Weldon (R-Pa.), a senior member of the House Armed Services Committee who has laboriously pieced together information about China's technology acquisition infrastructure. Weldon concludes: "It would have been bad enough if the Clinton-Gore Administration had been merely asleep at the switch—but it's far worse than that. By relaxing controls and export policies, the Clinton-Gore Administration actually assisted China in its efforts. This is a blunder of monumental proportions, and the blame can be laid clearly at the feet of this Administration."[16]

Although it might be tempting to dismiss such claims as partisan rhetoric, Weldon has backed them up with a carefully constructed diagram, "The China Connection," which depicts all of Beijing's state organs and the interconnecting agencies and fronts that make up China's high-tech acquisition apparatus. Despite its complexity, the Weldon chart is not likely to be complete. The web of entities it traces, however, gives us a good idea of how China over the last 25 years has labored to upgrade its military-industrial complex.

Only one example is needed to show how the PRC's strategy works. At the top of the chart is the all-powerful Central Military Commission, which for the last few decades has been the locus of power in China (quite separate from the CCP's politburo). Just below the CMC is the General Staff Department, whose Second Department is the equivalent in Chinese military intelligence to the Soviet's old military intelligence arm, the GRU. The PLA Second Department, in turn, is the connecting link to the China International Trust and Investment Group; that entity is tied to the Asia Satellite Telecommunications Company, which has its headquarters in Hong Kong. Any purchases made, for example, by Asia Satellite would be at the behest ultimately of the CMC and its secretariat in the General Staff Department. This example of the kinds of links among China's principal military and political organs—with front companies operating in Hong Kong, the United States, and elsewhere—could be easily replicated in dozens of other cases.[17]

The upshot is this: with no U.S. government requirement to identify their customers, American corporations do not know the identity of the end user. The Chinese have made access to such knowledge even more difficult by creating, as stated earlier, over 1,000 front companies in the United States. In most cases, ties between those firms and the Beijing government are unknown to the U.S. corporations doing business with them. Sales to those companies, and their reexport of items (often through Canada) to China, now occur regularly and without the licenses that would be required if it was known that the items were for export.

Such indifference is not the only dereliction of duty by current policymakers, however. They have, for example, made a hash of the U.S. nonproliferation policy, which affects not only China but also many other nations, including Iraq, India, and Pakistan. One must be realistic about the inherent limitations of nonproliferation policy, however. Since the days when President Kennedy openly worried about the nuclear club growing to a score or more nations, unrealistic hopes have been attached to the goal of nonproliferation. No matter how good the policy, or how vigorously it is enforced, and no matter the level of cooperation among our allies, weapons of mass destruction cannot forever be kept out of the hands of have-not nations, especially when their leaderships—Iraq's comes to mind— are determined to acquire and deploy nuclear weapons. Deterrence remains America's crucial line of defense. But skill, toughness, and perseverance can delay the spread of such weapons, perhaps even for a significant amount of time, giving the United States and its allies time to build appropriate defenses—for example, against ICBMs.

Those qualities have not been the hallmarks of this administration. Indeed, despite the tough words spoken in his 1992 campaign and early in his first administration, President Clinton has presided over the most relaxed approach to nonproliferation in U.S. history, and that laxness is no more abundantly apparent than in Washington's policy toward China. Once again Representative Weldon has put together a time line that dramatically demonstrates the above observation. According to the congressman's research, there are in a five-year period alone no fewer than 15 cases in which China, in defiance of American law, covertly transferred key U.S. technology to third nations. From mid-1994 to mid-1995, China sold dozens, maybe hundreds, of missile guidance systems and computerized machine tools to Iran. Those actions, among others, may have violated the Iran-Iraq Arms Non-proliferation Act, the Arms Export Control Act, and the Export Administration Act. Yet, four years later, no clear determination has been made, and, of course, no sanctions have been imposed.

In September 1995, Weldon reported, an electromagnetic isotope separation system for uranium enrichment also was sent by Beijing to Tehran, violating similar U.S. laws and agreements. In late 1997, the China Great Wall Industry Corporation sold telemetry equipment to Iran for its Shahab-3 and Shahab-4 medium range ballistic missiles. No sanctions were imposed despite the flouting of similar U.S. laws.[18]

Other militarily ambitious countries, such as Pakistan, have also been the objects of Chinese largesse. For example, in August 1996, U.S. intelligence learned that Beijing had exported an entire plant for the manufacture of M-11 missiles or missile components, once again in violation of the Missile Technology Control Regime, the Arms Export Control Act, and the Export Administration Act. Again, no sanctions were imposed.

The pattern over the years has become abundantly clear. Not only have security procedures regarding trade been abolished or relaxed, but those still nominally in force, especially for the reexport of sensitive technology to third countries, have no substance. The consequences of that supreme carelessness will be felt in the coming years. The question now is how to prevent even worse consequences.

The failure to meet even the basic standards of prudent conduct raises troubling questions about the behavior of President Clinton. The key question is whether he may have been compromised, as the evidence uncovered in various, albeit unconcluded, investigations of the "China connection" with the 1996 campaign-financing irregularities suggests. As one Clinton official said, "The president is deaf on this subject." The issue, of course, is why he cannot or will not hear the alarm bells that have been going off in the past few years.

Indeed, his disinterest has had a powerful effect on even the Defense Department, which historically has raised the greatest bureaucratic barriers to trade with national security implications. Yet in both terms of the Clinton administration, the president's secretaries of defense have never appealed any White House decision on sensitive technology exports, despite staff recommendations that they do so.[19]

Realistically, little or nothing will be done within the executive branch on these questions until there is a change of administration, when a thorough review of our trade and security policy must be a major priority. Business as usual won't work and cannot remain in place for long, despite the inevitable slow start that marks any new foreign policy team.

The outlines of such a review are clear enough. First, the intelligence community must prepare a Special National Intelligence Estimate on the damage to national security. This must be done across-the-board. The SNIE should be completed within 90 days of the new administration. Second, the new president should immediately order an interagency task force under the leadership of the NSC to review existing procedures on trade and security and to make recommendations for the president's signature. Among other options, this group should consider the reestablishment of the authority of the Pentagon's currently downgraded DTSA. The Commerce Department's role in technology export issues should be rescinded and the authority placed once more with the State Department, whose assets in this area need to be strengthened.

In addition, and at a minimum, China's actions invite the resurrection of a COCOM-type system to reduce the flow of militarily useful technology to Beijing's military by U.S. allies as well as American companies. The Wassenaar Agreement needs to be either strengthened or abandoned. It cannot continue as it is, offering the illusion rather than the reality of providing effective safeguards on technology transfers to problematic regimes.

That, of course, will not be easy to accomplish. The post–Cold War mentality is firmly in place with nearly all our allies—an attitude that the United States in the last few years has greatly encouraged by its own actions and lack of leadership. Restoring leadership in this area will take time and patience and will never work completely smoothly—as COCOM did not. On the intelligence side, the new administration can help its cause by sharing sensitive information demonstrating how a lax security policy has endangered the interests of the West. The United States can also show the way by defining clearly what cannot be exported to China or other potentially hostile nations. Broad-brush bans won't work; pointed prohibitions might.

Finally, thwarting espionage directed at the United States by China and other nations is our responsibility. Consequently, the next administration needs to rebuild its counterintelligence capabilities, which, like our other national security assets, have been allowed to wither. It is not, for example, sufficient for the DOE to conduct its own internal investigation of what went wrong at the national laboratories. An interagency effort presided over by the NSC and the president's national security adviser is needed to review and replace counterintelligence procedures in all relevant agencies, not just the DOE, scarcely the only department that has failed to meet the standards expected by the American people.

Trading with China: Caveat Venditor

In the 20th century U.S. perceptions of China have ranged from the sentimental to the xenophobic. Policy based on either perception is wrong. For example, China was not destined to become the largest democracy on earth after World War II, as envisioned by President Franklin Roosevelt. The Chinese Communists were not simply agrarian reformers either. In the last two decades, China has changed greatly since Mao's mad rule. Nevertheless, the Middle Kingdom, despite economic development and burgeoning trade and investment with the West, remains an authoritarian state, and most investment decisions are centrally controlled. On the other hand, it is not quite the dire enemy U.S. officials envisioned during the Vietnam War.

China is an emerging great power with ambitions of its own that do not coincide with the West's, especially after the demise of the Soviet Union. Its political evolution is completely uncertain, and 5,000 years of Chinese civilization does not assure us of a quick and happy outcome. Rather, it suggests the opposite. At a minimum, China's present leadership is intent on making its country Asia's leading power, a power that, inter alia, still seeks to regain control over Taiwan by any means. China also seeks the expulsion of U.S. military power from the region, thus making its own force projection capabilities the greatest in Asia. U.S. policy, even in the Clinton administration, must be to limit, if not thwart, those ambitions. But to do so requires a critical component: a trade and security policy that complements rather than frustrates that central policy objective of the United States in this century. Much hard, sustained work lies ahead if that is to be accomplished.

Notes

1. Patrick Tyler, *A Great Wall: Six Presidents and China: An Investigative History* (New York: Public Affairs, 1999).

2. There is a peculiar form of amnesia at work here. There were many, even at the height of the Cold War, who dismissed the importance of ideology in the actions of both the Soviet and Chinese elites, because, contrary to evidence, that assumption did not seem *reasonable*. We know better now, even though the same analysts who were wrong about it then are maintaining the same proposition now. For more on that precise point, with examples, see John Lewis Gaddis, *We Know Now: Rethinking Cold War History* (Oxford: Clarendon, 1997), pp. 289–91. Gaddis's discussion of Stalin's ideologically driven belief that the next war would be between the capitalist nations is a good example. The Soviet dictator simply refused to understand that Western Europe and the United States were not at dagger's point or that his actions in Eastern Europe, Germany, in particular, would bring about the creation of NATO, an alliance based on democratic values as well as national security interests.

3. Author's interview with James Lilley, April 15, 1999.

4. From an unclassified summary of a CIA National Intelligence Estimate, quoted in the *Washington Times*, September 10, 1999, p. A-22.

5. James Mann, *About Face: A History of America's Curious Relationship with China from Nixon to Clinton* (New York: Knopf, 1999). The Carter administration had little time to formulate a trade policy toward China, since normalization of relations came late in the president's first (and last) term. Nevertheless, William Perry, then under secretary of defense for research and development, recommended (after a September 1980 trip to China) that the United States find the ways and means to assist the PLA in modernizing its 1950s guerrilla-style military into a modern force. For a discussion of the report that Perry would later mischaracterize, see ibid., pp. 111–13.

6. Quoted in Mann, p. 262.

7. Quoted in ibid., pp. 260–64.

8. William Jefferson Clinton, Letter to Edward McCracken, September 15, 1993, p. 1. Emphasis added. Three weeks earlier, however, the administration was in another mood. On August 25, it banned all satellite sales to China after Beijing was caught selling M-11 missiles to Pakistan. Months later, waivers were being granted that, in effect, made the August sanctions moot.

9. Ibid., p. 2.

10. Ibid.

11. Kenneth R. Timmerman, "Partners in Crime," *American Spectator*, August 1999, p. 30.

12. The DTSA's new chief in the Clinton administration was David Tarbell, who had once opposed U.S. efforts to deny the Soviets Toshiba's ultrasilent propeller technology.

13. Stephen D. Bryen, Testimony to the Subcommittee on International Trade and Finance, Senate Banking Committee, 106th Cong., 1st sess., June 24, 1999, p. 2.

14. U.S. House of Representatives, "Memorandum for Full Committee Hearings on Encryption Prepared for the Committee on Armed Services," 106th Cong., 1st sess., June 30, 1999, p. 3. The bill to be considered was H.R. 850, the Security and Freedom through Encryption Act.

15. Author's interview with Michael Maloof, April 26, 1999.

16. Curt Weldon, News release, May 27, 1999.

17. For example, in California, the China Aero-Technology Import-Export Company, a Chinese state-owned corporation, has created at least a dozen different other front companies that have purchased, among other things, machine-tool dies designed to manufacture spare parts for the F-14 fighter, which is not in the inventory of China but of Iran, a nation with whom China has long had a military-supply relationship. For more detail, see Kenneth R. Timmerman, "California Take-Out," *American Spectator,* October 1998, pp. 35–41.

18. Weldon.

19. Interview with Maloof.

13. China's Trade Regime at the End of the 1990s: Achievements, Limitations, and Impact on the United States

Barry Naughton

Following the landmark agreement with the United States, China will most likely enter the World Trade Organization in 2000 or 2001. Compliance with WTO requirements will expose Chinese businesses to new competitive pressures, require major modifications of the Chinese trading regime, and force substantial adjustment costs. Why is China evidently willing to pay those costs and assume significant new obligations? After all, under the existing system, without WTO membership, Chinese trade has grown rapidly, and China has emerged as a major participant in the world trading system. China already has access to the markets of most major developed countries, including the United States. Indeed, by U.S. calculations, China's trade surplus with the United States was to surpass $65 billion in 1999. With such an apparently favorable situation for China, some observers had argued that China would not be willing to make the concessions necessary to reach agreement with the United States. Agreement seemed especially elusive after May 7, 1999, when the U.S. bombing of the Chinese embassy in Belgrade plunged the U.S.-Chinese relationship into a serious crisis. And yet, despite obvious continuing strains in the bilateral relationship, on November 15, 1999, the Chinese leadership signed on the dotted line and committed itself to extensive new market-opening obligations.

Chinese government leaders clearly believe that WTO membership is in their own interests. This chapter argues that one important motivation behind the drive to join WTO is the desire to overcome serious flaws in China's existing trade regime and to move forward to a qualitatively different, more unified, and more open trade regime. I have termed the existing trade regime "dualistic," and while it has had important successes, it also has important, distinct shortcomings. Since 1995, the growth of China's foreign trade has slowed substantially. Without doubt, much of the explanation for the trade slowdown lies with external economic factors beyond China's control. The Asian financial crisis had a severe impact on China's exports during 1998 and 1999. Under those circumstances, it is not surprising that trade was a less dynamic force in transforming the domestic economy than it might have been under more robust economic conditions. Nevertheless, the relative slowdown in the growth of trade also reflects problems in devising a successful post-1995 model of trade reform.

Until 1995, successful reform relied primarily on opening a dualistic trading regime under which exporting firms were able to import supplies without duties or administrative obstacles. Much of the growth of trade came from firms operating under that relatively open set of rules. Since 1995, the emphasis of trade reform has been on moving toward a more unified—but also more open—set of rules to cover the entire external sector. However, those efforts have met with limited success. Adverse economic conditions have made it more difficult to devise a successful gradualist reform strategy, and some reforms have been frustrated by administrative weaknesses and inconsistencies in policy. It is conceivable that the relative lack of success of recent trade policy reforms has contributed to China's willingness to make dramatic concessions on market-opening initiatives associated with membership in the WTO.

In this chapter, I describe the evolution of China's trading regime through the end of the 1990s. The primary purpose is to shed light on the relative achievements and shortcomings of Chinese trade reform and to highlight remaining potential gains from trade. That perspective also sheds light on the trade relationship between the United States and China. It shows that the frustrations felt in the United States over the chronic trade deficit with China, and over the continuing limitations on access to the Chinese market, are structurally related to the nature of the Chinese trading regime. The particular fashion in which trade flows have responded to the incentives in the trade regime helps explain why the current situation—although frustrating—imposes relatively modest costs, if any, on the United States. I illustrate that point by presenting two "fables" of the hard disk drive (HDD) industry. The two fables help to illuminate the ways in which the Chinese trade regime is costly to the

Figure 13.1
CHINA'S TOTAL FOREIGN TRADE

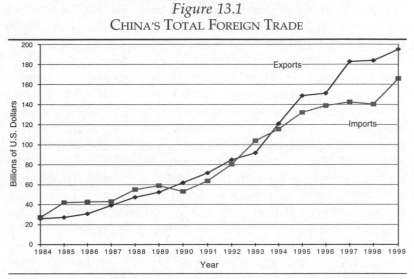

SOURCE: *China's Customs Statistics* (Beijing: General Administration of Customs, monthly, various issues).

Chinese economy and to clarify the nature of the U.S. deficit with China.

In the following section I first present a quick overview of recent quantitative developments in China's trade. That is followed by a discussion of trends in China's dualistic trade regime. I describe policies adopted in the late 1990s that were intended to lessen the differences between the two trade regimes, with the objective of eventual integration and liberalization of the overall regime. Next, looking predominantly at the import side of the ledger, I examine some measures of openness of the Chinese economy. Those measures lead us to emphasize the continuing limits on openness in the Chinese economy. Finally, I examine the impact of those institutional features on U.S.-Chinese trade. I conclude with some speculations about the motives underlying China's recent initiatives on WTO membership.

Recent Trade Developments: An Overview

Figure 13.1 shows overall trends in China's foreign trade through 1999 in current U.S. dollars.[1] While long-run growth has been impressive, growth has slowed markedly since 1995. The nominal value of exports actually declined throughout the second half of 1998 and the first half of 1999, until rapid recovery in the second half of 1999 boosted the growth rate to 6.1 percent for the year as a whole. (The unit price of exports fell substantially during 1998–99, so real export growth probably continued even during the 1998–99 export contraction.) Export growth resumed in mid-1999 and reached 6.1 percent for the year. Growth in 1999 surpassed expectations of most observers—and of the Chinese government—and reflected the speed of the recovery in Asia during 1999. Despite the relatively strong performance in 1999, the medium-term export growth trend has clearly shifted downward. Between 1984 and 1995, nominal exports grew 17 percent annually; between 1995 and 1999, growth dropped to 7 percent annually. Indeed, only one year (1997) of those four displayed robust growth. The picture is similar for imports. Between 1984 and 1995, imports grew almost as fast as exports, at 15.4 percent annually. Since 1995, import growth has also dropped to just below 6 percent annually. Again, the pattern has been three years of stagnation and one (1999) of growth. The growth in 1999 largely reflected a crackdown on smuggling that diverted previously contraband goods to legal channels (discussed further below). Overall import growth has been slowed by the weakness of Chinese domestic demand in recent years.

With gross domestic product growth remaining relatively robust in China throughout that period, the ratio of trade to GDP has declined, reversing earlier patterns. After growing steadily to a peak value of 44 percent in 1994, the total trade (exports plus imports) to GDP ratio declined to 34 percent in 1998 and then ticked up to 36 percent in 1999. The reduction in the trade to GDP ratio has been caused by both real appreciation of the Chinese currency and slower growth of real trade compared to real GDP. During 1999, imports—at least legal imports—grew substantially, so China's recorded trade surplus shrank from $43.6 billion to $29 billion.

The Dual Trading Regime

China's trade continues to be characterized by a strongly dualistic trading regime.[2] Chinese trade policies affect different types of traders in different ways. The most open part of the trading regime I label the "export-processing" (EP) regime. Under that regime, exporters are permitted to bring imported inputs into the country duty-free, with a minimum of administrative interference and regulation. The adoption of the EP regime was closely associated with a welcoming policy toward foreign direct investment (FDI) in export-oriented sectors. Creating an open trading regime was necessary to attract from Hong Kong, Taiwan, and nearby Asian countries export-oriented producers that were seeking to relocate because of rising wages and costs. As a result, the EP regime is closely associated with foreign-invested enterprises (FIEs). In "processing and assembly" trade, foreign firms outside China maintain ownership of materials and consign them to Chinese firms for processing, then manage the export of finished goods; in "import-processing" trade, foreign-invested firms inside China purchase imported inputs, process them, and export the finished goods themselves. In the following discussion, I aggregate both forms of processing trade into the EP category. Some domestic firms also participate in EP trade, and there is no reason why the EP regime should be limited to FIEs; but in practice the association is quite close. FIEs enjoy privileges under the EP regime that are shared by only a small fraction of domestic enterprises.

The growth of trade conducted by FIEs under EP provisions contributes substantially to Chinese economic development. EP trade reflects increasing Chinese participation in the complex division of labor among Asian economies. EP trade was initially pioneered by textile and garment producers. In recent years, though, it has become increasingly important in electronics and telecommunications equipment. Now, almost half of EP exports are electronic or machinery products.[3] EP trade has generated a powerful export-led boom in Guangdong Province, which originated 55 percent of all EP exports in 1998. Besides generating foreign exchange, EP production in Guangdong supports an estimated 20 million jobs. Workers come to Guangdong from all over China, and, besides earning wages and making purchases, they remit substantial sums back to their home villages. Last year, remittances through the postal system from two important export cities in Guangdong Province, Shenzhen and Dongguan, to outside the province surpassed 10 billion yuan (over U.S.$1.2 billion) for each city. Such remittances probably do more to combat poverty in interior China than do all the programs of the central government.[4]

Despite those beneficial features, EP trade is regarded with some suspicion in China, and there are ongoing debates about its economic impact. The debates usually take as a starting point one important characteristic of EP trade: the share of in-China value added as a proportion of the total value of the export commodity is quite low. Commonly, China value added is estimated to be 20 percent or less of export value. In addition, however, many critics of EP trade regard it as low-tech, low-skilled trade. In their view, both the direct and the indirect benefits to China of EP exports are quite modest.[5] As we will see below, that view of EP trade contains some elements of fact but is seriously incomplete.

During most of the 1990s, the actual operation of the EP regime was even more open than the formal legal provisions had indicated. Tax breaks were routinely given to FIEs. Geographically, FIEs were concentrated in Guangdong and Fujian Provinces, where provincial authorities routinely facilitated the most liberal interpretation possible of trade regulations. Smuggling and diversion of inputs to the domestic market made the local economy even more open to world-market forces than would otherwise have been the case. Smuggling has been substantial: though difficult to quantify, every indication is that smuggling accounts for well over U.S.$10 billion annually.[6] In a sample of customs fraud cases investigated in 1997, 63 percent were related to EP trade, even though EP imports were 49 percent of total imports.[7] Conceivably smuggling became even more serious in the first half of 1998. World market prices for bulk commodities such as diesel fuel and heavy chemicals dropped so low that it became profitable to smuggle in entire freighter loads.

Figure 13.2 shows that firms operating under the EP regime have continued to provide the majority of the impetus for trade growth. FIE exports continued to climb through the first half of 1999, when they accounted for 47 percent of total exports. Exports produced under EP provisions (i.e., by processing duty-free imports) accounted for 58.5 percent of total exports in the first half of 1999. Overall, EP exports increased 12 percent annually in 1995 and 1998, only half the 24 percent annual rate between 1990 and 1995, but still respectable. Figure 13.3 shows that EP trade growth ebbed in 1998–99, but did not contract significantly, and resumed growth in the second half of 1999.

The alternative to the EP trade regime is the "ordinary trade" (OT) regime (*yiban maoyi*). Ordinary trade is conducted primarily by trading companies, which were all state owned until 1998. Manufacturers may also receive trading rights, but those are limited generally to export of their own products. Most significant, importers are

Figure 13.2
EXPORTS BY TRADE REGIME AND OWNERSHIP

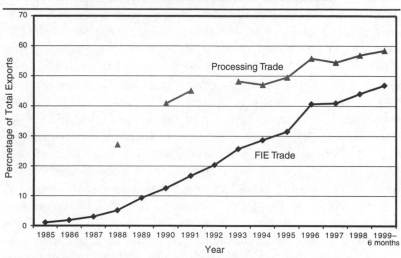

SOURCE: *China's Customs Statistics* (Beijing: General Administration of Customs, monthly, various issues).

Figure 13.3
EP TRADE: EXPORTS AND IMPORTS

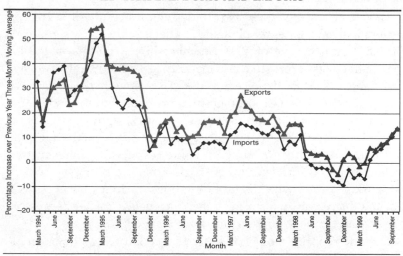

SOURCE: *China's Customs Statistics* (Beijing: General Administration of Customs, monthly, various issues).

limited to a specific, designated set of trading rights, or "scope of operation." Thus, there is always an implicit degree of conditionality limiting the ability of importers to import.[8] Important steps have been taken to lower tariffs and reduce nontariff barriers in the OT trading regime. However, pending WTO accession, the basic features of the OT regime are still intact. Most fundamental, foreign companies do not generally have the right to import goods and then market them directly to Chinese customers. Instead, the foreign trading companies (FTCs) must first import the commodities into China, where they are then released to domestic distribution networks. As a result, there are very strong incentives to restrict competition, limit innovation in marketing, and allow noneconomic objectives to interfere with market forces.[9] In recent years a few exceptions have slightly liberalized the OT regime: foreign-invested retailers can import commodities up to 30 percent of their total sales, and a handful of foreign-invested trading companies have been licensed. But those exceptions are small cracks in the wall, particularly compared with what WTO membership will bring. China has agreed, effective immediately on WTO accession, to cease limiting trading rights to authorized FTCs. All businesses will in principle have the right to import and market goods directly to Chinese businesses and households.

The coexistence of these two trade regimes results in a trading system with a high degree of dualism. That is particularly significant for China on the eve of WTO membership. Exporters in the EP regime have easy access to world markets, few administrative delays, and very low taxes. Exporters in the OT regime increasingly have the legal authority to export their own products, but they still must cope with substantial administrative obstacles, significant taxes on imported components or materials, and other aspects of the domestic trade and regulatory regime. In some respects, China's system resembles that of Thailand, where high tariffs protecting the domestic market coexist with liberal exemptions of duties for exporters. But the degree of dualism in China is arguably greater because of greater government bureaucratic interference in China.

The different types of Chinese trade respond to economic conditions in different ways. OT trade is fairly responsive to real exchange rates and to export promotion policies, such as tax rebates and

Figure 13.4
OT Trade: Exports and Imports

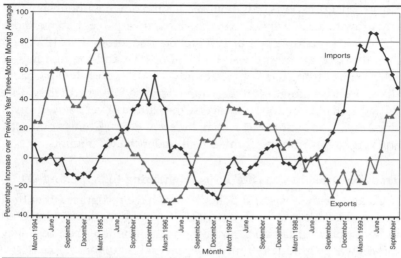

Source: *China's Customs Statistics* (Beijing: General Administration of Customs, monthly, various issues).

preferential lending programs. Figure 13.4 shows trends in OT growth rates: exports and imports respond in opposite directions, as we would expect if trade growth is driven primarily by exchange rates and macroeconomic conditions. Exports soared and imports dropped after the initial 1994 devaluation; in 1995–96 currency appreciation, a robust domestic economy, and problems with the export tax rebate program led to a shrinkage of exports and a surge in imports. During 1997, the pattern was reversed, as the tax rebate program was rehabilitated, and slowing in the domestic market, combined with direct-export credit supply, refocused exporters. Therefore, we again saw a pattern of expanding exports and stagnant imports. During 1998, however, although some of these conditions persisted, adverse exchange rates eventually overwhelmed the picture. Exports were again declining by midyear, and in the fourth quarter of 1998, imports began to take off. OT demonstrates a clear pattern of cyclical responses to fluctuating economic conditions.

More important, the OT regime has performed poorly in recent years. Through 1995, although EP was an increasing share of total

243

trade, overall growth was sufficiently robust that OT exports were also growing quickly, at 15 percent annually between 1990 and 1995. Since then, OT exports have bounced up and down without showing any growth, and 1998 OT exports were only 4 percent above those of 1995. Exports dropped in 1996, rebounded strongly in 1997, and then dropped again in the second half of 1998 and the first half of 1999. With a strong recovery after midyear, OT exports will probably show positive growth for the whole year 1999. Nevertheless, that growth will not be enough to reverse the pattern of very slow growth since 1995. The simple fact is that, in recent years, China's domestic enterprises have not performed well under the OT regime.

Trade Reforms in the Late 1990s: Tightening EP, Opening OT

Chinese economists and policymakers have recognized that they have a dualistic system. From 1995, it was increasingly expressed in both policy discussions and actions that the intention of policy reform was to gradually unify the rules and regulations. The desire to unify the trading regime has been partially driven by the perceived need to comply with WTO rules on "national treatment." National treatment as interpreted in WTO agreements means that countries may not discriminate against imported commodities—only the taxes and regulatory arrangements agreed to as part of the accession process are allowed. Because of the close link in China between types of enterprise (foreign-invested or domestic) and types of trading regime (EP or OT) under which goods are transacted, it is clear that national treatment in the Chinese context will mean phasing out many of the discriminatory rules that treat foreign-invested firms differently from domestic ones. Chinese leaders have generally accepted the need for a "level playing field" as part of WTO membership.[10] Central government leaders have also sought to unify the trading regime in order to increase tax revenues and close tax loopholes. Moreover, in a broader context, FIEs are playing an increasingly prominent role in the Chinese domestic economy (not just in exports) and, as a result, have been eliciting debate. One strand of debate focuses on the rapid success foreign firms have had in dominating certain segments of the Chinese consumer markets (such as film and soft drinks), wiping out Chinese brands in the process. Another strand emphasizes that FIEs have been absolute to leverage favorable treatment under Chinese law and manipulate competition among local governments for investment in order to pile up concessions in tax, pricing, and land-use provisions.[11] These issues led to a serious concern about unfair competition and an announced determination to limit unfair privileged treatment received by FIEs. Finally, the desire to unify the trade regimes was a recognition that the earlier stages of trade reform had been successful but that the current hybrid system had both advantages and defects. It was hoped that by gradually unifying the system, the best points of both might be combined in a new more open and more uniform system.

Most of the major policy initiatives the government has implemented in the intervening three years fit into the general framework of unifying the two regimes—that is, there has been a consistent effort to reduce the separateness and special privileges of the EP system, while increasing the openness of the OT system. In addition, there has been a concerted effort to unify regulations, particularly by reducing tax breaks given to FIEs. Following the crackdown on smuggling and military involvement in business, there has also been a significant reduction in the de facto openness of the EP system.[12]

However, the government's initiatives have been relatively unsuccessful. The government has certainly not been able to combine the best of both systems. Despite efforts to tighten the EP regime and open the OT regime, the differences between them persist. That is not necessarily the "fault" of policymakers in the Chinese government. They have been buffeted by the shocks coming from the Asian financial crisis. Those shocks have reduced China's bargaining power with foreign investors, increased China's vulnerability to import surges (due to fluctuations in exchange rate), and decreased demand for the country's exports. Naturally, this has made it much harder to implement policy changes smoothly and in line with government objectives.

Tightening the EP Regime

There have been a number of initiatives to tighten the EP system. The most important have involved simply more rigorous enforcement of existing rules. But these initiatives are nonetheless important changes in the de facto operating environment for traders. I list some of the most important.

- A full-scale campaign against smuggling was launched in midyear 1998. Inevitably, since the military was deeply implicated in smuggling activities, tackling smuggling meant attacking the privileges the military had developed in the economy.[13] Early in 2000, a huge scandal, involving high-level corruption, blackmail, and allegations that a single government company smuggled in several billion dollars' worth of contraband, began in the southern city of Xiamen. While the struggle over corruption is inevitably highly politicized, the fact that such a huge operation could be exposed reveals both the scope of the problem and the serious effort that has begun to address the problem.

- Deposits are now required for some duty-free imports, and this, combined with increased record keeping, makes it more difficult to divert export-processing materials to the domestic market. For example, EP exporters are now required to keep logbooks with the weight of all imported components shown and then verify that exports contain the requisite weight of total components. The previous, relatively lax system represented an implicit subsidy to exporters. Because they were able to profit from duty-free domestic sales of imported materials, exporters could gain additional revenues from the process of exporting. The system was similar to Korea's practice during that 1960s and 1970s of granting a generous "wastage allowance" on imports purchased by exporters at favorable exchange rates. Such a practice allowed an implicit subsidy.[14]

- EP exporters are being classified into four grades (A through D). "Trustworthy" enterprises, in category A, will continue to operate the EP system essentially as before, importing materials without deposits and reporting transactions to the customs authorities. Category A enterprises have never had any serious violations of regulations or bad audits. Category B enterprises are considered "basically trustworthy" and have only a few record-keeping requirements. Enterprises in categories C and D have experienced serious violations in the past. They will be required to pay significant deposits on imported materials and meet more stringent record-keeping requirements. According to some initial surveys, 40 percent or more of enterprises in Guangdong may be in categories C and D.[15] This represents a significant tightening of the overall system.

- There are current moves to impose additional restrictions on specific types of raw materials: cotton, steel, and petroleum products. In this system, exporters importing these products for processing would have to pay all the tax, which is rebated on export.

- Taxes on foreign investors are being increased. In 1995 the Chinese government proposed an end to tariff exemptions on equipment imported as part of foreign investment. In that year, duty-free imports of machinery for foreign investment projects were $18.7 billion. That figure subsequently rose to $24.9 billion in 1996 (as investors scrambled to get equipment in before the tax break expired), before declining. In 1998, though, the total was $14.5 billion, a decline of only 23 percent since 1995. In other words, policymakers had declared that they would end tax exemption for foreign investment but instead succeeded only in reducing it by one-quarter. That failure no doubt reflects a certain loss of bargaining power by the Chinese government vis-à-vis potential foreign investors. In 1995 it seemed as if all multinational corporations were desperate to get into the Chinese market. With the Asian downturn, many Asian and Western companies feel that they have great freedom to pick the locale of future investments and can insist that the Chinese provide tax breaks. At the same time, the Chinese government has traditionally been comfortable with a discretionary regime, in which duty-free import is authorized for projects in specific sectors. That is the current situation, with duty-free status approved in priority sectors and for specific projects. During the first three-quarters of 1999, realized foreign investment dropped 7 percent, but duty-free equipment imports dropped 31 percent, so some tightening of tax breaks continues.

Opening the OT Regime

At the same time the government was tightening regulations for the EP regime, it was moving forward with measures to liberalize the OT regime. Those measures, which received a lot of attention abroad and in the Chinese press, were clearly related to China's campaign to join the WTO. Important commitments were made at the time of major Asia-Pacific Economic Cooperation meetings and were followed by swift unilateral action. The most important measures included the following:

- Lower tariffs. China has cut tariffs repeatedly—indeed, almost annually—since a recent high point in 1992. The average nominal tariff declined from 43 percent in 1992 to 17 percent in 1999. It was recently announced that the further reductions in 2000 would lower the average nominal rate to 15 percent, and a official with the Ministry of Foreign Trade and Economic Cooperation claimed that China would meet its promise to APEC to cut the average tariff on imported industrial goods to 10 percent by 2005.[16]
- Expanded grant of trading rights, including extending trading rights to some joint ventures and private companies. During 1998, three joint venture trading companies were given permission to set up but only in the Special Economic Zones of Pudong and Shenzhen. By the end of June 1999, 142 private domestic Chinese firms were licensed to engage in some kind of export or import business. In the case of both joint venture and private companies, the grant of expanded powers was used to implement some regional distribution goals: the joint venture trading companies were used to encourage foreign firms to relocate to Pudong, and the private exporters were used predominantly in inland provinces. Thus, 14 of the first 61 private firms were in Sichuan Province, and only 9 were in Guangdong Province.[17]
- Phaseout of some nontariff barriers (NTBs).
- Increase in the rate of value-added tax (VAT) rebates. Full rebate of the (usually 17 percent) VAT was tried in 1994–95, but abuses led to a scaling back of the system. The rebate levels have been systematically increased since 1997.

However, despite those measures, not all movement was in the direction of liberalizing and unifying the trading regime. Largely because of external and internal economic shocks, policy changes in the trading regime were inconsistent and sometimes unsuccessful. The net impact of various measures has been to somewhat increase the degree of domestic protection provided by the overall trading regime. This can be seen in a number of areas. First, the crackdown on smuggling has tended to push trade into the OT regime, and a stress on revenue collection has affected actual import duty rates. That can be seen most clearly by comparing collected customs revenues with the total value of imports. Customs revenue has traditionally been small, much smaller than that implied by posted tariff rates, because of the large number of statutory exemptions (in the EP regime) and ad hoc remissions (in the OT regime) granted. In the 1990s, tariff take as a proportion of total imports was generally in the 5 to 6 percent range and tended to decline over time. The smuggling crackdown increased legal imports but increased the realized tariff take even more. Tariffs collected in 1999 jumped 78 percent from 1998, and customs revenues as a share of the total value of legal imports increased from 5 to 7.8 percent.[18]

Second, measures taken to protect the renminbi against speculative pressures have made it more difficult for importers to get financing to pay for imports. The result has been a slowing of imports into China and reduction in trade growth.[19] Third, there is substantial evidence of increased use of informal nontariff barriers to control potential import surges of low-priced Korean steel, petrochemical products, and a whole range of commodities in which a small number of state-owned companies have substantial market power. These policies mutually reinforce policies to crack down on smuggling and misinvoicing of EP trade. The overall effect of the measures has almost certainly been to temporarily increase the overall degree of protection provided by the trade regime.

Those measures are to some extent short-term responses to serious policy dilemmas. Since the Asian financial crisis first erupted, Chinese policymakers have committed and recommitted to a "no devaluation" promise. In the face of unmistakable signs of eroding Chinese competitiveness, that pledge increasingly involves serious costs to the Chinese economy. These costs are particularly important because China is already going through a major restructuring and downsizing of the public-enterprise sector. The change in institutional features of the Chinese urban economy is a large topic that should be the subject of a separate chapter. It is important to note here that the persistence of weak domestic demand for several years, combined with intensified competition from private firms, township and village enterprises, and FIEs has wreaked havoc on the public-enterprise sector. A few numbers illustrate the point. The total number of employees of state-owned manufacturing enterprises peaked at 35 million in 1992. Since then, the number of state industrial workers first began to drift down, and then dropped precipitously. At the end of 1998, there were only 18.8 million state manufacturing workers.[20] Not coincidentally, unemployment also skyrocketed, leaping from 5 million to 6 million in 1992, to around 15 million in 1998. While the Chinese government has obviously made a policy decision to facilitate the shrinkage of the state sector, it also faces the need to cushion the blow of higher unemployment. The need to stimulate the domestic economy conflicts to some extent with the promise to not devalue the currency.

In struggling to adapt to these economic rip currents, China has so far adopted mainly stop-gap measures. A large program of domestic infrastructure investment has been rolled out. The program is a reasonable pragmatic policy to shore up weak domestic demand and was reasonably successful in stabilizing growth rates in 1999. However, large-scale investment programs such as this entail systemic risks and costs that might significantly affect economic policy in the future. Restructuring the financial system will be somewhat more difficult in the wake of a renewed massive program of government-financed infrastructure investment. While fiscal policy is expansionary, real interest rates are extremely high, in part to prevent capital flight. Thus, Chinese economic policy is to a certain extent hostage to the desire to defend an (overvalued) exchange rate. Internationally it is a familiar pattern—measures for trade liberalization fail in an environment of currency overvaluation. Stop-gap measures contribute to both protection and further overvaluation, potentially locking policymakers into a vicious cycle. China still has many opportunities, including dramatic liberalization as part of WTO membership, to break out of that destructive cycle. In the short run, though, adverse macroeconomic conditions have undermined a gradualist policy of incremental unification of the trading regime.

Evaluation

The limitations of the dualistic trade regime are becoming increasingly apparent. Exporters operating under the OT regime have been relatively unsuccessful in recent years. That has undermined the effort to give Chinese domestic firms a major role in continued trade growth. Abuse of the liberal provisions of the EP regime is depriving the Chinese government of desperately needed revenues. Lack of flexibility in the dualistic regime has hampered effective response to fluctuations in external economic conditions. Moreover, the EP regime appears increasingly ill suited to meet the requirements of the current stage of Chinese economic development. The technological sophistication of EP exporters has increased markedly as machinery and electronics have emerged as the largest industries operating under EP provisions. As technical levels have risen, it becomes clearer that China loses in the segregation of EP activities into a kind of enclave economy. For EP producers, links with suppliers and customers outside China are actually easier to maintain than links with more proximate domestic suppliers and customers. The dualistic regime reinforces separation from the rest of the economy of high-tech exporters, and reduces the potential spillover effects that successful exporters might provide to the local economy. This can be illustrated by the first fable of the HDD industry.

First Fable of the HDD Industry

China assembles HDDs and produces some of their components, especially labor-intensive components such as heads. Yet all the heads, and all the assembled disk drives, are exported. All output is exported, even though many of the heads are ultimately installed in drives in China, and many of the drives are ultimately installed in personal computers in China. For example, Seagate, a U.S. company, has two facilities for assembling disk drives in China. The total export of disk drives from these two plants in 1998 was over 10 million units, with a value around $1.5 billion. According to company estimates, a minimum of 1.5 million hard drives are reimported into China and installed in personal computers sold in China.

Why are these drives exported and then reimported? Because for exporters to continue to operate under the EP regime with minimal restrictions, they must export all output. Otherwise, imported inputs would be subject to duties, and VATs would be charged on a portion of output value. Moreover, because widespread smuggling makes the trading regime porous, Chinese producers paying taxes would not be able to compete in the domestic market with smugglers, who can purchase outside China the products produced under an essentially zero-tax regime. In response to those incentives, the Seagate assembly plants have made very few links to local suppliers and no

(continued next page)

> direct links to local customers. Their supply and sales chains
> all lead across Chinese borders. As a result, Seagate's neighbors
> in China have few opportunities to learn by example, or to
> begin supplying low-tech components or supplies to these
> high-tech factories. The dualistic regime stops spillovers from
> initial investments in the HDD industry from contributing
> directly to China's development.

U.S.-Chinese Trading Relations

U.S.-Chinese economic tensions persist because of the large U.S. deficit with China. This deficit is so large because China's EP exports are directed primarily to the U.S. market. Indeed, of direct Chinese exports to the United States in 1997, 71 percent fell under the EP regime, a higher percentage than in any other major country.[21] Moreover, the trade conducted under the EP regime accounts for the entire U.S. deficit with China. When OT and other provisions are combined, the United States has a small trade surplus with China (including commodities exported to China as part of U.S. investment in that country). But the huge deficit under the EP regime overwhelms the tiny surplus under other trading arrangements. The United States' share of China's EP exports is three times as large as its share of China's EP imports. By contrast, the share of the three newly industrializing economies of Taiwan, Korea, and Singapore in China's EP imports is more than three times their share of China's EP exports. Their surplus with China on the EP account is over 80 percent of the U.S. deficit with China on the EP account.[22] China's position in global-manufacturing chains is frequently the point of final assembly before goods are exported to the United States. However, this final assembly typically represents a small portion of the total value of the goods. Table 13.1 shows the main U.S. imports from China. Nearly all of them are produced under the EP regime. The most important product in the "Electrical Machinery" category is the telephone; the most important "Machinery" products are computer components and peripherals. These are precisely the areas in which growth of EP trade has been so rapid in recent years.

Table 13.1
MAIN U.S. IMPORTS FROM CHINA, 1998

	Billion Dollars	Percentage of Total
Electrical machinery	12.8	18%
Toys and sports equipment	10.6	15%
Shoes	8.0	11%
Machinery	7.6	11%
Apparel	5.7	8%
Total	71.2	100%

SOURCE: STAT-USA®/Internet, U.S. Department of Commerce.

Table 13.1 shows that U.S. imports from China fit overwhelmingly into one of two categories: labor-intensive, low-tech products, such as stuffed animals (almost $2 billion in 1998!) that are no longer produced in the United States in significant quantities; and labor-intensive assembly of high-tech products. These high-tech products are often the result of production chains that contribute to the profitability of U.S. corporations. This can be exemplified by a second fable, again from the HDD industry.

The Second Fable of the HDD Industry

The United States imported almost $.6 billion worth of assembled hard drives from China in 1998. The United States exports only a few million dollars' worth of HDDs to China, so we have an apparent HDD trade deficit of over a half billion dollars.

However, the story is much more complex. First, all the HDDs produced in China and imported to the United States are produced by American companies. Since those HDDs are produced by U.S. companies, some of the revenue accrues to U.S. citizens. Moreover, the HDD factories in China are typical EP producers in the sense that in-China value added is a small share of the total value of the commodity. In the example of Seagate, described in the first fable, none of the major components of HDDs produced in Seagate's Wuxi facility is produced

(continued next page)

in China. Instead, the components are sourced throughout Asia and assembled in China. A very generous approximation of the value added within China, including wages, overhead, and a portion of transport costs, is, at most, 10 percent of the total value added. Most of the value of an HDD comes from research, design, and prototype creation, plus management of the supply chain, logistics, and marketing, which is done primarily in the United States. According to various estimates, at least 60 percent of the wage bill of a typical U.S.-based HDD producer is earned in the United States.[23]

An approximation of the value shares of the $1.5 billion in output produced by Seagate in China yields the following results (no company proprietary data were available for this approximation): U.S. citizens earn about $900 million from the total U.S.-Chinese trade in HDDs, while Chinese citizens earn about $150 million (according to generous assumptions). Citizens of other Asian countries, especially Singapore, Malaysia, and Thailand, earn another $400 million or so. What is most striking is that U.S. citizens earn about $120 million from the production of HDDs in China, which are destined to be installed in Chinese computers, while Chinese citizens earn less than $60 million from sales *in the United States* of HDDs assembled in China. That is true even though sales of HDDs assembled in China are about four times larger in the United States than in China Thus, U.S. citizens earn more revenue from this activity than do Chinese citizens, notwithstanding the fact that trade flows show a lopsided pattern of large U.S. imports. It is hard to see why the United States should be concerned about this "trade deficit."

Reassessing the Openness of the Chinese Economy

In an earlier section, measures of openness were presented, in the traditional manner, by examining total trade as a share of GDP. China's openness increased dramatically through 1994 and then declined moderately through 1998. It is interesting, however, to examine openness in more detail from the perspective of imports, as well. Of course, since China has been running a trade surplus,

Figure 13.5
IMPORT/GDP RATIOS

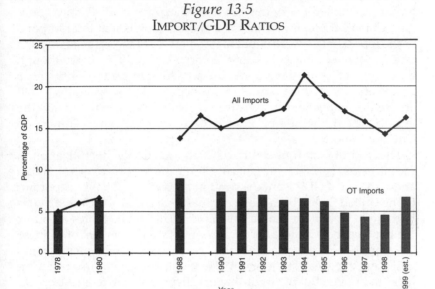

SOURCE: *China's Customs Statistics* (Beijing: General Administration of Customs, monthly, various issues).

import openness is somewhat less than export openness. Imports peaked at 21 percent of GDP in 1994, declined to 14.6 percent in 1998, and rebounded to 16.5 percent in 1999. But it might also be interesting to look at China's openness to specifically OT imports. After all, at least in theory, EP imports come solely to supply export production. Only OT imports can be sold openly on the Chinese market and represent direct competition to Chinese domestic firms. The size and trends of China's openness to OT imports are surprising. As Figure 13.5 shows, openness to OT imports probably peaked sometime in the late 1980s and has been declining since. Since 1996, OT imports have been less than 5 percent of China's GDP. By this measure, China's openness to trade is similar to what it was in 1978!

But the system is more restrictive even than the numbers show. In most years, OT imports are dominated by a few government-run FTCs. Thus, in both 1996 and 1997, imports by the 10 largest FTCs were very large, accounting for more than half of all OT imports.[24] We can take this analysis a step further. Instead of looking at the top 10 FTCs, let us look at the top 500. As far as can be determined these are all state-run corporations. These FTCs are big firms, and, having accounted for 79 percent of SOE exports in 1996, they dominate China's trade. But what is far more telling is that total imports of the top 500 FTCs were equal to 99.5 percent of the value of imports of state-owned companies and enterprises in 1996! Even though thousands of firms have some kind of foreign trade rights, those rights are, in practice, largely confined to exporting and a small amount of importing that is directly related to export. Outside the top 500, the thousands of other FTCs have a very small impact on Chinese imports.[25]

The institutional framework of OT trade, despite liberalization in recent years, continues to sharply limit the size of total OT trade, and its share of GDP is modest and not increasing. That is important to the United States, because in comparative terms, the United States does quite well in the China OT market. The United States accounts for 17 percent of Chinese OT imports and takes 11 percent of Chinese OT exports.[26] That is precisely the area in which WTO membership will have the greatest impact. WTO membership will increase China's trade overall, but it will have a disproportionate effect on OT trade. EP trade is already conducted in a fairly liberal environment, but OT trade will grow much more rapidly in the wake of the WTO's elimination of restricted trading rights and other barriers. Given the opportunity to sell directly to the Chinese market, U.S. companies should perform well, at least maintaining their share of rapidly growing Chinese OT imports.

Conclusion

U.S. firms are frustrated by their inability to export directly to the Chinese market. They are legitimately frustrated: the Chinese trading regime makes such exports extremely difficult. However, those limitations on trade hurt both the Chinese and the American economy. Ironically, it is not the flood of "cheap Chinese imports" that harms the U.S. economy, since those products would not be produced in the United States in any case, and in many cases are part of production arrangements that strongly benefit U.S. companies and workers. But the restrictions on export to China hurt both U.S. businesses and Chinese businesses and consumers. Moreover, the dualistic system is increasingly less able to serve Chinese developmental interests. From that perspective, it is easy to see that WTO membership has the potential to benefit both countries.

That perspective may also provide some small measure of understanding for the renewed Chinese emphasis on gaining WTO membership quickly. Zhu Rongji's remarkable package of reforms brought to Washington in 1999 represents a very substantial departure from past positions. I suggest that alternative trade liberalization strategies have run into, if not exactly a dead end, then certainly a series of setbacks that make continued progress on the same path uncertain. Thus a more radical alternative—rapid liberalization in the context of WTO membership—naturally looks more appealing. We cannot say that China's trade reforms have failed, but we can say that in the last few years, successes have been relatively few and far between.

Of course, that is not the sole reason for progress on WTO membership. Certainly, the breakthrough in 1999 was made possible by a number of factors. Zhu's personal style and leadership were important positive factors. The possibility that a new "millennium round" of global trade talks would "move the goalposts" by adopting new liberalization measures put additional pressure on China to settle now. Noneconomic motivations were also important for Chinese leaders. The desire of the Chinese leadership for the prestige of membership in the last major multinational club in which China is not yet a member is significant, as is the desire to de-politicize trade and avoid annual reviews by the U.S. Congress. And of course the simple fact that Chinese policymakers recognize that the benefits of increased trade and integration in the world economy underlie all those other factors.

Contributing to those factors, however, is that the lack of success of unilateral gradual trade reforms in recent years naturally increases the pressure to try a different approach. Thus, the perspective advanced here helps explain recent Chinese policy moves. But it also includes an implicit warning. China is still not reaping the gains from international trade to the extent that it could and should. Concerns about adequate food supplies, China's huge potential impact on world markets for some commodities, and national security issues explain in part the limitations on China's integration into the world economy. But inconsistency and hesitation in trade reform explain part of it as well. There are still large economic gains to be reaped. Further progress in export development, establishment of a stable equilibrium exchange rate, and more rapid technological progress are all likely to require greater openness to imports. WTO membership could have a substantial positive impact if it contributes to that openness and, in the process, contributes to a more balanced and mutually advantageous economic relationship between China and the United States.

Notes

1. Unless otherwise stated, trade and trade regime data come from *China's Customs Statistics* (Beijing: General Administration of Customs, monthly, various issues). Some recent data are also taken from China's Statistics Information Consultancy Service Centre, *China's Latest Economic Statistics* (Hong Kong: China Statistical Publishing, semimonthly).

2. Barry Naughton, "China's Emergence and Future as a Trading Nation," *Brookings Papers on Economic Activity* 2 (1996): 273–344.

3. Sun Shuohong, "The Influence of Foreign Investment on China's Foreign Trade" (in Chinese), *Guoji Jingmao Tansuo*, no. 6 (1998): 21–24.

4. PRC Ministry of Foreign Trade and Economic Cooperation, *Zhongguo Duiwai Jingji Maoyi Baipishu* (China White Paper on Foreign Economics and Trade) (Beijing: Jingji Kexue, 1999), pp. 410–11; and author's interviews with PRC officials, Beijing, August 1999.

5. For discussion, see articles in *Guoji Jingmao Tansuo*, no. 2 (1999).

6. Total revenue from smuggling can be derived by aggregating estimates of the most important categories of smuggled goods (cigarettes, automobiles, integrated circuits, etc.) or by calculations based on the volume of apprehended contraband. Contraband seized in 1998 was worth over 10 billion yuan (U.S.$1.2 billion). The best customs agencies in the world are generally assumed to be able to apprehend a maximum of 10 percent of total contraband. (Author's interviews with PRC officials, Beijing, August 1999.)

7. "Electronic Processing of Trade Will Formally Begin in May" (in Chinese), *Guoji Jingmao Tansuo*, no. 2 (1999): 11.

8. For more on the trading companies, see Will Martin, "The Role of State Trading," in *China in the World Trading System: Defining the Principles of Engagement*, ed. Frederick M. Abbott (Boston: Kluwer Law International, 1998).

9. For a detailed study on the operation of this system for steel imports, see Ian Dickson, "Institutions Affecting Integration between Chinese and International Steel Prices, 1992–1996," M.A. thesis, Department of Economics, University of Adelaide, 1998.

10. It is important to note that these discriminatory regulations often provide advantages to FIEs that are not available to domestic firms. Such advantages are not excluded by WTO rules, nor does the principle of national treatment apply generally to firms (as opposed to goods). However, as international agreements increasingly cover service providers, as well as goods producers, and as China seeks to align its regulatory framework with international principles, there are clear pressures to expand the concept of national treatment. Indeed, within China, national treatment is often understood as equal treatment of foreign-invested and domestic firms.

11. See, for example, Sun Xuewen, "Some Problems Related to FIEs in China and Appropriate Policy Responses" (in Chinese), *Dangdai Zhongguo Shi Yanjiu*, no. 4 (1997): 55–63.

12. This has been accompanied by a certain amount of recentralization of political authority over Guangdong Province, which contributes to the same effect.

13. See, for example, *China to Disband Firms Run by Law, Army Bodies*, Xinhua News Agency, July 31, 1998, reprinted in British Broadcasting Corporation, Summary of World Broadcasts, part 3, Asia-Pacific, August 3, 1998, p. FE/D3295/G.

14. This assumes that the ability to divert imported materials to the domestic market bears some kind of positive relationship to exports.

15. Matthew Durham and Deng Ju, "New MOFTEC Regulations Unify Processing Trade Mechanisms," *China Law and Practice* (December 1999): 35–37; and author's interviews with PRC officials, Beijing, August 1999.

16. "China Vows Tariff Cuts despite Stalled WTO Bid," Ministry of Foreign Trade and Economic Cooperation, July 2, 1999, http://www.chinamarket.com.cn.

17. "China Grants Ex-Im Trade Rights to 41 Private Companies, Bringing Total to 61," *China Online*, February 11, 1999, http:/chinaonline.com/issues/econ_news/ currentnews/secure/C00011101; Yao Sufeng, "Approaching Standards in International Trade: Permitting Non-publicly Owned Enterprises into the Foreign Trade Arena," *Guoji Maoyi*, no. 3 (1999): 20-22; and "Private Firms Gain Foreign Trade Rights," Ministry of Foreign Trade and Economic Cooperation, July 7, 1999.

18. Data are computed from "China's 1999 Tax Revenue Increased over 13%," *China Online*, January 13, 2000, http://chinaonline.com/issues/econ_news/currentnews/ secure/C00011101. See also, "China Credits Smuggling Crackdown for Surge in Customs Revenue," *Inside China Today*, June 7, 1999, http://invest.insidechina.com.

19. Thomas E. Jones and Margaret H. Maher, "China's Changing Foreign-Exchange Regime," *China Business Review*, March–April 1999, 26–33.

20. Data are according to *1999 Zhongguo Tongji Zhaiyao* (1999 Statistical Abstract) (Beijing: Zhongguo Tongji, 1999), p. 34. The sudden drop from 1997 to 1998 reflects some lag as workers laid off in earlier years were gradually taken off enterprise rosters.

21. Françoise Lemoine, "Les Délocalisations au coeur de l'expansion du commerce extérieur chinois," *Economie et Statistique*, no. 326–27 (1999): 63–64. Lemoine uses Chinese data incorporated into the International Trade Center databank in Geneva for these calculations. Chinese exports to the United States through Hong Kong are not included in this figure but presumably have an equal or higher proportion of EP trade.

22. Lemoine, Table 6. Again, this excludes that part of the total U.S. deficit that derives from imports from China through Hong Kong. The database does not allow us to decompose this part of U.S.-Chinese trade into separate trade regimes.

23. Peter Gourevitch, Roger E. Bohn, and David McKendrick, "Who Is Us? The Nationality of Production in the Hard Disk Drive Industry," Report 97-01, Data Storage Industry Globalization Project, Graduate School of International Relations and Pacific Studies, University of California, San Diego, March 1997.

24. This conclusion follows from the fact that total imports of the 10 largest FTCs were over 60 percent of total OT imports. We know that (using 1998 numbers), of total state-owned enterprise (SOE) trade, well over half is OT. But the big FTCs do not export very much, so they don't have much need to import inputs for export processing. In 1998 SOEs exported $97 billion and imported only $60 billion; thus, SOE exports equaled 162 percent of their imports. But the total amount of exports of the top 10 FTCs amounted to only 26 or 32 percent of their imports (in 1996 and 1997, respectively). The extent to which SOEs (including state-owned FTCs) engage in EP imports is likely to be related most closely to the total volume of the SOEs' exports.

In addition, we know that the biggest imports under EP provisions are textiles (especially synthetic fibers), plastic, and electronic components. A quick inspection of the top 10 list indicates that none of the big FTCs is likely to be a major importer of those inputs, except possibly electronic components for instruments. That follows from the fact that the main function of the large FTCs is to manage and coordinate imports for the domestic market, especially imports of investment goods and necessary raw materials. Thus it would be unlikely if FTCs did very much EP business. Assume therefore, very generously, that FTCs' share of EP imports by SOEs would equal their share of SOE exports. The large FTCs accounted for about 7 percent of SOE exports in both 1996 and 1997, so subtract 7 percent of SOE EP imports from total large FTC imports to conservatively correct for that factor. By this calculation the 10 largest FTCs account for more than 54 percent of total OT imports.

25. Since the numbers for the top 500 FTCs and for the total import and export of SOEs are collected through different channels, it would be inappropriate to make too much of the near equality of total imports from the top 500 FTCs and from all SOEs. Possible lack of comparability among data sources means that the differences between FTCs and SOEs could be much larger. Nevertheless, the conclusion is robust: large state-run FTCs overwhelmingly dominate import trade. Data are from http:// www.moftec.gov.cn/moftec/business/html/our_recommendation/top/96f500ae.htm; and *China Customs Monthly* (Beijing), no. 12 (1996): 14–15.

26. Lemoine, Table 6. Again, this reckoning does not include indirect U.S. imports through Hong Kong.

PART IV

LOOKING TO THE FUTURE

14. Freedom: Can China Embrace It? Can Hong Kong Keep It?

Martin Lee

In 1949 two boys were taken by their respective fathers to Hong Kong. One boy was 11 and the other was 12. I was the younger one. The older boy, Tung Chee Hwa, is now chief executive of Hong Kong. If you ask people in Hong Kong why they are living and working in Hong Kong instead of in China, they will probably tell you it was because of the very important decision made decades ago by their fathers, grandfathers, or great-grandfathers—to take the entire family from the motherland to Hong Kong.

Why? To be free. They could not have gone for wealth, because Hong Kong was then very poor. People went there because they wanted to be free. And that is why so many left Hong Kong before the handover in 1997.

Freedom gives luster to this Pearl of the Orient—Hong Kong. But, in China, they separate political freedom from economic freedom. They will allow people to enjoy the latter but not the former. How long can that last? How can you allow the economic half of the genie to come out of the bottle but keep the political half inside? In fact, you either have freedom or you do not.

The Erosion of Freedom and the Rule of Law in Hong Kong

In Hong Kong, unfortunately, we are, beginning to lose our freedoms, both political and economic. China has always wanted to control the goose that lays the golden egg. Beijing was already setting up institutions of control before the British left. The Basic Law, of which I was one of the drafters, was promulgated in April 1990. It is not a very good constitution because it is very restrictive. China was able to control the executive branch through its own appointed chief executive, Tung, who in 1949 left China for Hong Kong with his father, a shipping magnate. China also controls the legislature— although the Democratic Party and its allies won two-thirds of the votes, we got only one-third of the seats. China is now attempting to control the courts, and I am afraid that before long China will succeed.

In January 1999 the Court of Final Appeal laid down a landmark decision dictating how the courts in Hong Kong should construe the Basic Law. The court construed certain articles of our constitution, the Basic Law, in a way that refused to accept the government's submissions. The government then went to Beijing and effectively had that interpretation overturned by the Standing Committee of the National People's Congress.

The government sent the following message to the world: If you should be unfortunate enough to be involved in litigation with the Hong Kong government, and if you should lose in the Court of Final Appeal, then that is indeed final for you. But if you should win in the Court of Final Appeal, then don't jump for joy because it is only semifinal and the NPC could later overturn it.

The message to the judges in Hong Kong was, "You naughty boys, you knew what we wanted from you and you didn't deliver. So we'll have to correct you. In the future you can reject our submissions again, but we will ultimately overturn your decision." I am afraid that soon those judges will start questioning whether they are doing the community a service or a disservice by not conforming to the government's wishes.

The judges will ask, How should we rule when we know the government is wrong? Do we uphold the law according to our judicial oath and defend the rights and the freedoms of our people? If we do that, what happens? How long will our decisions last? Two months? Once the judges start asking themselves those questions, Hong Kong will be no different from China or Singapore, where the government always wins. And that will be the end of the rule of law. So even the Hong Kong judiciary is very much under threat.

Cronyism is also hurting Hong Kong. Let me give you two examples. The first involved a publishing tycoon who was in a conspiracy with three of her senior executives. The investigating authorities recommended prosecution, and the director of Public Prosecutions agreed that all four should be prosecuted. But the secretary for justice, the equivalent of the U.S. attorney general, decided to prosecute the three but not the boss. Her reason? Very simple. Prosecution of the boss could possibly have resulted in the loss of 2,000 jobs.

Following that logic, entrepreneurs in Hong Kong who have only a small number of employees will be subject to prosecution, but those with 2,000 or 20,000 employees will escape prosecution. But there was another reason—this rich publishing tycoon happened to be a long-time family friend of the chief executive.

In the other case, a large piece of residential land, in demand by every land developer in Hong Kong, was given to the son of a Hong Kong tycoon, Mr. Li Ka-shing, to develop as a "Cyberport"—without calling for open tender of bids. The result was that 10 property tycoons issued a public statement criticizing the government. Where is the level playing field? Cronyism has already crept in. For years I have been saying that, if we in Hong Kong cannot export our rule of law to the mainland, the mainland will export its corruption and cronyism to Hong Kong. And it is happening.

Even religious freedom has been affected. I am not saying that people are being put into prison because of their religious beliefs, as they could be in China. However, the pope was not allowed to visit Hong Kong even though the Basic Law says that there shall be religious freedoms in Hong Kong, including the right to be associated with religious groups outside Hong Kong. Why can't the pope visit Hong Kong? If we are really to enjoy this high degree of autonomy under the "one country, two systems" principle, then why not allow the pope's visit? .

One Country, Two Systems

The one country, two systems principle was the brainchild of Deng Xiaoping. He wanted to open China's economy to the outside world, but he knew that it would take a long time for China to catch up with Hong Kong. He wanted China to assume sovereignty over Hong Kong so his name would go down in history as the leader who, by winning Hong Kong back from the British (and Macao back from the Portuguese), wiped away the shame of the Opium War and colonialism. But Deng did not want to drag Hong Kong down with China, which was still developing its economy. That is why he advocated the policy of one country, two systems. You keep your way of life, your rule of law, your level playing field, and your freedoms, he advocated, and China will take 50 years to catch up.

That was his plan, but it has been difficult to implement. China has 1.2 billion people; we have only 6.5 million. Establishing equilibrium between Hong Kong and China is like a game of seesaw between a small boy and a giant. Besides encouraging Hong Kong to stay at one end of the plank, China, at the other end, needs to move toward the center until equilibrium is struck, or there will be no game. But the opposite is being done now. China is staying at the far end, and Tung and his administration are moving Hong Kong toward the center. There is no game and there is no equilibrium. Despite that problem, Deng has done a marvelous thing for China: he has gotten rid of communism.

China's Dilemma

What is the way forward for China? On the one hand, China wants to control people, but, on the other hand, it wants its people to prosper. So, you have troops stationed in Beijing and businesspeople celebrating in Shanghai. You need a psychiatrist to get the right balance.

China's leaders should look to Taiwan as an example. Only a decade ago the Chinese people in Taiwan were just as suppressed by the Kuomintang government as their counterparts in mainland China were by the Chinese Communist Party. In both places dissidents were either thrown in prison or driven overseas. But look at Taiwan today. There are democratic elections. Of course, the rule of law is still weak, but the people are free and prosperous. The Kuomintang is still in charge, but it must work hard to win elections.[1] Why can't the leaders on the mainland do the same? Why don't they look at Hong Kong, where we still have a pretty good system of law, although it is beginning to go down the slippery slope? If we can keep what we have—and it is much easier to keep what you have than to develop what you don't have—we would be able to provide a shining example for China. Instead of being mired in "socialism with Chinese characteristics," China could move forward toward a real market system and the rule of law.

Hong Kong used to be very corrupt but now it is well under control. The Chinese leaders have been talking about the rule of law, but only *talking* about it. Because to implement the rule of law would mean that all the leaders, without exception, would have to comply with the law. That is something they do not want to do.

China's leaders feel very insecure. Look at the way they have reacted to and dealt with the Falun Gong. Why do the leaders feel so insecure? It is because they know they no longer have the mandate. They know that they cannot convince the people. Actually, they should encourage people to practice religion because most religions teach people to love one another, to resolve problems by peaceful means, and to love God or Buddha. But the Chinese leaders don't want that. They want to control people's minds. But how can they?

China's Destiny

What do I feel as a Chinese person? I cannot visit my motherland. The government will not let me in. Not only me. Practically all of the popularly elected legislators are not allowed in.

But when I look at my motherland I see a country much stronger than before. I do not think anybody will look at my Chinese face and say, "Look, you weakling, coming from this weak country China." No they won't say that. But am I really proud of my country? The day when I will be truly proud is the day when I know that the rights of every citizen in China are respected and protected by law. That day will have to come because the whole world is marching toward democracy, freedom, human rights, and the rule of law. China's leaders cannot block that tide for long.

Note

1. In March 2000, the Kuomintang lost in the presidential election but promised a peaceful transfer of power to the Democratic Progressive Party's Chen Shui-bian.

15. Hong Kong's Role in Freeing China: A Trojan Horse That Self-Destructs

Yeung Wai Hong

> The nationalists of all countries have succeeded in convincing their followers that only the policies they recommended are really advantageous to the well-being of the whole nation and of all its honest citizens, of the *we;* and that all other parties are treacherously ready to sell their own nation's prosperity to foreigners, to the *they.*
>
> —Ludwig von Mises

On July 1, 1997, Britain handed Hong Kong to China. On that day, something else went China's way, too. A train car equipped to operate on cataract patients crossed the border. The Hong Kong tycoons who donated the hospital car did not intend the symbolism; subtlety has never been their strong suit. Nevertheless, there was the hope that Hong Kong would, after it became a part of China, help open China's vision to liberty and a free market.

That hope was by no means unfounded. Hong Kong had, for 20 years, been the beacon for China's march toward a free market. It was only reasonable to expect that, after claiming Hong Kong, China would redouble its effort to liberalize.

Sadly, that hope was soon dashed. This is not the usual story of a totalitarian regime setting out to bury capitalism. Instead, a capitalist Hong Kong has become interventionist because the change of sovereignty has dictated a nationalist, hence interventionist, posture. In two short years, the Trojan Horse that was to free China has turned on itself and gone down the path of self-destruction.

That self-destruction began when the new government announced, as its first act of office, a five-year plan to raise homeownership from 65 to 75 percent of households. That was to be accomplished by heavy subsidies and stepped-up construction of public housing.

Then the government abolished English as the language of instruction for virtually all secondary schools. To jump-start the economy with technology, the government gave a prime-site property to the son of Hong Kong's richest man, Li Ka-shing, to develop a "Cyberport"—Hong Kong's answer to Silicon Valley. Most recently, to fulfil its plan to turn Hong Kong into Asia's playground, the government is luring Disney with a U.S.$3 billion "bribe" to build a theme park.

Overnight, Hong Kong turned from Milton Friedman's "last bastion of capitalism" to a centrally planned crony economy with Chinese characteristics. Hong Kong's self-destruction notwithstanding, China will undoubtedly continue to liberalize. With rising expectations that come with 20 years of opening up, it has little choice. However, without Hong Kong there as a beacon, the pace of China's liberalization will be slower than has been seen in the last 20 years. Thus, as it marks its 50th year under communist rule, China might have just seen the best days of market reform.

Hong Kong's Role in Freeing China

In the years after the collapse of socialism, it was common to ask why China had fared better than Russia in economic reform. One reason was that China was less collectivized than Russia, and thus reform was relatively easier for China. But even more important, as Milton Friedman pointed out, was that China, not Russia, had Hong Kong.

Hong Kong's importance to China predated the start of reform in 1978. For some 30 years, Hong Kong was the entrepôt through which China earned most of its foreign exchange. To millions of Chinese living under communist deprivation, Hong Kong was the difference between life and death.

During the bleak days of the Great Leap Forward, in the early 1960s, parcels of food from Hong Kong helped alleviate widespread famine brought on by the collectivization of agriculture. The number of China-bound food parcels was so great that, in 1962, the government-run Hong Kong postal service was even able to turn a profit.

Once the reform was under way, Hong Kong was the first to provide China with capital and commercial know-how. Hong Kong businessmen and traders visiting China helped lift the aspirations of the entire nation. There is perhaps no better indication of Hong

Kong's influence on China than the city of Shenzhen, one of China's four Special Economic Zones.

Shenzhen's Edge

At the beginning of reform, four coastal cities—Shantou, Zhuhai, Xiamen, and Shenzhen—were designated Special Economic Zones. Of the four, only Shenzhen has taken off in any significant way. It developed from a sleepy border town of 30,000 to 40,000 people into China's showcase of reform with more than 3 million people. Former communists, such as Boris Yeltsin, and incumbent communists, such as Fidel Castro, all came to Shenzhen to learn about economic reform.

That was not unlike the heyday of the Cultural Revolution, when communist apologists from the West made their pilgrimage to Dazhai, the Maoist commune that was supposed to have pulled off communist miracles, as would a magician pulling a rabbit out of his hat.

Shenzhen owes its meteoric rise as China's most capitalist city—before the handover of Hong Kong—not so much to a sleight of hand as to its proximity to Hong Kong. That proximity greatly lowered Shenzhen's information cost of adopting "the Hong Kong system" wholesale. That cost advantage has put Shenzhen well above not only the other three Special Economic Zones but also the rest of China.

For example, when it started looking for ways to fund its infrastructure, Shenzhen adopted Hong Kong's leasehold system and auctioned off land. It is not difficult to see why Shenzhen would take to that system: over the years, depending on the stage of the business cycle, proceeds from land auctions have provided the Hong Kong treasury with a third to a half of its revenue.

In addition to a ready source of revenue, the leasehold system is also a face-saving way for a communist regime to establish private property rights while the state continues to own the title to the land. Once property rights are established, the next logical step for China is to copy Hong Kong's mortgage-financing practices. Once both are in place, China will be well on its way to privatizing its housing market.

Hong Kong even had a hand in shaping Shenzhen's appearance. Despite its relative abundance of land, the city's skyline has taken on the Hong Kong look of high-rise buildings—a sign of prosperity.

At the street level, Hong Kong's success in deterring crime by police officers on beat is taken to heart in Shenzhen, which is one of the few Chinese cities that has put its police force on beats.

However, not all the ideas that spilled over to Shenzhen were considered good or wholesome—at least not in the eyes of the Chinese authorities. Although gambling is prohibited in China, Shenzhen punters can now, thanks to underground syndicates, bet on Hong Kong horseracing as easily as millions of their counterparts over the border do. Horseracing has become so popular that producing racing forms is among the most lucrative underground publishing activities in Shenzhen.

Hong Kong in Vogue

Hong Kong's influence on China is by no means confined to Shenzhen. Outside Shenzhen, Hong Kong investors now have the run of the Pearl River Delta. They have set up export-oriented manufacturing activities that employ upward of 4 to 5 million workers in Guangdong Province alone.

While American investments in China—those by General Motors and Chrysler, for example—have made headlines, Hong Kong is the largest "foreign" investor in China. Hong Kong's investments account for some 60 percent of the total foreign investment on the mainland.

One has only to go to Wangfujing Road, in the heart of Beijing, to dispel any doubts about Hong Kong's "economic dominance" over China. This "Champs Elysées" of China's capital is essentially carved up by a handful of Hong Kong companies. At one end of the boulevard is the Palace Hotel (owned in part by Hong Kong's Peninsula Hotel Group) and at the other end is the Oriental Plaza (developed by Li).

Even that most Chinese of human activities—cooking—is not immune from Hong Kong's influence. *The Economist* noted recently that Hong Kong not only "sets the bar for China's culture vultures generally," but when it comes to Chinese cuisine, Hong Kong's influence is "pervasive."[1] Had Russia its own Hong Kong, would its reform not have fared better? It does not take an optimist to see that the removal of the political boundary separating Hong Kong and China should hasten China's march toward a free market.

The Curse of Nationalism

Were it not for the curse of nationalism, Hong Kong would have given China's reform a bigger push. That curse went beyond China's exercising its claim over Hong Kong; the bane of nationalism set Hong Kong on a course—as if by fate—away from free-market capitalism toward interventionism.

Mainland China's assumption of sovereignty over Hong Kong was raw nationalism in action. The "one country, two systems" principle that was to govern postcolonial Hong Kong testified to that: by explicitly leaving Hong Kong's socio-political system alone, the Chinese acknowledged that it was claiming merely the title to Hong Kong. The substance of government, based on private property and the rule of law, was to be left in the hands of "the Hong Kong people"—albeit, the few chosen by Beijing.

That China's totalitarian regime would explicitly abdicate the substance of government underscores two things: first, that China conceded that communism is inferior to capitalism; second, that the concession was, however, not sufficient to overcome nationalistic pride. But for that sense of nationalistic pride, how could the Chinese leadership—having conceded defeat in a contest between economic systems—justify its territorial claim on Hong Kong, thus putting at risk all that Hong Kong had contributed to China since the inception of communist rule?

This overriding nationalist pride has, from that start, compelled the new Hong Kong government to assume a more activist role than the government had done under British rule. The new government cannot put a distinctive Chinese stamp on Hong Kong's free-market capitalism by keeping its hands off. In that sense, the change of sovereignty preordained the unraveling of Hong Kong as we know it.

Hong Kong Unraveled

Hong Kong began to unravel almost immediately after the change of sovereignty. On July 2, 1997, only the second day after the handover, the Thai baht was devalued. That triggered a series of devaluations that has come to be known as the Asian financial crisis.

If it had remained under British rule, Hong Kong would have benefited from such a crisis: flight capital from Southeast Asian countries had always seen Hong Kong as a safe haven, the "Switzerland of the East." Until the spring of 1996, when mainland Chinese

273

missiles were flying across the Taiwan Strait, Taiwanese money was still pouring into Hong Kong. That influx of flight capital stopped after the handover.

In fact, flight capital did not flood into Hong Kong; instead, the Hong Kong dollar and the stock market came under speculative attack almost as soon as the baht was devalued. The attack went on relentlessly for more than a year. Eventually, the new government in Hong Kong was forced to take extraordinary measures to preserve its ill-conceived nationalist pride.

Hong Kong Gone Insane

The new government perceived what was a run-of-the-mill episode as a foreign conspiracy against Hong Kong under Chinese rule. The government fought that "foreign aggression" by spending U.S.$15 billion to nationalize some 10 percent of the stock market. Milton Friedman called that flagrant intervention "insane."[2]

To be fair, Hong Kong fell victim to nationalism even before the handover. The new government is merely exacerbating a situation that has been going on for some time. To ensure that Hong Kong can weather the change of sovereignty—putting to rest the suggestion that only the British could bring prosperity—Beijing initiated, at the beginning of 1997, injections of capital into Hong Kong to prop up the stock and property markets.

That injection brought both the property and stock markets to record levels. However, the unintended consequence was that the infusion of new capital set the stage for the inevitable contraction to follow. In two years, property prices were to fall by half and the unemployment rate was to double, to more than 6 percent. At the same time, the economy went into a tailspin.

Such a disastrous outcome evidently ran counter to Beijing's wishes. Even if Beijing had not shown displeasure, nationalist pride nevertheless would have required the Hong Kong government to restore prosperity by whatever means.

The means the government has chosen are all interventionist old hats—massive infrastructure projects, huge budget deficits, an industrial policy with a hi-tech twist, and the like. In other words, the new government is aggressively pursuing everything that Hong Kong is not.

Among those interventionist schemes, the so-called Cyberport project stands out. The project smells heavily of cronyism. Is it coincidence that Li is the most important patron of the chief executive and that the government granted his son the site for the development without calling for the open tender of bids?

Regardless of the Cyberport's efficacy as a high-tech project, it has touched off a rush for land among developers to claim their own piece of real estate in the name of various "ports"—for example, a Chinese "herbal port" or an American "silicon port."

The Demise of Judicial Independence

Nationalism has not only turned Hong Kong interventionist, it is also undermining Hong Kong's judicial independence and, hence, the rule of law. Two examples illustrate the point.

Hong Kong's Basic Law guarantees the right of abode to offspring of Hong Kong citizens born outside Hong Kong. What the drafters of the Basic Law did not realize was that there would be so many of those people. Official estimates suggest that there could be as many as 1.7 million people. (Though that number did not go unchallenged, the thought that a government known for its integrity might even think of tampering with statistics to shape public opinion underscores how far Hong Kong has sunk in two short years.)

Once the government realized that so many people could settle in Hong Kong, it asked Beijing to overturn Hong Kong's Court of Final Appeal judgment that confirmed these people's rights.

The sudden increase in population was nothing new to Hong Kong, a city of refugees. In fact, almost overnight, on the eve of the communist takeover on the mainland, Hong Kong's population soared from half a million to about 2 million. At that time, up to a third of the population slept on the streets.

Cardinal Wu, of Hong Kong's Catholic church, recalled that statistic in a compassionate plea to let in all those who have the right to settle in Hong Kong—if that is what it takes to preserve the Basic Law.[3] However, the government thought otherwise. It was concerned that a surge in population would create a tremendous fiscal drain on a government and an economy already suffering from recession.

Worse, such an influx of people could once again turn Hong Kong into a city of refugees, with millions of people sleeping on the streets.

Coming so soon after the handover, that disastrous scenario would be a great loss of face to the motherland. If destroying judicial independence, hence the one country, two systems principle, would save face for the mother country, so be it.

In the end, Beijing acceded to the Hong Kong government's request to intervene, and Hong Kong's Court of Final Appeal gained a new name: the Court of Semi-Final Appeal.

Cronyism Rules

The Sally Aw case dealt Hong Kong's rule of law another mortal blow. Publisher Sally Aw is a close friend of C. H. Tung, the first chief executive of the new Hong Kong government. Tung remained on the board of Aw's company until he started his "campaign" for the chief executive office. When Tung became chief executive, his younger brother, C. C. Tung, succeeded him as a member of Aw's board.

Aw has an even more important qualification than merely being a close friend of the Tung family. She is a member of Beijing's National People's Consultative Council, an honorific position generally bestowed on those who have been "useful" to the Chinese government.

Soon after the handover, the government prosecuted three of Aw's executives for defrauding the public by fabricating one of her newspapers' circulation figures. A court later found all three guilty. Though investigators named Aw as a coconspirator, she escaped prosecution. Secretary of Justice (known as attorney general under the British) Elsie Leung gave "public interest" as the reason for not prosecuting Aw.

Leung explained what she meant by "public interest." First, because Aw is a newspaper publisher, to prosecute her would lead the world to think that Hong Kong suppresses freedom of the press. Furthermore, Aw's company employs thousands of people. Should she go to jail, as her employees did, her business would be ruined, and her employees' livelihood would be jeopardized.

In the public's mind, though, it was clear that the biggest "public interest" of all was Aw's connections to both Beijing and C. H. Tung.

Conclusion

It is difficult to exaggerate the positive influence that a capitalist Hong Kong has had on China. That influence went much further than the mere infusion of Hong Kong money and human capital. A prosperous, capitalist Hong Kong based on private property rights and the rule of law has provided China with an excellent role model. In prescribing one country, two systems as the principle by which to govern postcolonial Hong Kong, Deng Xiaoping acknowledged Hong Kong's positive influence in helping China along the road to a free market. He clearly wanted that influence to continue after 1997.

It is one thing for a hardened communist like Deng to concede defeat in a contest between economic systems; tragically, it is quite another for a totalitarian regime that built its legitimacy on nationalism to renounce a claim on what it deems to be territory lost to imperialist aggression.

China thus had to have Hong Kong back. However, the Chinese leadership knew that, for the time being, the capitalist square peg could not fit into a socialist round hole. So the leadership tried to buy time with the one country, two systems principle, hoping that the Chinese characteristics would eventually reconcile the two.

What the Chinese did not bargain for was the nationalist, hence interventionist, pursuits of the new Hong Kong government following the handover. Such pursuits are, however, inevitable. Without a popular mandate, the Hong Kong government must gain Beijing's confidence to stay in office. It cannot do that by prosecuting Beijing's friends.

Furthermore, nationalist pride dictates that the new government must be seen to be doing more for the people than the colonial British "oppressor" had done. That government can do this only by pursuing an activist and interventionist agenda. The intention to keep its "hands off" notwithstanding, the sad thing is that the Hong Kong government simply cannot afford to leave things alone. Until China can exorcise the curse of nationalism, there is little hope that Hong Kong can avert this course of self-destruction.

The backlash from Hong Kong's unraveling has already begun to emerge in China. It does not take a stretch of imagination to suspect that Hong Kong's massive intervention in the stock market influenced the Chinese government to talk up its market earlier this year.

Hong Kong has provided both the means and the inspiration for China to reform. Reform in turn has given China the heft to assert its claim on Hong Kong. Should an interventionist-bent Hong Kong lead China astray in its reform, Hong Kong the Trojan Horse could very well turn into China's poison pill.

Notes

1. "Chinese Food Renaissance Fare," *The Economist,* July 3, 1999.
2. Erik Guyot, "Nobel Laureate Hits Hong Kong for Share Buys," *Asian Wall Street Journal,* September 3, 1998, p. 1
3. Cardinal Wu, "God Is Love," Pastoral Letter, May 1999.

16. Taiwan in China's Future: Flash Point, Model, or Partner?

James R. Lilley

One rarely gets the chance to speak as one wishes on China; therefore, I am pleased to have this opportunity. To discuss whether Taiwan is a partner, a flash point, or a model for China, the following three aspects are worth exploring. First, I would like to draw on an important stream in Chinese historical thinking that has long been overlooked. In my mind, the great Chinese novel *The Romance of the Three Kingdoms* offers the most relevant example of how the Chinese think about themselves and the world around them. Then, I will discuss the intricacies and complexities of interaction between Taiwan and China. Finally, I will explore the power equation between China and the United States. It is important that we realize that the U.S.-Chinese relationship did not begin with the Nixon trip at the height of the Cold War, or the finger pointing over "who lost China?" in the 1950s. China does not need to be a highly politicized issue in American foreign policy.

Chinese Historical Thinking

Sunzi, the great Chinese military strategist of over 2,000 years ago, is always relevant when thinking about China strategically, but *The Romance of the Three Kingdoms* is the book people should read to understand the Chinese perceptions of history, which underlie much Chinese political action.[1] It is important to recognize that the *Three Kingdoms* starts with the sober reflection: "Empires wax and wane: states cleave asunder and coalesce," and ends—120 chapters later—with a similar and rather cynical reflection: "Kingdoms have vanished as in a dream, the useless misery is ours to grieve."[2] This realistic reflection is not prevalent in current Chinese discourse about themselves.[3]

The *Three Kingdoms* is concerned with the nature of human ambition, the will of heaven, and the actions of clever, ruthless men. As

279

the title suggests, the three key players are three kingdoms, all vying for power and control of Zhongyuan—the traditional heartland of the Chinese nation. The three contending kingdoms are Shu, Wei, and Wu.

Shu is the continuation of the Later Han dynasty. Functionally, we can draw a parallel between it and the Communist government from Mao Zedong to Deng Xiaoping to Jiang Zemin. Both perceived themselves to be the orthodox heirs of the previous era.

The leader of Shu was Liu Bei, who is described as someone whose earlobes touched his shoulders and whose hands hung below his knees. He could even see backward past his ears. He is half legend and half man. Similarly, Mao was reported by the state media to be a superman who swam the Yangtze River—the longest river in China—reports with the background of many legends and myths in mind.

Wei is the major contender for power in the *Three Kingdoms*. The patriarch of that house was Tsao Tsao. Tsao Tsao was a man able enough to rule the world. However, because he did not succeed in taking it over, he has been left in history as someone who was wicked enough only to disturb it. Tsao Bei, Tsao Tsao's son even said, "I understand how it was that the virtuous rulers of antiquity got their power."[4] Tsao Tsao's counterparts in contemporary Chinese politics include Lin Biao, at one time Mao's chosen successor, and the Gang of Four, the extreme radicals under Chairman Mao's eccentric wife Jiang Qing. These people are the challengers, who win battles and lose battles, but do not stay for long, and thus are viewed as agitators in the general flow of Chinese history.

Wu is less important in the power struggle as told in the *Three Kingdoms*, because historical tales in China are often depicted with two sides, the *Han* (the upright and virtuous) versus the *Zei* (the thief).

The *Three Kingdoms*, according to the great scholar of China, C. H. Brewitt-Taylor, is a vast, long landscape-painting scroll—a continuous spectacle with only a single episode visible at any one time. The epic surges forward like a great wave, ever moving against the swelling sea of human ambition. The pageant ends when, after a series of pointless battles, a general of Wei usurps the throne and establishes hegemony over the two other kingdoms.

In contrast with the *Three Kingdoms*, Lao-tzu's *Daodejing*[5] says, and I paraphrase: Do not worry when your authority does not intimidate people; do not impoverish them or harass their lives. And for the very reason that you do not harass them, they will cease to turn away from you. Perhaps Lao-tzu's wisdom can be applied to Taiwan today.

Therefore, in China's intellectual discourse, there are historical tales of brutality, cunning, and manipulation alongside benign, gracious sentiments from philosophers and poets. That duality is not unique to China; however, it is very deeply accepted and imbedded in Chinese thought. It manifests itself today in principles and pragmatism, in China's sanctimony about itself and sarcasm and skepticism toward its adversaries. Keeping this duality in mind is helpful for understanding the nature of China's relationship with Taiwan.

China's Bucking a World Trend

Today, two forces pull and push at the world. Pushing the world closer together is the growing economic interdependence and globalization of markets. Proponents hope to see the emergence of economic regions where capital and goods can move across borders freely. Others anticipate that efficiency will be achieved when many economic decisions are made by multinational houses of finance instead of national governments.

On the other hand, nationalism cuts into economic integration and tries to pull the world apart. Protectionism, nontrade barriers, security issues such as who controls telecommunications, and *Juche*, the weird autarkical policy of North Korea, have all been cited ad nauseum. Instead of softening political borders, economic development has become a tool of mercantilists and nationalists.

There was hope among some people that rising economic expectations would lead to more open societies and to democracy. But a number of Asian leaders apparently had something else in mind: authoritarian rule in politics and heavy government intervention in the market. Apprehension about this illiberal trend has been expressed in books such as *Asia Rising* and *Japan as Number One*.[6] And the Chinese diaspora has been alternately described as either an instrument of the People's Republic of China or a vast international force leading the way to greater economic integration.

In China, catchwords such as "sacred sovereignty," "historic borders," and "unity" thwart attempts at greater integration. And increasingly, such terms as "anti-imperialism" and "anti-hegemony" are becoming code words directed against the United States. This is a departure from China's past rhetoric, which was composed of grievances against foreign big-nosed bullies and a century of humiliation. The new rhetoric puts Chinese protests on a more aggressive platform.

It is ironic that the most serious and strident defense of nationalism comes from Communists—Fidel Castro, Slobodan Milosevic, and Jiang Zemin—who depart from the communist theology that the international communist movement should supplant individual countries' preoccupation with national boundaries.

Taiwan as a Partner

Taiwan and China have come close to being partners economically. Since 1987, Taiwan's investments in China have grown phenomenally, to an estimated $40 billion and 40,000 enterprises. Taiwan has been one of China's largest external investors.

Politically, though, there is a snarling disparity. The difference is like a huge sumolike wrestler—powerful and flabby, insecure and greedy—meeting the little guy—mean, hard, and loud but populist in a genuine way. The schoolyard bully meets the defiant little guy.

Taiwan and China might look alike, talk alike, or even sing alike, but they quarrel incessantly. Our challenge then, is to move the conversation away from such issues as missiles, theater missile defense, one China, two Chinas, three kingdoms, one state, two states, one China, one Taiwan—which all belong to an arcane, unsolvable, and complex Chinese problem—to economic partnership, particularly in this time of financial stress in Asia. All over Asia, economic systems are being threatened—in Indonesia, North Korea, and other countries—and money that should have been appropriated for investment has flowed instead to arms purchases, military buildups, and force-modernization programs. Unfortunately, the United States is part of the problem, as our arms and our technology industry have been heavily involved.

At the same time, Beijing has yet to learn how to be a partner. Beijing's imperial edicts, reminiscent of those of earlier dynasties such as the Manchu, tend to try to impose order on neighboring countries. For instance, the February 1992 law passed by the National

People's Congress included provisions on the Spratly islands, Taiwan, and the Senkaku islands and brooked no challenge. China has reserved its right to use force. This imperial attitude directly conflicts with principles of self-determination and the democratic processes that are needed to achieve peaceful integration.

I may have painted a stark picture, but this must also be looked at against the backdrop of thousands of deals and exchanges at the highest level between China's political leaders and Taiwan's businessmen. For instance, Douglas Hsu of Taiwan Far Eastern Textiles—who once had his magazine put a picture of himself and Lee Teng-hui on one page and himself and Jiang on the adjacent page—said to me, and I paraphrase: I am an industrialist. I have enough problems building plants, I should not be worried about missiles back and forth. This is a cloud—if it stays there, China will pay a price. As if reflecting the general sentiment of Taiwanese businessmen, Taiwanese investments in China have been on a steady decline since 1998, and went down a further 30 percent in the first half of 1999. In contrast, Taiwanese investments elsewhere in the world went up 10 percent in the first half of 1999.

But economic cooperation continues despite the statistics, just at a slower pace. For instance, Evergreen Corporation has been investing heavily in China, especially in the coastal areas. And this close relationship has translated into a gentle push to open the "three links"—direct mail, transportation, and trade. This is for the sake of efficiency and for keeping a competitive edge. Cooperation and communication are also under way in other less politically sensitive areas: Paul Hsu, a leading lawyer in Taiwan, is hoping to streamline intellectual property rights practices between the two sides by holding legal seminars in Shanghai. The seminars are well attended.

There has always been hope that economic integration would lead to more conciliatory gestures in the political realm. If Wang Jun, the son of the old revolutionary Wang Zhen, could play golf with Jeffrey Koo, a leading businessman in Taiwan and cochairman of the U.S.-Taiwan Business Council, when he visited Taiwan, the possibilities are perhaps endless. In fact, Jeffrey Koo said to me when he was in Alaska, en route to China, "We can deal with China—you Americans often get it wrong. If you would stop flexing or alternately cringing, we could probably work things out among ourselves."

The concept of one China is like a beautiful rainbow with a pot of gold at the end—and it remains ephemeral. For now, the PRC has adopted the equivalent of former West Germany's Hallstein Doctrine, which insisted on one Germany. It is noteworthy, however, that although Chancellor Willy Brandt's opening to the east effectively ended Hallstein's vision of one Germany, the abandonment of that doctrine did result in a unified Germany in the end. Under that same logic, is it likely that, if China were to officially recognize Taiwan, there would be a unified China further down the road?

Not in the foreseeable future, but rainbows, which argue for a brighter future, must exist. Perhaps a more realistic way of looking at the cross-strait situation is to consider the Marxist-Hegelian concept of thesis, antithesis, and synthesis. In a more local context, Confucius's Doctrine of the Mean advises its students to always take the middle path, avoiding extremes. Singaporeans and other well-intentioned people have also been contributing various proposed solutions to this arcane game between China and Taiwan, but with limited success. Singapore did, however, host the first cross-strait meeting in April 1993. There was also a second meeting in Shanghai and Beijing, but the third meeting appears to have been postponed by China.

The paradigm of economics driving Taiwan and China toward greater partnership in other areas has merit. For example, an education task force created within Taiwan's Executive Yuan decided in August 1999 to adopt the pinyin system of romanization of Chinese characters used by the PRC. According to Hong Kong finance secretary Donald Tsang, Hong Kong has already adopted the pinyin system. In Taiwan, however, the decision was not made on political grounds. The government felt that linguistic matters should be handled pragmatically, for economic reasons.

The decision was about business. For instance, ACER, the largest computer company in Taiwan, has withdrawn from its semiconductor fabrication project to invest $1 billion in developing Internet software and exploring the potential for e-commerce in China. Microsoft may dominate English-language Web sites, but ACER hopes to dominate the Chinese portion of the Internet. A uniform system for romanization of Chinese characters could quicken the pace of both business and information exchange and avoid much confusion—especially when both sides are diverging more and more on the *Chinese* rendition of characters. A fairly convincing case can be made that, as economic partners, China and Taiwan are moving in the right direction.

Another factor that ties Taiwan and China together is culture, as was amply illustrated when Koo Chen-fu, the distinguished Taiwanese businessman and head of the Straits Exchange Foundation, made his epochal trip to Beijing in 1998. He sang *Kong Chengji* ("Strategy of the Empty City")—to a full house, and brought the audience to its feet clapping. This was a noteworthy moment, because Koo, a native Taiwanese, appeared to know more about traditional Chinese culture than did most of the Chinese present. He sang with such a flourish and dignity that he earned the admiration of his Chinese hosts, who tend to be very protective of, but somewhat uninformed about, their culture.

The cultural affinity is no illusion. Koo even stated: "We have a special relationship with China, it is based on common culture, history, language, understandings. We share this with you." It is a shame that agreements reached between Wang Daohan, former mayor of Shanghai and head of China's cross-strait organization, and Koo Chen-fu—two superior men whose sense of brotherhood is reminiscent of the peach garden oath of *The Romance of the Three Kingdoms*—are oftentimes thwarted by the political ambitions of others and by intervention from forces higher up.

Taiwan as a Flash Point

Conflict across the Taiwan Strait is part of a 63-year-old civil war, which started when the Communists and the Nationalists split in 1927. In the early years of that conflict, millions died in combat or as the result of floods and shortages of food. But since the military confrontation in Quemoy in 1958, almost no Chinese have died in combat. This has been the case for the past 42 years. Taiwan, therefore, is not Kosovo, Kashmir, or Korea, where much blood has been spilt.

Rhetoric has often crowded out reality, however. For instance, Mao was reported to have said to a high-ranking visitor that China could wait for 100 years to unify with Taiwan. When the same visitor later asked Jiang if Mao's policy had changed, Jiang reportedly said yes. It is now 87 years instead of 100.

The reality is that there are anecdotes and comments from China that often imply different things. Taiwan is not an immediate flash point, although there are arguments and incidents—not all originating from China—to support such a view. For instance, in a recent meeting, a well-known U.S. strategist on China talked about a preemptive strike that China might make against Taiwan. But when I asked the Chinese military officer sitting next to me what he thought of the assessment, he said, "He really doesn't know much about China's strategy—we are not suicidal."

China has, on the other hand, often fought wars on its periphery—sometimes successfully, sometimes not—against India, Vietnam, Korea, the Soviet Union. But Chinese willingness to fight can be distorted by Americans as well. In 1996, an American military attaché commented to me, "A million Chinese would die to take Taiwan." In reality, China altered its aggressiveness against Quemoy in 1958 after fewer than 50 casualties.

Another misconception is the view that any Chinese leader who compromised on Taiwan could not stay in power. The reality is that the congressional passage of the Taiwan Relations Act was followed shortly by the nine-point Peaceful Reunification Proposal by Ye Jianying—a marshal in the People's Liberation Army and close associate of Deng. Likewise, Deng did not fall from grace after Washington's F-16 sales to Taiwan. In fact, two months after the U.S. sale China and Taiwan agreed to disagree on a one-China formula, and five months after that, negotiators from Taiwan and China sat down in Singapore for their first significant talks since 1949. Jiang was not removed from power in March 1996, when he had to back down in the face of U.S. aircraft carriers patrolling close by the Taiwan Strait. Jiang wisely declared victory and went home.

The fact is, Taiwan can become a flash point only if it is made into one—by bungling on the U.S. side, provocation on the Taiwanese side, and overreaction on the Chinese side.

It would be unwise for the United States to fight another land war in Asia. At sea, China cannot match us militarily. In air power, China is improving its missile technology and is compiling an arsenal in preparation for asymmetrical warfare, but time remains on our side. Our technological edge in advanced weaponry is still considerable. However, the hollowing out of our military and our tendency to cut back on overseas commitments provide opportunities for our rivals. China is a continental nation facing a string of island nations along its eastern coast. With memories of the Opium Wars in the 19th century and the Japanese invasion from the sea in 1931, China has historical reasons to feel that its east coast is exposed and vulnerable. Added to that, the eastern coast is once again its richest area.

China has legitimate reasons to want to defend itself and extend its reach to the surrounding archipelagoes, but in doing this it must come to terms with the United States. Our interests intersect, but there is still room for compromise.

Taiwan as a Model

A high-level Chinese Foreign Ministry official asked me in 1989, before the Tiananmen Square episode, "How did Taiwan do it? What was their way of moving up the scale in economic development?" We had a long conversation on this subject, and in my response I relied heavily on books by economists from Yale and Taiwan regarding Taiwan's economic miracle.

Another question was posed to me at that time. It concerned China's entry into the General Agreement on Tariffs and Trade (superseded by the World Trade Organization). When talking about the issue, I would try to tell my Chinese hosts that it was really in their best interest to let Taiwan join simultaneously, and they should even help Taiwan get into the GATT. The point I tried to make was that economic development is superior to confrontation.

China does not have to be at constant odds with Taiwan. In fact, China draws many lessons from Taiwan. Special Economic Zones in China are modeled in part on Taiwan's Special Export Zones. Taiwan, China, and Hong Kong are trying to synthesize their banking laws and have held conferences on this subject, although progress has been slow; China has not yet even worked out details with Hong Kong. Another good example of China's emulating Taiwan is the export of Taiwan's sugar industry to Sichuan Province. The industry is becoming obsolete in Taiwan, but with Taiwanese sugar mill machinery and the abundance of arable fields in China, a sugar export industry is being introduced in Sichuan.

Taiwan as a political model is not yet acceptable to China. Nevertheless, village elections in China today are reminiscent of earlier local electoral developments in Taiwan. What is happening in China bears a certain similarity to Taiwan under the early presidency of Chiang Ching-Kuo. At first, the government in Taiwan closely controlled "free" village and *xian* (district) elections. It was 20 years before elections reached the national level in Taiwan, and opposition groups, such as the Democratic Progressive Party, rose in stature to pose a legitimate challenge to the ruling party. Beijing could benefit from Taiwan's evolving experience.

The U.S. Role

The United States has been drawn into an intricate drama akin to *The Romance of the Three Kingdoms,* whether we like it or not. We have ties to both sides: the recognition of China, the adoption of the Taiwan Relations Act, security guarantees, arms sales to Taiwan, and international cooperation with China.

Cooperation with China has included bringing down the USSR. Such cooperation included monitoring from northwestern China Soviet nuclear and missile developments, orchestrating a political solution in Cambodia, and defeating the Soviet invasion in Afghanistan. More recently, U.S.-PRC efforts have included some Chinese cooperation on East Timor. There are still basic philosophical differences regarding international intervention, as reflected in the Kosovo conflict, but, as demonstrated by the case of East Timor, even China has to go along with the international norm when it does not have valid arguments against it. What could China object to when the host nation, Indonesia, accepted the intervention of international forces?

As for Taiwan, it is probably more secure today without U.S. troops on its territory—it does not have to deal with the ensuing social fallout that is likely to happen with the presence of U.S. troops. Its own advanced military is the first line of defense against military attack.

The United States has kept a balance in the region. We have military deployments near Taiwan, in the East China Sea, and in the South China Sea. Our troops, however, are concentrated mostly in Japan and Korea, and they are becoming sitting ducks for missile attacks. The United States must think these deployments through strategically: we should consider changing our concept of forward deployment in East Asia, as well as accurately projecting the kind of conflicts we might have to face there.

This is a long-term question—it is important that we keep a solid military presence in Asia, because it is wanted by the countries in the area and has been important for stability and economic growth. The immediate priority, however, should be WTO entry for China and Taiwan. The United States needs to realize that it is imperative that China and Taiwan enter the WTO as closely together as possible.

Simultaneous entry is crucial to peace, because both sides could then deal with each other as equals within the WTO and would use WTO mechanisms to negotiate specific problems—possibly, the establishment of sea links, air links, and mail links—which could lead to other forms of communication and confidence-building measures.

We do not want any military surprises in the Taiwan Strait, and there are ways in which surprises can be averted. Increasingly sophisticated commercial satellite technology can now give real-time coverage of a large area. With geosynchronous satellites over the Taiwan Strait commercially available, no one could move a tank, a sampan, a cruiser, or a destroyer without being spotted. I realize this is perhaps premature, but it is the sort of action that could be worked on once the ball gets rolling—once we get away from the endless semantic struggles and posturing between the two sides concerning the Taiwan Strait.

It is important at this moment that the United States insist that the subject be changed from military to economic matters. We must try to influence the agenda. And we should be able do so, because we should have learned from our past mistakes. We are not going to link human rights concerns with China's normal trade relations (NTR) status. At the same time, we are not going to have a cause célèbre; seminal events such as President Lee Teng-hui's trip to the United States in 1995 weaken stability. We must handle Taiwan with greater skill, not with condescension. We know that when we mess up our Taiwan policy, our China policy is inevitably affected. On the other hand, if we get our Taiwan policy right, Chinese forces will move ahead in their own way as they did in 1987, when unprecedented progress was made in opening trade and in protecting U.S. intellectual property rights in both China and Taiwan.

The United States should not lean to either side in these Chinese semantic arguments—although we have tended to do that—because the repercussions, if mishandled, can affect our whole policy. If we take a position on the "three noes"—no independent Taiwan, no two-China policy, and no support for Taiwan in international organizations where statehood is a requirement—which circumscribes Taiwan's international flexibility, Taiwan will react. If we do not discourage China from imposing its own version of one China—namely, China is the PRC and Taiwan is part of the PRC—Taiwan will react. These are internal battles from which the United States should stand aside. We can influence what people do and keep the exchanges peaceful, but the internal games—like those described in *The Romance of the Three Kingdoms*—are best kept between the two parties that are struggling for power.

So in the end, I am left with a sense of optimism, because despite the complexities and intricacies of Chinese-Taiwanese ties, it appears that our own dialogue with China is moving away from the narrow focus on arm sales, or theater missile defense versus missile deployments, and is beginning to approach more diverse issues, such as solving the dangerous problem of North Korea. We should work together to establish a peaceful, prosperous environment in the 21st century. Our interests should coalesce, not be cleaved asunder.

Notes

1. *The Romance of the Three Kingdoms* (Tokyo: Charles E. Tuttle, 1960).
2. Ibid., vol. 1, p. 1.
3. Ibid., vol. 2, p. 623.
4. Ibid., vol. 1, p. ix.
5. Lao-tzu, *Tao teh ching*, ed. Paul Sih (New York: St. John's University Press, 1961), pp. 103 and 106.
6. Jim Rohwer, *Asia Rising* (New York: Simon and Schuster, 1995); and Ezra Vogel, *Japan as Number One: Lessons for America* (Cambridge, Mass.: Harvard University Press, 1987).

17. Political Change in Post-Mao China: Progress and Challenges

Minxin Pei

The post-Mao era (1976 to the present) has seen the most rapid progress in economic development in Chinese history. Most quantitative measures suggest that the Chinese economy has experienced a significant structural transformation and, to a lesser extent, attendant institutional changes.[1] China's progress in political reform, however, has been much slower. Although some important institutional changes are beginning to take place, especially in the strengthening of legislative institutions, the development of a legal system, and the experimentation with rural self-government, the overall pace of political reform significantly lags behind that of economic reform and development.[2] The lack of dramatic progress toward democratization has led some analysts to question the connection between market-oriented reforms and political liberalization and casts doubt on whether China is actually following the gradualist Taiwanese model of democratization.[3] The disparity between China's economic modernization and its political development has been a serious source of friction, not only domestically between new socioeconomic conditions created by market reforms and old and increasingly dysfunctional political institutions, but also externally between China and Western industrial democracies, which have grown impatient with China's slow pace of democratization and more assertive in demanding quick improvement.

This chapter examines the process of political change in post-Mao China and explores the prospects for political liberalization. The first section studies the restoration of political order following the calamitous Cultural Revolution (1966–76). The second section assesses the emerging trends of institutional pluralism. The third section probes the implications of the disparity between the pace of economic reform and that of political change.

Restoration of Political Order

The first priority of the Deng Xiaoping regime on its assumption of power in 1979 was to restore China's most basic political norms and institutions, which were devastated by the Cultural Revolution. That effort consisted of two components: establishment of rules and norms governing intraelite conflict and distribution of benefits and formulation of a new social contract revamping state-society relations.

New Elite Norms

A key lesson learned by the victims of Mao's Cultural Revolution (many of whom were members of the ruling elite) was that a political system risked implosion if it did not have a set of norms to provide personal security for the ruling elite. During the Mao era, political life for the members of the ruling Chinese Communist Party who had run afoul of the faction in power was, as Hobbes put it, "nasty, brutish, and short." There were no formal or informal rules and procedures governing internal power struggles and limiting penalties to the losers. Consequently, victims of intraregime conflict were not protected by due process. They faced disastrous consequences, not just to their political careers and personal security, but to their families. Such an environment fostered a zero-sum political mentality among the ruling elite, who would fight their political enemies with no mercy and win at any cost to avoid losing everything (should their opponents prevail). Thus a vicious cycle—lack of institutionalized security guarantees to the members of the ruling elite providing incentives for totally unrestrained struggle for power—emerged under Mao's rule and constituted the main source of instability among the elites and in the political system.

It was not a surprise that one of the first steps taken by Deng was to end this vicious cycle. He accomplished this task not only by rehabilitating almost all of the victims of Mao's purges but also by establishing a new set of rules to limit intraelite power struggles. Formally, most of these rules were enshrined in *Dangnei zhengzhi shenghuo de ruogan zhunze* (Some Principles on the Party's Internal Politics), issued in 1980. Among other things, this document specified the basic procedures for resolving political differences within the CCP. Deng's effort to repair the CCP's internal norms did not eliminate serious internal power struggles, nor did Deng himself abide by those procedures at the critical junctures of such struggles (e.g., his dismissals of Hu Yaobang and Zhao Ziyang as CCP general secretary in 1987 and 1989, respectively). However, those new norms seem to have become binding. With the possible exception of Bao Tong (Zhao Ziyang's chief aid who received a jail sentence on trumped-up charges in 1989), no losers of intraelite power struggles experienced the physical abuse and other types of persecution characteristic of the Maoist regime.[4] More important, the new norms effectively ended the practice of large-scale purges, also characteristic of the periodic political campaigns launched under Mao. Typically, top-level political infighting ended with the dismissal of a senior leader and a few of his key followers. The political system was spared convulsive top-to-bottom witch-hunts. Those norms may have substantially contributed to stability of the elite in the post-Mao era. A recent study of the mobility of Chinese provincial leadership shows that, although massive purges of provincial leaders routinely accompanied power struggles at the top prior to the 1980s, provincial leadership remained very stable during the Deng era, indicating greater security of China's ruling elite.[5]

In addition, Deng devised two institutional reforms to manage intraelite conflict and install a more merit- and education-based promotion system within the elite. The first reform—limited competition for some leadership positions in the party and the government—provided a subtle mechanism for removing the most controversial figures on both ends of the ideological spectrum to ensure a centrist leadership orientation. Over the years, that scheme seemed to have worked as designed, as many such controversial figures (more hard-liners than soft-liners) lost elections for important positions (such as memberships on the Central Committee). The second reform, which combined mandatory retirement of government officials and promotion based on educational qualifications, removed a key source of intraelite conflict and ushered a new generation of leadership into key decisionmaking positions. The stabilizing effect of a more institutionalized process of elite promotion and retirement cannot be exaggerated because, without such a system, as was the case in the Mao era, upward mobility would remain low and unpredictable, and frustration within the lower ranks of the ruling elite would accumulate, making intraelite struggle for power and position more likely and more frequent. Since its implementation in 1982, the mandatory retirement system has increased the circulation of the elite within the regime and revitalized it with fresh blood.[6] More than 5 million government officials had been forced into retirement by the end of 1989. In 1989, of all government officials, only 1 percent was older than 60, while 80 percent were younger than 50.[7]

The emphasis on educational qualifications as a key criterion for promotion has brought about a fundamental transformation within China's ruling elite.[8] That change is reflected in the increasing share of government officials who have received a higher education. According to official sources, of the 4.55 million government officials in 1989, 23 percent had received a higher education and 25 percent had been educated in vocational schools. Educational requirements seem to be higher for those in the upper echelons of government. In 1998 nearly 60 percent of government officials in the State Council and its ministries had received a higher education, mostly in natural science or engineering.[9] The improvement, in both age profile and educational qualifications, of members of the CCP Central Committee was similarly impressive. In 1982 the average age of a member of the committee was 59, and about 55 percent of the members had received a college education. In 1997 the average age had dropped to 56, and nearly 93 percent of the members had received a college education.[10] It is difficult to gauge the effects of the homogenization of the ruling elite on policy in the post-Mao era. On the surface, homogenization certainly seems to have greatly expanded the centrist base and reduced ideological rivalry within the ruling hierarchy. If that is the case, Deng's strategy of rebuilding the norms within the CCP must be considered a major success of his regime.

China's New Social Contract

Two decades after the end of the Mao era, the broad contours of a new social contract have become more identifiable. This contract consists, implicitly, of several key provisions that seem to be honored by both the state and society. The overall consequence of the implementation of such a contract has been a significant expansion of personal (but not political) freedom and a considerable decline in the level of political repression. The expansion of personal freedoms (such as travel, residence, employment, and access to information) has been the result of an implicit commitment by the state to withdraw from the private realm. In all likelihood, the post-Mao regime hoped to win back some popular support by abandoning most of the draconian practices of the Mao era that restricted, politicized, and criminalized otherwise fully legitimate private behavior. In the last two decades, this process of withdrawal has been gradual but substantial. Despite several conservative attempts to reverse this process (such as the Anti–Spiritual Pollution campaign in 1983 and the periodic crackdown on pornography), the degree of state intrusion into the private sphere has declined dramatically. In the economic sphere, the withdrawal of the state has been the most dramatic and far-reaching, with the gradual decline of the state-owned enterprises (SOEs) and the rapid rise of private and semiprivate enterprises. In the cultural sphere, the state's hold on mass entertainment, popular lifestyle, and personal values has been seriously eroded as a result of the rise of market forces and increasing public assertiveness of personal rights. In the social sphere, limited relaxation of state control, growing influence of the market, and rising interest in forming associations have led to a considerable increase in the number and variety of unofficial or semiofficial organizations engaged in diverse social, cultural, and civic activities.[11]

Another important component of the new social contract is the reduction of political repression. Compared with the totalitarian Maoist regime, which carried out massive and indiscriminate repression through repeated political campaigns and displayed complete disregard for the basic legal rights of Chinese citizens, the post-Mao regime has adopted a more "soft-authoritarian" approach to political repression.[12] Massive repression of the general population has been replaced by selective repression of a small group of individuals who openly challenge the CCP's rule. Moreover, such selective repression is implemented through the post-Mao regime's legal system instead of through mass campaigns. Of course, the post-Mao regime's record of honoring the new social contract is not totally spotless. On three occasions, the regime came very close to breaking it: the 1983 Anti–Spiritual Pollution campaign, the 1989 Tiananmen crackdown, and the 1999 anti–Falun Gong movement. But a close examination of those incidents shows that, despite the regime's harsh rhetoric and initial missteps, repression was carefully controlled and eventually curtailed. Whether repression in post-Mao China has really decreased is controversial. Most critics of China's human rights practices maintain that it remains high. They cite the 2,000 to 3,000 political prisoners in the Chinese penal system and the 200,000 to 300,000 inmates in the *laojiao* (reeducation-through-labor) camps, whose punishment was administratively, rather than judicially, determined. Empirical evidence, however, shows a very different picture. Strictly measured, the level of political repression (defined as physical persecution of the regime's opponents) has fallen dramatically from the Mao era to the post-Mao era. Although political repression may be high by the international standards of the post–Cold War era, it is very low by China's historical standard. Take, for example, the percentage of political prisoners (categorized as "counterrevolutionaries"): data collected by Chinese researchers show that, as of 1980, about 13 percent of all inmates in Chinese jails were counterrevolutionaries; in 1989, only .5 percent were. Historical data from Sha'anxi Province show that the percentage of counterrevolutionaries in its jail system averaged 33 percent between 1953 and 1968.[13]

Embryonic Institutional Pluralism

Progress toward political liberalization has been relatively slow in the post-Mao era. The last two decades witnessed brief periods of political openness that were quickly followed by conservative backlash, as was the case in the Democracy Wall movement of 1978–79, the debate about alienation under socialism in 1982, the political reform debate in 1986–87, the political liberalization leading up to the Tiananmen Square movement in 1989, and the "Beijing Spring" of 1998. That track record of political reform disappoints even the most ardent believers in the positive relationship between economic development and democratization because, despite a more than quadrupling of China's gross domestic product in the last two decades, the Chinese political system has attained few ostensibly democratic institutions.

However, it is premature to dismiss the link between market-oriented economic development and democratization in China. First, the process of economic reform is only about two decades old and evolved from a very elemental foundation characterized by a host of unfavorable socioeconomic conditions. Given the experience of other developing countries in which democratic institutions grew gradually (such as South Korea, Taiwan, and Mexico), this evolutionary process could take a long time (almost four decades in South

Korea and Taiwan, and much longer in Mexico). It is wrong to simply claim that democratization in China will not occur in the future because it has not occurred yet. Second, democratization can be conceptualized as a phased development. Although the final breakthrough may be sudden and dramatic (with the replacement or the overthrow of the previous regime), most of this development typically occurs with little drama or outside notice. The final break-through can be preceded by years, if not decades, of slow and frequently interrupted development of some of the basic social and political infrastructure of democracy (such as a freer press, civic organizations, independent courts, and institutional pluralism). The focus on political change, therefore, must be on the gradual emergence of such infrastructure.

In the following section, I examine three important trends that constitute institutional pluralism: China's emerging legislative, judicial, and electoral institutions.

Legislative Institutions

The post-Mao era witnessed a gradual emergence of the National People's Congress, the country's constitutionally supreme lawmaking body, as an increasingly assertive institution that has deftly capitalized on its new constitutional status. At the subnational level, the provincial and municipal People's Congress has also gained considerable institutional clout (especially in the elections and confirmation of senior provincial and municipal executives and monitoring of local government bureaucracies).[14] Given its critical importance as China's supreme lawmaking institution, the NPC's evolution over the last two decades has attracted most of the scholarly attention.

The degree of institutional assertiveness and maturity of the NPC can be measured by several indicators, such as legislative output, organizational development, and symbolic assertion of constitutional prerogatives.

Legislative Output. Measured by the number of laws passed by the NPC, legislative output dramatically increased in the post-1979 era. In the two decades since 1978, the NPC has passed 165 major laws, amended 32 laws, and issued 88 resolutions. Judged by legislative output, the NPC has become increasingly productive.[15] The 8th People's Congress passed more than twice the number laws than the

5th Congress did and nearly doubled the total legislative output achieved during the 5th Congress. There were several explanations for the NPC's growing legislative output. First, it could be directly related to the NPC's growing institutional power and autonomy, which enabled it to influence the legislative agenda. Second, the choices of the chairmen of the NPC Standing Committee could also have a significant impact on the NPC's legislative output. Wan Li and Qiao Shi, who, respectively, chaired the 7th and 8th NPC Standing Committee, were known to be more liberal than their predecessors, Ye Jianying and Peng Zhen. Third, many major laws required long periods of time to draft, and legislative compromises were reached only after long negotiations among the major players involved in the legislative process (the NPC's own legislative staff, the state bureaucracy, the CCP, and the legal community).

The rapid pace of legislation has dramatically reshaped the Chinese legal system. At the end of 1994, of the 130 laws in effect, only six had been passed before 1978. Of the 81 NPC resolutions in effect, only five had been passed before 1978; of the 356 State Council regulations in effect, only 45 had been issued before 1978; of the 203 rules made by various ministries, only 9 had been promulgated before 1978.[16] It is worth noting, moreover, that the government's top legislative priority since the late 1970s has been the passage of laws governing economic activities and practices. That is evident in that nearly one-third of all legislative output consisted of such laws and about 40 percent of all freestanding laws may be classified as economic laws.

Organizational Development. Prior to its resurgence, the NPC did not have much of an organizational structure. Its permanent staff was less than a dozen; its technical legislative capacity (research and drafting) and ability to influence the content of legislation was minimal; its own internal operating rules and procedures were nonexistent.[17] In the last two decades, the NPC has experienced substantial organizational development along those lines. The NPC has gained a sizable permanent staff (more than 2,000 at the end of the 1980s), acquired a significant technical capacity for drafting laws, established specialized legislative committees that are influential in drafting and debating proposed legislation, and set up clear operative rules and procedures.

The organizational development of the NPC has begun to affect its legislative activities and its relationship with the CCP and the state bureaucracy. Before the NPC gained its current organizational stature, the legislative body dutifully passed—with no amendments—the legislation desired and drafted by the State Council. Since 1983 (when the NPC Standing Committee for the first time voted down a draft law proposed by the State Council) it has blocked the passage of several laws because its deputies opposed certain provisions (e.g., the Highway Law proposed by the State Council in 1999 was shelved because some members of the NPC Standing Committee objected to the fuel tax contained in the law). However, the most potent weapon of the NPC was not outright defeat of a government-proposed bill but the group's bargaining power at various stages of the legislative process. The enhanced power of the NPC led some observers to believe that no major laws can pass the NPC without its own legislative input in the form of drafting and bargaining. The NPC signaled its coming of age in 1993 by announcing its own legislative plan (such plans used to be drawn by the State Council) and its intention not to consider proposed legislation not contained in the plan.[18]

Symbolic Assertion of Constitutional Prerogatives. Political institutions gain power not simply by organizational capacity and influence but also by constant symbolic assertion of their authority and prerogatives. In the case of the NPC, this type of assertion is expressed in the following forms:

- Voting against laws in order to register opposition, even though such opposition fails to block their passage. It is notable that some of China's laws were passed with a large number of deputies (as many as one-third) voting against those laws (such as the People's Bank Law and the Education Law in 1995).
- Using its power of confirmation to express disapproval of the CCP's personnel decisions. In the March 1995 session of the NPC, 20 to 33 of the deputies voted against the nominations of two CCP Politburo members to be vice premiers. Similar incidents have been reported in the provinces, where deputies in local people's congresses rejected the CCP's nominees for provincial executive positions and selected write-in candidates.
- Voting against major government reports in order to register discontent with the bureaucracy's performance. In the 1996 session, 30 percent of the NPC deputies openly opposed the report

given by the Supreme Procurate on law enforcement and anti-corruption. Twenty percent of the deputies voted against the report given by the chief judge of the People's Supreme Court. In the March 1997 session, 848 deputies (32 percent of all deputies) refused to support the annual report of the People's Supreme Court, and 1,065 (about 40 percent) of the deputies voted against the annual report of the Supreme Procurate. Such public display of discontent forced the government to take specific steps to address the issue of corruption in the judicial system.[19]

The causes for the gradual rise of the NPC are complex. Two leading American scholars of the NPC, Michael W. Dowdle and Murray Scot Tanner, argued that the CCP's voluntary withdrawal from the legislative arena was an important factor. In their view, the relocation of the day-to-day control of lawmaking from the CCP to the NPC allowed the institution to assert its constitutional prerogatives more effectively.[20] Second, the norms of constitutionalism and procedural legitimacy may be taking root and becoming a factor in forcing the CCP leadership to take into account the NPC's constitutional status and institutional interest. In the post-Mao era, when a personalized ideology no longer has any appeal or legitimizing power, such norms, however incipient, may have worked to the advantage of the NPC. Third, the NPC also owes its growing clout to the appointments of several CCP heavyweights as chairmen of its Standing Committee: Ye Jianying, Peng Zhen, Wan Li, and Qiao Shi. Their individual standing within the CCP hierarchy conferred a considerable amount of bargaining power on the NPC. Fourth, the generational changes in the composition of China's ruling elite have transformed the rank and file of NPC deputies. Toward the end of the 1990s, the NPC had seen a significant rise in the representation of the intelligentsia, government officials, and ethnic minorities (from 28 percent in 1978 to 50 percent in 1993). Correspondingly, the percentage of deputies representing workers, peasants, and the People's Liberation Army decreased (from 62 percent in 1978 to less than 30 percent in 1993).[21]

Ultimately, the institutional authority and the legitimacy of the NPC must be measured by how the Chinese public perceives them. Unfortunately, no systematic studies have been conducted to investigate this issue. One opinion poll conducted in 1994 suggested that the NPC might be gaining a degree of public respect. Along with China's fast-changing media, the NPC was found to be an important channel through which ordinary citizens could voice their views and redress injustice. In a similar poll conducted in 1988, 43 percent of the respondents said that they would go to the "relevant authorities" (i.e., party and state officials) to lodge complaints; only 38 percent of the respondents gave that reply in 1994. In contrast, the media and the People's Congress gained influence as forums in which to air private grievances, with nearly a quarter of the respondents saying that they would choose the media to voice their complaints (compared with only 9 percent in 1988). Twenty-two percent said that they would lodge their complaints with the deputies of the People's Congress (compared with 13 percent in 1988).[22] Official figures also show that more than 100,000 private citizens write to the NPC requesting assistance each year. The Chinese press often reports individual NPC members' frequent intervention in cases of abuse of power by government officials.

Judicial Institutions

Legal reform has become one of the most important institutional changes in China since the late 1970s. Initially introduced as part of the post-Mao regime's efforts to establish a "socialist democracy and legal system," China's legal reform has produced profound changes in the country's legislative institutions and processes; in its criminal, civil, procedural, and administrative laws; and in its professional legal community. Within China, the changing legal institutions have begun to play an increasingly important role in governing economic activities, resolving civil disputes, enforcing law and order, and setting the boundaries between the power of the state and the autonomy of society.

China's progress in legal reform becomes all the more remarkable when we consider the state of the country's legal system at the end of the Mao era. The politicization and systematic weakening of the legal system began in the late 1950s—with the abolition of the Ministry of Justice and the system of professional legal representation in court proceedings. Legislative output also fell precipitously as the NPC's lawmaking power waned—the NPC passed only 16 pieces of legislation during 1959–66 (averaging fewer than two per year). The Chinese legal system on the eve of the Cultural Revolution was thus rudimentary at best. Only a relatively small number of laws had been passed in the previous 17 years and few of those laws explicitly protected personal liberties or property rights. Indeed, the pre-1966 system did not have some of the most basic laws, such as a civil code; a criminal code; citizenship law; criminal, civil, and administrative procedure laws; not to mention many civil and administrative laws governing economic activities. Such a skeletal system completely collapsed during the Cultural Revolution. The NPC ceased to function. With the exception of one piece of legislation issued in 1975, not a single law was passed. In this period, the directives of the Communist Party Central Committee served as laws. The constitutional amendments made in 1975 and 1978 formally deprived the NPC of its constitutional status as the "sole legislative body."

In a strict sense, China did not have much of a legal system when Deng gained political supremacy in late 1978. On the legislative front, the newly revived NPC was an inactive legislature (which passed only five pieces of legislation during 1978). Its constitutional power of lawmaking remained greatly diminished and was shared with the CCP. Most of the laws passed before 1966 were outdated and thus no longer applied to China's new political and social conditions; furthermore, nearly all the laws urgently needed to govern a post-totalitarian society and a transition economy did not exist. The judiciary, devastated by the Cultural Revolution, was, along with the professional legal community, in great need of rebuilding.

A central feature of the pre-1979 Chinese legal system was the small number of laws that constituted it. According to a 1987 report issued by the Legal System Work Committee of the NPC, 134 laws were issued between September 1949 and the end of 1978. Of the 134 laws, 111 were declared invalid for a variety of reasons: 11 were annulled by new laws; 41 were superseded by new laws; 29 ceased to be enforced or applicable because of changes in circumstances; and 30 had expired. Only 23 laws—about 17 percent of the total— remained valid (and some of those were being revised).[23] An examination of the list of legislation issued by the central government during 1949–78 and declared invalid in 1987 shows that a majority of the legislation were not major laws but rather simple, event-specific NPC resolutions (such as resolutions on issuing public debts, amnesties for civil war criminals, and dates of elections of NPC

Table 17.1
GROWTH OF LITIGATION, 1978–96 (ACCEPTED CASES)

Year	Commercial	Civil	Administrative
1978		285,000	
June 1979–			
Dec. 1982	49,000		
1981		658,000	
1982		770,00	
1983	44,000	747,000	
1984	85,700		
1985	226,600	846,000	
1986	308,393	989,409	632
1987	367,156	1,213,219	5,240
1988	513,615	1,455,130	9,273
1989	690,765	1,815,385	9,934
1990	598,314	1,851,897	13,006
1991	563,260	1,880,635	25,667
1992	650,601	1,948,786	27,125
1993	894,410	2,089,257	27,911
1994	1,053,701	2,383,764	35,083
1995	1,278,806	2,718,533	52,596
1996	1,519,793	3,093,995	79,966
1997	1,483,356	3,277,572	90,557

SOURCE: *Zhongguo falu nianjian* (China Law Yearbook) (Beijing: China Law Yearbook Publishing, various years).

deputies). Indeed, approximately 52 of the pre-1979 laws (39 percent of the total legislative output) can be considered major laws. Of those laws, only 14 remained effective as of 1994.[24]

The rapid pace of reform since 1979 has fundamentally changed the legal landscape. As described earlier, the 200-plus laws passed by the NPC have filled some of the long-standing legal void and appear to have started to play a role in governing China's increasingly complex economic and social activities.

Legal Reform and Economic Activities. Several indicators show that China's legal reform has had a powerful impact on economic transactions, although the precise extent of this impact remains difficult to measure. First, the rising rate of litigation suggests that an increasing number of economic actors are relying on the courts to protect their rights (Table 17.1). We assume that economic actors make careful calculations when deciding whether to litigate to resolve their commercial disputes. In most cases, we assume that their decisions to initiate legal action are based on their assessment that the benefits of litigation would outweigh the costs of litigation or of resolving the same disputes in other ways. Given the direct and indirect costs of litigation in a political environment that is generally hostile to private property, rational economic actors are unlikely to initiate legal action if they judge their chances of success to be minimal. These assumptions lead us to believe that the continual increase in the rate of litigation is a sign that the legal system, in general, and the courts, in particular, may be delivering at least some of the benefits sought by the litigants. Data on rates of litigation show a dramatic increase in commercial, civil, and administrative lawsuits since the early 1980s. This should be considered as evidence that the Chinese legal system is gradually performing a more effective and important role in resolving various conflicts in Chinese society. Specifically, the rapid increase in the number of commercial (economic) cases accepted by the courts of first instance from an average of 15,000 a year in 1979–82 to more than 1.5 million a year in 1996 (a 100-fold increase) demonstrates that the legal system has become an important arena in which to resolve economic disputes.[25]

Second, as a direct measure of the importance of the legal system, the total monetary claims in the commercial disputes accepted by the Chinese courts and the average size (measured in monetary terms) of each dispute have risen considerably over the last two decades. The total amount of monetary claims in commercial disputes adjudicated by Chinese courts rose from 21.5 billion yuan in 1989 (1.27 percent of GDP) to 330 billion yuan in 1997 (4.5 percent of GDP).[26] The average amount of each commercial dispute increased from 31,900 yuan in 1989 to 222,000 yuan in 1997. These are the two important trends that support the basic assessment that China's emerging legal system is beginning to have a substantial impact on governing economic activities. It is unlikely that those claims are inflated, because Chinese courts do not award punitive damages. Moreover, Chinese litigants do not have an incentive to inflate monetary claims because the litigation fees assessed by the courts are based on those claims (the higher the claims, the greater the court costs borne by the litigants). This suggests that litigants are willing to take greater risks in seeking legal recourse.

Potential Political Effects. Legal reform has yet to demonstrate that the monopolistic power of the CCP has been effectively constrained. There is, however, tentative evidence suggesting that the current legal reforms may eventually produce such effects. First, legal reform has not only raised the public's awareness of its legal rights but also provided institutional channels through which such rights can be defended. This is evident in the increase in the number of cases filed against the government under the Administrative Litigation Law passed in 1989 (from 600 in 1986 to 90,000 in 1997). Analysis of official data shows that about 40 percent of plaintiffs obtained favorable decisions or mediation through this system.[27] Another indicator of the rising level of rights consciousness is the number of personal rights lawsuits (such as libel, defamation, unauthorized use of personal portraits, and other matters) filed by ordinary citizens. In 1988 the courts accepted 2,434 such cases; in 1997, 8,650 such cases were filed in the courts.[28]

Over time, China's emerging professional legal community has the potential to constitute an autonomous social group capable of concerted political action. Official data show that the number of lawyers rose from 31,000 in 1988 to 98,900 in 1997.[29] A notable trend in the growth of China's legal community is that most of the newly founded law firms are private or cooperative partnerships. In 1991, only 73 (2 percent) of China's 3,706 law firms were cooperative partnerships. In 1997, 2,957 (35 percent) of the country's 8,441 law firms were private or cooperative partnerships.[30] This trend of privatizing the legal profession will inevitably increase the economic independence of Chinese lawyers and have a powerful impact on their incentives.

It is conceivable that, before the launch of a full-scale democratization transition (which in other countries has normally been initiated by reformist leaders or precipitated by a regime collapse), China's new legal system could become a political arena in which the monopoly of power by the CCP might be contested and constrained. It could be the "backdoor" through which a gradual process of democratic transition could be introduced. Compared with other forms of political reform that directly challenge the CCP's rule (such as open elections and a multiparty system), gradual legal reforms present no imminent threat to the one-party dictatorship and, in the short term, may even serve some of the interests of the ruling elite and win allies inside the regime.

Electoral Institutions

Self-governing local political institutions, such as village committees chosen through semicompetitive elections, emerged in China in the wake of sweeping economic changes.[31] The CCP leadership allowed this experiment in order to arrest the rapid erosion of its authority and organizational infrastructure in rural areas after the dismantling of the communes in the early years of the reform. Official CCP figures painted a grim picture of the disintegration of its rural political infrastructure. The Organization Department of the CCP reported that only a quarter of the party's 730,000 rural branches were considered "good" in terms of effectiveness and organizational cohesion; 7 percent were labeled "backward" and 8 percent were considered "paralyzed."[32] The specter of a power vacuum in China's 930,000 villages was so alarming that it prompted some top CCP leaders, most notably a leading conservative, Peng Zhen, to support some form of limited rural self-government. Like agricultural reform, the initiative of rural self-government originated from below when peasants in some areas spontaneously held unauthorized elections to form village governments in the early 1980s. A conservative proposal for direct appointment of village officials by the government was rejected by the CCP leadership. Under the relentless pressure of Peng (who was chairman of the NPC Standing Committee), the NPC passed "The Draft Organic Law of the Village Committees" in 1987, establishing and defining the legal status and administrative functions of village committees. It was revised in 1998. The final version contained many procedural improvements (such as the mandatory requirement for secret balloting).

The initial experiment in rural democracy was disappointing. Between the second half of 1988 and 1989, fewer than half of the provinces held the first round of village elections on a trial basis. The post-Tiananmen political backlash against liberalism temporarily halted this reform. The experiment was resuscitated only after Deng's famous tour of southern China in 1992, which spurred a new round of economic reform. By the end of 1995, 24 provinces (of 30) had passed local legislation on electing village committees. Official data show that village elections have been held in all 30 provinces (excluding Tibet). Fujian and Liaoning, two provinces considered leaders in the experiment, had held six rounds, while 19 other provinces had held three to five rounds.[33]

Although village committees elected by rural residents are not, according to the Chinese constitution, a form of local government, they perform critical administrative functions such as fiscal management, economic development, implementation of government policies, and provision of public services. Most village committees have five to seven members: chairman, vice chairman, and three to five members. (The size of the committee varies with local population; a Chinese village has about 800 to 3,000 residents.) The village committee acts as an executive council in charge of daily administrative decisions. In theory, the highest decisionmaking body is the village representative assembly, which normally consists of about 30 members. Some reports suggest that the most important economic decisions (such as those involving large capital expenditures) are made by the assemblies. Assemblies also play an important role in the nomination of candidates for village chairmen. In areas that have fully established this governance structure, village committees and village representative assemblies are elected concurrently. Although at present most Chinese villages have elected village committees, official reports indicate that, by 1994, only about half of the Chinese villages had set up such assemblies.

The short history of village elections, diversity of local conditions, and lack of accurate national and regional data make it impossible to generalize about the progress of rural self-government. Published accounts portray a complex but incomplete picture. Unfortunately, the best data available come from provinces that have implemented this experiment most effectively (such as Fujian and Liaoning) and are hardly representative. Fujian Province is considered the most progressive jurisdiction because it has held six rounds of village elections, achieved relatively high voter turnout, and adopted secret ballots and covered voting booths. Elections in Fujian have become more competitive, with the number of nominees for village committees rising by 300 percent from 1989 to 1997. The province has also introduced absentee ballots and election monitors, abolished fraud-prone proxy voting, and extended voting time from two to eight hours. Estimates of how village elections are held in other areas differ widely. Some academic researchers estimate that between 10 and 20 percent of villages have implemented the electoral procedures well, while other observers put the figure slightly higher.[34]

A legitimate concern often expressed by observers of village elections is that members of the ruling Communist Party dominate newly established village committees. A survey of village committees carried out in the early 1990s found that about 60 percent of elected members of village committees and 50 to 70 percent of chairmen of village committees were party members. It was estimated that about 20 to 50 percent of the members of representative assemblies were party members.[35] Skeptics of China's village elections may justifiably regard this as evidence of the political insignificance of the experiment. The reality, however, may be more complex. Members of the ruling party win these elections not because such elections are inherently uncompetitive but because party members may be the strongest candidates. Candidates who are party members usually have name recognition, a good education, and the advantages of incumbency. Ever ready to recruit fresh blood, the ruling party frequently co-opts winning nonparty candidates by offering them party membership.

Studies of village elections suggest that the success of the experiment is unrelated to such factors as the level of economic development.[36] The leading provinces in this experiment are neither the wealthiest nor the poorest. Fujian and Liaoning are among the upper-middle-income provinces in China. However, there is evidence that the laggards in this experiment are mostly the poorest provinces. A study on village elections shows that the most important variable is the leadership provided by provincial authorities in charge of local elections and by consistent government efforts to enforce and improve electoral procedures.[37] That finding highlights the dilemma of democratic reform in an authoritarian system: no initial democratic opening is possible without some support from elements within the regime. The uncertainty of intraregime conflict over reform makes progress of democratization slow, uncertain, and ambiguous.

The most fascinating but least known aspect of village elections is their effect on local governance. Anecdotal evidence suggests a link between democracy and good governance in villages that have effectively implemented this reform. Official publications report that law and order improved measurably in villages with elected committees. Fiscal management became more transparent and less corrupt.

Village elections have received some limited external assistance, especially in the late 1990s when the Western donors identified village elections as a promising development. The European Union donated $12 million in 1998 to support elections-related programs. American nongovernmental organizations such as the Ford Foundation, the Carter Center, the Asia Foundation, and the International Republican Institute provided funds and technical advice.

As a newly established channel for political participation, village elections may be taking root as an institution. Poll data collected from villages indicate a rising level of democratic consciousness. A 1996 survey of 5,000 peasants reported that 80 percent cared about the election of the members of the village committee and 91 percent were concerned with the management of village affairs, especially the budget. In addition, villagers may be gaining experience as they repeat the electoral process. Electoral procedures may improve and produce more accountable local administrations. Village elections and village committees may assume more importance and change the political landscape in rural China because those institutions can provide ambitious individuals with a certain degree of popular legitimacy and power to counter the dominance of the ruling Communist Party. Reformist elements inside the regime have also invested enough political capital in this experiment and seem to be encouraged by the initial results. The central government has announced plans to train as many as 1.5 million local officials in elections management in order to improve the electoral process in villages. Finally, village elections could, by their success, increase pressure on the government to expand similar democratic experiments. In December 1998, Buy, an impoverished township of 16,000 in Sichuan Province held a competitive election for mayor, without receiving approval from provincial or central authorities (the township leaders did get an informal endorsement from the county leaders). Although the central government initially criticized the township for holding an "illegal election" on the grounds that it was not sanctioned by the existing Chinese constitution, official media eventually hailed the event as a bold experiment, and the authorities did not, significantly, annul the results of the election.

However, we should adjust our expectations of village elections to the political reality in China. The CCP has consistently rejected genuine democratization as a future political goal and suppressed, often by violent means, any form of organized political opposition. Despite the obvious value of village elections, Chinese leaders have given this experiment low political priority. Lack of top-level political commitment will deprive this experiment of momentum and support in addressing several thorny political issues, including a redefinition of the power and the role of the CCP in villages and the party's relationship with elected village committees, the legality of political opposition groups in villages, and the relationship between the elected village officials and the unelected township officials who exercise considerable administrative power over the former. Those unresolved issues will make the prospects for village elections uncertain.

Therefore, it would be premature to bet the future of China's democratization on village elections. This experiment is a small and tentative step toward democratization. Its progress has been slow and uneven. In the best-case scenario, the experiment may have started a gradual process of political participation for nearly 80 percent of China's population. Should this experiment be expanded to the township or county level, it would constitute a qualitatively different leap of reform and could greatly accelerate China's long-delayed democratic transition.

Facing the Future, Grimly

The above analysis of the institutional development of the Chinese political system presents a mixed picture. On the one hand, this system is doubtless a significant change—if not a fundamental one— from the totalitarian Maoist rule and has acquired some of the basic institutional characteristics of a soft-authoritarian regime capable of further evolution toward a more open polity. On the other hand, the gains in institutional pluralism and civil society–building are very limited. Although the worst features of Maoist rule, such as indiscriminate mass repression, ceaseless political campaigns, and ruthless intraelite power struggle, have disappeared, the post-Mao regime has definitely retained the monopoly of power of the CCP and demonstrated convincingly its resolve to defend that power at almost any cost. Even the limited constraints placed on this monopoly should be recognized as the result of reluctant concessions made by the ruling elite who permitted or, in some cases, initiated partial reform for reasons of political expediency. The haphazard nature of political reform has made the future course of development not only uncertain and unpredictable but also fraught with risks that will only increase as the Chinese leadership continues to resist political reform.

Experience from other countries that have made the transition from authoritarian rule suggests that autocrats who seize the opportunity to reform from a position of strength have a better chance of retaining power in the post-transition phase or of striking a deal for withdrawal of the opposition. In contrast, those who resisted until the end fared much worse when their regime collapsed under the weight of misrule and total de-legitimization. China's leaders must heed this lesson because, if anything, their political system has the following structural and institutional flaws that will make their hold on power increasingly more precarious.

Narrowing Base of Support

The Maoist regime, for all its flaws and policy disasters, was nevertheless a regime with a broad base of social support among workers and peasants. However, pro-market reforms under Deng have seriously eroded the social base of the CCP. This change has come about, ironically, precisely because of the relative success of the economic reform in the post-Deng era. For the peasantry, market-oriented reforms have resulted not only in direct economic benefits and independence from the state; these reforms have also extensively eroded the CCP's political control in rural areas, leaving the party without a means of mobilizing rural political support. As for urban workers in state-owned enterprises, market-oriented reforms have begun to hurt their interests by making their jobs insecure and their benefits less generous. They blame their plight on the government and have begun to display their dissatisfaction openly and often violently. The only secure base of support for the party today is the bureaucracy, the military, the security apparatus, and the emerging crony-capitalists.

Organizational Deficit

Before the reform, the CCP controlled a vast network of social organizations that penetrated most segments of the population. Those social organizations included the official labor unions, women's associations, the youth league, and many professional associations. That situation has changed. Although nominally the party continues to control those social organizations, in reality things are quite different. Official organizations closely tied to the party, such as labor unions, women's associations, and the youth league, have lost credibility, enjoy little grassroots support, and cannot be expected to serve as instruments of control or political support for the CCP. Other organizations, notably religious groups and professional associations, have become more independent and will likely resist being manipulated by the party. As a result, the party can no longer rely on those subsidiary groups to help it maintain political control and resolve conflicts between the party and society.

Weak Institutions for Resolving State-Society Conflict

Another related weakness of the present Chinese political system is the absence of credible institutions that can represent people's interests and allow groups to articulate and advocate their interests in an institutional setting. In democratic systems, elections and legislative processes perform those functions. The absence of such institutions will result in the accumulation of collective grievances against the government that are likely to explode violently and with little warning.

No Effective Institutions for Resolving Conflicts within the State

China has no functioning formal institutions to resolve conflicts among the various components of the state. The absence of such institutions, typically provided for by federalism, causes cyclical opportunism characterized by frequent policy changes by the central government and resistance by local governments. Consequently, the policy environment is uncertain, and enforcement of laws is weak. In fact, the most serious problem facing China is not the absence of democracy but the absence of federalism.

In the short term, such flaws are not likely to contribute directly to a collapse of the ruling regime because the CCP will remain a dominant force of political authority and control and no credible alternative will emerge. Without political reform that addresses the above-mentioned institutional flaws, the post-Deng Chinese leaders will confront even more intractable challenges in the future. Failure to implement political institutional reforms could, either simultaneously or sequentially, lead to rising instability. First, failure to reform will reduce economic efficiency as the costs of insecure property rights, poor contract enforcement, and enormous rents become more serious. That will inevitably reduce the rate of growth, which will further exacerbate social tensions and damage the legitimacy of the CCP. Second, failure to reform will allow corruption to worsen, inequality to rise, and poor governance to persist, eventually causing a massive social crisis, as occurred in Indonesia in May 1998. Third, failure to reform will deepen division within the current moderate-conservative ruling coalition as the more liberal elements become disenchanted and frustrated with the slow pace of reform. A split within the elite will definitely lead to political instability.

As the People's Republic of China celebrates its 50th anniversary, its leaders and people are confronted with a set of choices that will determine not just the fate of the CCP but the future and aspirations of the Chinese nation.

Notes

1. For the best summary of China's economic achievement in this period, see The World Bank, *China 2020* (Washington: World Bank, 1997); and Angus Maddison, "Chinese Economic Performance in the Long Run," Organisation for Economic Co-operation and Development, 1998.

2. See Kevin O'Brien, "Implementing Political Reform in China's Villages," *Australian Journal of Chinese Affairs*, no. 32 (July 1994): 33–67; Kevin O'Brien, "Agents and Remonstrators: Role Accumulation by Chinese People's Congress Deputies," *China Quarterly*, no. 138 (June 1994): 359–80; M. Kent Jennings, "Political Participation in the Chinese Countryside," *American Political Science Review* 91, no. 2 (June 1997): 361–72; Minxin Pei, "Creeping Democratization in China," *Journal of Democracy* 6, no. 4 (October 1995): 64–79; Murray Scot Tanner, *The Politics of Lawmaking in Post-Mao China* (Oxford: Oxford University Press, 1998); Pitman Potter, ed., *Domestic Law Reforms in Post-Mao China* (Armonk, N.Y.: M. E. Sharpe, 1994); Tianjian Shi, *Political Participation in China* (Cambridge, Mass.: Harvard University Press, 1997); Stanley Lubman, ed., *China's Legal Reforms* (New York: Oxford University Press, 1996); Gordon White, Jude Howell, and Xiaoyuan Shang, *In Search of Civil Society: Market Reform and Social Change in Contemporary China* (Oxford: Clarendon, 1996); and Stanley Lubman, *Bird in a Cage: China's Post-Mao Legal Reforms* (Stanford, Calif.: Stanford University Press, forthcoming).

3. See David Zweig, "Undemocratic Capitalism: China and the Limits of Economism," *National Interest* (Summer 1999): 63–72; and Bruce Dickson, "China's Democratization and the Taiwan Experience," *Asian Survey* 38, no. 4 (April 1998).

4. Chen Xitong's case should not be considered one of power struggle. Chen went to jail for substantiated corruption in 1996.

5. Zhiyue Bo, "Economic Performance and Political Mobility: Chinese Provincial Leaders," *Journal of Contemporary China* 5, no. 12 (July 1996): 135–54.

6. For a study of the implementation of this system, see Melanie Manion, *Retirement of Revolutionaries in China: Public Policies, Social Norms, Private Interests* (Princeton, N.J.: Princeton University Press, 1993).

7. Those younger than 50 included 1.13 million officials in the government's administrative agencies, 2.56 million in state-owned enterprises, 1.81 million in nonprofit government institutions, and about 500,000 officials who retired in 1989. The total number of officials in various government agencies at all levels in 1989 was 4.55 million. *Zhongguo renshi nianjian 1988–89* (China's Personnel Almanac) (Beijing: Zhongguo renshi chubanshe, 1991), pp. 738, 742.

8. See Li Cheng and Lynn White III, "Elite Transformation and Modern Change in Mainland China and Taiwan: Empirical Data and the Theory of Technocracy," *China Quarterly*, no. 121 (March 1990): 1–35.

9. *Zhongguo renshi nianjian 1988–89*, p. 738.

10. Author's calculation based on official information from various sources.

11. For research on the growth of civic organizations in China, see Minxin Pei, "Chinese Civic Organizations: An Empirical Analysis," *Modern China* 24, no. 3 (July 1998): 285–318; Gordon White et al., *In Search of Civil Society: Market Reform and Social Change in Contemporary China* (Oxford: Clarendon, 1996); and Jonathan Unger, "Bridges: Private Business, the Chinese Government and the Rise of New Associations," *China Quarterly*, no. 147 (September 1996): 795–819.

12. Edwin Winckler first observed a similar trend in Taiwan in the early 1970s. See Edwin Winckler, "Institutionalization and Participation on Taiwan: From Hard to Soft Authoritarianism?" *China Quarterly*, no. 99 (September 1984): 481–99.

13. Lu Xueyi and Li Peilin, eds., *Zhongguo shehui fazhan baogao* (China's Social Development Report) (Shenyang: Liaoning renmin chubanshe, 1991), p. 379.

14. See O'Brien, "Agents and Remonstrators," pp. 359–80.

15. For studies of the NPC, see Murray Scot Tanner, "How a Bill Becomes a Law in China," in Lubman, *China's Legal Reforms*, pp. 39–64; Murray Scot Tanner, "The Erosion of Communist Party Control over Lawmaking in China," *China Quarterly*, no. 138 (June 1994): 381–403; Murray Scot Tanner, "Organizations and Politics in China's Post-Mao Law-Making System," in Potter, pp. 56–93; and Kevin J. O'Brien, "Is China's National People's Congress a 'Conservative Legislature'?" *Asian Survey* 30, no. 8 (August 1990): 782–94.

16. Legal System Bureau of the State Council, *Zhonghua renmin gongheguo xianxing falu xingzheng faqui 1949–1994* (Current Laws and Administrative Regulations of the PRC, 1949–1994) (Beijing: Zhongguo fazhi chubanshe, 1995).

17. For an excellent account of the organizational development of the NPC, see Michael W. Dowdle, "The Constitutional Development and Operations of the National People's Congress," *Columbia Journal of Asian Law* 11, no. 1 (Spring 1997): 3–25.

18. See ibid., p. 7. For substantial evidence of the NPC's growing legislative autonomy see Tanner, *The Politics of Lawmaking in Post-Mao China*.

19. Dowdle, p. 9.

20. See ibid.; and Tanner, *The Politics of Lawmaking in Post-Mao China*.

21. Minxin Pei, "Is China Democratizing?" *Foreign Affairs* 77, no. 1 (January–February 1998): 76.

22. *Far Eastern Economic Review*, December 7, 1995, p. 35.

23. *Zhongguo falu nianjian 1988* (China Law Yearbook 1988) (Beijing: China Law Yearbook Publishing, 1989), p. 250.

24. These laws were listed in Legal System Bureau of the State Council, *Zhonghua renmin gongheguo xianxing falu xingzheng fagui mulu 1949–1994* (List of Existing Laws and Administrative Regulations of the PRC) (Beijing: Zhongguo fazhi chubanshe, 1995).

25. See *Zhongguo falu nianjian*, various years.

26. Ibid., various years.

27. See Minxin Pei, "Citizens v. Mandarins: Administrative Litigation in China," *China Quarterly*, no. 152 (December 1997): 832–62.

28. *Zhongguo falu nianjian 1989*, p. 1081; and *Zhongguo falu nianjian 1998*, p. 1239.

29. Ibid., p. 1257.

30. There were no private partnerships in 1991. *Zhongguo falu nianjian 1992*, p. 874; and *Zhongguo falu nianjian 1998*, p. 1256.

31. Numerous studies have been done on village elections. See O'Brien, "Implementing Political Reform in China's Villages"; Melanie Manion, "The Electoral Connection in the Chinese Countryside," *American Political Science Review* 90, no. 4 (December 1996): 736–48; Daniel Kelliher, "The Chinese Debate over Village Self-Government," *China Journal*, no. 37 (January 1997): 63–86; Robert Pastor and Qingshan Tan, "The Meaning of China's Village Elections" (1999, photocopy); and Kevin O'Brien and Lianjiang Li, "Accommodating 'Democracy' in a One-Party State: Introducing Village Elections in China" (1999, photocopy).

32. Yu Yongyao, "Jiaqiang nongchun jicheng dangzuzhi jianshe" (Strengthening the Building of Grassroots Party Organizations in Rural Areas), *Zhongyang dangxiao baogaoxuan*, no. 19 (1995): 26–27.

33. Pastor and Tan.

34. Ibid.

35. China Rural Villagers' Self-Government Research Group and the Chinese Research Society of Grassroots Government, *Study on the Election of Villagers' Committees in Rural China: Main Report* (in Chinese) (Beijing: Chinese Social Science Publishing, 1993).

36. See Pastor and Tan; and O'Brien and Li.

37. Pastor and Tan.

18. China's Move to Market: How Far? What Next?

Thomas G. Rawski

Two decades of Chinese reform have delivered an astonishing economic boom. But China's great growth spurt may be nearing its end. This chapter surveys China's reform by asking whether the economy has evolved into a market system. Despite impressive changes in many areas, I find that the largely unreformed investment mechanism tilts China's whole economy toward patterns typical of planned rather than market systems. My analysis links China's declining economic momentum to investment structures that continue to waste vast amounts of capital. Current Chinese policy, which deploys short-run fiscal stimulus to combat structural problems, seems counterproductive. At the present juncture, policies focused on the promotion of domestic private business offer a unique opportunity to alleviate short-term weakness without compromising long-term reform objectives.

What Is a Market System?

Market systems have occupied the core of economics at least since Adam Smith's famous comment on the human "propensity to truck and barter." Surprisingly, economists have no clear definition of market economy. Efforts to specify the meaning of a market system are not easy to find. The comprehensive *New Palgrave Dictionary of Economics*, for example, contains no discussion of "market economy" or "market system." Edward Green defines a market system as one in which the economy operates through "a profusion of coalitions

The author thanks participants in the 28th Sino-American Conference on Contemporary China, held at Duke University, June 12–14, 1999, for comments on an initial draft and gratefully acknowledges information and explanations provided by Nicholas Lardy, Li Jingwen, Liu Shucheng, and Zheng Yuxin without implicating them in what follows.

doing things independently and without coordination" in pursuit of financial gain.[1] While this definition omits the state, it surely implies that the function of government is to create a stable and predictable background that allows individuals to assess the benefits and costs of joining coalitions (firms, projects, contracts, etc.) and to prevent illicit groups (of thieves, extortionists, etc.) from disrupting legitimate activity.

This formulation implies that the pricing of commodities and services, the allocation of resources, the choice of technologies, and other fundamental determinants of economic structure and change depend primarily on the nature and the operation of voluntary coalitions. Since economists emphasize the importance of marginal decisions, evidence that government action influences the conduct of economic activity need not vitiate the primacy of voluntary coalitions.

The importance of public policy in any market economy—recall that even in colonial Hong Kong, government controlled the scarcest factor, land, and conducted large-scale operations in education, housing, and health care—complicates any effort to differentiate between market and nonmarket systems. Since extensive government intervention is found everywhere and typically extends far beyond enforcement of clearly specified laws and regulations, evidence of frequent ad hoc interventions in market operations is not sufficient to establish that China (or any other national system) remains outside the realm of market economies.

The relation between governments and market systems is anything but clear. Any but the most rudimentary market system requires a foundation of supportive government regulation. American experience shows that market systems can retain their fundamental character even under intrusive regulation. This means that conclusions about the "marketness" of an economy cannot rest on straightforward criteria such as the extent of price controls, the size of official bureaucracies, or other readily denumerable elements. Instead, they require delicate judgments about the scope of voluntary coalitions, the extent of supportive regulation, and the impact of official intrusions on market outcomes.

Has China Become a Market System?

Has reform propelled China into the ranks of market economies? Some observers do not hesitate to offer an affirmative answer: "Chinese leaders did not intend to bring a market economy to China when they launched their reform program. . . . However, the reform creates its own path to a market economy."[2] Efforts by American trade negotiators to obtain Chinese acceptance of a "nonmarket economy" designation well into this century may be dismissed as attempts to shield powerful domestic interests from market competition, but *The Economist* forcefully advances the opposite perspective, arguing that "China's economy . . . is still largely controlled by the state. Prices are fixed, monopolies common and subsidies legion. Its laws are opaque and often applied arbitrarily. Even if China does away with import quotas and dismantles tariff barriers, its markets will not be free in any meaningful sense."[3] What is the scope of market forces in China's economy? A brief review of the evidence on the scope of the market in China's growing economy may resolve this sharp clash of views.

Allocation of Commodities

There is overwhelming evidence that market forces now play a dominant role in allocating commodities. Tables 18.1 and 18.2 show that, by the mid-1990s, market determination of commodity prices had become the norm. Although government intervention remains common, the primacy of market forces in determining the pricing and distribution of commodities is beyond dispute. Major distortions of relative prices, such as the long-standing underpricing of energy and industrial materials, have virtually disappeared, in part because of pressures arising from the growing openness of China's economy.

Confirmation of that judgment comes from the structure and behavior of commodity prices, which display phenomena associated with market systems. Even in sectors dominated by state enterprises and closely monitored by central ministries, press accounts routinely report that domestic sales, prices, and profits respond to national and global market trends in ways that exactly parallel observations from market systems. Thus we read that "China's steel imports skyrocketed" because of "the plunging price of steel products on the international market . . . triggering fears [of] . . . a negative influence on the domestic steel market."[4] Similarly, "diesel fuel prices have risen to their highest level" in several years following "the reduction in diesel fuel imports" after "prices on the international market . . . reached their highest point" in several years; as a result, "many domestic petrochemical factories have increased production."[5]

319

Table 18.1
LOCUS OF PRICE DETERMINATION IN CHINESE COMMODITY
MARKETS, 1990–96 (PERCENTAGE)

	State Order	State Guidance	Market Forces
Retail commodities			
1990	29.8	17.2	53.0
1991	20.9	10.3	68.8
1992	5.9	1.1	93.0
1993	4.8	1.4	93.8
1994	7.2	2.4	90.4
1995	8.8	2.4	88.8
1996	6.3	1.2	92.5
Agricultural products			
1990	25.0	23.4	51.6
1991	22.2	20.0	57.8
1992	12.5	5.7	81.8
1993	10.4	2.1	87.5
1994	16.6	4.1	79.3
1995	17.0	4.4	78.6
1996	16.9	4.1	79.0
Production materials			
1990	44.6	19.0	36.4
1991	36.0	18.3	45.7
1992	18.7	7.5	73.8
1993	13.8	5.1	81.1
1994	14.7	5.3	80.0
1995	15.6	6.5	77.9
1996	14.0	4.9	81.1

SOURCES: Guo Jianying, "Proportion and Changes for Three Types of Prices," *Zhongguo wujia*, no. 11 (1995): 10–12; *Zhongguo wujia nianjian 1996* (China Price Yearbook 1996) (Beijing: n.p., 1996), p. 388; and ibid., 1997, pp. 479–81.

Efforts to attenuate the workings of the price system now arouse vociferous opposition from critics who extol the virtues of untrammeled competition with arguments that are instantly recognizable as standard themes of "free-market" advocacy. When mounting deflationary pressures prompted efforts to curtail "unethical competition" by enacting minimum prices, critics insisted that "any firm

Table 18.2
SHARE OF PRICES DETERMINED BY MARKET FORCES IN 1994, BY
COMMODITY TYPE AND PROVINCE (PERCENTAGE)

	Retail Sales	Agricultural Commodities	Production Materials
National average	90.4	79.3	80.0
Provincial figures			
Beijing	79.0	94.2	68.8
Tianjin	89.0	. . .	72.4
Hebei	88.8	88.8	81.3
Shanxi	97.4	80.9	71.6
Liaoning	96.4	90.4	82.5
Jilin	91.8	85.9	84.4
Heilongjiang	87.8	81.2	51.9
Shanghai	94.9	91.7	78.3
Jiangsu	92.8	77.4	77.8
Zhejiang	92.8	76.5	90.6
Anhui	91.9	81.7	85.5
Fujian	91.9	91.0	87.1
Jiangxi	84.6	74.7	74.9
Shandong	89.0	73.5	73.3
Henan	87.2	60.0	68.0
Hubei	90.2	72.7	71.1
Hunan	85.2	79.3	86.5
Guangdong	92.6	98.8	93.0
Guangxi	90.2	81.2	88.9
Hainan	93.7	. . .	87.2
Sichuan	89.2	80.6[a]	78.1
Yunnan	93.6	67.3	81.7
Shaanxi	84.3	77.2	87.3
Gansu	87.8	85.0	77.9
Qinghai	70.7	77.5	77.7
Ningxia	80.6	81.5	72.0
Xinjiang	92.1	74.2	60.1

SOURCE: Guo Jianying, "Proportion and Changes for Three Types of Prices," *Zhongguo wujia*, no. 11 (1995): 10–12. The source provides no data for Guizhou, Inner Mongolia, or Tibet.

NOTE: Ellipses are used if no data are available.

[a]Corrects obvious misprint in source.

should be entitled to institute desired price-cuts as long as its actions do not result in a market monopoly. . . . The true danger comes from all forms of monopoly under the backing of administrative power singing enticing tunes like 'safeguarding the normal market order.'"[6]

Allocation of Services

Although systematic information about the allocation of services is not readily available, abundant anecdotal evidence indicates that gradual reform has cumulated into extensive commercialization. Housing, education, health care, telecommunications, transport, wholesale and retail trade, meals, entertainment, personal care, banking, finance, insurance, law, and accounting, formerly the exclusive province of systems controlled by government officials, are increasingly available through parallel networks of market-based suppliers accessible to anyone willing to pay the going price. Substantial commercialization is visible even in sectors like banking and railways, in which traditional suppliers retain overwhelming market shares.

Allocation of Labor

Long viewed as a lagging segment of Chinese reform, the market for labor has expanded rapidly during the late 1990s. The emergence of disturbing phenomena that were not tolerated under the planned economy provides the clearest possible evidence of major change in the labor market. Recent developments include mass layoffs in state enterprises, steeply rising unemployment among previously tenured urban workers, virtually uncontrolled mass migration of rural workers seeking nonfarm employment, the rise of private business as the largest source of new formal employment, and a large and growing differential between women's and men's wages.[7] The depth of official commitment to market forces is evident from the minister of labor and social security's advice, offered during the spring festival holiday season, to state enterprises "afflicted with the scourge of low efficiency and surplus employees"—"lay off redundant labourers to pull the companies out of the quagmire."[8]

Allocation of Ownership Rights

Restructuring of ownership rights via merger, divestiture, bankruptcy, or liquidation of corporate assets is a central component of any market system and one that hardly existed in prereform China. The scale of property-rights transfers remains modest, with annual volume of perhaps renminbi (RMB) 1 billion in the late 1980s and RMB 10 billion during 1990–95—small figures when compared with state-owned fixed assets amounting to RMB 5,298 billion for industry and RMB 9,642 billion for all economic sectors.[9]

Yet shareholding corporations, which accounted for only 5.5 percent of industrial assets in 1995, contributed 44.2 percent of the reported asset transfers in that year.[10] With the share of assets held by various types of shareholding entities rising steeply—the number of state enterprises fell by 24,000 in 1998,[11] while local governments, particularly in China's southern provinces, sold large numbers of town and village enterprises (TVEs) to private buyers or reorganized them as shareholding cooperatives—it seems reasonable to anticipate that a major expansion in the frequency and the scale of property-rights transactions.

Technology

China has achieved great strides in the commercialization of research, development, and technology transfer. New patent and trademark systems provide rudimentary protection to entrepreneurs. Research institutes and universities face stringent financial pressures that compel efforts to produce marketable products. Despite well-documented complaints about theft of intellectual property rights, the contractual transfer of specialized equipment, proprietary technologies, blueprints, and know-how across China's international borders, provincial boundaries, and administrative systems has become a routine feature of commercial life. Success stories associated with companies like Haier, Changhong, and Baosteel demonstrate that Chinese firms can acquire new technology and use it to improve product quality and enhance their domestic and international competitiveness.

Market-Supporting Institutions

Chinese newspapers and journals are filled with information about the (often incomplete) development of market-supporting institutions, which have expanded immensely over the past two decades. The legal system illustrates this history of massive, though uneven progress. China's legislatures, long dismissed as "rubber stamp" bodies, continue to expand their influence and power. Legislative seats, previously regarded as devoid of influence, have become a venue for fierce competition. Legislators regularly challenge, and occasionally reject, official reports and proposals. The courts, formerly meek recipients of government and party instructions, demonstrate growing independence. Business periodicals inform readers about contracts and lawsuits, evidently because managers and entrepreneurs increasingly apply such knowledge in their everyday work. Demands that government itself submit to the "rule of law" now come to the fore, as legislators contemplate measures that would "require government officials to meet . . . legal standards" and the *People's Daily* intones that "all are equal before the law. . . . No government department or worker has the privilege to supersede the Constitution or the law. All must follow the law . . . and accept the supervision of the people's congresses."[12]

Capital Market

To this point, the evidence uniformly supports the notion that, despite wide differences from economic patterns observed in most nations belonging to the Organisation for Economic Co-operation and Development, China deserves recognition as a market system. Investigation of the market for capital, however, shows that this conclusion is premature.

Like other segments of China's economy, the market for capital has made important steps in the direction of a market system. Stock exchanges in Shanghai and Shenzhen transact shares of several hundred corporations. In place of the socialist monobank we see a moderately independent central bank supervising a financial system comprising four large state-owned banks, each lumbering in the direction of commercial operation, surrounded by a host of smaller institutions.

Investment finance, formerly dominated by government grants, now depends mainly on enterprise funds. This can be seen in Table 18.3, which shows that funds for investment projects come mainly from retained earnings, issues of shares or bonds, and other funds assembled by enterprises. The share of government grants is less than 5 percent for state firms, and less than 1 percent for firms outside the state sector (including foreign-linked enterprises). The share of domestic bank loans, including some offered to state enterprises on concessional terms in response to government pressure, is less than one-fourth of investment spending in the state sector and less than one-sixth elsewhere. The combined share of official

Table 18.3
SOURCES OF FUNDS FOR INVESTMENT SPENDING IN 1997
(PERCENTAGE)

	Total	State Sector	Others
State grants	2.8	4.7	0.7
Domestic loans	19.2	23.0	15.0
Foreign investment	10.8	5.1	17.1
Own funds	55.6	52.7	58.9
Other	12.9	14.3	11.4
Total	101.3	99.7	103.0

SOURCE: *Zhongguo tongji nianjian 1998* (China Statistics Yearbook 1998) (Beijing: Zhongguo tongji chubanshe, 1998), pp. 188–89.

NOTE: Figures do not add to 100 percent because of inconsistencies in the underlying data.

grants and domestic bank loans in investment finance, which might be viewed as a crude measure of official involvement or of nonmarket influences in capital allocation, is surprisingly small—just over one-fourth in the state sector and less than one-sixth elsewhere.

With more than three-fourths of investment spending funded through channels—retained earnings, share offerings, bond issues, interenterprise transfers, individual subscription, foreign borrowing, and direct foreign investment—that respond primarily to profit expectations, investment appears to qualify for the list of economic categories in which market forces prevail. That impression turns out to be mistaken.

Information on seasonal changes in gross domestic product, reproduced in Figure 18.1, shows quarterly figures for nominal GDP from 1995-Q1 to 1998-Q3 along with projections through 1999. The data in Figure 18.1 show a consistent pattern. Output rises sharply in the fourth quarter and declines precipitously in the first quarter. There is modest expansion in the second quarter and little change in the third quarter. This pattern is typical, not unusual. Projections for 1998–99 show the same features, which also appear in data for 1980–95 (not shown). Figure 18.2, which shows the percentage change in nominal GDP from quarter to quarter, illustrates the regularity and scale of seasonal fluctuations.

These data show that the world's most dynamic economy regularly shrinks during 3 months of each year and stagnates for another

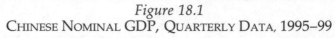

Figure 18.1
CHINESE NOMINAL GDP, QUARTERLY DATA, 1995–99

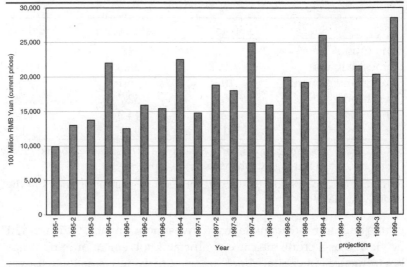

SOURCES: *Zhongguo renmin yinhang tongji jibao* (People's Bank of China Quarterly Statistical Bulletin) no. 1 (1997); Zhu Yunfa et al., "Analysis of China's Trends and Prospects from Economic Performance in the First and Second Quarters of 1997," *Shuliang jingji jishu jingji yanjiu*, no. 3 (1997): 4; Zhang Yanqun, "Analysis and Forecast of Quarterly Economic Situation for 1998–1999," in *1999 Zhongguo jingji xingshi fenxi yu yuce*, ed. Liu Guoguang et al. (Beijing: Shehui kexue wenxian chubanshe, 1998), p. 80; and Yunfa Zhu and Yanqun Zhang, "Quarterly Analysis and Forecast of the Chinese Macroeconomy," in *PRC 1998 Economics Blue Book*, ed. Guoguang Liu et al. (Hong Kong: Hong Kong University Centre of Asian Studies, 1998), p. 139.

quarter, with all the growth occurring in the second and fourth quarters.[13] The enormous seasonal fluctuations dwarf comparable variations in any market system. In the United States, for example, quarterly GDP fluctuations between 1875 and 1995 are limited to plus or minus 9 percent.[14]

There is nothing mysterious about the fluctuations revealed in Figures 18.1 and 18.2. The seasonal profile is typical of a socialist economy driven by planned investment. The socialist calendar is punctuated with regular bouts of storming, or "shock work" (ϫϫ ϫϫ), "the spurt of activity before the end of each planning period . . . in an attempt to achieve 100 percent fulfillment, with a subsequent period of slack until the next target date approaches."[15]

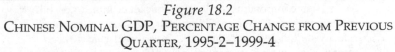

Figure 18.2
CHINESE NOMINAL GDP, PERCENTAGE CHANGE FROM PREVIOUS
QUARTER, 1995-2–1999-4

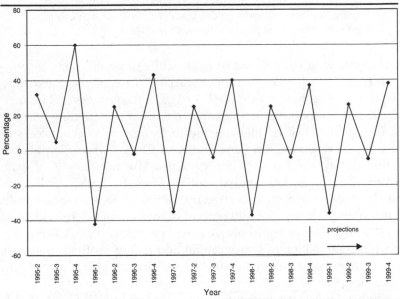

SOURCES: *Zhongguo renmin yinhang tongji jibao* (People's Bank of China Quarterly Statistical Bulletin) no. 1 (1997); Zhu Yunfa et al., "Analysis of China's Trends and Prospects from Economic Performance in the First and Second Quarters of 1997," *Shuliang jingji jishu jingji yanjiu*, no. 3 (1997): 4; Zhang Yanqun, "Analysis and Forecast of Quarterly Economic Situation for 1998–1999," in *1999 Zhongguo jingji xingshi fenxi yu yuce*, ed. Liu Guoguang et al. (Beijing: Shehui kexue wenxian chubanshe, 1998), p. 80; and Yunfa Zhu and Yanqun Zhang, "Quarterly Analysis and Forecast of the Chinese Macroeconomy," in *PRC 1998 Economics Blue Book*, ed. Guoguang Liu et al. (Hong Kong: Hong Kong University Centre of Asian Studies, 1998), p. 139.

Disaggregation of the GDP figures (not shown) reveals that huge fluctuations in investment drive the seasonal patterns displayed in Figures 18.1 and 18.2. This suggests that limited reform of investment, which accounts for roughly two-fifths of Chinese aggregate expenditure, may lie at the root of China's growing economic difficulties. That possibility has not escaped the attention of Chinese economists:

Many basic components of a "pure" market economy are still in their incipient stage in China, although market-oriented reform started two decades ago. *Government-guided investment mechanisms,* a State-controlled banking system and dominant State-owned enterprises . . . *still run in a framework molded primarily on the previous planned economy.*[16]

Anyone who visits China or reads Chinese publications encounters frequent reference to capital scarcity, for example, "generally capital remains in short supply"[17] or "capital shortages still exist."[18] Elementary economics teaches that if capital (or anything else) is scarce, profits will be high for the lucky few who gain access to the scarce resource. But profit rates in China have fallen almost continuously for the past two decades. The tribulations of state enterprises are all too familiar. But we also observe steep declines in the profits of rural collective industries, where after-tax profit rates plunged from above 20 percent of total capital during 1978–82 to less than 10 percent in nearly every year since 1987.[19] The unexpected combination of scarce capital and falling profit rates signals the presence of serious defects in China's capital allocation mechanism.

Chinese investment spending may generate weak financial outcomes, but what about product flows? Here again, we encounter unmistakable evidence of difficulty, this time from information about rates of capacity utilization. In 1995 the utilization rate for China's steel-refining capacity, which then amounted to 169 million annual tons, was only 56 percent.[20] Even though output never came close to 1995 capacity, new investment pushed refining capacity to 190 million tons, nearly double the expected 1999 output of 104 million tons.[21]

This history of excessive investment recurs in sector after sector. China's 1995 industrial census revealed that the average utilization rate for equipment in 111 product lines was 66 percent, with half the figures falling under 55 percent.[22] In 1996 utilization rates for 600 of 1,000 product lines fell below 60 percent. A 1999 report, presumably referring to conditions in 1998, stated that "at present, nationwide utilization rates are below 60% for half of all industrial products."[23] Data for Guangdong, one of China's most dynamic provinces, and one with only a small legacy of older state enterprises, show that "of 320 types of production equipment [apparently for

1998] . . . 52% have utilization rates below four tenths, and 22 types have utilization below two tenths."[24] Reports of overcapacity span a broad range of industries, including steel, glass, cement, chemicals, machinery, motor vehicles, fertilizer, textiles, garments, appliances, paper, coal, and oil refining.

Evidence that industrial investment projects often fail to produce commodities as well as profits provides further proof that China's economy is riddled with massive waste of capital. The magnitude of waste—including roughly 100 million tons of excess capacity in both steel refining and cement manufacture[25]—far exceeds anything that might be attributed to individual incompetence, theft, or fraud. After two decades of market-leaning economic reform, why does China continue to direct vast quantities of investment funds into ill-considered projects?

Chinese analysts and external observers point to a number of institutional factors, such as soft-budget constraints and "investment hunger." There is also a long history of negative real interest rates, which make it profitable to attempt projects with low payoffs. But none of those factors seems capable of explaining either the scale of misallocation or its persistence throughout a reform process that has hardened firms' budget constraints, denied investment funds to growing numbers of weak firms, and, most recently, produced steep increases in real interest rates.

The influence of government administrators over investment decisions stands out as the most likely explanation of long-standing low returns to capital. At the macrolevel, government agencies use annual investment and credit plans[26] to control the size of overall investment. And at the microlevel, efforts to expand the independent management capabilities of enterprise managers and bank executives have failed to eliminate the key role of government offices in investment decisions.

Although government agencies value profits, which remain the leading source of tax revenue, many other motivations influence their view of investment alternatives. Officials may plunge ahead with industrial projects that seem certain to fail. Even though a 1995 report indicated that "float glass production lines which have started construction or preparatory work" have a "combined annual output capacity . . . [that] far surpasses actual demand and will cause a surplus on the market," an official announced "plans to build some

329

float glass projects with foreign investment in the central and western regions to seek a balanced distribution of float glass projects."[27]

The aim of projects may be to create or preserve employment or to postpone the bankruptcy or closure of specific enterprises. Political motives often come into play, as when officials ordered the rebuilding of stonework to remove designs associated with the banned Falun Gong movement or when Beijing welcomed "the completion of five new office projects in celebration of the 50th anniversary of the founding of the People's Republic of China," even though a surplus of office space, with a 30.2 percent vacancy rate at the end of 1998, meant that "they are unlikely to be sold or rented out in the short term."[28] These matters are well understood by Chinese economists:

> It is widely recognized that the root cause for the low efficiency of China's economy lies in overly duplicated industrial structures and overflowing similar products. . . . Behind the duplicated industrial mix is a diseased investment decision-making mechanism. *Most investment projects are funded not based on an investor's pursuit of profit maximization, but on administrative power.*[29]

Summary

Despite huge progress in the direction of market operation, it is not yet possible to classify China's economy as a market system. China remains outside the realm of market economies because of an unreformed investment mechanism, which remains largely controlled by public officials rather than by the profusion of independent coalitions typical of market systems. Administrative management of China's investment system leaves its distinctive imprint in the form of a seasonal macroeconomic roller coaster. No true market system can produce the seasonal fluctuations shown in Figures 18.1 and 18.2, which are characteristic of plan-driven socialist economies.

Why Is China's Economy Sagging?

After two decades of boisterous growth China's economy is now in difficult straits. While official figures show continued high growth, the frequency with which Chinese authors speak of "glut," "depression," "slide," "stagnation," and "grim conditions" suggests that domestic as well as foreign observers doubt the credibility of government statistical reports.

Whatever the exact circumstances, declining growth, falling profits, protracted deflation, rising unemployment, and the associated fall in confidence of the Chinese people have dimmed China's economic prospects.[30] China's leaders attribute these difficulties to a shortfall in aggregate demand resulting from a combination of domestic and international circumstances: Chinese households save too much, and the Asian crisis has hammered the growth of exports and foreign investment. Current policy features two components: deficit spending and other short-term measures intended to bolster aggregate demand, combined with long-term initiatives designed to extend the process of gradual, market-oriented reform.

That diagnosis is mistaken and the policy misconstrued. Weakness in the economy, which predates the Asian financial crisis of 1997–98, runs much deeper than China's leaders appear to believe. The difficulties are structural rather than cyclical. Short-term pump priming exacerbates structural problems and undercuts long-term reform objectives. A policy built around a major effort to expand the scope of domestic private business holds the promise of resisting short-term decline without compromising long-term goals. Despite initiatives in that direction, ideological constraints hinder the promotion of private business and, consequently, the prospects for an early exit from China's present economic doldrums.

To explain why, I offer the following propositions:

1. Data falsification has exaggerated recent growth.
2. Slower growth set in prior to the Asian financial crisis.
3. Inefficient use of capital has retarded job creation.
4. Keynesian deficit spending cannot cure structural defects.
5. Private business offers the best chance to revive growth.

Deep Decline in Growth Performance

Falsification of economic statistics, formerly of major significance only in the data for rural industry, exploded in 1998 after the government had identified 8 percent annual growth as a compulsory target. China's statistical authorities rejected GDP figures supplied by the provinces. After unspecified informal adjustments that supposedly "squeezed out the over-reported part," the State Statistics Bureau announced real growth of 7.8 percent for 1998.[31] Table 18.4 contrasts official measures of 1998 performance with alternative indicators suggesting more modest outcomes. Only a painstaking reconstruction of 1998 statistics can provide firm conclusions about output growth. In the meantime, it is clear that the range of possibilities includes growth amounting to less than half of official claims.

The Falloff in Growth Performance Antedates the Asian Crisis

China's success in quelling strong inflationary pressures sparked claims that the economy had achieved a "soft landing" in 1994–96. Evidence from the labor markets shows that conditions in the real economy were anything but soft. Table 18.5 calculates absorption of labor into formal employment as a percentage of increments to the labor force. The years 1990–95 witnessed an unprecedented labor-market boom that sucked millions of workers from the informal sector (including household farming) into formal employment, mainly in rural industry (TVEs) and private business. In 1996 absorption of labor into formal employment suddenly plunged from 140 percent to less than two-thirds of annual labor force growth. The ratio of new formal employment to labor force increment turned negative in 1997. Fallout from the Asian crisis of 1997–98 contributed to a further decline of employment in 1998, with more to come as downsizing continues and enterprises begin to sever ties with furloughed personnel who remain on the employment rolls.

The Collapse in Job Creation Due to Wasteful Investment

Every economy wastes resources. The experience of Japan and Korea illustrates the capacity of dynamic economies to sustain rapid growth despite massive waste. Assigning valuable resources to occupations that deliver no returns effectively partitions the economy into two components, one dynamic, the other stagnant. As the share of the stagnant component grows, a constant overall growth rate requires ever-faster growth from the dynamic sector. That is increasingly difficult because a large stagnant component not only consumes resources but also disrupts the operation of dynamic firms, for example, by choking the banking system with nonperforming loans. The result is an eventual falloff in growth.

This process is now visible in China, where protracted waste of investment funds has inflicted frightening financial pressures on governments, which are the main owners of capital, and their clients:

Table 18.4

ALTERNATIVE INDICATORS FOR GROWTH OF GDP AND MAJOR COMPONENTS, 1997–98 (PERCENTAGE)

Category	Standard Measure		Alternative Indicator	
Industrial output	SSB figures:	8.9	Electricity output	2.8
Aggregate investment	SSB figures:	14.1	Steel output	5.4
			Steel consumption	≈4[a]
			Cement output	4.7
Aggregate consumption	Retail sales:	9.6	Wage bill	−0.6
			Department store sales	≈0?[b]
Aggregate output	Real GDP:	7.8	Freight transport	−0.9
			Energy use	−1.6
			Airline passenger traffic	3.4

SOURCE: Except as noted, *Zhongguo tongji zhaiyao 1999* (Statistical Survey of China 1999) (Beijing: Zhongguo tongji chubanshe, 1999), pp. 6, 7, 11, 16, 35, 55, 104, 112.

NOTES: SSB refers to China's State Statistics Bureau.
GDP is equal to the sum of A. Wages and salaries
  B. Interest, rent, dividends
  C. Profits (including net farm income)
  D. Taxes

The nominal value of items A (certainly), B (almost certainly), and C (probably) declined in 1997–98. Government revenue rose by 13.9 percent. The implicit GDP deflator for 1997–98 is −1.5 percent.

[a] "With net steel imports declining . . . the increase in consumption of steel materials reached about 4%" in 1998. "1998 Market Prices for Steel Materials: Trends, Analysis, and Forecast for 1999," *Zhongguo wujia,* no. 3 (1999): 8.

[b] "Among the country's 234 large-sized shopping malls, 61.7 percent saw negative sales growth" in 1998. Chandong Wang, "Retailers Suffer As Market Plunges," *China Daily,* January 30, 1999, p. 4.

Table 18.5
SECTORAL CONTRIBUTIONS TO LABOR ABSORPTION, 1980–97

	1980–90	1990–94	1994–95	1995–96	1996–97
Labor force increment (millions)	215.5	32.9	7.5	9	7.5
Absorption (percentage)					
Formal sector	49	141	143	63	−34
State	11	26	7	−2	−27
Collective	5	−8	−17	−14	−19
Other	1	18	17	8	20
Private	3	27	64	32	45
TVE	29	84	112	72	−1
Xiagang	0	−6	−40	−33	−53
Informal[a] sector	51	−41	−43	37	134

SOURCES: Zhongguo tongji zhaiyao 1998 (Statistical Survey of China 1998) (Beijing: Zhongguo tongji chubanshe, 1998), p. 32; and Thomas G. Rawski, China's Prospects for Full Employment, International Labour Office Employment and Training Papers no. 47, Geneva, 1999, Tables 1 and 2. Xiagang figures: 2 million for 1994, 3 million for 1995 and 1996, 4 million for 1997. "Measures Suggested to Reduce Unemployment," China Daily, January 29, 1999, p. 4, gives figure for 1997 and a cumulative total of 8 million at year-end 1996.

[a]Residual, including self-employed farmers and unemployed workers. Note that xiagang workers remain associated with their units and are therefore included in the employment totals.

publicly owned state and collective enterprises, state-owned banks, and public-sector employees. These pressures take the form of dwindling profits, slow growth of tax revenue, and accumulation of bad debt. The most dramatic consequence is xiagang, best translated as "furlough," or "on-the-job layoff," which began in 1993 and has increased rapidly from 1996. Twelve million workers were furloughed in 1998, and a further 7.5 million in the first half of 1999.[32] Those changes are enormous: by percentage, the scale of layoffs far surpasses the postwar experience of any major market economy.

Keynesian "Pump Priming" Not the Answer to Structural Difficulties

Chinese economists recognize that the anticipated "multiplier effects" of recent deficit spending have not materialized. Official media credit short-term interventions with adding 1.5 percentage points to overall growth in 1998.[33] The costs associated with that modest gain are large. Efforts to ramp up aggregate demand promise fresh cohorts of hastily selected and poorly implemented investment projects. Predictably, the quality of bank assets and the proportion of loan obligations fulfilled by borrowers continued to decline in 1998.[34] In addition, the administrative measures that accompany the drive to boost spending obstruct long-term reform by reversing efforts to commercialize the state-owned banks and to reduce ad hoc official interventions in enterprise management. The benefits of 15 months of pump priming are scant: the (unknown) rate of overall growth continues its downward drift, while China's gravely flawed investment mechanism continues to direct resources into outlets that have a long history of waste and mismanagement.

Private Business Offers the Best Opportunity for Renewed Growth Momentum

Current policy concentrates investment funds in the very sectors responsible for the excess capacity that is dragging the economy down. To escape structural difficulties, China must reduce the resources available to the old, failed investment mechanism. But with the economy sagging and mass unemployment now a reality, it is not feasible to curtail spending in any major sector, however incompetent, in the absence of fresh sources of demand. With former "growth poles"—rural industry, exports, joint ventures, foreign investment—largely dormant and with little prospect for their rapid revival, private business offers the only opportunity for an investment boom that could rekindle China's dwindling economic momentum.

That observation is rooted in economic reality, not ideology. Officially recognized private businesses (excluding family farms and other sources of informal work) have created more jobs since 1994 than have the combined efforts of state, shareholding, collective (rural and urban), and foreign-invested businesses. The policy issue is simple. Private business is already the most dynamic sector of

China's economy. How much additional investment resources could private business absorb, and how much additional employment could private entrepreneurs create, if the government initiated a sweeping assault on the obstacles that currently limit the flow of resources into private business?

No precise answer is possible. We know, however, that formidable barriers confront would-be entrepreneurs. Private businesses have little access to credit. They are easy targets for predatory officials. Government agencies and state-run banks are permeated with an anti-business culture. Even though private-sector borrowers repay 90 percent of their loans[35]—perhaps double the figure for state-sector debtors—bankers eschew loans to private borrowers, evidently because defaults by private clients are more dangerous to bankers' careers than defaults from public-sector borrowers.[36]

Local governments, particularly, but not exclusively, in the south, have begun to lavish resources and energy on the promotion of private business. Growing attention to the potential of private business is visible at all levels—for example, the passage of a constitutional amendment recognizing the legitimacy of private property and the contribution of private entrepreneurship to the national economy, followed by preparations for implementing legislation.[37] But enthusiasm for such efforts seems to decline at the higher levels of the administrative ladder. No national leader has stepped forward to champion the cause of the private sector. News that "China will launch a nationwide campaign to clean up all the random charges and fees imposed on foreign-invested companies" prompts an obvious query: what prevents China's leaders from supporting employment growth with a concerted effort to "clean up all the random charges and fees imposed on" businesses established and operated by *Chinese* entrepreneurs?

Conclusion

Despite immense progress toward the creation of a market system, a largely unreformed investment mechanism tilts China's whole economy toward distinctively nonmarket behavior patterns, most visible in the continuation of huge seasonal fluctuations driven by investment plans. China's economic downturn, which appears far deeper than official statistics would indicate, is structural, not cyclical. Its sources are domestic, not international. A long history of wasteful investment spending is the root cause of China's economic woes. Current policy seems shortsighted, inconsistent, and poorly aligned with economic realities. Without major policy shifts, the chances of rekindling high-speed growth seem remote. Accelerated development of private business stands out among available economic options. Promoting private business, the most dynamic sector of China's economy, offers the unique prospect of boosting short-term demand while advancing (rather than obstructing) long-term reform goals. Official policy offers growing recognition and support to private business, but the legacy of anti-business ideology dictates a cautious approach, especially in Beijing. The resulting ideological constraint on the pace of private business growth could prove very costly to China's economy in the coming years.

Notes

1. Edward Green, "What Is a Market Economy?" Notes for a panel discussion at a meeting of the Allied Social Science Associations, San Francisco, California, January 1996.

2. Weiying Zhang and Gang Yi, "China's Gradual Reform: A Historical Perspective," Working paper E1995001, China Centre for Economic Research, Beijing University, Beijing, 1995, p. 16.

3. "China and the WTO," *The Economist,* April 3, 1999, p. 15.

4. Yan Zhang, "Steel Import Rise Causes Concern," *China Daily Business Weekly,* May 31, 1999, p. 2.

5. Wei Gao, "Profits Fall As Record Diesel Price Makes Mark," *China Daily,* December 25, 1996, p. 5.

6. Jianlin Li, "Let Market Function according to Its Rules," *China Daily,* May 4, 1999, p. 4.

7. See Thomas G. Rawski, *China: Prospects for Full Employment,* International Labour Office Employment and Training Papers no. 47, Geneva, 1999; and Margaret Maurer-Fazio, Thomas G. Rawski, and Wei Zhang, "Inequality in the Rewards for Holding Up Half the Sky: Gender Wage Gaps in China's Urban Labor Markets, 1988–1994," *China Journal,* no. 41 (1999): 55–88.

8. Zuoji Zhang, "Social Security Instrumental to SOEs Reform," *China Daily,* February 6, 1999, p. 4.

9. *1996 Zhongguo guoyou zichan nianjian* (State Assets Yearbook 1996) (Beijing: Jingji kexue chubanshe, 1997), p. 451.

10. Ibid., p. 76; and *Zhongguo tongji nianjian 1996* (China Statistics Yearbook 1996) (Beijing: Zhongguo tongji chubanshe, 1996), p. 414.

11. "State's Property Grows Fast Last Year," *China Daily,* August 7, 1999, p. 1.

12. Yang Xu, "Supervision Law Urged by Deputies," *China Daily,* March 13, 1999, p. 2; and "Officials Urged to Follow Law," ibid., July 8, 1999, p. 4.

13. This explains the Chinese practice of comparing partial-year output totals with "the same period of last year" rather than with the previous month or quarter. That approach permits commentators to avoid the question of why, for example, output

in the first quarter of 1999 was projected to be nearly 40 percent below the figure for 1998-Q4.

14. "Taking the Business Cycle's Pulse," *The Economist*, October 28, 1995, pp. 89–90 (citing Victor Zarnowitz, *Business Cycles: Theory, History, Indicators, Forecasting* [Chicago: University of Chicago Press, 1992]).

15. Alan A. Brown and Egon Neuberger, "The Traditional Centrally Planned Economy and Its Reform," in *Comparative Economic Systems: Models and Cases*, ed. Morris Bornstein (Burr Ridge, Ill.: Irwin, 1984), p. 370.

16. Jianlin Li, "Uneven Results Raise Questions," *China Daily*, February 12, 1999, p. 4. Emphasis added.

17. Kunrong Shen, "Foreign Investment Helpful," *China Daily*, July 31, 1998, p. 4.

18. Fureng Dong, "Clarifying Ideas on Economy," *China Daily*, June 11, 1999, p. 4.

19. Charles C. L. Kwong, "Property Rights and Performance of China's Township-Village Enterprises," in *China's Economic Growth and Transition: Macroeconomic, Environmental and Social/Regional Dimensions*, ed. Clement A. Tisdell and Joseph C. H. Chai (Commack, N.Y.: Nova Science, 1997), p. 496.

20. Chen Jiagui, "China's Industry Has Entered the Crucial Period for Raising Quality," *Guangming ribao* (Beijing), June 2, 1997, p. 7.

21. "Steel Output Cut to Boost Development," *China Daily*, June 23, 1999, p. 4.

22. Calculated from *Zhongguo tongji nianjian 1997* (China Statistics Yearbook 1997), pp. 454-55.

23. Chen Hao and Qi Guanyi, "Specific Features of China's Buyer's Market and the Strategic Choices Facing Public Investment," *Touzi yanjiu*, no. 1 (1999): p. 16.

24. Li Chao, "Guangdong Economic Review for 1998 and Development Policy for 1999," in *1999 nian Guangdong: jingji xingshi fenxi yu yuce* (Guangdong in 1999: Analysis and Forecast of Economic Environment), ed. Li Chao and Li Hongchang (Guangzhou: Guangdong renmin chubanshe, 1999), p. 45.

25. According to Dashan Xu, "Cement, Glass Firms to Be Closed," *China Daily*, June 11, 1999, p. 5, 1998 cement production and capacity were 536 and 700 millions tons, respectively.

26. Credit plans, supposedly eliminated in 1997, continue to operate. Thus "an important development in 1998 is that we truly include the nurture of credit for enterprises outside the public sector in the Central Bank's credit plan. Prior to that, the share of nonpublic economy in bank lending was less than 1%." Li Xiaoxi, "Analysis and Forecast of China's Economic Situation," *Zhongguo gongye jingji*, no. 1 (1999): 10–14.

27. Yu'an Zhang, "Glass Industry Urges Interior Investments," *China Daily*, July 4, 1995, p. 5.

28. Craig S. Smith, "In China's Religious Crackdown, an Ancient Symbol Gets the Boot," *Wall Street Journal*, September 8, 1999, p. B1; and Dashan Xu, "Surplus to Grow in Office Market," *China Daily Business Weekly*, April 19, 1999, p. 5.

29. Jianlin Li, "Economy Good, despite Severe Crisis and Flood," *China Daily*, December 30, 1998, p. 4. Emphasis added.

30. Poll results from 1998 show that unemployment has replaced social order as "the main worry" of Chinese residing in major cities, only 12 percent of whom "expressed confidence that their lives would improve significantly in the next five years." Jin'gen Jiang, "Corruption Tops List of Major Concerns," *China Daily*, August 28, 1999, p. 1.

31. Binglan Xu, "Statisticians Seek Reliability," *China Daily Business Weekly*, February 15, 1999, p. 1.

32. Bin Shen and Lan Bing, "Nation to Reverse Money-Losing Firms," *China Daily*, April 26, 1999, p. 1; and Yan Wu, "Laid-Off Workers to Get Extra Pay," ibid., August 30, 1999, p. 1.

33. "Treasury Bond Issuance Aid to Economic Growth," *China Daily*, September 1, 1999, p. 4.

34. Xie Ping, "Challenges Facing China's Financial Reform," *Zhongguo gongye jingji*, no. 4 (1999): 24; and Kan Ren, "Central Bank Chief Reaffirms Money Policy," *China Daily*, July 30, 1999, p. 5.

35. According to Prof. Dong Fureng of the Institute of Economics, Chinese Academy of Social Sciences, Lecture at the University of Melbourne, Melbourne, Australia, July 1999.

36. This is the apparent point of Fan Gang, "Overcoming Credit Crunch and the Reform of the Banking System," *Jingji yanjiu*, no. 1 (1999): 7, note 1.

37. Yan Meng, "Draft Law May Help Individual Enterprises," *China Daily*, August 25, 1999, p. 5.

19. Finishing China's Economic Reform: Challenges and Pitfalls

David D. Li and Ling Li

There is a fundamental disparity in the recent history of the Chinese economy. On the one hand, the performance of the economy, as measured by the growth rate of output and increases in the standard of living, has been impressive. In fact, it is miraculous in comparison with other formerly socialist economies undergoing reforms. On the other hand, China's progress toward building a market economic system has been rather limited in comparison with that of better-reformed East European countries, such as Poland, the Czech Republic, and Hungary. For instance, 20 years after reform began in China, the market for corporate control is still largely missing, as most large enterprises are still tightly controlled by the state. The credit market as normally defined is nonexistent; the largest creditors are non-market-oriented state banks. The housing market is very limited; most land and apartments are owned by the government and are not easily traded. Concomitantly, a labor market in urban areas is, at best, emerging. There is no properly functioning wholesale market for grain and fertilizers, as the state monopolizes the distribution of those goods. Land for agricultural production is still controlled by collectives and not freely tradable. In a word, the Chinese economy is still halfway between a socialist economy and a market economy.

The fundamental disparity raises three important questions. First, why and how has China achieved its enviable economic performance before complete market institutions are in place? Indeed, a large literature has emerged trying to address this question.[1] This chapter is not intended to make a contribution to that line of inquiry. Second, is China showcasing a new type of economic system that is different from both socialism and market economy and superior to both in stimulating economic performance? Unseemly as the question is, there are people who have been arguing that such is the case.[2] We

341

do not share this view. As will be shown below, we believe that major problems have been accumulating in the Chinese economy. Unless China finishes the reforms that will lead to a market economic system, sustained growth is impossible for the Chinese economy.

Here, we are concerned with the third question, what are the remaining reforms China must accomplish to complete its journey to a market economic system? We shall identify those reforms that China urgently needs to accomplish. In addition, we shall identity the challenges facing China's reformers and the pitfalls to which they must pay particular attention lest the reforms stall or go astray.

Unfinished Reforms in China

There are six critical economic reforms China must accomplish to complete its journey to a market economic system:

1. State-owned enterprises (SOEs) must be put on a commercial basis.
2. The financial sector must be opened to competition and market forces.
3. International trade and investment need to be further liberalized.
4. The labor market must be more flexible to increase allocative efficiency.
5. Agriculture needs to be decontrolled to allow greater productivity.
6. China's government needs to rest on the rule of law.

In fact, it is imperative for China to accomplish those reforms quickly in order for the economy to stay on a growing path. During the past two decades China has avoided tackling the hard-core issues of the six reforms. That is due to the necessity of sequencing the reforms, which is driven mainly by considerations of political economy. As a result, fundamental problems have accumulated that threaten continued growth of the economy.

Transforming the SOEs

SOEs have been a major problem in the Chinese economy for the past decade. The symptoms are prominent and painful. With the gradual entry of nonstate enterprises, such as private or collective enterprises and foreign enterprises, most SOEs have been outcompeted in the marketplace. Many consequences follow: sales are slow; inventories accumulate; production capacities are idle; workers are underemployed, furloughed, or laid off; debt payments, tax payments, and payments of trade credits are delayed or delinquent. In today's Chinese economy, other than a few high-profile and highly publicized cases, most SOEs in industries that allow entry of nonstate enterprises are having serious problems.

Asset stripping, which is an extreme consequence of unchecked insider control, is another major problem of Chinese SOEs. Not only does asset stripping aggravate the financial performance of SOEs, it also brews a potential financial crisis by rendering many SOEs worthless and by leading them to default on their debts to banks. Moreover, asset stripping is widely regarded as an extreme form of corruption of government officials and has given rise to enormous complaints against reforms in general.[3]

It is not surprising to see the problems of SOEs mushrooming, since until very recently SOE reforms had been rather limited and superficial. The theme of the SOE reforms of the 1980s was granting autonomy and incentives to SOE managers and employees. The centerpiece of the SOE reform was the so-called contract responsibility system, that is, letting SOE managers (and employees) sign performance contracts with their supervising government agencies. Although those reforms had some positive initial impact on SOE efficiency, by the early 1990s problems began to emerge.[4] In retrospect, the cause was very clear. Unlike performance contracts in a market economy, which are backed by a legal system involving rights of property owners, the contracts between SOE managers and their government supervisors were nothing but glorified bureaucratic agreements. Such agreements are subject to frequent renegotiations prompted by either side. As a matter of fact, by the early 1990s most SOE managers had lost interest in such contracts. The contract-based reform came to a stop.[5]

It is high time to deal with the problems of the SOEs. Their poor financial performance is crippling the banking sector and brewing a potential financial crisis. Their unemployment problem is destabilizing society. Their poor corporate governance, which allows for asset stripping, is generating massive social discontent and negative public opinion about reform in general.

The top leadership in China is obviously well aware of the seriousness of the SOE problem. However, it is not clear that the leaders have embarked on the right track and committed themselves to fundamentally transforming the SOEs. Judging from public speeches and proclaimed policies, the government's objective seems to be very narrow-minded and myopic. The main goals of the government leaders, it seems, are to help SOEs become profitable and to minimize the impact of unemployment caused by SOE reform. To those ends, various policies that effectively subsidize SOEs have been designed and implemented: privileged loans, reduced debt burdens, and even anti-competition policies (e.g., prohibiting "excessive" price competition). An extremely worrisome outcome is that, in the short run, those policies may be effective and many SOEs may turn profitable so that the senior leaders may proclaim their SOE reform successful. However, since the fundamental defects of SOEs persist, performance of SOEs will deteriorate soon after. The so-called SOE problem is not really resolved.[6]

What is needed is a massive and fundamental transformation of the Chinese SOEs. Strictly speaking, the SOEs, so long as they are SOEs, are not reformable. An SOE, by definition, represents a control rights structure under which the government (i.e., bureaucratic agencies) functions as an active and large control rights and cash-flow rights holder. Once in such a position, no government or bureaucratic agency can resist the temptation of direct intervention in its SOEs in order to advance its own noneconomic objectives. For example, there are few cases in which the government can resist the temptation to bail out financially distressed SOEs.

According to this analysis, the task of transforming SOEs is twofold at its core. First, there should be a smooth retreat of the government from the SOEs. The government must be transformed from an active and large shareholder of the SOE to a passive and (necessarily) small shareholder of the newly transformed enterprise. The change must be smooth so that the government as well as the state banks can avoid losing an enormous amount of financial assets and insiders are prevented from usurping enormous real control rights. Second, new institutions of corporate governance need to be established, so that nongovernment outside investors are able to monitor and discipline the insiders effectively. The Russian experience of mass privatization offers negative lessons in this regard.

Reforming the Financial Sector

The financial sector is perhaps the least reformed sector of the Chinese economy. It is overwhelmingly dominated by a few large state-owned commercial banks and has been essentially closed to foreign investment and competition. Stock markets are very small and the corporate bond market is negligible, so bank deposits are, by far, the most important way for households to accumulate financial assets.

The key feature of the Chinese financial sector can be characterized as mild financial repression. That is, through state monopoly of the financial (mostly the banking) sector and control of international capital flows, the government maintains a below-market rate of return for holders of financial assets. That enables the government to collect implicit taxes on households' financial assets. The financial repression is mild because, for most periods during the past two decades, real interest rates on bank deposits were positive. Thus, households remain interested in accumulating financial assets in bank deposits. The trend of financial deepening, a key feature of economic development, has not been hampered in China. The implicit taxes that the government collects from the financial sector are often referred to as quasi-fiscal revenue. It comes from three sources: the increase in the stock of cash issued, the wedge between the market interest rate and the deposit rate, and the state banks' non-interest-bearing reserves with the central bank.[7]

So far, the Chinese government's decision to maintain mild financial repression by delaying drastic reforms of the financial sector has been purposeful and arguably very wise. It has been purposeful in that, from early on, the Chinese policymakers have understood the importance of financial deepening as an instrument to fight inflation. The political cost of inflation is very clear to the policymakers, and mild financial repression avoids inflation. Specifically, the key way to fight inflation is to attract household savings and manage aggregate demand by offering positive real interest rates on bank deposits. At the same time, the huge amount of quasi-fiscal revenue, which is as high as revenue from explicit taxes, has provided the central government with a badly needed addition to tax revenue.[8] Understanding this mechanism very well, the Chinese policymakers have been leery of any tendency to divert household savings to places other than the state banks. Thus, financial reforms have been very slow.

Despite those defensible economic rationales, the Chinese financial sector has to be reformed in order for the economy to continue along a high-growth path. There are two major reasons for this. The first is efficiency. As a result of the state monopoly, the financial sector has been very inefficient in channeling savings into productive outlets. In fact, the central government has been diverting a significant amount of the accumulated household deposits to nonproductive and profit-losing projects, mostly SOEs. The large state-owned banks are accustomed to directing loans to established state-owned enterprises. They are inexperienced in lending, and often reluctant to lend, to start-up enterprises led by entrepreneurs. This is very costly to the whole economy, since the start-ups have proved to be the driving force of economic growth in emerging market economies. To a great extent, the Chinese government's current difficulties in trying to spur economic growth are due to the lack of effective channels for extending credit to small and private enterprises.

The second reason that reforming the state sector is urgent is that, without reform, the current situation may not be sustainable. Because of the inefficiency of the financial sector, nonperforming debt as a proportion of the banks' total loans has been increasing. As of now, it is roughly 30 percent of total loans outstanding, equivalent to 27 percent of total gross domestic product. The level of nonperforming debt is manageable today, since it is essentially owed by the state to household depositors. In fact, a simple calculation reveals that the ratio of required interest payments on national debt to government revenue is similar to that of the United States in the mid-1990s. Moreover, since the Chinese government still holds the majority shares of state enterprises listed on the stock market, it should be able to mobilize enough financial resources to service current national debt. However, without reform, the debt level may easily increase very rapidly. To finance state debt, high interest rates will have to prevail, to the detriment of future economic growth.

Reform of the Chinese financial sector will prove to be very tricky. It has to balance two potentially conflicting objectives. The government has to find ways to help the existing state banks solve the bad-debt problem. Direct injection of capital may not be a feasible solution, since that involves increasing the central government's budget deficit. A more plausible solution is to require the state banks to continue attracting household deposits so as to dilute the proportion of bad loans and to increase provisions for nonperforming debts.[9] But that may conflict with the second reform objective, namely, to introduce new financial institutions and new financial products, which take household savings away from existing banks. There are no obvious solutions, and it seems that reform of the financial sector will be a long and gradual process.[10]

Liberalizing International Trade and Investment

Although international trade and investment are areas in which China's reform has been very successful by many standards, much reform is still needed in order for China to be a fully open market economy. There are two critical issues that must be dealt with properly. The first is nontariff barriers to trade. There are many implicit import restrictions that are not reflected in tariffs, which are scheduled to come down significantly—especially if China enters the World Trade Organization. The most significant nontariff barrier consists of many restrictions that make it difficult, if not impossible, for foreign manufacturers to set up direct sales channels in China. Those restrictions give domestic manufactures an artificial advantage.[11] That not only reduces consumer welfare; it also will not improve the long-term efficiency of domestic producers.

The second task of reform, which is more difficult and more critical than the first, is phasing out pervasive entry barriers to foreign direct investment (FDI). FDI, defined as cross-border investment for direct corporate control, is the most effective form of international capital flow that brings in technology transfers, generates knowledge spillover, trains professional employees, and promotes market-oriented reforms. Despite being the second most popular destination of FDI in the world, China still has a lot of potential to attract much more FDI. Currently, many sectors are almost completely closed to FDI, including financial services, retail sales, and telecommunications. Not surprisingly, these are exactly the sectors in which domestic producers are extremely inefficient by world standards. Introducing strong international competitors in those areas has the greatest potential for improving consumer welfare, enhancing economic efficiency, and spurring economic growth. For example, allowing foreign entry to the telecommunications sector will dramatically improve the quality and lower the cost of services. Very likely, this will generate enormously positive externalities to the Internet service industry, high-tech industries, and financial services. Needless to say, opening those sectors to international competition will be initially traumatic for existing domestic firms. Very quickly, however, all the other benefits to the whole economy—including higher employment, greater efficiency, stronger growth, and higher wage rates—will overwhelm the costs.

The recent agreement between the Chinese and U.S. governments on China's accession to the WTO is an important step toward China's trade liberalization. The comprehensive and bold agreement covers all areas discussed above. There is no doubt that membership in the WTO would be an important step forward in China's trade liberalization. However, equally sure is that the implementation of such a bold trade agreement, assuming that China's bid for membership is successful, will be full of tricky and controversial issues. Those issues reflect the difficulties of trade liberalization discussed above. We remain cautiously optimistic in this regard.

Labor-Market Reforms

China's labor-market reform has to deal with three problems at the same time. The first one is how to make peace with the current cohort of SOE employees who were hired before and during the early days of reform (i.e., the early 1980s). Those employees were hired with a promise of lifetime tenure and various employment benefits, such as free housing and zero-cost medical care and pensions. In exchange, their monetary wage is lower than their marginal product. Obviously, the promises are inconsistent with the basic premise of a functioning labor market. With reform, those SOE employees are potentially the biggest losers. But, because they are politically vocal and relatively well organized—the workers' union was still intact when they were hired—a successful labor-market reform should find ways to compensate, at least partially, their welfare loss. Thus, labor-market reform is likely to be financially costly to the government.

The second problem is to establish the supporting institutions and related markets that are essential to the proper functioning of the labor market. At the top of the list is the housing market. Without a functioning housing market, workers cannot move from locations of lower productivity to locations of higher productivity. The challenge in creating a housing market is to release the huge housing stock that has not been tradable in the marketplace. More specifically, once the stock is privatized, who will get the windfall, which is the capitalized future housing benefits? To avoid massive discontent, SOEs and government agencies must credibly commit to using the revenue from housing sales to compensate people who were promised but have not been allocated apartments or houses.

In addition to establishing full-fledged housing markets, the other goal of labor-market reforms is to establish market-oriented social security programs to provide medical insurance and pensions. To the credit of China's reformers, certain reforms have already been implemented.[12] However, currently, medical insurance and pension plans are managed by individual municipalities, rather than provinces or nationwide agencies. In addition, only urban SOE employees are covered by those programs. Employees of collective and private enterprises are not covered. It is, therefore, difficult for midcareer employees to migrate to different cities or provinces for new job opportunities. Employees stick to SOE jobs because better-paid non-SOE jobs do not have comparable nonwage benefits. That is apparently hampering the emergence of a nationwide labor market, especially for skilled labor. The next step of reform has to remove or reduce those obstacles.

The third problem that China's labor-market reforms have to deal with is the huge amount of labor migrating from rural to urban areas. The magnitude of the migration and the potential gain in economic efficiency associated with it are unparalleled in modern economic history. But the flooding of an enormous amount of labor into urban areas is potentially very disruptive. It threatens to lower the quality of life of city residents and the productivity of urban sectors that rely on highly skilled labor. Because growth of those sectors is highly complementary to that of sectors employing low-skilled labor, unrestricted and unregulated labor migration into urban areas is extremely damaging. Therefore, China's labor-market reforms have to strike a balance between regulating an orderly flow of migrating labor and helping rural labor find employment opportunities in urban areas.

Agricultural Reforms

China's economic reform started in the agricultural sector, but 20 years later major problems still remain in that sector and further reforms are needed. A fundamental problem is that Chinese policymakers have attached too much importance to grain production and so have retained too much control over the grain market and other related markets. As a result, wholesale markets for grain and major production inputs (such as fertilizers) are missing. The state still functions as monopolist and monopsonist in those markets. The proclaimed rationales for government monopoly and monopsony are the provision of insurance to farmers and the maintenance of self-sufficiency in grain production. Both objectives, although questionable, could be achieved via indirect intervention in a fully functioning market. The current system not only generates a wasteful oversupply of grain products, it also has created an enormous inefficiency that in the end is borne by the farmers. For example, the local branches of the state grain procurement agency offer very poor services and often delay cash payments to farmers. Thus, a key step of further agricultural reform involves liberalization of the markets for agricultural products and inputs.

Very interestingly, establishing private land ownership should not be an outright objective of further agricultural reform. Currently, land (except private plots for households' self-consumption) is still owned by the collectives. Farmers own only a long-term use right to land. Surveys of farmers reveal that the status quo is preferred, by a wide margin, to private ownership of land. That is not surprising, as the system of private land ownership functions well only in a market environment. Studies of post-Soviet agriculture show the same tendency. Therefore, the objective of reform should be to liberalize markets relevant to agricultural production. Meanwhile, the reform should create a free-choice environment in which farm households can voluntarily opt for private land ownership in due course.

Reforming Government

Contrary to conventional belief, China implemented a swift and effective reform of its bureaucracy well before economic reforms in the urban sector began.[13] The reform, initiated by Deng Xiaoping soon after the Cultural Revolution, induced retirement of old revolution veterans (by offering relatively lucrative compensation), imposed strict age and education requirements for each level of government positions, and effectively abolished lifetime tenure of officials in any government position. Those reforms laid a solid foundation for the success of subsequent economic reforms.[14]

However, there are still serious problems with China's massive government bureaucracy. It is hard to exaggerate the importance of drastic structural reforms of government to continued good economic performance. First, government agencies are still overly expansive and intrusive. The scope of control of government agencies has to be reduced. Moreover, different agencies overlap with each other in their scope of control, causing enormous frictions and confusion. For example, any significant government decree is cosponsored and signed by three or more agencies. With so many agencies responsible for a policy, its implementation and enforcement are destined to be difficult. To the credit of the incumbent reformist policymakers, an extensive reform was carried out in 1998 to streamline the central government. The total number of ministries was reduced from 50 to 29.

The second problem is that the workforce in most government agencies is so large that the marginal product of labor is most likely negative. Layoffs of government employees are a must. A significant percentage of central government employees was furloughed in 1998 and eventually will be laid off. The current problem is how to implement similar and more effective reforms of local governments. Related to that, the third problem is that the average salary of government employees is low. It is very low in comparison with the average pay of similarly educated and experienced business professionals. Coupled with the fact that many government officials still enjoy excessive control over many economic activities, this creates an ideal environment for the epidemic of corruption. Greatly increasing the average salary of government officials after reducing the number of officials and imposing a moderate amount of monitoring should go a long way toward reducing the prevalence of corruption.

Challenges Facing the New Reformers

The remaining reforms in China are more challenging than the ones of two decades ago, since they have to be implemented in a changed political economy. Moreover, the economy is more efficient than it was when reform began, so efficiency gains are more difficult to realize. Thus, the new reforms will have a harder time compensating potential losers. A case in point is the SOE reform. In the early 1980s profit incentives were very poor in SOEs and inefficiencies were easy to identify. Reforms at that time provided incentives to SOEs by giving profit shares to employees. Both the employees and the government benefited from the increase in work effort. Current SOE reforms, on the other hand, require that many of the SOEs be transformed into nonstate enterprises or simply liquidated, generating a large number of laid-off workers. Theoretically, the net revenues gained through such transactions could be used to compensate the unemployed workers. In reality, claimants to such savings (e.g., banks needing to recapitalize because of nonperforming loans) already existed. Therefore, it is difficult to arrange credible mechanisms through which laid-off workers could be compensated.

Making it even more challenging for the reformers is that the people who lose under the new reforms are more vocal than their predecessors. The main reason is the much liberalized press and mass media. The volume of traffic on the mass media in today's China is enormously bigger than it was before, so the government simply cannot control the wide spectrum of opinions on most nonpolitical issues. Virtually every social group in the economy has its representatives and voices in the market of ideology. The potential and perceived losers under reform are particularly active and often win the sympathy of the general population.

At the same time, the central government is in a much-weakened position for implementing reforms. Ironically, like the liberalization of the press and mass media, this is an outcome of desirable political reform. The administrative branch of the state, where many reform initiatives arise, is increasingly monitored and interfered with by the National People's Congress. Because the NPC is susceptible to the mass media and popular opinion, the job of determined reformers in the government is much more difficult than before. Moreover, there are a few recent cases in which ministries of the central government, representing the interests of large SOEs, have openly fought against the central government's reform policies. This is obviously unprecedented.[15]

Finally, when the economy is open, part of the benefit of reform goes to outsiders. It is difficult to collect taxes from outsiders to compensate the losers under reform. For example, compare the reform of allowing FDI into an industry with that of allowing entry of only new domestic firms to compete with SOEs in the industry. In the first case, international practice must be honored with respect to the FDI firm for the sake of maintaining China's international credibility. Therefore, there are limits to taxes on the FDI firm. There are many more ways to squeeze the profit of a new domestic entrant to compensate losers.

Pitfalls of New Reforms

Two major pitfalls threaten to stall the reforms or to lead them astray. The first pitfall is letting short-term problems take priority over long-run objectives. Currently, there are a few seemingly urgent short-run issues that beset the central government reformers: a slowing of economic growth, a rising unemployment rate, a surge of income inequality, and massive complaints about corruption. Painful as they are, such short-run issues should never overwhelm efforts to achieve fundamental reforms. After all, such problems are nothing but manifestations of the need for fundamental reforms. They are at most a part of the cost of reform. Unfortunately, because of the ever-louder representations of the losers under reform and the diminishing authority of the reformist government, resources and attention tend to be devoted to the short-run issues. A case in point is the ongoing drive in China to stimulate domestic demand. In the name of stimulating growth, many nonviable SOEs are subsidized and their debt burden relieved. Taxes on interest on household savings are levied and price competition among producers is curbed. Those policies clearly tend in the wrong direction.

The second and perhaps the most deceiving pitfall is the introduction of improper reforms or even anti-reform measures in the name of "convergence with international practice." Examples are the newly devised taxes on interest on bank deposits, the possible implementation of real-name bank accounts (abolishing prematurely the existing Swiss-style anonymous bank accounts), and enforcing a progressive personal income tax. Those measures are extremely counterproductive. One has to bear in mind that there are critical infrastructural institutions in modern market economies that make many of the so-called international practices function well. At the top of the list of such infrastructural institutions are democracy, the rule of law, and the division of powers that together constrain and curb the tendency of state predation.[16] Without those important institutions limiting the behavior of the state, a lot of the international practices may well become convenient instruments for the government to use to interfere in the economic activities of citizens and hamper private incentives. Moreover, one must bear in mind that some international practices are simply inefficient institutions that today's mature market economies themselves are trying to abolish.

Conclusion

We make three main arguments in this chapter. First, we argue that China's economic reform, which started in 1978, is far from being finished. Instead, many reforms have been delayed until now. Without strong efforts to complete those reforms, the Chinese economy may not be able to stay on its growing path. Second, we argue that there are many challenges facing the reformers. The challenges are to find credible ways to compensate the ever more vocal losers under reforms. Third, facing those challenges, the reformers must watch out for two pitfalls. One is that short-run issues tend to overwhelm long-term objectives of reform. The other and more deceiving one is that in the name of "convergence with international practice," many inefficient and actually counterreform institutions are introduced.

Notes

1. For a survey, see Yingyi Qian, "The Institutional Foundations of China's Market Transition," in *Proceedings of the World Bank's Annual Conference on Development Economics 1999*, ed. Boris Pleskovic and Joseph Stiglitz (Washington: World Bank, forthcoming). For an example of research motivated by the first questions, see Chongen Bai et al., "Anonymous Banking and Financial Repression: How Did China's Reform Limit Government Predation without Reducing Its Revenue?" Economic Center for Policy Research Working Paper, 1999.

2. See, for example, Zhiyuan Cui, "Disintegrating the Bundle of Property Rights: A New Interpretation of China's Reform," Department of Political Science Working Paper, MIT, 1994; and Zhiyuan Cui, "Whither China? The Discourse and Practice of Property Rights Reform in China," Department of Political Science Working Paper, MIT, 1998.

3. He Qinglian, *Xian Dai Hua De Xian Jing* (The Pitfalls of Modernization) (Beijing: Jing Re Zhong Guo Chu Ban She, 1998), p. 106. He Qinglian complains about problems with China's reforms. She launches her case against the ongoing reforms almost entirely from the observations about the asset stripping of SOEs. She claims that, between 1982 and 1992, 25 percent of state assets were lost in various ways to asset stripping.

4. Theodore Groves et al., "Autonomy and Incentives in China's State Enterprises," *Quarterly Journal of Economics* 104, no. 1 (1994): 183–200, document some of the improvement in SOE efficiency due to granting managers autonomy and incentives. Gary Jefferson and Thomas Rawski, "Enterprise Reform in Chinese Industry," *Journal of Economic Perspective* 8, no. 2 (1994), seem to be more optimistic about China's SOE reform as a result of their estimations of productivity growth in the 1980s.

5. See Wu Jingliang, *Xian Dai Gong Si Zhi Du Yu Qi Ye Gai Ge* (Modern Enterprise Systems and Enterprise Reform) (Tien Jin: Tien Jin Ren Min Chu Ban Che, 1994), for a careful analysis of the failure of the contract responsibility system. Dong Fureng and Tang Zhongkun, *Zhong Guo Guo You Qi Ye Gai Ge: Zhi Du Yu Xiao Lui* (China's State Enterprise Reform: Institutions and Efficiency) (Beijing: Zhong Guo Ji Hua Chu

Ban She, 1992), chap. 12, document the reluctance of SOE managers to continue the contract responsibility system reform in the early 1990s.

6. In September 1999 an annual plenary meeting of the Central Committee of the Chinese Communist Party was in session. It was reported that a major debate erupted during the meeting. One side argued for the drastic measure of selling most SOEs. The other side insisted on mild measures aiming at helping SOEs overcome their current difficulties. See Willy Wo-Lap Lam, "Party Leaders Argue the Fate of State Firms," *South China Morning Post,* September 20, 1999. The final report of the meeting was a compromise calling for the "retreat" (i.e., privatization) of SOEs in some sectors and the "strengthening" of SOEs in other sectors, including high-tech industries.

7. It should be noted that the rapid increase in the money supply in China, as reflected in the dramatic increase in the M2-to-GDP ratio from around 50 percent to over 110 percent from the early 1980s to the late 1990s, has been driven mostly by rapid monetization of economic activities, especially in rural areas.

8. Bai et al. calculated quasi-fiscal revenue over the years of reform. They found that it has been as high as revenue from explicit taxes.

9. See David Li and Shan Li, "The Corporate Debt Crisis in China: Analysis and Policy Proposal," in *The Reformability of China's State Sector,* ed. G. J. Wen and D. Xu (River Edge, N.J.: World Scientific, 1996), for a discussion of jointly resolving the non-performing-debt problem and pushing for SOE reform and for a proposal of debt-equity conversion that aims to restructure simultaneously both the control rights and the financial structure of the SOEs.

10. For a proposal to gradually introduce nonstate banks without aggravating the financial woes of the existing state banks, see Shan Li, David D. Li, and Yijiang Wang, "Zhong Guo Shang Ye Ying Hang Ti Zhi Gai Ge De Zheng Ce Jian Yi" (A Policy Proposal of Reforming China's Commercial Banking System), in *Yin Qi Gai Ge He Fa Zhang Di Qu Xing Jing Rong Zhong Xin De the Ce Lue* (The Bank-Enterprise Relations and Strategies of Developing Regional Financial Centers.), ed. Chun Chang, Decheng Zheng, and Yijiang Wang (Beijing: Zhong Guo Jing Ji Chu Ban Che, 1997).

11. See Hong Song, "Gong Ye Yiu Shi, Bi Jiao Yiu Shi He Jing Zheng Yiu Shi" (Industrial Advantage, Comparative Advantage, and Competitive Advantage), *Guo Ji Jin Ji Ping Lung* (July–August 1999): 5–9.

12. See Ling Li, "Family Insurance or Social Insurance—Policy Options for China's Social Security Reform," *International Journal of Economic Development* (forthcoming), for discussions of major problems of China's social security reform.

13. David D. Li, "The Changing Behavior of Chinese Bureaucracy during Reform," *American Economic Review* 88, no. 2 (May 1998).

14. David D. Li argues in ibid., pp. 393–97, that political reform should be broadly defined to include reform of the bureaucracy. According to that view, China's political reform has not lagged behind its economic reform.

15. For an outstanding recent case, see Ian Johnson, "China's Wu Looks to Derail WTO Talks: Fiery Minister's Internet Edict Hampers Negotiators' Delicate Efforts," *Asian Wall Street Journal,* September 20, 1999, p. 7.

16. As F. A. Hayek argued, the root of the doomed experiment of socialism is an unconstrained and totalitarian government. Thus of first-order importance to the postsocialist reform is finding ways to reduce the scope of control of the government rather than simply to superficially copy many secondary institutions of modern market economies. Friedrich A. Hayek, *The Road to Serfdom* (Chicago: University of Chicago Press, 1944).

Contributors

Ted Galen Carpenter is vice president for defense and foreign policy studies at the Cato Institute. Carpenter is the author or editor of 10 books, including *NATO's Empty Victory: A Postmortem on the Balkan War*, *NATO Enlargement: Illusions and Reality*, *Delusions of Grandeur: The United Nations and Global Intervention*, *The Captive Press: Foreign Policy Crises and the First Amendment*, *Beyond NATO: Staying Out of Europe's Wars*, and *A Search for Enemies: America's Alliances after the Cold War*. His work has also appeared in various policy journals, including *Foreign Affairs*, *Foreign Policy*, *National Interest*, *World Policy Journal*, *Mediterranean Quarterly*, *Korean Journal of Defense Analyses*, and the *Journal of Strategic Studies*, as well as in major newspapers throughout the United States, Europe, and East Asia. Carpenter holds a Ph.D. in U.S. diplomatic history from the University of Texas. He is a member of the Council on Foreign Relations and serves on the editorial boards of *Mediterranean Quarterly* and the *Journal of Strategic Studies*.

James A. Dorn is a China specialist at the Cato Institute and Cato's vice president for academic affairs. He is also editor of the *Cato Journal* and director of Cato's annual monetary conference. His research interests include trade and human rights, economic reform in China, and the future of money. He has edited nine books, including *China in the New Millennium: Market Reforms and Social Development* and *Economic Reform in China: Problems and Prospects*. His articles have appeared in numerous publications, including the *Financial Times*, the *Asian Wall Street Journal*, the *South China Morning Post*, the *Hong Kong Economic Times*, *Investor's Business Daily*, and the *Australian Financial Review*. He has been a visiting scholar at the Central European University in Prague and at Fudan University in Shanghai and is currently a professor of economics at Towson University in Maryland. Dorn holds a Ph.D. in economics from the University of Virginia.

Mark A. Groombridge is a research fellow with the Center for Trade Policy Studies at the Cato Institute. His current research interests include intellectual property services and China's entry to the World Trade Organization. Before arriving at Cato, Groombridge was the Abramson Research Fellow at the American Enterprise Institute and associate director of its Asian studies program. He is the coauthor (with AEI's Claude Barfield) of *Tiger by the Tail: China and the WTO*. Groombridge has written widely on international economic issues in such publications as *Barron's*, the *Journal of Commerce*, the *Hong Kong Economic Times*, the *Journal of World Intellectual Property*, the *Australian Financial Review*, and the *American Enterprise*. He has been featured on CNN, the BBC, and other media outlets. Groombridge received his Ph.D. in political science from Columbia University.

Stefan Halper is a former White House and State Department official who writes a nationally syndicated column from Washington. He is also the host of *This Week from Washington* and *Reminiscences* on Radio America. Halper's work on foreign policy issues has been published nationwide in newspapers and magazines, including the *New York Times*, the *Baltimore Sun*, the *Wall Street Journal*, the *Weekly Standard*, and the *Los Angeles Times*. He holds a Ph.D. from Oxford University.

Selig S. Harrison is a senior scholar of the Woodrow Wilson International Center for Scholars, a fellow at the Century Foundation, and director of the Century Foundation Project on the United States and the Future of Korea. A former Northeast Asia bureau chief of the *Washington Post*, he is the author of six books on Asia, including *China, Oil and Asia: Conflict Ahead? Japan's Nuclear Future;* and *India: The Most Dangerous Decades*. He served as a senior associate of the Carnegie Endowment for International Peace for 22 years and is a former senior fellow in charge of Asia studies at the Brookings Institution.

Martin Lee is chairman of the Democratic Party (and its predecessor, the United Democrats of Hong Kong, established in April 1990), Hong Kong's most popular political party. He has led his party to electoral victories since the first democratic popular elections to the territory's Legislative Council (through Functional Constituency) in 1985 and has been reelected in every election since. A barrister, Lee was appointed Queen's Counsel in 1979 and chaired the Hong Kong Bar Association from 1980 to 1983. He served from 1985 to 1989 as a member of the Basic Law Drafting Committee, the body appointed by Beijing to draft Hong Kong's post-1997 constitution, until his expulsion in the aftermath of his denunciation of the Tiananmen crackdown. Lee has received international recognition for his efforts to defend Hong Kong's free society and the rule of law.

David D. Li is an associate professor of economics and associate director of the Center for Economic Development at the Hong Kong University of Science and Technology. He is also a research fellow of the Center for Economic Policy Research (CEPR), the William Davidson Institute of the University of Michigan, and the National Center for Economic Research (NCER) at Tsinghua University. From 1992 to 1997, he was an assistant professor of economics at the University of Michigan. From 1997 to 1998, he was a national fellow of the Hoover Institution at Stanford University. His research has been published in various professional journals, including the *American Economic Review, European Economic Review, Journal of Comparative Economics, Journal of Finance,* and the *RAND Journal of Economics.* He is also a frequent contributor of op-ed articles to newspapers in English and Chinese. Li received his Ph.D. in economics from Harvard University.

Ling Li is an assistant professor of economics at Towson University in Maryland and a vice chair on the Baltimore-Xiamen Sister Cities Committee. From 1982 to 1987, she taught at Wuhan University, first in the physics department and later in the economics department. Her research interests include economic development, economic growth, health economics, and the economics of aging. She has numerous publications in refereed journals and books, including *Global Economic Review, International Journal of Public Administration, International Journal of Economic Development,* and *China's Tax Reform Options.* Li received her Ph.D. in economics from the University of Pittsburgh.

James R. Lilley is resident fellow of Asian Studies at the American Enterprise Institute. Before joining AEI in January 1993, he served as assistant secretary of defense for International Security Affairs from November 1991 to January 1993. Lilley was also the U.S. ambassador to the People's Republic of China from April 1989 to May 1991, U.S. ambassador to the Republic of Korea from 1986 to 1989, and the second director of the American Institute in Taiwan from January 1982 to May 1984. He was an adjunct professor at the Johns Hopkins School of Advanced International Studies, a fellow at Harvard University's Institute of Politics, and the Philip M. McKenna Visiting Scholar at Claremont McKenna College. Lilley also directed the Institute for Global Chinese Affairs at the University of Maryland and later served as its senior adviser. He is the coeditor of *Beyond MFN: Trade with China and American Interests*, and *Crisis in the Taiwan Strait*. He has also written numerous pieces for the *Washington Post*, the *Washington Times*, the *New York Times*, *U.S. News & World Report*, and *Foreign Policy*.

Liu Junning is an independent scholar in Beijing. He is the author of several books, including *Peking University and the Liberal Tradition in Modern China; The Phenomenon of Power: A Liberal Perspective;* and *Conservatism, Republicanism and Constitutional Democracy: Studies on Liberalism*. He is also the editor of *Res Publica*, the first academic journal since 1949 dedicated to liberal ideas, and the translator of *The Third Wave: Democratization in the Late Twentieth Century* by Samuel P. Huntington. He received his Ph.D. in political theory from Beijing University.

Robert A. Manning is currently C. V. Starr Senior Fellow and director of Asian studies at the Council on Foreign Relations. Prior to that he was a senior fellow at the Progressive Policy Institute. He is also a consultant to the U.S. Institute of Peace, a regular contributor to the *Los Angeles Times* Sunday "Opinion" section, and a contributing editor to the *Japan Times*. Manning has written, edited, or contributed to more than a dozen books, including *The Asian Energy Factor: Myths and Dilemmas on Energy, Security, and the Pacific Future* (forthcoming); "Waiting for Godot: The Asian Security Environment," in *The U.S.-Japan Alliance, Past, Present, and Future;* and "Going for the Brass Ring," in *The Foreign Relations of North Korea*. He has also written widely on international affairs in professional and policy journals such as *Asian Survey, Survival, Foreign Affairs,* and *Foreign Policy.* From 1989 to March 1993, Manning was advisor for policy to the assistant secretary for East Asian and Pacific Affairs at the U.S. Department of State and in 1988-89 he served as an advisor to the office of the secretary of defense.

Mao Yushi is director of the Unirule Institute of Economics and a member of the international advisory group PECC (Pacific Economic Cooperation Council). He was a visiting scholar at the department of economics at Harvard University on a Ford Foundation Fellowship during 1986. From 1984 to 1993, he was a senior fellow at the Institute of American Studies, Chinese Academy of Social Sciences. He is the author of many books, including *The Future of Chinese Ethics, Who Prevents Us from Being Well-Off?* and *The Principle of Optimal Allocation, Economics and Its Mathematical Foundation.* His articles have appeared in many scientific journals such as the *Journal of Economics Surveys, Ethics and Environment Policy,* and the *International Journal of Solar Energy.*

William McGurn is a member of the editorial board and chief editorial writer for the *Wall Street Journal.* He began his career with the *American Spectator* in Bloomington, Indiana, and from 1989 to 1992 served as Washington bureau chief for *National Review.* Prior to rejoining the *Journal* in 1998, he served as senior editor for the *Far Eastern Economic Review* in Hong Kong, as deputy editorial page editor for the *Asian Wall Street Journal* in Hong Kong, and as editorial features editor for the *Wall Street Journal Europe* in Brussels. A member of the Council on Foreign Relations, McGurn is the author of *Perfidious Albion: The Abandonment of Hong Kong.*

Barry Naughton is an economist who specializes in China's transitional economy, focusing on issues relating to industry, foreign trade, and macroeconomics. He has recently been named the first So Kuan-lok Professor of Chinese and International Affairs at the Graduate School of International Relations and Pacific Studies of the University of California at San Diego. His study of Chinese economic reform, *Growing Out of the Plan: Chinese Economic Reform, 1978–1993* (New York: Cambridge University Press, 1995), won the Masayoshi Ohira

Memorial Prize. His most recent work is the edited volume *The China Circle: Economics and Technology in the PRC, Taiwan, and Hong Kong*. Naughton is currently engaged in a study of provincial economic growth in the People's Republic of China.

Marvin C. Ott is a professor of national security policy at the National War College and a faculty fellow at the Institute for National and Strategic Studies, National Defense University. Previously, he was an associate professor at Mount Holyoke College, senior manager at the Congressional Office of Technology Assessment, senior East Asia analyst at the CIA, chairperson for Southeast Asia at the Foreign Service Institute (State Department), senior associate at the Carnegie Endowment for International Peace, and deputy staff director of the Senate Select Committee on Intelligence. He is the author of more than 70 journal articles, newspaper op-eds, and book chapters on Asian, East European, intelligence, and technology assessment topics. He has been a regular commentator on the CNN program *Business Asia* and an occasional commentator on National Public Radio. Ott holds a doctorate from the Paul N. Nitze School of Advanced International Studies, Johns Hopkins University.

Minxin Pei is a senior associate at the Carnegie Endowment for International Peace. Previously, he taught East Asian political economy and international relations at Princeton University. He is the author of *From Reform to Revolution: The Demise of Communism in China and the Soviet Union*. His articles have appeared in the *New York Times*, the *Washington Post*, the *Los Angeles Times, Foreign Affairs* and the *Asian Wall Street Journal*. Pei is associate editor of *World Politics* and a member of the editorial board of the *Journal of Contemporary China*. He holds a Ph.D. in political science from Harvard University.

Thomas G. Rawski is a professor of economics and history at the University of Pittsburgh. He specializes in China's contemporary economy and modern economic history. His books include *Economic Growth and Employment in China, China's Transition to Industrialism, Economic Growth in Prewar China* as well as several edited and collaborative volumes. He has also published numerous articles on the dynamics of China's transition from plan to market. His recent work includes studies on productivity growth, wage and employment behavior, institutional change, innovation, and measurement issues in China's rapidly changing economy. Rawski spent the 1999–2000 academic year at Harvard University's Fairbank Center for East Asian Research, where he worked on several China-related projects, including a book on the foundations of China's economic growth.

Peter W. Rodman is director of national security programs at the Nixon Center in Washington, D.C. He was a deputy assistant to the president for national security affairs under President Reagan and special assistant to the president for national security affairs under Presidents Reagan and Bush. In the Nixon and Ford administrations, Rodman served on the National Security Council staff as a special assistant to Henry Kissinger. Rodman is the author of a history of the Cold War in the Third World, *More Precious Than Peace,* and of a series of annual strategic assessments published by the Nixon Center, the most recent of which is *Drifting Apart? Trends in U.S.-European Relations.* Rodman was educated at Harvard College, Oxford University, and Harvard Law School.

Yeung Wai Hong is editor and publisher of *Next* magazine. Yeung's interest in applying market solutions to public policy issues led him to leave a Hong Kong–based merchant bank and go into publishing in 1990. In addition to *Next,* Yeung's publishing group, the largest print media group in Hong Kong, publishes three other magazines as well as a daily newspaper and books. Yeung has taught economics and worked in government agencies and financial institutions. He received his education in economics in the United States.

Kate Xiao Zhou is an associate professor of comparative politics and political economy of East Asia in the department of political science at the University of Hawaii. Her main research interests include the dynamics of transition from central planning to markets, Chinese economic development, Chinese business, globalization in East Asia, comparative studies of businesses, and Asian entrepreneurship. She has published articles on political economy and women's studies, along with a book, *How the Farmers Changed China: Power of the People.* She received a Ph.D. in politics from Princeton University.

Index

Cato Institute

Founded in 1977, the Cato Institute is a public policy research foundation dedicated to broadening the parameters of policy debate to allow consideration of more options that are consistent with the traditional American principles of limited government, individual liberty, and peace. To that end, the Institute strives to achieve greater involvement of the intelligent, concerned lay public in questions of policy and the proper role of government.

The Institute is named for *Cato's Letters*, libertarian pamphlets that were widely read in the American Colonies in the early 18th century and played a major role in laying the philosophical foundation for the American Revolution.

Despite the achievement of the nation's Founders, today virtually no aspect of life is free from government encroachment. A pervasive intolerance for individual rights is shown by government's arbitrary intrusions into private economic transactions and its disregard for civil liberties.

To counter that trend, the Cato Institute undertakes an extensive publications program that addresses the complete spectrum of policy issues. Books, monographs, and shorter studies are commissioned to examine the federal budget, Social Security, regulation, military spending, international trade, and myriad other issues. Major policy conferences are held throughout the year, from which papers are published thrice yearly in the *Cato Journal*. The Institute also publishes the quarterly magazine *Regulation*.

In order to maintain its independence, the Cato Institute accepts no government funding. Contributions are received from foundations, corporations, and individuals, and other revenue is generated from the sale of publications. The Institute is a nonprofit, tax-exempt, educational foundation under Section 501(c)3 of the Internal Revenue Code.

CATO INSTITUTE
1000 Massachusetts Ave., N.W.
Washington, D.C. 20001